# The Government of the Fifth Republic

# The Government of the Fifth Republic · *French Political Parties and the Constitution*

By J. A. LAPONCE

UNIVERSITY OF CALIFORNIA PRESS

*Berkeley and Los Angeles, 1961*

*University of California Press*
*Berkeley and Los Angeles, California*
*Cambridge University Press*
*London, England*



*Library of Congress Catalog Card Number: 60-14656*
*Printed in the United States of America*
*Designed by Marion Jackson Skinner*

*A mon père, en souvenir*
*de la rue Saint-Guillaume*

# *Acknowledgments*

I wish to acknowledge the help given me by the Committee on Research and by the Institute of Social and Economic Research of the University of British Columbia, which contributed part of the traveling expenses of four consecutive visits to France between 1956 and 1959.

I owe a debt of gratitude to the many politicians, civil servants, and party officials who attempted to answer my queries and who were gracious enough to show no annoyance at the development of a new form of question period, that of academicians from North American universities.

My special thanks are due to Mr. Gordon R. Elliott, who read the entire manuscript and suggested many stylistic improvements.

Of course, I am solely responsible for any misstatement of fact and for any error of interpretation.

J. A. L.

*The University of British Columbia*

# *Contents*


*1* The End of the Fourth Republic, *1*

*2* Parties and Ideologies, *14*

*3* The Communist Party, *28*

*4* The SFIO, *45*

*5* The Radical Party, *70*

*6* The MRP, *85*

*7* The Independents, *109*

*8* The UNR, *122*

*9* Minor Parties, *140*

*10* Parties and Pressure Groups, *156*

*11* The Drafting of the 1958 Constitution, *167*

*12* The Executive, *182*

*13* Parliament and the Legislative Field, *210*

*14* Elections to the National Assembly, *221*

*15* Organization, Powers, and Functions of the National Assembly, *249*

*16* The Senate, *277*

*17* The Other French Constitutional Organs, *288*

*18* The Community, *302*

Conclusion, *317*

Appendix, *321*

Notes, *369*

Selected Bibliography, *385*

Index, *401*

# *Tables*

IN TEXT:


1 Vote on the Investiture of de Gaulle, National Assembly, June 1, 1958 *12*

2 Communist Votes in General Elections, Metropolitan France, *42*

3 SFIO Revenues and Expenditures, 1958 *63*

4 Distribution of MRP Membership, *105*

5 Referendum, September 28, 1958 *180*

6 Election, December, 1958 *187*

7 Voting in Thirty-third District of Seine, 1958 *240*

8 Voting in Fifty-third District of Seine, 1958 *241*

9 Voting in Seventh District of Bouches-du-Rhône, 1958 *242*


IN APPENDIX:


I Prime Ministers of the Fourth Republic, *323*

II Elections to the Constituant and National Assemblies in Metropolitan France, 1946–1958 *324*

III Seats in the Constituant and National Assemblies in Metropolitan France, 1946–1958 *324–325*

IV Memberships of Parliamentary Groups, October, 1959 *325*

V Major Votes in the National Assembly, *326–327*

VI Population over Nineteen Years Old, *328*

# I *The End of the Fourth Republic*

The Fourth Republic might have lived much longer. For a long time parliaments, like mad kings, could have put to death governments guilty of not having done what the parliaments themselves had prevented or forbidden. For yet a long time French politicians could have made their sorrows or their delights of the subtle game of shifting majorities and ministerial coalitions. But the Republic was ill. Under a seeming activity which was superficial agitation, she was paralyzed by internal tensions. She disintegrated under the shock of the events of May 1958. De Gaulle's forecast was fulfilled; the time had come when the question was not even one of seizing power but of picking it up.

On May 13, 1958, a group of students, meeting with little opposition from the guards, stormed the government building in Algiers, and were allowed to stage the disorder fitting to insurrections. A "Committee of Public Safety" was formed. Soon controlled by the army and Gaullist politicians, it called on France to give herself a government led by General de Gaulle.

In Paris, the National Assembly, not believing in the possibility of an army rebellion but sensing that grave events were in the making, hurriedly invested Pierre Pflimlin as prime minister, thus ending a ministerial crisis which had lasted almost thirty days. The choice of Pflimlin was bad. Not that he lacked character or governmental experience but because he was thought, rightly or wrongly, to be committed to a "liberal" solution in Algeria, a liberal policy against which the settlers and the army had just rebelled fearing that such a policy might lead to the complete withdrawal of France from North Africa.

Two weeks after he had become prime minister, Pflimlin resigned, although he still had a parliamentary majority. In a bloodless struggle for the allegiance of the army, of the police and of public opinion, Algiers had beaten Paris. The legal government, rather than letting events go to their humiliating conclusion, wisely abandoned the contest. On June 1, the National Assembly invested General de Gaulle, gave him emergency powers, and entrusted his government with the drafting of a new constitution.

## The Protagonists

In the crisis of May, 1958, there were four major protagonists: the European settlers in Algeria, the army, the Fourth Republic, and de Gaulle.

About 1,200,000 people of European origin live in the towns and on the coastal plains of Algeria. They are at home there. Algeria is their province, France is their country. Like the Americans who established themselves in Texas or California after the annexation of these territories to the United States, they do not think that they have ever left their country behind but, on the contrary, that they have helped to push its frontiers forward. Established in an area which, before their arrival, was politically and economically backward, they transformed it thanks to their techniques, their investments, their energy, and the help given by the government. Separated by language, religion, and customs from the Moslem world in which they lived, they developed a feeling of racial and cultural superiority. They opposed the granting to certain categories of Moslems the French citizenship as proposed by the Blum government of 1937; they disliked de Gaulle's giving of such citizenship to a limited number of Moslems in 1944; and in 1957 they opposed the creation of a common electoral roll. Long before the beginning of the Algerian war in 1954, the settlers thought that extending the rules of democracy would jeopardize their supremacy. They had the normal reaction of socially dominant groups numerically in the minority: they feared that majority rule would crush them; they saw in their privileges the condition of their survival. There never was in Algeria any legal segregation as in South Africa or in some states of the United States, but there was a social and psychological segregation which helped the Moslem insurgents to separate each community by hatred and fear.

When the Moslem insurrection which had begun in the out-of-the-way mountains spread to the rest of Algeria, the settlers, as any citizens would, expected their government to maintain the public peace. The sending of nearly half a million soldiers, the increase in military expenditures, were not considered as favors but as the results of normal governmental obligations. As the Algerian war continued, the settlers began to blame the government for the delay: they found arguments for suspecting an eventual betrayal in the doubts and in the crises of conscience of some politicians, newspapermen, and writers in metropolitan France. The Communists were not the only ones to propose negotiations with the rebels. Socialists, Radicals, and Christian Democrats publicly expressed the idea that the solution to the Algerian problem could not be imposed by force. The editor of a conservative magazine wrote that France's former colonies were costing her more than they benefited her; [1] a right-wing writer, a contributor to *Le Figaro*, suggested that the settlers be resettled in France.[2] Writers with no Communist sympathies protested against the brutal methods used by certain army units to combat terrorism.[3] Meanwhile the majority of Frenchmen, badly informed of the conditions in Algeria, remained largely indifferent to the war. The French of France and the French of Algeria lived in a completely different psychological climate: to the one group, war was far away; to the other, it was a daily presence. What to one group appeared as an objective search for a solution or a criticism of methods, seemed to the other a questioning of war aims and a preparation for treason. The opposition between Frenchmen separated by the Mediterranean was not, of course, absolute. In metropolitan France, certain politicians,[4] newspapers, and organizations, in particular veterans' organizations, shared the apprehensions of the settlers, but nevertheless, on the whole, metropolitan France had kept her peace psychology and, if the Algerian war had penetrated national consciousness more than the Indochinese conflict, it had not come to the fore.

The continuation of the war, the lack of understanding between France and Algeria, the weakness, the irresolution of the governments, all had led the settlers to a state of mental rebellion against Paris. A set of circumstances—historians will have to tell which were fortuitous and which were planned—turned this latent revolt into an open rebellion against the legal authorities.

The government was not so badly informed that they could not have forecast the settlers' rebellion; it was not unknown in Paris that tension in Algiers could lead to grave disorders. But French politicians, on the whole, did not want to believe the warnings sent by Robert Lacoste, the minister resident in Algeria, and refused to think that the army could join an insurrectional movement.

An army is meant for victory. But the French army which had been at war for the past twenty years had not known victory, unless under foreign command. The successes gained under Eisenhower could not erase the disaster of 1939, the defeat of Indochina, and the humiliation of Suez. At last this army saw in Algeria the victory needed. In Algeria they found at last this just cause which they did not have in Indochina. They had come to Algeria not to protect and maintain the privileges of a minority of European settlers, not to crush a people by force but to bring to Algerians, Moslems as well as Europeans, French justice and civilization; they had come to keep for France her African extension and thus to maintain the door open to the wealth of the Sahara and prevent the establishment of hostile forces on the southern flank of NATO. The army which had never adapted itself to the type of conflict waged in Indochina, understood that the war they wanted to win was a war of a new type. It was not a war of destruction, but of construction, a war where physical violence counts less than ideologies. It was a psychological war. The strength of the rebellion lay less in their 40,000 guns than in their myth of independence. To this myth, the army opposed that of integration. To a humiliated people they offered equality. The army believed that nearly all Moslems would have liked to side with France but that the irresolution of passing and short-lived governments had thrown them into a position of neutrality. The army thought that, if the government made clear and definite that France would not leave Algeria, the Moslem masses would help in routing the rebels. But such a government would have to be a true government speaking with authority for the nation as a whole and most of all a government secure in office, not one which had been invested for six months as the nation's caretaker.

Early in 1958 the officer corps, seeing the Gaillard government waver in its Algerian policy and accept foreign arbitration in the affair of Sakhiet, feared that Paris had entered with Arab nationalism a series of concessions which would end in the withdrawal of France from Algeria. Military leaders [5] were ready to accept an idea which was gaining strength in Algeria as well as in France: only the formation of a de Gaulle government could redress a highly compromised situation. Only such a government, respected in France and in foreign countries and guaranteed not to be overthrown by a divided parliament, only such a government would have enough authority to introduce the reforms necessary for integrating the Moslem community to France and, having proclaimed the will of France, enough authority to remain in Algeria and rally the Moslem masses to her. So thought the army. Although its conception of the future of Algeria was different from that of the settlers, the army shared with them the fear that the government's will to fight would weaken. When, in May, 1958, hearing of Pflimlin's candidacy to the premiership, Lacoste said that a "diplomatic Dien Bien Phu" was to be expected,[6] the army, like the settlers, thought that the politicians were "once again" preparing a betrayal. This the army would not accept and, after having been for over a century "la grande muette," reëntered politics.

The Fourth Republic did not lack politicians of talent and character and has some notable achievements to its credit, such as the modernization of the economy and the move toward European integration, but its constitutional structures were so badly adapted to its party system that even better statesmen could not but have floundered in the midst of institutions which precluded coherent leadership.

The parliamentary system had degenerated into Assembly government because of the divisions between and within political parties. Cabinets were little more than committees of the legislative body, trying their best to satisfy the contradictory wishes of their many masters. Each of the political groups which had invested a coalition government tended to act as though the executive were under its sole control. This multiple paternity had disastrous effects. For a parliament to treat its government as a still irresponsible child is unwise, but when, in addition, the parliament expects this child to obey the contradictory orders of its many fathers, the system becomes absurd. Understandable then, this paralysis of the will to act, this lack of energy, these crises of schizophrenia to which French governments were subject. By acting, the government could not but risk antagonizing one of its creators. The great temptation was not to move. In order to arouse the government from its torpor, ministers would threaten to tender their resignations, parties would serve motions of want of confidence. After six months, the cabinet, at the end of its *élan vital,* would usually disintegrate. The overthrow of a government had, paradoxically, become a means of government. The Fourth Republic had, in the words of one of its prime ministers, developed a system of government-by-crisis.[7]

The resignation or overthrow of a cabinet had become a means of obliging the executive to act or the Parliament to unite. The opening or the prolongation of a ministerial crisis was used by parliamentary factions to impose their views on the executive. Rare were the occasions—the Suez expedition was one—when the government was backed by a solid parliamentary coalition with which to collaborate. More often the executive was subject to the continuous attacks of parliamentary minorities. The political groups which had invested a government could have tried to settle their differences among themselves. According to the old technique of logrolling, they could have tried to obtain satisfaction for as many of their claims as possible but without expecting to obtain satisfaction for them all. These methods were used of course but, while seeking a compromise, parties and groups always kept in reserve the overthrow of the government as their last bargaining card. The irresponsible use of that power led to frequent dismissals of governments by coalitions of minorities with nothing in common but their dissatisfaction.

Once a ministerial crisis had been "opened," the blackmail of prolongation of the crisis replaced the blackmail of overthrow of the government. It has been noted that under the Fourth as compared to the Third Republic, a cabinet's span of life tended to become shorter. Another evolution which had the same causes and was as nefarious as the first led to the lengthening of ministerial crises. While under the Third Republic the *interregnum* between governments was rarely more than a few days, under the Fourth Republic it tended to last a few weeks. The duration of the crises leading to the formation of the last six governments of the Fourth Republic was as follows: Mendès-France, 6 days; Faure, 18; Mollet, 28; Bourgès-Maunoury, 22; Gaillard, 36; Pflimlin, 27 days.

During a crisis, parties and pressure groups put all their weight to bear on the government which was in a process of formation, in order that as many of their claims as possible be in the government program. Parliamentarians had become so used to these periods of bargaining in the absence of an executive, that most of them did not realize the danger of the game. The crisis of May 13, 1958, was in the logic of the system. European settlers and the army acted as pressure groups. Already ill-equipped to resist the pressure of ordinary groups, the Fourth Republic could not resist that of the army.

The misfortunes of the Fourth Republic disprove the saying that in politics men are more important than institutions. The contrary may not be any more valid but would be of greater practical value. One should put his hopes of good government on sound institutions rather than on sound politicians. The humiliating end of the Fourth Republic should be remembered as a warning that democracies not producing strong and stable executives are threatened in their very existence. The morality proposed by La Fontaine in the fable of the dragon with many heads and the dragon with many tails is valid for political systems. The many-headed animal seemed better fitted for battle than the many-tailed. An obstacle was in the way, a hedge, which the single-headed dragon negotiated easily, but in which the many-headed monster so entangled himself that he died there of inanition.

After the failure of the *Rassemblement du Peuple Français* (RPF) and its dissolution in 1953, de Gaulle had withdrawn from active politics. Realizing that he could not force history, he decided to make himself available in the event that history were to come his way. He knew that, in a country humiliated by its loss of strength and status, he incarnated victory and national *grandeur*. He knew that in the event of a serious crisis, the nation would turn to him. In other times he had divided the French by his uncompromising attitude toward Petain, by bringing Communists into the government, by the nationalizations, by the creation of the RPF; but in 1958, after three years of retirement, he had become the symbol of national unity. Just as Churchill, retired from politics, identifies himself with Great Britain far more than with the Conservative party, de Gaulle, in his silence, identified himself more and more with France. One may find irritating that when speaking of himself, de Gaulle would sometimes say "de Gaulle" instead of "I." This is a sign that he was conscious of having himself become a myth as necessary to the France of 1958 as that of the monarchy to Great Britain: a symbol of survival under adversity.

After May 13, three alternatives were open to de Gaulle: side with Algiers against Paris; come to the rescue of Pflimlin; let the crisis develop to the point where both contestants, Paris and Algiers, would have no other recourse than his arbitration. In choosing either of the first two solutions, de Gaulle would have destroyed his own myth; in choosing the latter course he remained faithful to it and thus preserved his chances as supreme umpire.

### MAY 13–JUNE 1, 1958

May 13 was followed by a period of waiting and observation during which the contestants set their claims. It lasted until May 24, when the creation of insurrectional committees in Corsica precipitated the decline of Pflimlin's government which ended with General de Gaulle's investiture as prime minister on June 1.

The soldiers and civilians who formed the committees of Public Safety in Algeria agreed to keep Algeria French, but they were divided in their political conceptions. A group, of which Dr. Lefèvre and Colonel Thomazo were representative, had nothing but contempt for "Democracy and its rigmarole" and would have willingly substituted a corporatist or fascist system. Others, such as General Massu, L. Delbecque, and J. Soustelle, had for their primary purpose the bringing back of de Gaulle to power. Moslems such as Sid Cara understood integration as meaning equality between Europeans and Moslems; P. Lagaillarde understood it as a continuation of the *status quo*.

Pflimlin, hoping that the insurrectional committees would be paralyzed by their internal dissentions, tried to outwit Algiers. General Salan, commander-in-chief in Algeria, whose authority was recognized by the committees of Public Safety, was confirmed by Paris in his functions and given increased powers. It was hoped in Paris that the army, having given vent to its dissatisfaction would naturally return to obedience. The Bank of France was authorized to transfer to Algeria the funds without which the Algerian administration would have found operating difficult, and troop reinforcements as well as supplies were sent to Algiers from metropolitan France.

For a while, Pflimlin seemed about to win. General de Gaulle had said, on May 15 in an ambiguous statement, that he was ready to assume the powers of the Republic but, at a press conference on May 19, he had let it be understood that he would not defy the legal authorities. Pflimlin had strengthened his cabinet by bringing Socialists into it, in particular Guy Mollet who had remained popular after the Suez expedition, and Jules Moch who was remembered for the authority with which he had broken the insurrectional strikes of 1947. The National Assembly thought that it had weathered the storm. When Pflimlin tried to take the initiative and proposed a rapid reform of the constitution, the Assembly, jealous of its prerogatives and anxious to show that it could not be panicked into making hasty decisions, postponed from May 23 to May 26 the discussion of constitutional reform. In the meantime Corsica joined the Algerian movement.

The government had been warned that the few hundred paratroopers stationed in Corsica were ready to lend support to the establishment of committees of Public Safety. Police forces were dispatched to the island for maintenance of order. These policemen joined the paratroopers in helping to push aside the legal authorities peacefully.

Without the support of the army, or the police, or a public opinion which had maintained a detached and spectator-like attitude, Pflimlin was left with no alternative but to tender his resignation to President Coty on May 28. The way was open for de Gaulle's return to power, but an obstacle was still in his way, the investiture by the National Assembly. De Gaulle needed the support not only of the right-wing and center groups but also of the Socialists. Without such support he risked defeat or an investiture by a slim majority. On May 27, before Pflimlin's resignation, a joint meeting of the Socialist parliamentary group and of the party executive committee (*Comité Directeur*) had decided by a vote of 117 to 3 with 1 abstention that the Socialists would "in no circumstances . . . rally to the candidacy of General de Gaulle which . . . was and will remain a challenge to republican legality." [8] The resignation of Pflimlin, the fear of a possible *coup d'état* by the military, and the pressure put on them by Mollet (their secretary general) made the Socialists revise their positions. By writing personally to de Gaulle on May 25, to outline the reasons for his opposition to the general's return to power, by the very fact of writing over the head of his prime minister, Mollet had established contact between de Gaulle and the Socialists.[9] A subsequent exchange of letters between Vincent Auriol and de Gaulle had the same effect. After the resignation of Pflimlin, Mollet tried to convince his Socialist colleagues that the choice was between de Gaulle and an army dictatorship. At a caucus meeting, 30 Socialist deputies took Mollet's side, 41 dissented. With the guarantee that about half of the Socialist parliamentary group would vote for him, de Gaulle presented his cabinet to the National Assembly on June 1. He was invested by 329 votes against 224 and 32 abstentions. Notable among those who voted against de Gaulle were: P. Mendès-France and E. Daladier (Radicals), F. Mitterand (UDSR); F. de Menthon (MRP), P. Isorni (Independent), G. Defferre, C. Lussy, C. Pineau, R. Verdier (Socialists). Most overseas representatives abstained; F. Houphouët-Boigny was one of the few to vote for de Gaulle. Forty-two Socialists finally supported the general, 49 voted against him.

Before attempting to form a government and before attempting to obtain the investiture, de Gaulle had invited the delegates of the parliamentary groups to meet him. First he received the representatives of the Socialist group, then the representatives of all parliamentary groups in the National Assembly except the Communists who had refused the invitation. He outlined a program of reforms and defined the means required for the execution of such a program. The objective was threefold: to bridge the gap between civilian and military power, to find a solution for Algeria within a French context on the basis of equality between Europeans and Moslems, and finally to reform the constitution in order to insure the stability of the executive. De

Gaulle asked that emergency powers be delegated to him for a period of six months, that he receive authority to draft a new constitution and, in order that his government be one of national union, that all major parties except the Communists be repre-

TABLE 1

VOTE ON THE INVESTITURE OF DE GAULLE, NATIONAL ASSEMBLY, JUNE 1, 1958

| Party | For | Against | Abstentions or not present |
|---|---|---|---|
| Communists | 0 | 141 | 1 |
| Progressives | 0 | 8 | 0 |
| Socialists | 42 | 49 | 3 |
| African Socialists | 2 | 0 | 0 |
| UDSR-RDA | 10 | 4 | 6 |
| MRP | 70 | 3 | 1 |
| Radical-Socialists | 24 | 18 | 0 |
| RGR | 14 | 0 | 0 |
| Dissident Radicals | 12 | 1 | 0 |
| PRA | 4 | 0 | 11 |
| Independents | 86 | 1 | 1 |
| Farmers | 10 | 0 | 1 |
| Farmers for Social Action | 7 | 0 | 1 |
| Social Republicans | 15 | 0 | 3 |
| Poujadists | 30 | 0 | 0 |
| No party | 3 | 1 | 4 |

NOTE: The tabulation does not include four deputies who were on leave: two Social Republicans, one Independent, one PRA.
SOURCE: *Le Monde*, June 3, 1958.

sented. He promised not to include representatives of the committees of Public Safety in his government, at least for the present.

The government formed by de Gaulle included civil servants and politicians. The three key ministries, Foreign Affairs, Interior, and National Defense, were given to civil servants, the other ministries were allocated to the major parties. Four ministers without portfolio, Houphouët-Boigny (RDA), Jacquinot (Independent), Mollet (Socialist), and Pflimlin (MRP), formed a sort of inner cabinet. Michel Debré (Social Republican) received the Ministry of Justice and Antoine Pinay (Independent), the Ministry of Finance and National Economy. The cabinet had the symbolic value wanted by de Gaulle: it affirmed the continuity of the Republic and the gathering of the nation. From this rally of parties, only two groups were excluded, the Communists and the Poujadists.

De Gaulle asked parliament to delegate to his government the right to rule by decree for six months and the right to draft a new constitution. The National Assembly, by 322 votes to 232, gave him emergency powers and delegated constitutional power by 350 votes to 161. Parliament then put an end to its session and in fact if not in law, to the Fourth Republic.

## May 13: An Evaluation

When an army tries to impose its will on the civilian authorities, when the people witness with indifference if not with sarcasm the paralysis of their parliament, when a nation finds no other solution to its difficulties than to entrust its fate to one man, democracy suffers a defeat. In that sense May 13 was a defeat for the French Republic. But if May 13 has ended the process of dissolution of governmental authority in which France was engaged, if it has been the salutary shock which enabled the French parliamentary system to reform itself, then the long-range effects will have been beneficial.

The memories of the crisis of May, 1958, will, for years to come, weigh on the political consciousness of France. To find a political event of similar importance one would probably have to look back to the Commune of 1870. The Fourth Republic had been a mere continuation of the Third; the Fifth marks a turn in the evolution. The failure of Assembly government has been made so evident that French politicians will probably not wish to "return to their vomit." This, however, is of course, far from certain.

# 2 *Parties and Ideologies*

In his study on French politics, A. Thibaudet gives this advice to the would-be founder of a political party: "Do not put economic interests on your flag." [1] French political parties present themselves to the electorate as the incarnation of ideologies. The only party which achieved any success while identifying itself with the protection of the financial interests of a limited and well-defined section of the electorate, the *Union et Fraternité Française* of Pierre Poujade, lasted only two years as a parliamentary force. As soon as the discontented shopkeepers who had voted for the UFF were given the alternative of voting for a man, de Gaulle, and for a party, the UNR, which had no sympathy for their economic plight but could give a more ideological form to their discontent, they deserted a party closer to their pocketbook for a party closer to their heart. Symptomatic also is the fact that farmers' parties have never had any significant following.

French political parties are not, as they tend to be in the United States, mere roads of access to the machinery of government. The prospective politician cannot plan a career as he would an automobile journey. Admittance to a French political party and promotion within its ranks is usually subject to one's adherence to a particular ideology.

### Ideologies

There are many "isms" and practically all can be found in France. In listing the major political philosophies which divide the French, one must risk either oversimplication or confusion. Aware that in trying to avoid both one might only succeed in avoiding neither, one can recognize nine major *idées-force:* communism, democratic socialism, economic liberalism, political liberalism, anticlericalism, Christian democracy, conservatism, nationalism, and Europeanism.

If such political philosophies as anarchism, Trotskyism, Titoism, fascism, racism, corporatism, Maurrassism, monarchism among others, have been excluded it is because, whatever their past or future importance, they have not at present a major role in the ideological struggle.

### Communism

Just as France was made to believe by her kings that she was the elder daughter of the Church, she is thought, by French Communist leaders, to be the elder daughter of the Bolshevik revolution. But while the kings thought that their position of supremacy and prestige among Christian rulers allowed them some privileges and justified their Gallicanism, French Communists think of their position as one of increased responsibility to orthodoxy and to ultramontanism. The French brand of communism closely resembles the Russian, at least as far as ideology goes. Little original contribution to Marxist thinking has been made by French Communists; their work has been one of glossary comments. One would look in vain for a French Lenin or a French Mao Tse-tung. The Communist ideology in France is Marx as interpreted by the orthodox Russian commentators. It has adopted Marx's interpretation of history and its inevitable term, the classless society; it has adopted also, Lenin's definition of the role of the Communist party as the conscience of the proletariat, the duty of which is to hasten the revolution by increasing the class consciousness among workers and by giving the final blow to a dying capitalism; it has accepted Stalin's conception of the leadership of Russia in determining the actions and tactics of all Communist parties.

### Democratic Socialism

Socialism has, in common with communism, a deterministic conception of history and an ideal of equality among men. But while communism sees in the democratic form of government, as practiced in "capitalist" nations, a temporary stage destined to perish with capitalism itself, socialism thinks that democratic government in its representative form is the historical achievement of a quest for greater freedom and greater justice and that, far from having to be replaced, the existing democratic system has to be extended. The Socialists think further that of all associations, it is the state which, in its present form, can provide greater freedom and equality, and that consequently the state should increase its sphere of action. The economy of the nation should no longer be left to a chaotic and hazardous existence but should be regulated by the government in such a way that distribution of goods is on a just basis and that private property is not a means of oppression. "An economy controlled by the state, itself controlled by the people," sums up the major French brand of socialism. One could also find, although more diffused, another type of socialism, a socialism inherited from Phroudhon which calls for a stateless form, one to be realized through professional organizations or communal units. There also the major contention is maintained that freedom would be preserved by the controlling of the groups by their own members.

Socialism, which at first was presented as a philosophy primarily for the benefit of workers, has now lost its exclusiveness. Indeed, one of its major points of difference with communism is that it has moved away from the notion of class conflict and substituted for it that of social justice. The framework of its thought has been more and more society as a whole, rather than one section of society.

### Economic Liberalism

Liberalism in the European sense of the term does not necessarily describe, as in the United States, a "progressive" or "left-wing" position. Economic liberals believe that the government should refrain from interfering with the economic process, except to maintain or strengthen competition. Thus, while they entrust the state with the maintaining of the rules of the game, they think that economic decisions should be left to the individuals. Economic liberalism does not necessarily imply political liberalism and may be associated, as under Napoleon III, with authoritarian governments.

### Political Liberalism

Political liberalism calls for restraint by the state in dealings with the citizens and proclaims the supremacy of the individual endowed with inalienable rights. Political liberalism restricts the state to the role of a benevolent policeman who intervenes only when public order is seriously and directly menaced. Political liberalism finds its charter in the Declaration of the Rights of Man and Citizen of 1789, which defines the rights of the individual against the state as the right to express freely one's opinions and to communicate them to others, the right to acquire and dispose of property, and the right to move freely. The guarantees of such rights are that restrictions on the individual can only be set by laws which must apply to all equally and must be passed by the people themselves either directly or through their representatives. Such representatives have to be chosen by the people and to be responsible to them.

### Anticlericalism

Anticlericalism is an outgrowth of political liberalism. While the latter philosophy aimed at liberating man from the state, anticlericalism aimed at liberating the individual from the church.

At first the two ideologies were so linked that they could not be easily separated and many thought that anticlericalism was only one of the aspects of political liberalism. The Catholic church had been so closely identified with the monarchy and the feudal system that the liberal revolution of 1789 against the monarchy and the aristocracy, turned also against the Church which had failed to detach itself in time from the sinking *ancien régime*. During the nineteenth century and even more in the twentieth, political liberalism and anticlericalism branched. In its present form, anticlericalism is a philosophy denying the church any role in secular matters, not only in the administration of the country, but also, for example, in the education of children and in the providing of social benefits. In its extreme, anticlericalism would like to reduce the church to a folklore society.

### Christian Democracy

Christian democracy originated in the nineteenth century from a desire to reconcile French Catholics with the Republic. In the twentieth century it gave itself the ideal of combining the principles of liberalism and those of socialism which were consistent with Christian ethics. From liberalism, Christian democracy took the proposition that the state is subordinate to the individual and that man's freedom of choice should be preserved as much as possible; from socialism, Christian democracy took the concept of the state's responsibility for the welfare of society as a whole and the obligation made upon the government to intervene in order to mold a society from which men could benefit more equally. Christian democracy added that the major objective of the state was not the material welfare of the people; it was to create a society in which men could live according to Christian morals while refusing the state the right to enforce such morals.

### Conservatism

The philosophy of conservatism cannot be easily defined. One could argue that it is more an attitude of mind than a full-fledged philosophy of politics. But diffuse and badly formulated as it may be, conservatism implies a certain concept of society and of the state in its relations with individuals. The easiest way of defining conservatism is to recognize its two extreme boundaries, extreme authoritarianism on one side, political liberalism on the other. The various shades of French conservatism are obtained by the blending of a form of conservatism inherited from the monarchists and the Bonapartists on the one hand and a form of conservatism inherited from de Tocqueville on the other. The first may be called authoritarian conservatism, the second libertarian conservatism. Conservatives welcome or accept in democracy what democracy implies in terms of freedom, but are afraid of, or at least have objections to, its equalitarian implications. A government controlled by the multitude is a potential, if not an ever-present, danger to the established order and its natural hierarchies. Conservatives have not overcome the old fear that such a government may act as a leveler, an equalizer of private wealth, power, and prestige. As the economic liberal thinks that there is a natural economic order, the conservative thinks that there is a natural social order. When this social order is not menaced, authoritarian and libertarian conservatives draw close to each other and tend to become undistinguishable. When this order is menaced, or when at the time of a national crisis such as that of 1940, authoritarian systems of government are offered as alternatives to democracy, then the two branches tend to separate.

### Nationalism

Nationalism in France has taken various forms. But on the whole, nationalism has been a reaction against policies or ideologies thought to question the integrity or the independence of French territory or culture. After the restoration of the monarchy in 1815, nationalism was a republican doctrine, the monarchy being thought by republicans as a foreign import depending on outside help and trying to erase the heritage of the Revolution. At a later date nationalism changed camps and was raised against international socialism, then against international communism.

Since the Second World War, nationalism has taken on a new aspect, the opposition to the merger of France with other European nations. The national ideology is now one which calls not only for the preservation of a traditional French culture against ideologies believed tinted with un-French ideas, but it also calls for the preservation of France as is; it is then a refusal to see her disappear into larger entities, such as the proposed United Europe, or an Atlantic Alliance too closely controlled by the United States. It may also be a will to maintain a greater France, that which includes overseas possessions in Africa; it is then a refusal to grant independence or even autonomy to former colonies.

### Europeanism

Among the various ways proposed to answer the challenge of the United States of America and the Soviet Union, one, the creation of United States of Europe, has taken precedence over such projects as a French-African union, a Mediterranean confederation or a Latin union. The idea of unifying Europe is not new but, since the First World War and especially since the Second, it is presented in an entirely new context. The projects of European union devised by Sully, Bernardin de Saint Pierre, Rousseau, or Victor Hugo were closer to the dreams of Gary Davis than to the modern projects for unifying Europe. Before the First World War, such a union was contemplated, not to answer the challenge of outside forces but to achieve perpetual peace through the grouping of nations which had been warring against each other under a single authority, an effort at establishing a rule of law over nations torn by external conflicts.

The more recent projects were not prompted by a vague desire for universal peace but found their reason in the natural tendency of weak nations, close to one another, to form a common front against stronger and farther-away states; they were based also on the assumption that western European nations had certain values in common which should be preserved.

Not love and longing for brotherhood made some postwar

politicians contemplate a merger of European nations but the analysis of economic and political factors. However, although contemplated as a marriage of convenience, the unification of Europe has now achieved the force of a myth. Europeanism has become an "*idée-force*" which appeals to sentiment as well as to reason. It appeals to the desire of belonging to a powerful and influential political entity, to the desire of expanding one's frontiers, to the desire of burying old conflicts and hatreds and replacing them by new ones, as much as it appeals to economic and material interests.

Such are the major ideologies around which the electorate clusters, at least for the present. New ideologies may emerge or minor *idées-force* suddenly come to the fore. From the Algerian problem may be born an opposition between integrists and racists; from economic difficulties, a dormant fascism may gain strength; from political instability monarchism may possibly regain the ground lost in the past eighty years; from upheavals in the Communist leadership either in France or in the Soviet Union, national communism of the Tito brand may replace the present Communist orthodoxy. For more than one reason France is "the paradise of the intellectuals." Not only does the present multiplicity of ideological struggles contribute to the richness and diversity of the intellectual landscape, but so does the feeling that the future is open for yet different types of ideological conflicts and tensions.

### Ideologies and Political Parties

Some of the major ideologies find their incarnation in a single party, others in more than one. The Communist ideology finds its embodiment in the Communist party; the social democratic in the Socialist party; the Christian democratic in the MRP and a few splinter groups. Economic liberalism is represented by the Independents, the various Radical groups, and the UNR; political liberalism principally by the Radicals; anticlericalism by the Socialists, the Communists, and the Radicals; conservatism by the UNR and the Independents; Europeanism mainly by the Socialists and the MRP; nationalism in its anti-European form by right-wing groups, although not universally; and nationalism in its anti-Communist form by all the non-Communist parties although at varying intensity.

Notable is the overlapping of ideological groupings. For example, nationalism separates Communists and Socialists, but anticlericalism links them; Europeanism relates Socialists and MRP but anticlericalism separates them.

Some parties are not separated by ideologies but solely by personalities or short-range programs. The difference between the Radicals and the Republican Center, between the Independents and the UNR, or between the MRP and Georges Bidault's Christian democracy are not fundamentally ideological. Although ideology is the firmer and more durable basis for the opposition between political groupings, it is not the only one. Political parties are differentiated not only by their ideologies, but also by their immediate programs, by the vested interests of their leadership, by their different electorates, by the regional and sectional interests with which they may have become identified. The opposition between the Radicals and the Socialists is not limited to the opposition between socialism and economic liberalism; it covers the opposition between profit-making and salaried people, as well as the opposition between the different geographical areas in which each of these two parties have their strongholds.

The political parties in the first parliament of the Fifth Republic can be classified from the various ideologies which they represent or pretend to represent.

| Ideology | Political Party |
|---|---|
| Communism | Communists |
| Democratic socialism | SFIO |
| Economic liberalism | Independents, Radicals, Republican Center |
| Political liberalism | Radicals, Republican Center |
| Anticlericalism | Communist party, SFIO, Radicals |
| Christian democracy | MRP, Bidault's Christian democratic group |

| Ideology | Political Party |
|---|---|
| Democratic conservatism | UNR, Independents |
| Nationalism (anticommunism) | All parties but the Communists |
| Nationalism (anti-Europeanism) | Communist party; and groups of varying importance within other parties, in particular the UNR. |
| Nationalism (Greater France) | Independents, Bidault's Christian democratic group and right wings of UNR, MRP, Radicals, and Socialists. |
| Europeanism | MRP, SFIO, and groups in other parties. |

Not mentioned is the Algerian parliamentary group, which is not properly speaking a political party, but a group unified on the sole issue of Algeria's integration to France. The members of this group tend, on the whole, to represent the philosophies of nationalism, economic liberalism, and conservatism, but some want a corporate or fascist state structure.

### Left, Right, and Center

The now universal notion of Right and Left originated with the revolution of 1789. In the first National Assembly, the supporters of the king sat on the right of the chairman, the opposition to the king, on the left. Those without definite opinions sat in the middle. Such seating arrangement corresponds to the three basic alternatives offered to a legislator: return to the past, status quo, or innovation.

The general tendency in the nineteenth century for political parties to emerge on the left and in the course of their existence to move toward the right, together with the universal belief in the march of humanity toward greater and greater enlightenment, made popular the notion that progress is on the left and conservation on the right.

From the political conflicts of the nineteenth century and early twentieth century, modern France has inherited a traditional association of certain ideologies with either the Left or the Right. On the Right one finds: conservatism, economic liberalism, and nationalism; on the Left: communism, democratic socialism, political liberalism, and anticlericalism. The more recent ideologies of Christian democracy and Europeanism have not yet become clearly associated with either.

The personalization of political and ideological conflicts has resulted in a mythological characterization of the Left-wing and Right-wing temperaments. As sophisticated a writer as E. Berl contends that one can tell a Right-winger from a Left-winger by the very way he dresses or smokes.[2] The baggy pants and the pipe of Edouard Herriot were obviously on the Left, the neat suits of Paul Reynaud obviously on the Right. Seen from the Left, the Left-winger exudes generosity, goodheartedness, and, short of being folksy, is humane and simple in his ways. But seen from the Right, the same person is a masochist, a hypocritical masochist at that, a man who delights in torturing his own soul while making others bear the cost of easing his crises of conscience. On the other side of the picture, the Right-winger is either a healthy realist, with sound ideas, a man who does not question God's and nature's work but tries to make the best of it, a man who enjoys life as it comes, or on the contrary a narrow-minded person, systematically hostile to new ideas, overbearing, cold, distant, and egoistic. And, of course, the Left-winger has morals neither for himself nor for others, while the Right-winger has no morals for himself but plenty for others.

Not all is absurd in these myths. They are ways of saying that the monarchy was on the Right and the republic on the Left; that order was on the Right, and the questioning of order on the Left; that liberty and sympathy for the poor are on the Left, while authority and the preservation of one's financial interests are on the Right. These associations of ideas are not peculiar to France. André Siegfried's observation that Frenchmen have their heart on the left and keep their wallet on the right, applies not only to Frenchmen, but is universally true.[3] Also universal is the picture of Justice, with the sword, symbol of authority in the right hand and the balance, symbol of equality, in the left hand.

The already-noted nineteenth-century tendency for parties to rise from the left and to die on the right made the left or center seats in the assemblies preferred ones. The seating of the Communists on the extreme left has perhaps rendered left seats less attractive, but the dislike for extreme right seats has remained general. The fights by the RPF in 1952 and the Poujadists in 1956 to be seated closer to the center are illustrative of the importance of the notions of left and right in determining the elector's attitude. Walter Lippmann observed correctly that opinions are, for a large part, images in our heads.[4] The graphic reproduction by the press of the seating arrangement of parties in the assemblies probably influences, to some extent, the voting behavior of the electorate.

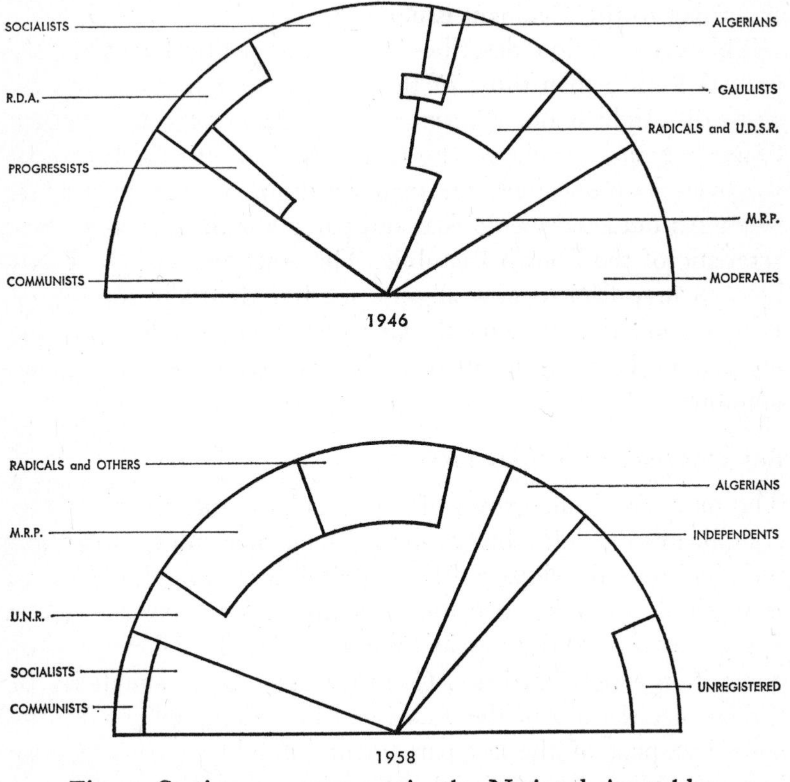


Fig. 1. Seating arrangement in the National Assembly, 1946 and 1958.

The traditional classification of parties as either Left or Right seems to have been done on the basis of three major tests: attitude toward a monarchy, attitude toward the church, attitude toward the system of free enterprise. The more favorable, the more to the Right; the more hostile, the more to the left. Only two parties, the Communists and the Socialists, are hostile to monarchical structures, church influence, and free enterprise. These parties are consistently associated with the Left by French politicians as well as by political analysts. Similarly the Independents and the UNR, because they score in the same column on the three tests mentioned, are universally considered as Right-wing parties. Other parties such as the MRP and the Radicals, not having the same solid pattern of likes and dislikes on political, religious, and economic matters, appear either as Left or Right according to the dominant issue.

This classification describes better the political conflicts of prewar France than those of the 1950's. Belonging to the Left or to the Right is not determined by a party's attitude toward France's major problems, the future of Europe, the future of the overseas possessions, the modernization of economic structures. An outdated ideological and party alignment was a characteristic of the Fourth Republic. The emergence of the UNR in 1958 may lead to new alignments, but traditions are strong and for some time to come the electorate will probably continue to associate Left and Right with dated conflicts of interests and opinions.

### Bonapartism and Gaullism

The more fond one grows of a particular game, the more one complicates the rules, but as the rules become too complex and too rigid, one develops a desire to abolish all complications, to start afresh. Whether because of fondness for it or from other reasons, party politics has in France a natural tendency to become increasingly intricate. Compare the relative simplicity of the first legislatures of the Third and Fourth republics with the esoteric aspect of the last parliaments of both regimes. Under both republics the continual splintering of parties and groups and the growing party antagonism tended to jam the democratic machinery. The pulling out, simultaneously, in all directions resulted in an ever increasing loss of energy for an ever greater *immobilisme.* The ultimate consequence was the dying of exhaustion in order to stand still. As politicians and public opinion became aware of such fatal consequences, a desire for an umpire grew, for an arbitrator above politics or at least above the petty politics of the day who could disregard the old rules, the old classifications, the old customs. The call to Doumergue in 1934 and to de Gaulle in 1958 are examples of the bypassing of its elected representatives by a public opinion which "wants to be governed" and wants to force its parliamentarians to delegate power of decision to a single man who, because of his prestige or past achievements, is trusted to impose the best solutions for the nation's problems. Bonapartism, in that sense, is not properly speaking a permanent ideology but rather a temporary discarding of ideological alignments in order that a system of government be re-formed or set to work again. The Bonapartist parties of the Third Republic, such as those founded by General Boulanger in the late nineteenth century and by Colonel de la Rocque in the 1930's, failed to obtain their objectives and did not survive their leaders. In 1958, on the contrary, the Gaullists succeeded in bringing General de Gaulle back to power. Assured of lasting as long as the general remains in power, the Gaullist party may try to guarantee its further survival by giving itself an ideological basis. Whether the UNR will succeed in turning itself into a French Conservative party is one of the unknowns of the Fifth Republic but the logics of French politics would indicate that if the gaullists wish to survive de Gaulle they can only do so by ceasing to be a purely Bonapartist party devoted to maintaining a particular leader in power.

# 3 *The Communist Party*

At the end of the nineteenth century, the French Socialist movement was divided between two tendencies, revolutionist and reformist, each represented by a number of separate parties. In 1905, Jean Jaurès succeeded in bringing the various groups together into a single party organization, the SFIO. The collaboration between reformists and revolutionists was uneasy even before the war of 1914, but the war itself and then the Russian revolution brought to the breaking point the tension between the two tendencies. In 1920 Lenin sent to the French Socialist party as well as to other Socialist parties throughout the world, the so-called 21-point ultimatum calling on Socialist parties to agree to a basic catechism of Marxism, to overhaul their organizations, to exclude the reformists and to accept the authority of the Third International. The SFIO met at Tours in 1920 to consider the ultimatum. A majority of the delegates,

3,000 votes against 1,400, decided to accept Lenin's terms and thus founded the French Communist party. As most members of the SFIO followed their delegates, the French Communist party started with a large membership, estimated in 1920 at about 100,000, but in less than three years it dropped to 40,000.[1] The party was torn by internal disputes and purges. Many of its adherents returned to the old Socialist party. In the election of 1928, the Communists made the mistake of treating the SFIO as an enemy; the decision to maintain Communist candidates against the Socialists on the second ballot cost the party nearly 40 per cent of its votes. Its parliamentary representation in the Chamber of Deputies dropped to less than 3 per cent. In 1932 the Communists reached their lowest point in terms of popular vote as well as parliamentary representation, 8.4 per cent of the votes and 2 per cent of the seats. The party seemed on its way to extinction. The SFIO, which had by 1932 almost regained the voting strength it had before the First World War, seemed to have defeated the revolutionists in the contest for the allegiance of the working class. The depression, the formation of a Socialist government, then the war, not only saved the Communist party but by 1945 also made it the largest French party in terms of membership as well as of electorate.

Following the election of 1932, France entered a period of social and economic tensions. The fear of fascism, the fear also that the country might be more seriously hit by the depression than she already was, and the change in Comintern tactics led to the formation in 1936 of an electoral alliance between Radicals, Socialists, and Communists. The Communist vote almost doubled to 15.4 per cent while for the first time since 1919 the Socialists lost electoral support. The Communist party, now well controlled by its leaders and in particular by its secretary-general, Maurice Thorez, swelled to an estimated 350,000 members. In the following years the party played both the governmental and the opposition cards; it offered its votes to the government led by Socialist Léon Blum but refused to accept seats in the ministry. Their being allied to long-established parties such as the Radicals and the Socialists gave the Communists respectability, their remaining outside the government enabled them to take the leadership of the strikes which spread throughout France. Although in the minority the Communists began their systematic and well-coördinated conquest of all key positions in the *Conféderation Générale du Travail* which were to put them in control of the largest trade union movement after the liberation.[2] While gaining social status, they had not lost dynamism.

The party emerged from the war with even greater respectability, having succeeded this time in draping itself in nationalist garb during the *Résistance*. This feat was all the more remarkable in that the war had not started well for the party and might have left it with a durable stigma. Thorez had deserted the army in October, 1939, and had gone to Russia, after Communist organizations had been disbanded by the Daladier government. Furthermore it seems well established that, following the occupation of Paris by the Germans, some Communist leaders approached the occupation authorities with the hope that, in keeping with the spirit of the German-Russian pact of 1939, French Communists would obtain privileged treatment. The German invasion of Russia enabled the French Communist party to take a solidly anti-German and patriotic stand, and to establish itself as one of the major political forces behind the *Résistance* movement. At liberation, the party leadership resisted the pressure of activist groups which would have used the Communist-armed underground to seize power during the period of transition preceding the firm establishment of de Gaulle's government. Maurice Thorez and Jacques Duclos analyzed the situation as unfavorable to an uprising; the Allied forces would not have accepted the establishment of a Communist regime in France. The teachings of Marx and Lenin as well as the experiences of 1848 and of the Commune of 1870 had taught Communist strategists that an abortive *coup d'état* or revolution would have been a serious setback to them. The Communist maquis were ordered by the Communist party either to disband or to accept integration into the regular French forces. The party chose to play the card of legal and electoral action. In his desire for national unanimity, prompted by the thought that Communists would be better controlled and would be less likely to create social disorder if closely associated to the government, and influenced finally by the Socialists' wish to see the Communists share ministerial responsibility, de Gaulle offered cabinet positions to Communist leaders, thus introducing them to the sanctum of the executive and giving them an aura of legality. In 1945 the party claimed to have a million members and obtained 26.1 per cent of the votes in the general election. Excluded from the key ministries, the Communists endeavored, with limited success, to infiltrate the administrative machinery. Hoping to attract further support from the centrist electorate, the party associated itself with the "colonial" policy of repressing by force nationalist disturbances in Indochina and Algeria, and it called on workers to accept necessary financial sacrifices and to increase their productivity. The many Communist mayors and local councilors were instructed to establish personal records as good, sound administrators. But the party failed in its attempt at forming a new popular front with the Socialists. The latter accepted collaboration with the Communists in the government provided that the MRP be party to the alliance. As the years passed, the Communists found themselves more and more isolated in the tripartite governments, and began to wonder whether they would not be better in the opposition, from where they could lure the Socialist electorate. In 1947 Paul Ramadier, then prime minister, expelled the Communists from his government after they had refused to vote the military budget. The party, which had contemplated a voluntary withdrawal but not an expulsion, then made a serious attempt at paralyzing the economic life of the nation by launching a series of strikes. With the help of Jules Moch, Ramadier restored order and thus proved that one could govern without Communists in his cabinet. After 1947 the party lost members as well as authority over its supporters. Only with difficulty could it rouse its troops to action, whether for strikes or street demonstrations. The party did not lose electoral strength until 1958, however. For the ten years following their expulsion from the cabinet, the Communists maintained their national vote at about 25 per cent. Only in 1958 did it drop sharply to about 19 per cent.

Since 1947 the Communist party has been in a difficult tactical position. Unable to gain power either legally or by force, the party endeavored to keep its revolutionary apparatus in good shape while maintaining as large an electorate as possible, thus closing neither the legal nor the revolutionary avenues to power.

### Organization

Based theoretically on the principle of democratic centralism which calls for the subordination of the lower echelons to the higher ones but which as a counterpart calls for the election of officers by the ordinary members, the Communist party organization is in fact based on the principle of coöptative centralism.

There are four major echelons in the organization: those of the cell, of the section, of the federation, and of the national organs.

### The Cell

Except for an unknown but probably limited number of "Communists in hiding" attached directly to national headquarters, members of the party belong to grass root organizations, the cells. Those are classified into three groups: the workplace cells, the homeplace cells, and the rural cells. The first type is organized on the basis of the place of work, the second on the basis of residence, the third combines both residence and place of work. The membership of a cell varies roughly from three to eighty members. When a cell contains more than fifty members the party usually divides it, if proper leadership for a new cell can be found. The party prefers workplace cells to homeplace cells. Composed of members having in common their work rather than their place of residence, a workplace cell can be used far more effectively to maintain and develop class consciousness among workers. But the frequent changes of working shifts, the unwillingness of members to stay for cell meetings after working hours and the fear of losing one's job have been obstacles to the growth of these cells. In 1955 the work cells were only about 20 per cent of the total number, the homeplace cells accounted for 45 per cent, and the rural cells for 35 per cent.

The functions of the cell are thus defined by the party rules: "The duties of the cell are: The accomplishment of the party's work among the working population through systematic propaganda and agitation, through recruiting, through diffusion of party literature . . . through intervention in all political conflicts."

As a matter of principle cells meet once a week or at least once every fortnight. Extraordinary meetings are called to discuss a particular question, a strike for example. At regular meetings, the cell's secretary delivers a report analyzing political and other developments during the week. Then a general discussion takes place during which the "better educated" members analyze local and national or international events in terms of party doctrine. After the secretary's report and the general discussion which are compulsory, the cell deals with its own problems such as propaganda, collection of fees, meetings of ancillary organizations.

Each cell divides the work of organization among the members of its executive known as "bureau." Theoretically elected every six months or every year, the bureau is in fact selected by coöptation under the supervision of a delegate from the local section. Administrative work and political leadership is concentrated in the hands of the secretary.

Individual cells are autonomous. If they coördinate action, they do so through the superior echelon, the "section"; their financial resources are obtained from membership fees, of which they receive a 25 per cent share, and from occasional collections or money drives. The party is organized financially on the principle that money moves upward but not downward. Assistance from higher echelons takes a material instead of a financial form: literature and posters, for example.

### The Section

The section, which groups a varying number of cells, has no fixed geographical basis. Large factories such as Renault have a section of their own but most sections have control over all cells of an area, whether workplace cells or homeplace cells.

Each cell sends a varying number of delegates to a section

convention; one delegate and one additional representative for every five members. The convention meets in principle three times a year. Its main function is to review section activities and to select an executive. The latter is selected, like that of the cell, by coöptation, with the higher echelon, the federation, having a right of veto over candidacies. The section executive committee varies from fifteen to thirty-five members; a majority of its members should be workers. From among the members of the executive committee, a bureau is selected by the members of the outgoing bureau under the supervision of the federation's secretary. General leadership of the section is in the hands of a section secretary who is an important figure in the local party hierarchy. He maintains contact with the cells, he relays to the cells orders from the center and conveys to the center workers' reactions and grievances. The section secretary is usually a worker actually employed rather than a former worker on the party's payroll.

The section collects 25 per cent of the members' fees and of the various collections made by the cells.

### The Federation

The sections of a given *département* are grouped into a "federation." A few *départements* have been divided into more than one federation, for example in northern France where the mining area has been separated from the coastal area for tactical reasons.

Each section sends to a yearly federal convention a number of representatives proportional to membership. In selecting the candidates, effort is made to have a majority of workers, preferably under thirty years of age. These preferences throw light on the major function of federal conventions. They are not convened to elect executives or define policies, but to educate and promote future leaders. In order to prevent sclerosis of the *département* organization, a certain number of members of the executive are replaced each year. Such replacements do not necessarily mean demotion for the outgoing members. The number of executive officers varies from *département* to *départe-*

*ment*. In large federations such as that of Seine, it reaches sixty or more. The executive committee meets usually once a month. Its major function is to relay to the local organizations the tactical positions defined by the center. The true executive of the federation is its secretariat. The key position in the secretariat is that of federal secretary. In all large federations, the federal secretary and often his colleagues on the secretariat are party officials, giving full time to the party. The federal secretary is selected with utmost care by national headquarters. Preferably he must come from the working class [3] and be familiar with his *département;* he must also have a good training in Marxist doctrine and in communist strategy. Usually he will have received this training in the party's special schools for *cadres*.

The regular financial resources of a federation come from membership fees and local collections, 25 per cent of which accrue to the federation, and from the salaries received by the Communists elected to local representative positions.

The federations are responsible for much of the printing of propaganda material and for the organization of mass meetings or rallies.

### The National Level

According to the rules, the supreme party organ is the national congress which meets theoretically every three years. It is composed of delegates from the various federations selected by the federation secretariats in collaboration with national headquarters. In theory the congress is the legislative body for the party; it has sole authority for changes in program and doctrine. It is also supposed to select the national executive. In fact the role of the party congress is almost purely educational. The very atmosphere of a congress with its church-like silence and respectful attention is indicative. A congress is a solemn gathering of present and future leaders, a communion, an act of faith, a show of strength. All the speeches have been prepared with extreme care and checked and rechecked for orthodoxy. In the early years of the Communist party, discussions and debates originating from the floor were sometimes quite lively, but a public criticism of the speeches made from the rostrum would now seem shocking and utterly unacceptable. Any discussion of party line or of the acts of the leaders is confined to the political committee which meets in executive session, during the congress, to decide on new appointments to the national executive and to put in final form the motions to be submitted to a vote. The political committee includes the outgoing members of the political bureau and members selected by the national secretariat.

A few months before a congress, so-called "draft theses" (motions) are published in the Communist press. They are the object of formal discussions in the various local organizations, especially the cells. The national newspaper *l'Humanité* publishes a few letters to the editor on some of the draft theses. In 1956 a little more freedom than previously was allowed in the public criticism of the proposed theses. *L'Humanité* published some courteous and moderate objections to the party line. However, if a few dealt with the then crucial problem of the cult of personality, a larger number concerned the topic of birth control. But if there is not much discussion in public, the rank-and-file members are encouraged to speak freely at cell meetings. This discussion enables the leadership to know the reaction of their supporters to a proposed strategy and on the basis of such information to modify its position eventually.

The national congress elects a central committee and a finance committee. Their members are in fact selected by the political committee, itself dominated by the secretariat. The finance committee has a very minor and purely administrative role. The central committee is of greater importance. Among its seventy-one members one finds the national leaders, the secretaries of the major federations, important members of the ancillary organizations, particularly the CGT, as well as a few party intellectuals. In the central committee, the hard core leadership, which dates from before the war, surrounds itself with younger members. Some of them agglomerate to the group of stable leaders, others are rejected at following congresses. The turnover is usually about 20 per cent. As an exception, in order to emphasize that when the cult of personality was being criticized the party stood united, no member was dropped from the central committee in 1956.[4] In addition to its regular members, the committee has twenty-two alternates. A member of the central committee is usually expected to have served first as an alternate. In 1959 out of eleven new members, ten were selected from the alternates, one from the finance committee.

The central committee selects from its members a politbureau and a secretariat. The politbureau is composed of fourteen members and four alternates; the secretariat of six members is headed by a secretary-general. Since 1956, three members of the secretariat must come from the politbureau, the three others from the central committee. Although the congress of 1956 emphasized that the politbureau was the higher executive organ, the actual direction of the party is in the hands of the secretariat and more particularly in those of its secretary-general who since 1936 has been Maurice Thorez.[5] The choice of members for the politbureau and for the secretariat is made by the secretary-general. It is not known precisely what role the Russian Communist party plays in the selection of the French Communist hierarchy. The influence of Moscow was clearly recognizable in the changes of leadership which took place in the 1920's. In 1923 for example the Comintern forced the party secretary to resign although his "Centrist" policy had been approved by a majority of the French party congress. It is doubtful that Moscow could now as easily impose its own choices.

The major financial resources of national headquarters include a 25 per cent share of membership fees and of local or national collections and the salaries of Communist representatives in parliament. The loss of one hundred forty seats in the National Assembly in 1958 resulted in a loss of 40,000,000 francs a month [6] (about $80,000). The contributions made by foreign Communist countries could not be determined.

### The Secret Apparatus

In addition to the surface organization, the Communist party maintains an underground structure. The effectiveness of this secret organization was demonstrated during the Second World War. In September, 1939, the Daladier government dissolved the Communist party and all other organizations associated with the Third International, jailed thousands of party and trade-union leaders, and banned the Communist papers. The party continued nevertheless its activity, published newspapers clandestinely, and maintained contact with members. The normal organization was replaced by one better adapted to illegal action. The cells were replaced by groups of three members contacting each other only through the higher echelons. Unlike the surface organization, the underground fulfills Lenin's definition of the Communist party as a small and tightly organized group of professional revolutionaries entirely devoted to an ideal.

### Ancillary Organizations

The many groups and organizations controlled by the Communist party belong to two categories, the membership organizations and the commercial organizations. The most important of the membership organizations is the *Confédération Générale du Travail* (CGT) which groups a majority of industrial workers affiliated to a trade union. The CGT includes Communists and non-Communists but the first have complete control of the leadership. The secretary general, Benoit Frachon, is a member of the party's politbureau. Among other unions controlled by the Communist party are the *Conféderation Générale du Commerce et de l'Industrie* and the *Commerçants, Artisans et Petits Industriels;* they have but a small following.

Other important membership organizations include the French Women's Union (*Union des Femmes Françaises*) and a great number of specialized organizations such as those for newspapermen, writers, veterans, tenants, and children among others. These organizations are open to non-Communists of Progressive leanings but are always controlled by members of the party hierarchy.

The major commercial organizations include printing, editing, and distributing companies such as *Editeurs Français Réunis* and *Editions Sociales,* as well as libraries and the *Banque Com-*

*merciale pour l'Europe du Nord* which is used for financial transactions with Communist countries and in which all major French Communist organizations have an account.

PARTY LEADERSHIP

Since 1936 the position of secretary general has been held by Maurice Thorez who had entered the party secretariat in 1929. Taken gravely ill in 1950, Thorez spent the following three years in the U.S.S.R. The leadership of the party remained theoretically his but was in fact assumed by the other members of the secretariat together with the influential members of the politbureau. The absence of Thorez and the lack of any precise rule for taking decisions led to personal conflicts among lesser leaders. A. Marty backed by C. Tillon wanted to inherit Thorez's powers. Countered by J. Duclos, B. Frachon, and J. Vermeersch, however, Marty and Tillon were downgraded, then expelled. Duclos assumed the *interim.* Since his return to France in 1953 Thorez has again taken full control of the party machine but his bad health, which keeps him away from Paris most of the year, obliges him to rely more heavily than before on his lieutenants, in particular on J. Duclos, J. Vermeersch, B. Frachon, J. Servin, F. Billoux, E. Fajon, Waldeck-Rochet, and L. Casanova.

The top leadership of the party, represented by Thorez, Duclos, and Frachon has been in control since the 1930's. Purges have been infrequent since Thorez's appointment to the secretariat but they have affected such important members of the hierarchy as Barbé and Celor in 1931–1934 and Tillon, Marty, and Lecoeur in 1954. Because of purges and because also of the practice of renewing the membership of the politbureau by about 20 per cent at each national congress, the top *directorate* has been able to surround itself with a renewed body of advisers.

All members of the secretariat and of the politbureau and most members of the central committee are professional politicians. The party gives its secretary general the possibility of a bourgeois existence, but purposely gives only a modest salary to other leaders.

## Membership and Electorate

Around the top party leadership gravitate the small group of party officials and the mass of ordinary members who divide themselves into active and occasional militants. The party officials include all those who work for the party full time and draw their salary from it. A. Brayance estimates them to be about 2,000 in the Paris area,[7] where they are mostly concentrated. They are entirely devoted to the party. Among the ordinary members, active militants number probably less than 70,000 but no reliable figures are obtainable. The total party membership, that of the card-carrying members who have paid at least part of their yearly fees is known only approximately.[8] According to the figures given at the party congress of 1959, the total number of cards sent by national headquarters to local organizations between January and May numbered 425, 150.[9] Even if such figures could be considered reliable, one would still not know how many cards were actually sold. The party rarely gives figures on actual membership. These have to be deduced from various sources. In 1956, for example, Marcel Servin,[10] saying that the party had gained 50,000 new members in a year, added that this number represented twice the members of 1934. Previously, Thorez [11] had given for the end of 1933 a figure of 45,000. Considering that membership was claimed to have increased from 1933 to 1934, the figures given by Thorez and Servin show a great discrepancy. There were 25,000 members according to Servin; at least 45,000 according to Thorez. The difference is to be explained either by assuming that figures given by the party are pure invention or that the actual number of members was about half that of cards sent to the local organizations by party headquarters. Party membership in 1960 could be estimated at anywhere from 200,000 to 400,000. The number of members in 1959 was probably much lower than that of 1956. Membership which had reached its peak in 1945–1946 when claimed to be about a million, has declined ever since and has fallen to its prewar level.

According to party sources,[12] the party's social composition was as follows in 1959: factory workers, 40.3 per cent; agricultural workers, 5; farmers, 8.2; civil servants, 12.2; school teachers, 2.7; shopkeepers and artisans, 6.7. Men accounted for 78.1; women, for 20.2. The distribution by age group was: under twenty-five, 5.6 per cent; between twenty-six and forty, 38.3; over forty, 56.2. The Communist party attracts more young people proportionally than any other party in France.

Membership in the Communist party, at least among active Communists, has deep psychological effects. Communists have the feeling that they are a minority, that they live in hostile surroundings, but they are convinced that history flows their way. The party gives a meaning to their material difficulties and gives them hope for the future. The class consciousness instilled into them makes them naturally conceive adherence to the party as the normal form of loyalty to other workers. In the dechristianized industrial suburbs of the big cities, the Communist party has replaced the church, and acts like one in offering men an all-embracing philosophy of life as well as a political program. The Communist lives in a Communist world, reads Communist newspapers, novels, or comics and becomes used to a Communist vocabulary. His intellectual contacts with non-Communists are often limited to the radio and the movies. Frequently attachment to the party is not for ideological reasons and has no deeper roots than loyalty to the surrounding group. For example, the behavior of Communists drafted in Algeria has shown that most transferred their loyalties to the new army group.

Since the creation of the party, the Communist electorate has oscillated between 8 and 28 per cent of the total vote in the general elections.

If one excepts the decline of 1932, the Communist electorate has grown in size at each election from 1924 to 1946, stabilized itself between 1951 and 1956, after a slight decline from the peak of 1946, and dropped significantly in 1958. The French Communist electorate is, proportionally, one of the largest outside the Communist world; in the West it comes third after the Finnish and the Italian.

According to a sample survey made in 1952 by the *Institut Français d'Opinion Publique*,[13] the Communist electorate was composed of the following groups (in per cent):

| | | | |
|---|---|---|---|
| Industrial workers | 44 | Civil servants | 4 |
| Nonworking women | 22 | Retired people | 3 |
| Agricultural workers | 10 | Businessmen, shopkeepers | 3 |
| Employees | 6 | Industrialists and cadres | 1 |
| Farmers | 5 | Professional people | 1 |

Industrial workers compose the largest single group and, together with farm hands, make the majority. Nearly 65 per cent of this electorate is composed of salaried people; independent farmers and farm hands account for another 15 per cent, while profit makers are only 10 per cent.

TABLE 2

COMMUNIST VOTES IN GENERAL ELECTIONS, METROPOLITAN FRANCE (In per cent)

| | | | |
|---|---|---|---|
| 1924 | 9.8 | 1946 | 26.2 |
| 1928 | 11.4 | 1946 | 28.6 |
| 1932 | 8.4 | 1951 | 25.9 |
| 1936 | 15.4 | 1956 | 25.9 |
| 1945 | 26.1 | 1958 | 18.9 |

The Communist electorate is not only largest, it is also best distributed geographically. In 1956 no single *département* gave less than 5 per cent of its votes to the Communists and in 1958 only two; the Manche and the Deux-Sèvres, did so. In 1958 only 18 of 90 *départements* gave less than 10 per cent of their votes to Communist candidates. These *départements* of relative Communist weakness are located in eastern France, along the German border and in western France in the belt extending from the Poitou to western Normandy. The former are in industrial, the latter in agricultural areas. Elsewhere, with the exception of the Basses-Pyrénées and the Haute Loire, the Communist party got more than 10 per cent of the votes. Its main strength comes from the industrial area which goes from Paris to the Belgian border, from the agricultural northern and western borders of the Massif Central and from the Mediterranean coast, which is industrialized in its eastern part and predominantly agricultural in the west. Better than other French parties of the Left, the Communists have avoided too pronounced a sectionalism.

## Doctrine and Tactics

The acceptance by French Communists of orthodox Russian communism as their doctrine has already been considered.[14] The French Communist party conceives its major role as increasing class consciousness among the workers, training and preparing a party elite for revolutionary and postrevolutionary tasks; its objective is also to weaken the "capitalist" camp and to paralyze the representative system of government by gaining the support of as many Frenchmen as possible. With these goals in mind the party leadership has to avoid two pitfalls which in its own terminology are called "sectarianism" and "opportunism." The sectarianist errs in giving sole attention to the party elite and the training of professional Marxist revolutionaries, while the opportunist errs in devoting himself exclusively to building a mass following. To avoid both sins, the party has tried to pursue at the same time the two aims of creating a small party of revolutionists and of winning the support of a large section of the electorate. Some of the seeming contradictions of the party are explained by the desire to prepare at the same time a revolution by force and a revolution by legal means. Denouncing war in Algeria satisfies the party doctrinaires, voting the military credits for Algeria is meant to impress upon the Socialists the feasibility of a popular front. The Communist party hopes that a Left-wing majority will eventually emerge from future elections as a reaction against the Right-wing first parliament of the Fifth Republic. They hope that the conditions of 1946 will reappear when Communists and Socialists had a majority in the National Assembly. They further hope that the Socialists will this time enter a governing coalition solely with the Communists. In the meantime their near elimination from the National Assembly in 1958, as a result of changes in the electoral system, will prevent the

Communist party from playing any significant role in the parliament. Compelled to what they think is only a period of parliamentary hibernation, they are giving greater attention to the trade unions which now remain their major political force.

How much Russia influences the tactical decisions of the French Communist party cannot be determined precisely, but it is beyond doubt that whenever deciding to interfere, Moscow was able to impose its own line. In 1922 the Fourth Congress of the Third International obliged French Communists to accept collaboration with the Socialists; in 1928 the Comintern reversed its attitude and ordered the treating of Socialists as class enemies; in 1934 Moscow called for a return to the earlier tactic of association with "bourgeois" parties and the formation of popular-front coalitions; in 1935, after the signing of the French-Soviet pact, Stalin asked French Communists to support rearmament and national defense; but in 1939, having allied himself with Hitler, he imposed an overnight change. The German attack against the U.S.S.R. in June, 1941, reversed again Moscow's orders to French Communists who were asked now to participate actively in the Resistance and to collaborate with non-Communist parties. Such collaboration lasted until 1947, when condemned by the newly created Cominform. In 1952 Stalin called again for a change of attitude and a return to the policy of the "open hand" to the Socialists. In 1959, the sudden reversal of French Communists on de Gaulle's Algerian peace proposals, first ridiculed then fully supported, is most likely to have resulted from a modification of the Kremlin's foreign policy. These tactical shifts imposed from above have cost the French Communist party some of its members; but the losses have been very limited and more than compensated by the benefits derived from these Communist great maneuvers which tested and proved reliability of the party machine.

# 4 *The SFIO*

The word *socialism* was probably coined by Pierre Leroux about 1830 in contrast to *individualism.*[1] However, the French socialist movement had begun earlier. At the end of the eighteenth century, Gracchus Babeuf and P. M. Buonarroti had founded a revolutionary organization which agitated for the abolition of private property and which, in 1796, attempted unsuccessfully to seize power. In the 1820's Saint Simon had proposed that the evolution of societies is due to changes in the rules concerning ownership and further suggested that the Roman law system of private property was by no means eternal; still in the first two decades of the nineteenth century Fourier had violently criticized the principle of free competition believed to reintroduce slavery under the name of salaried class, and had offered to reorganize society along the principles of association and coöperation; the workers' insurrection of 1831 in Lyon had shown the beginnings of class consciousness among the "fourth estate," the newly formed industrial proletariat.

After 1830, the socialist ideology proliferated. A. Blanqui called for the overthrow of the government by the working class and for the abolition of private property; L. Blanc advocated a system of full employment guaranteed and organized by the state in order to end poverty; V. Considerant and E. Cabet enlarged on Fourier's concept of a society divided into autonomous communities, the members of which would transfer all private properties to the group. F. Leroux saw in the state's controlling a large sector of the economy a cure to the growing impoverishment of the masses. Finally P. J. Proudhon while condemning the system of private ownership rejected both communism and authoritarian socialism in favor of a vague and badly formulated anarchism based on voluntary coöperation.

The revolution of 1848 was a short-lived success for the socialists. Allied with the Republicans they entered the government but soon the bourgeoisie found the socialists' questioning the existing order no longer acceptable now that the monarchy had been overthrown. Expelled from the cabinet, defeated at the polls, the socialists tried to impose themselves by force. At the end of a four-day battle in the streets of Paris the insurrection was crushed. Those among socialist leaders who had survived barricade fighting were jailed or exiled. The socialist movement entered a period of stagnation which lasted until the 1860's. From his jail Blanqui managed to regain authority over the discouraged revolutionary socialists and tried to arouse them. However the impetus for the relaunching of socialism came mainly from outside France; from the London International founded in 1864; from the German Socialist party; from the British trade-union movement then in full development. Marxism, thus far of little influence, gained ground among French socialists.

In 1871, following the defeat at Sedan, the fall of the Second Empire, the encirclement, then the capture of Paris, a revolutionary government of socialists and extreme republicans, the so-called Commune, seized power in the capital. After two months of violent struggle the Commune was defeated by Thiers and the regular army. As after 1848, the socialist movement was left completely disorganized.

In the 1880's a new generation of socialists, together with Blanqui, who had finally been released from jail, organized small socialist parties, the first modern political parties to be created in France. They were Guesde's French Workers party, Brousse's Socialist Workers Federation, Allemane's Socialist Workers party, Blanqui's and Vaillant's Central Revolutionary Committee, and Jaurès' Independent Socialists. At the turn of the century these various parties grouped themselves into moderates and extremists. The Broussists, the Allemanists, and the Independent Socialists formed the reformist French Socialist party, while the Guedists and the Blanquists founded the revolutionist Socialist Party of France. The first drew its doctrine in part from Marx but mainly from pre-1848 French socialists; the second mostly from Marx and Engels. In 1893, fifty socialist deputies entered the lower house; Guesde, Vaillant, Millerand, and Viviani were among them. In 1899 Waldeck Rousseau, seeking to form a wide pro-Dreyfus coalition cabinet offered a ministry to Millerand. The latter's acceptance provoked a crisis among socialists and further aggravated the conflict between reformists and revolutionists. Jaurès, who backed Viviani, led the first group; Vaillant and Guesde, who considered Viviani a traitor to his class, led the extremists.

In 1904 the Second International called its Sixth Congress to discuss the question of socialist participation in a bourgeois government. French Revolutionists had 41 votes; Reformists, 38. Jaurès, in the minority, accepting the majority's decision but making the most of this show of discipline, succeeded in unifying the two major French socialist groups. Thus was founded in 1905 the French Section of the International Workers Union (SFIO). The two major clauses of the founding charter placed the party to the extreme Left.

Art. 1. The Socialist party is a class party, the aim of which is to socialize the means of production and exchange, that is to say to transform the capitalist society into a collectivist or communistic society. The means used by the party (to achieve its goal) is the economic and political organization of the proletariat. Because of its aim and ideal, because of the means it uses, the Socialist party, while working toward the realization of short range economic reforms demanded by the working class, is not a reformist party but a party of class warfare and revolution.

2. The parliamentary representatives form a single group vis a vis all the bourgeois political fractions. The socialist parliamentary group must refuse to the government all the means which render possible bourgeois domination and maintenance of power; the parliamentary group must consequently turn down the military budget, the budget for colonial policy, secret funds and the whole budget.[2]

The newly formed party had in 1906 a membership of about 12,000; it reached 52,000 in 1910.[3] The same year the Socialists obtained 13 per cent of the seats in the Chamber of Deputies with 13 per cent of the votes; in 1914, at the last election before the war, they gained 17 per cent of the votes and seats. Membership had reached 72,000. The party had campaigned against the "three-year law," a conscription measure introduced by the government to prepare for the impending war. At an extraordinary congress meeting in July, 1914, Jaurès proposed to answer a declaration of war by a general strike. Jules Guesde objected that the sole effect of the strike would be to deliver the more socialistic to the least socialistic of the two nations at war. However, the congress supported the general-strike idea by 1,670 to 1,184 votes. Jaurès's success was not caused by a reversal in the relative strength of the reformists; it was rather due to Guesde's evolution from extremist positions to more conservative attitudes in the face of Germany's military threat. Jaurès was murdered by a fanatic the day France entered the war; Guesde joined the war cabinet.

Stunned by a military conflict they had thought impossible—they had believed that German socialists would prevent it—the pacifist socialists rallied to the defense of their fatherland; but as the war dragged on, the internationalists regained strength within the party. In 1916 a national congress passed a motion endorsing the government's war policy by a bare majority of 1,537 to 1,407.[4]

Following the war the Socialist party made remarkable gains. It obtained 22.7 per cent of the votes in the election of 1919; its membership rose to 180,000 in 1920. However the party was torn by the question of relationships with Moscow. Frossard, party secretary general, and Cachin, editor of *L'Humanité*, were sent on a mission to Russia. Both reported favorably on accepting Lenin's twenty-one-point ultimatum and on joining the Third International. An extraordinary congress was held at Tours in 1920 to decide this last point. For affiliation, 3,208 votes were cast; against, 1,022. The minority, led by P. Faure and L. Blum, withdrew from the party, but as the majority had decided to adopt the new name of Communist party, the minority was able to take with it the old name, SFIO. Only 50,000 of the 180,000 members, but fifty-four of sixty-eight deputies, remained with the SFIO. This difference of attitude reveals a source of conflict which was and has remained chronic: the opposition between parliamentarians and militants.

Separated from the Communists, the SFIO, between the two wars, shook off the Marxist program forced on them by the revolutionists following the unification of 1905. True, they continued to profess adherence to Marxism and fought the election of 1924 on the same platform as that of 1919, but behind the inherited phraseology, the beliefs were no longer the same. The SFIO became a reformist labor party. In 1924 the Socialists who had formed an electoral coalition with the Radicals, obtained 17 per cent of the seats in the National Assembly, while the Communists had only 10 per cent. Under the leadership of Léon Blum, the Socialists resumed an evolution which had commenced with Millerand's entry into the Waldeck-Rousseau cabinet, but which had been interrupted in 1905 for the sake of party unity. Although Blum refused to participate in the Herriot government of 1924, he gave parliamentary support to the Radical premier, and at a meeting of the party's national council, Blum was supported, by 1,157 votes to 730, in that Socialist parliamentarians be allowed to vote the budget provided it called for substantial social reforms. The same year, a national congress authorized them to enter coalition governments provided Socialists be given the premiership and a majority of cabinet posts. In 1927 the party revamped its electoral platform, proposing more moderate and more specific reforms. The party campaigned for women's suffrage, proportional representation, paid annual holidays, the nationalization of monopolies and public services, workers' participation in management of private enterprises, the abolition of private schools, the end of secret diplomacy, the preparation of a United States of Europe, and for the abolition of the Senate and of military courts. In 1932 following a general election which gave the SFIO 20 per cent of the votes and 21 per cent of the seats in the Chamber, a national party congress authorized by an overwhelming majority (3,682 to 154) participation in a bourgeois government; the only conditions were that the government agree to a minimum program of reforms including a cut in military expenditures, interdiction of private commerce of military weapons, balancing of the budget (by other means than reduction in expenditures for social services, schools, and agriculture), control of banking, and a forty-hour labor week. The Radicals would have welcomed Socialists in the government but rejected their minimum program. The Socialist party headquarter's subsequent decisions not to allow their parliamentarians to enter the cabinet provoked a conflict between parliamentary group and party leadership. The attempt made by the party to maintain its authority over the parliamentary group led to a serious split. Thirty-five parliamentarians out of 129, and 20,000 of the 140,000 adherents, left the SFIO, and under the leadership of Renaudel founded a dissident party, the short-lived Parti Socialiste de France. A second group of socialist deputies led by M. Déat and A. Marquet formed the Neo-Socialist party which later fell under Nazi influence. Notwithstanding these defections, the SFIO polled a victory in 1936, with 20 per cent of the votes and 24 per cent of the seats. Together with the Radicals and the Communists, the Socialists had formed an electoral coalition, the Popular Front, which obtained a majority of the seats in the Chamber of Deputies. The largest group in the winning coalition, the SFIO, was entrusted with the responsibility of forming the government: Léon Blum became France's first Socialist prime minister. His cabinet included Socialists and Radicals, the Communists having promised parliamentary support but having refused to take seats in the cabinet. The Popular Front electoral success led workers to believe that a new era was about to begin, that the capitalist system was about to disappear. Strikes combined with occupation of factories by strikers spread throughout France before Blum was officially installed as premier. Once in power the Socialists re-established order but failed to introduce any drastically new legislation. Blum's reforms were in essence comparable to Roosevelt's New Deal. A few armament plants were either nationalized or put under strict government control; collective bargaining between management and trade unions was organized legally; the working week was reduced to forty hours; paid holidays were made compulsory; wages, as a result of government arbitration between management and labor, were increased by about 15 per cent. But workers generally felt that they had been betrayed, that Blum had fallen prisoner to big business, that no serious structural reform had been even attempted. The Communist slogan "Blum à l'action" described the working-class disenchantment with the Socialist party—disenchantment which benefited the Communists, who appeared as a more truly working-class party than the Socialists. The Blum government episode convinced many leaders of the SFIO, although not Blum himself, that to ally themselves with parties to their Right while allowing parties to their Left to remain in the opposition was unwise. During Blum's term in office, the SFIO showed signs of internal tension. Marceau Pivert formed within the party an opposition group which, significantly enough, called itself the Revolutionary Left. The expulsion of Pivert at the national congress of 1938 was endorsed by only 4,904 votes to 3,033.[5]

The military defeat of 1940 and the formation of the Pétain government split the party asunder. A majority of the parliamentary group and the party's secretary-general, Paul Faure, joined the "defeatist" camp and backed the Vichy regime. Eighty Socialists out of 116 voted constitutional powers to Pétain and two of them, Faure and Belin, entered his government. The "resistants" followed Blum in his opposition to the new government. After all political parties had been dissolved, the SFIO reorganized itself clandestinely under the leadership of R. Verdier and D. Mayer. Unlike the Communists, the Socialists did not retain control over many of their adherents but succeeded in gaining or keeping control of a number of Resistance groups especially in northern France. Socialists were given important positions in de Gaulle's provisional government in exile [6] and one of their leaders, F. Gouin, was elected chairman of the Consultative Assembly. The first postwar election, that of 1945, gave 23.8 per cent of the votes and 25.7 per cent of the seats to the SFIO. The party had gained slightly as compared to 1936 but was only the third largest, coming after the Communists and the MRP. Caught between these two parties, the Socialists were, whether liking it or not, compelled to play the role formerly reserved to the Radicals, that of a Center party and consequently that of a governmental party.

The immediate postwar period bears the mark of the SFIO. The constitution of 1946, the nationalizations, the social-security scheme, and various other social reforms were the result of collaboration and compromise between the three parties in the government, the MRP, the SFIO, and the Communists; but as the SFIO was the axis of the coalition, the reforms reflected better the Socialist program than those of the other two parties. Blum wanted his party to accept without reservation the new role resulting from the growth in size of the Communist party, that of defending democracy while introducing as many Socialist reforms as possible. Opposition within and without the party prevented the Socialist leader from realizing a wide-open labor party which could have appealed to former Radicals as well as to Christian democrats. At its 1944 national congress, the SFIO chose to revive the clerical issue by demanding the abolition of government subsidies to private schools. In 1946, Blum's proposal to replace the old Marxian article 1 of the party rules by a new declaration of principles more adapted to the party's revisionist program was defeated at a national council. A majority of the delegates still hoped to regain the working-class electorate lost to the Communists. While the leadership wanted expansion to the Right, the rank and file wanted expansion to the Left. The failure of the SFIO to transform itself into a French version of the English Labour party was also due to outside obstacles. The party could not expand to the Right because of the MRP and because of the Radical hostility; it could not expand to the Left because the Communist electorate was faithfully behind its leaders who would not consider a merger with the SFIO unless on their own terms.[7]

A slight electoral setback in June, 1946, gave new vigor to the militant's hostility toward the parliamentarians, as usual accused of softness toward the government and of doctrinal betrayals. In 1946 the national congress took the unprecedented step of voting nonconfidence in its secretary general, D. Mayer, who was replaced by Guy Mollet. Further electoral setbacks and a decline in party membership convinced Mollet that the party should withdraw from the government. In 1947, he contributed to the defeat of the government led by his Socialist colleague, P. Ramadier. From de Gaulle's resignation in 1946 until 1947, three of the four prime ministers had been Socialists. From 1947 to 1951 Socialists participated in coalition ministries but did not hold the premiership. From 1951 to 1955 they withdrew completely into the opposition by not accepting ministerial positions. This opposition cure, supposed to be rejuvenating for a party, ended in 1955 when Socialist Pineau formed a cabinet. From 1955 to 1958, the SFIO participated in all ministries and Mollet headed the longest-lived government of the Fourth Republic, from January 31, 1956 to May 21, 1957.

Mollet who in 1947 had led the opposition to Mayer and Blum, accused of being too moderate, had by 1957 moved to an even more Centrist position than Mayer himself, now cast in the role of a Left-wing minority leader. The party leadership had been forced to gear its attitude on the party electorate rather than on the militants. Mollet's launching of the Suez expedition, his stand against the Algerian Moslem rebellion, his rallying to General de Gaulle after the crisis of May 13, all created unrest within the party. In January, 1958, A. Philip, one of the few party ideologists and one-time member of de Gaulle's provisional government, was expelled from the party for his attacks against the leadership's lack of respect for socialist principles. In July, 1958, D. Mayer, leader of the party during the Resistance, left the SFIO and together with Mendès-France launched the *Union des Forces Démocratiques* to rally the non-Communist opponents to de Gaulle. In September, 1958, E. Depreux and D. Mayer founded the Autonomous Socialist party for the purpose of grouping all socialists hostile to Mollet's leadership. Early in 1959, Vincent Auriol, former president of the Republic, announced that he had not renewed his membership card. To prevent further disintegration as well as to protest against the government's financial and economic policy, the SFIO refused to participate in the first government of the Fifth Republic, thus beginning its second postwar opposition cure.

### Organization

Notwithstanding the growing complaint among the rank and file that the party's internal structure is becoming too rigid and that freedom of discussion is disappearing, the SFIO remains of all French parties that with the most democratic organization in practice as well as in theory. The unification of 1905 had been made conditional to the adoption of a structure devised to prevent barring of political minorities from the party's governing bodies. Although the SFIO has since then been centralized and is more tightly controlled by the majority group, much remains of the original federation of parties, which had succeeded in combining discipline at the parliamentary level with factionalism within the party machine.

Until 1911 the grass-root organizations were the "groups" which, like the Communist cells, did not necessarily have a geographical basis. Since 1911, the lowest echelon is the section.[8] Theoretically each commune has one, the largest communes being divided into as many sections as required. In fact, there are much fewer sections than communes; according to party estimates there were in 1959 about 8,000 for more than 36,000 communes. A section has no fixed membership; it varies usually from around twenty members to slightly more than one thousand. Membership is determined by the buying of a permanent card, of an annual voucher, and of monthly stamps. The price of these items varies from federation to federation and often from section to section since the local organizations are left free to set membership fees.

Each section elects an executive committee by a majority vote. The committee, in turn, elects a section secretary who coördinates political and administrative work. The secretary is often chosen by national or departmental headquarters, especially in the less lively sections where candidates require much prompting to come forward.

The sections of a given department form a federation. The sections select, on the basis of proportional representation, delegates to a federation congress which meets at least once a year before the national congress. These delegates have a number of votes proportional to their section's membership. The federation congress elects an executive by a majority vote, passes motions, and elects representatives to the national congress on the basis of proportional representation. Membership varies greatly from department to department. Only two federations had more than 10,000 members in 1957, Nord with 13,400 and Pas de Calais with 11,800; six others had more than 2,000, Bouches-du-Rhône, Seine, Seine-et-Oise, Haute-Garonne, Gironde, and Haute-Vienne; most had less than 800. The most important position at the federation level is that of the federation secretary who coördinates the actions of the sections of his department. Unlike in the Communist party, the members of the federation executives and in particular the secretaries are not as a rule party officials. Their party activities are additional to their regular work. Only the richest federations, about ten of them, can afford to have any permanent staff, to help with administrative work. Before the war the federations were largely autonomous with regard to propaganda and would often distribute their own literature, but since the war national headquarters centralize all propaganda efforts.

The regular financial resources of the local organizations—not including contributions to electoral chests—come from the benefits made in selling membership cards and stamps. The yearly cards and monthly stamps are bought by the federations from national headquarters then sold at higher prices to the sections which, in turn, try to make as much profit as possible. A stamp bought for 70 francs from headquarters is sometimes sold for as much as 1,000 francs to the members. The small federations thus find themselves at a disadvantage. They are caught in a vicious circle: no members, no money; no money, no members. To alleviate this problem, party headquarters employ about fifteen "federal assistants" who are paid by the national organization and are sent to the federations which show possibilities of expansion but lack local resources. The federal assistants play the role of traveling organizers who, in close relation with national headquarters, endeavor to create or recreate sections throughout the departments, and to revitalize federation machines. The sending of federal assistants has been viewed by certain federations as an interference by the Center in their local affairs and in a few instances help has been refused, but on the whole the experiment has been successful.

At the national level the major organs are the national congress, the national council, the executive committee, and the national secretariat.

The national congress meets at least once a year. Each federation sends a number of delegates which varies according to the federation's declared membership. In 1958 the largest federation, Nord, had thirty delegates, the smallest, two; all but the four largest had less than ten delegates. These share among themselves their federation's votes, the number of which is also determined on the basis of membership. Each federation has one vote, plus one additional vote for each twenty-five members. In 1958, Nord had 429 votes, Vosges, 5. As at the federation level the number of delegates as well as the number of votes is determined by the number of yearly vouchers and stamps sold to a federation by national headquarters in the year preceding the congress. One voucher and twelve stamps are counted as one member. A federation may buy more cards and stamps than they actually can sell in order to get more votes in the congress. The lack of a national file of party members renders impossible the checking of the actual membership of the various federations, but although padding of membership lists is commonly done, there is no likelihood that it be done in such a way as to distort greatly the relative strength of the regional organizations. The delegates to a national congress are chosen by the federal congress through proportional representation. Before the federations hold their congresses, the motions which will be submitted to the national congress are circulated throughout the party. The local organizations are thus able to take a position on these motions and to choose their delegates accordingly. For example in 1957 the outstanding issue was the Algerian question. Among the motions proposed, three crystallized the opposition between various groups within the party: the motion submitted by E. Depreux and eighty other members of the party, the motion proposed by G. Defferre together with members of the Bouches du Rhône federation, and that proposed by the party secretariat. The first called for negotiations with the Algerian rebels and for the recognition of the legitimacy of Algeria's claim to national existence; the second accepted the principle of secret negotiations but rejected the promise of national identity; the third endorsed the policy of G. Mollet, then president of the council, to seek a political negotiation with the elected representatives of the Algerian people themselves after order had been restored. These motions were published in the party's *Bulletin Intérieur* in early June. Federation congresses were held in the three weeks remaining before the national congress called for June 27. The Nièvre congress gave 182 votes to the Depreux motion, 160 to Defferre's and 109 to the secretariat's; the Bouches-du-Rhône, 316 votes from 367 to the Defferre's text; Gironde 1,493 from 1,806 to the secretariat's text. All other federations took a position on these and other motions and selected their delegates in such a way as to give proportional representation to the various factions.

The function of the national congress is double; it defines doctrinal and tactical positions and it elects the national executive.

The congress sits usually for three or four days. It first selects a number of committees, the most important of which is the motions committee, and makes an effort to have all major party factions represented. The committee on motions, which has about thirty members, studies the motions put before the congress; subject to overruling by the congress, the committee decides which motions shall be reported and debated. For each such motion the committee appoints a *rapporteur*. If the committee is not unanimous on a particular problem, as many *rapporteurs* are appointed as there are points of view. Voting on motions is according to the mandate system, each delegate casting as many votes as he has been assigned. These votes need not be cast as a block; they may be distributed among competing motions.

Between national congresses, supreme party authority rests theoretically with a national council which meets usually four times a year and more often if need be at the request of the executive committee. Each federation is represented by a single delegate but voting is according to the mandate system. The national council is often asked to settle urgent questions such as participation in or withdrawal from a government. For example, following the dismissal of Communist ministers from the government in 1947, a national council authorized Ramadier to stay in power by 2,529 to 2,125 mandates; in November, 1957, Socialists were allowed to participate to the Gaillard government by 2,087 to 1,732 mandates. The federation representative, usually the secretary, may and usually does split his votes according to instructions from his own federation. The national council can thus without distortion exercise the "legislative" functions normally assigned to the congress; the council can settle doctrinal and tactical problems, but cannot substitute itself for the congress in the election of the party's executive organs.

The national executive includes an executive committee, (Commité Directeur), a secretariat, a bureau, a conflicts committee and various other committees of lesser importance.

The executive committee is elected by the delegates to the national congress. Each delegate has only one vote. The candidates are listed alphabetically on the same ballot. Each delegate selects from the list of candidates forty-five names of his choice.

The forty-five candidates with the highest number of votes are declared elected, except that parliamentarians may not have more than twenty seats. By limiting the number of its own candidates to less than forty-five, the party leadership may allow minority representatives to obtain a seat on the executive, but ever since a majority system was substituted for proportional representation in 1946, the dominant group has always guaranteed itself a comfortable majority on the national executive. At the fiftieth congress in September, 1958, sixty candidates contested the election. Out of a possible 377 votes, 362 valid votes were cast. The candidate coming on top had 327 votes, the last candidate to be elected, 195; the minimum percentage of votes necessary to obtain election was thus 59 per cent. The minimum has sometimes been higher; a few congresses selected at random give the following figures: 1947, 54 per cent; 1950, 53 per cent; 1951, 62 per cent; 1953, 61 per cent; 1955, 59 per cent. Support by a bare majority of the delegates is usually not sufficient to insure election. The representation of minority fractions thus depends often entirely on the dominant group's willingness to share the executive with them.

Using the same procedure, the national congress also elects a conflicts committee which has disciplinary powers over members and local organizations, subject to appeal before the congress. Two-thirds of the members of the conflicts committee have to be nonparliamentarians. The women delegates, usually approximately a hundred, select a women's national committee which plays a minor role.

The executive committee selects from among its members a party secretariat composed of one secretary general, three vice-secretaries general and a treasurer; the committee also elects, still from among its members, a seven-man bureau which acts as the committee's representative.

The two dominant executive organs are the executive committee and the secretariat. The executive committee has important appointment powers. In addition to electing the secretariat and the bureau, it appoints the secretary general of the Socialist youth organization, the editors and governing boards of the party's national newspapers, *Le Populaire* and *Le Populaire Dimanche* and selects the senior members of the party's study groups, the function of which is to advise the party and the parliamentary group on legislation. More generally the executive committee is entrusted with executing decisions of the congress and council, with directing propaganda, with controlling members, with watching the parliamentary group and, if need be, with calling an extraordinary congress or a national council in order to settle a particularly important question. The executive committee, in collaboration with the parliamentarians, may have to determine electoral or parliamentary tactics. The committee meets at least monthly; decisions are taken by a majority vote. The bureau, which meets usually weekly decides matters of lesser importance and prepares meetings of the executive committee.

The secretariat, dominated by the secretary-general who since the war has always been a parliamentarian, is the source of party leadership. Although the secretary-general is not usually chairman of the parliamentary party, he combines in fact the functions of party machine and caucus leader. However, the secretary-general, whose decisions or advice may be reversed or ignored by the caucus, the executive committee, or the national congress, must rely more on his personal authority and prestige than on the party rules to impose his ideas. As secretary-general since 1946, G. Mollet gained this authority thanks to his ability as a party organizer and to his reputation as one of France's better statesmen. But on certain crucial occasions, even he could not avoid that either the parliamentary caucus or the national executive refuse to follow him. Although backed by the party congress and by the executive committee, the secretary-general could not prevent half of his parliamentary group in the National Assembly voting against the European Defense Community treaty in 1954. In 1958, notwithstanding a forceful plea in favor of de Gaulle and a threat to resign from the leadership, he could not prevent the majority of both the executive committee and the National Assembly caucus from opposing the general's investiture.

The relationships between parliamentary group and party executive have always been a difficult problem for the SFIO. The rules of 1905 provided that no parliamentarian could be a member of the executive committee, then known as the Permanent Administrative Committee (CAP). In 1913 parliamentarians were allowed one-third of the CAP seats, and CAP could give orders to the parliamentary group. However the parliamentary group sometimes refused to abide by the executive's decisions. In 1933 a majority of the parliamentary group, disregarding instructions from the CAP, voted the budget. An extraordinary congress called to deal with this situation dared do no more than vote disapproval of the undisciplined parliamentarian's action. Further insubordinations led to further censures and eventually to a split within the party. At other times the CAP was more successful. In 1929 the deputies who had decided to join the government bowed to the veto of a national council summoned by the CAP. But generally the executive was paralyzed by its inner conflicts, a consequence of its election by proportional representation, and was thus left with little actual authority over the parliamentary group. In 1944 the mode of election of the executive committee was changed to a majority system intended to give more cohesion and power to the party's highest executive body. However, while the executive committee gained in strength because of the change in its system of election, the parliamentary group gained in stature and independence because the party became more a governmental party and a party of personalities rather than a party of masses and of opposition. To end the constant conflicts between caucus and party machine, a joint committee in which the parliamentarians had the majority was created in 1949. Three years later the committee, entrusted with deciding the parliamentary group's tactics subject to congress orders, was abolished. The executive committee was again given authority over the caucus but they agreed that certain questions such as participation in a government and votes of confidence or censure would be settled at a joint meeting of the executive committee and of the parliamentary group. Such joint meetings give the majority to the parliamentarians unless the total number of deputies and senators were to fall under twenty-five. The more important decisions have to be taken by a two-thirds majority. Failing this special majority, the executive committee may take the decision by itself. The parliamentarians would lose their two-thirds majority if they were to fall under fifty; this has not yet occurred. The party executive cannot prevail against a unified parliamentary group, but may still play a role when the caucus is divided.

Because the secretary-general is not only the leading parliamentarian but also dominates, usually, the executive committee, the committee tends to become an instrument used by parliamentary leaders to enforce caucus discipline.

The committee is empowered to sanction members of the parliamentary group who vote against the congress or the joint committee's orders. The sanctions include warning, formal censure, suspension from party and parliamentary responsibilities, and finally expulsion—the last two may be appealed to the conflicts committee and eventually to the national congress.

The party's regular financial resources, excluding special election gifts, come principally from the membership fees and from the compulsory contributions made by the parliamentarians. The national organization's budget for 1958, not counting the election funds handled by an ad-hoc association known as *Socialist Friends*, may give an idea of the limited amount of financial support enjoyed by the national headquarters of one of France's major parties for its regular expenses.

In recent years party headquarters have increased the resources derived from membership fees by obliging the federations to buy from them a minimum 10 per cent of "high"-priced monthly stamps (25 instead of 4 cents). Socialist members of parliament are required to give the party 10 per cent of their parliamentary salary. Due to lack of readjustment when parliamentary salaries were increased, the contribution did not amount to more than 5 per cent in 1958. The steady decline in membership since 1945 has obliged the SFIO to reduce its permanent staff. In 1958 no more than sixty people were permanently employed by the party. Contributions from foreign countries, in particular from the British Labour party and from certain American trade unions, have been necessary to prevent the party's newspaper *Le Populaire* ceasing publication.

TABLE 3

SFIO REVENUES AND EXPENDITURES, 1958
(In dollars)

| REVENUES | |
|---|---|
| Cash on hand January 1, 1958 | 10,110 |
| Membership fees | 116,871 |
| Parliamentarians' contributions | 42,726 |
| Subscriptions to party publications | 2,022 |
| Various money drives and gifts | 5,773 |
| Total | 177,502 |
| **EXPENDITURES** | |
| General administrative expenses | 29,462 |
| General propaganda | 43,450 |
| Socialist International (contributions, delegates) | 5,438 |
| Salaries, pensions | 74,418 |
| Modernization of national headquarters | 900 |
| Elections and Referendum | 21,580 |
| By-elections contributions | 2,100 |
| Total | 127,348 |

SOURCE: Parti Socialiste 51$^{e}$ Congrès National, *Bulletin Intérieur,* No. 110 (May, 1959).

## ANCILLARY AND RELATED ORGANIZATIONS

The party maintains a number of specialized organizations such as Socialist Students, Socialist Young People or the Jean Jaurès Club. These groups lack vitality. The more active Socialist youth organizations had been a source of annoyance to the party because they sometimes assumed radical positions and were unwilling to submit to party orders. In 1947 the Socialist Young

People organization was summarily beheaded of its leadership; the ensuing crisis has not been surmounted.

Although in close sympathy with the SFIO, the Socialist union CGT-FO is not organically linked to it. However, the SFIO is of all parties that on which CGT-FO has greatest influence. The union centainly plays an important role in maintaining for the party the support of a section of the working class. Other unions such as the Autonomous Syndicalist Federation which groups certain categories of iron workers and the Lay Primary School Teachers Union are also close to the SFIO.

### The Leadership

Unlike the Communist party but like other French parties the SFIO abounds in leaders and potential leaders. Prominent among them are the parliamentarians who have held important posts in the government. They include F. Gouin, P. Ramadier, C. Pineau, and G. Mollet who were prime ministers in the Fourth Republic; J. Moch who made a reputation as minister of the interior; R. Lacoste, former minister-resident in Algeria; A. le Troquer, a former president of the National Assembly; G. Defferre, who played an important role as minister for the French Union; M. Lejeune who devoted himself to the economic promotion of the Sahara; and A. Gazier who often held the post of minister of labor. Nonparliamentarians have been less influential. SFIO men reaching top positions in the party, such as G. Brutelle and P. Herbaut, do so as full-time party officials. The most influential is undoubtedly Mollet who, without the prestige enjoyed by Léon Blum until the war, has succeeded in gaining recognition both as party organizer and parliamentary leader.

### Membership and Electorate

The Socialist party which reached a prewar peak of 280,000 members in 1937 and an all-time high of 350,000 in 1946 had approximately 100,000 members in 1959, most of them local politicians.[9] Only in certain areas, such as the mining north, has the party maintained a following large enough to justify a claim at being a mass party. Two federations, Nord and Pas-de-Calais, accounted for about one-fifth of the total membership. Like all French parties other than the Communists, the Socialist party is primarily a politician's syndicate. Increasingly difficult is the recruiting of members not expecting electoral rewards. If, on the model of the British and Swedish Socialist parties, the SFIO were to adopt a system of indirect membership enabling trade unions to affiliate themselves to the party and if CGT-FO were to accept such an affiliation, the party would thus gain about 100,000 to 200,000 members. But the old syndicalist tradition of nonallegiance to a political party, militates against such a merger. Unless the Communist party were to lose its hold on the working class and without a transfer of loyalty from the Communists to the SFIO, the SFIO has little chance of becoming again a mass party. The classical conflict between parliamentarians and militants has now become one between national and local politicians.

A survey made in 1951 showed that the party membership was composed mainly of older men and that most of them were either workers employed by the state, civil servants, or white collars.[10]

Of those surveyed, 88 per cent were men; 69 per cent were more than forty years old; salaried people accounted for 58 per cent and pensioners for 12 per cent. Classified by occupation the membership was divided as follows:

| | | | |
|---|---|---|---|
| Civil servants | 24.9 | Employees | 8.8 |
| Workers | 24.3 | Farmers | 7.4 |
| Pensioners | 12.8 | Professional people | 2.6 |
| Artisans and businessmen | 12.3 | No profession | 7.4 |

According to the author of the survey, about 40 per cent of those listed as civil servants were workers employed by the state. Workers would thus be the largest group with about 35 per cent of the membership, but unlike in the Communist party most workers, still according to the author, were either state workers with a guaranteed stable salary or workers in middle-size or small private industries.

The Socialist electorate which had reached 22.7 per cent in 1919 before the split from the Communists, had not succeeded before the Second World War in regaining its 1919 percentage. Its peak was in 1932 with 20.7 per cent. The elections of 1936 which brought the Socialists to power had given them only 20 per cent of the votes. Their highest postwar percentage was 23.8, in 1945. After that time, the SFIO lost steadily; it obtained 21.1 per cent in June, 1946; 17.9 per cent in November, 1946; 14.5 per cent in 1951. Since 1951 the party has ceased to decline but has failed to make any significant gain. It obtained 15 per cent in 1956 and 15.5 per cent in 1958.

According to the survey of 1952, the Socialist electorate was composed as follows (in per cent):

| | | | |
|---|---|---|---|
| Nonworking women | 28 | Retired people | 7 |
| Industrial workers | 25 | Employees | 4 |
| Farm workers | 9 | Industrialists, cadres | 4 |
| Civil servants | 9 | Businessmen | 3 |
| Farmers | 9 | Professional people | 1 |

The party's electoral basis is wider than that of its membership; proportionally more women and more workers vote Socialist than join the party. However of all French parties the SFIO is that which has among its electors the highest proportion of civil servants and employees and, together with the Radicals and the Communists, that which obtains the least support from women.

Geographically the Socialists have their stronghold in the industrial North (Nord, Pas-de-Calais, Ardennes), in the winegrowing South along the Mediterranean coast, and in isolated *départements* such as Landes, Basses-Alpes, Haute-Vienne, and Doubs. In 1958 the party obtained more than 30 per cent of the votes in seven *départements*, Ariège, Aude, Belfort, Landes, Pas-de-Calais, Pyrénées-Orientales, and Haute-Vienne. It is weak in the Paris area.

### Doctrine and Program

At the end of his political career Léon Blum, reflecting on the state of Socialist doctrine in France, saw socialism as a mere outgrowth of democracy. To him there could be no divorce between political and economic power. As the people wanted to rule themselves politically, they would also want to rule themselves economically; as an extension of the suffrage had stripped the bourgeoisie of its political power, the extension of state control over the economy would strip the former ruling class of its economic power. Although not exclusively theirs, the postwar nationalizations were made under the Socialist's inspiration, the transfer of production of coal, gas, and electricity from private to public property, the nationalization of the major banks, the establishment of a compulsory social-security scheme for salaried people, were all in accord with the Socialist program. Since then the SFIO has proposed no new nationalization. The party now admits that transferring private into state ownership is not necessarily a gain for the Socialist cause. The objective is to prevent the wealthiest from being able to impose their rule on the rest of the citizenry and on the government. Since, in the opinion of the SFIO, the nationalizations after the Second World War have rendered less likely the possibility of private interests dictating to the government, the party now advocates only further but limited transfers of revenues through taxation.

The basic contention of socialism that profits made by individuals would not have been possible without the community of which the individuals are part, is no longer interpreted by French Socialists as creating obligations for the whole human community. French Socialist thinking now limits the field to the national community. Not infrequently one hears Socialists objecting to the full integration of Algeria to France on the ground that it would lower the French standard of living.

The SFIO assigns to the state the duty of helping the poor, the unemployed, and more generally those suffering from economic or social changes. The very composition of the SFIO's electorate inclines the party to give its preferences to the working class, to the urban population, and generally to salaried people, especially teachers and civil servants. In the South however the party identifies itself with the wine growers.

Although not necessarily favorable to rigid and over-all planning, the SFIO favors a controlled economy. The party has an instinctive distrust of the so-called "natural" mechanisms of economic liberalism. The party opposed Pinay's financial and economic measures of 1958–1959. The return to a policy of private instead of public investments, the use of indirect monetary controls instead of a direct regulation of production appeared to the Socialists as a step backward into the nineteenth century.

Among the points in the Socialist program which do not stem naturally from the SFIO's ideological positions, three stand out: acceptance of the quasi-presidential system inaugurated by the Fifth Republic, a liberal policy toward former colonies, and the desire to unify Europe.

French Socialists who when in opposition had been hostile to executive supremacy, when they led the executive became converted to the necessity of strengthening the government. Léon Blum at one time suggested a system of separation of powers. Toward the end of the Fourth Republic Guy Mollet proposed the election of a cabinet for a set term of office as in Switzerland. The constitution of 1958, notwithstanding its authoritarian features, was approved by a 70 per cent vote at the Socialist congress held before the referendum. When the SFIO again moved into the opposition in 1959, the party brandished again the old claim that democracy meant parliamentary supremacy. But Mollet without saying so probably agreed with Debré that creating a strong executive would serve the SFIO if it returns to power, and the party's center position makes this return most likely.

Under a Socialist premier and under a Socialist minister for the French Union the significant reforms of 1956 regarding the overseas were passed. The Defferre law of 1956 gave increased powers of self-government and autonomy to the overseas territories. The French Community of 1958, instituted on a voluntary basis, received the Socialists' complete approval. Regarding Algeria, the SFIO's position is not as clear cut. The party has endorsed de Gaulle's policy of letting the Algerians determine their own future but while Socialists such as R. Lacoste and M. Lejeune conceive this future exclusively within the French fold, others including Mollet want to leave the door open to solutions like partition, and a minority even accepts the prospect of complete independence.

Of all French parties, the SFIO is with the MRP the most European. True, the badly handled European Defense Community treaty met with much opposition from the Socialist parliamentary group, a majority of which refused to vote the creation of a European army, but the party has since approved the Common Market and the Euratom and generally support J. Monnet's proposals for political unification.

It is symptomatic of the SFIO's evolution that its most progressive proposals are on a political question such as the integration of Europe rather than on a reform of socioeconomic structures. Like the British or Swedish Labor parties, French socialists have ceased to adhere to their early dogma. But while British and Swedish socialists were able to do so without losing support from the working class, the SFIO when becoming a moderate party also became a middle-class party. As long as the Communists control 20 per cent of the electorate the SFIO cannot hope to become the French Labor party dreamed of by Blum and still hoped for by Mollet.

# 5 *The Radical Party*

In nineteenth-century Europe, parties campaigning to establish universal suffrage and parliamentary supremacy sometimes called themselves liberal as in Belgium, sometimes radical as in Switzerland. In keeping with the French habit of complicating the political vocabulary, French political liberals grouped themselves into a Radical Socialist party.[1]

Borrowed from English, the term Radical became accepted in French political circles around 1830 to describe the opponents of the monarchy who were unwilling to compromise with their republican ideals. Like English Radicals and latter English liberals, French Radicals fighting for universal suffrage considered it the single most important means of reaching the goal of liberty, equality, and fraternity set by the revolution of 1789. Introduced by the Second Republic in 1848 and confirmed by the Second Empire, universal suffrage disappointed the republicans because it did not prevent the establishment, and then the maintenance of Napoleon III's dictatorship. The ease with which the emperor could obtain the election of candidates favorable to the government convinced the Radicals that Frenchmen still had to be emancipated from their former rulers, from the clergy, and from the landed gentry. In the later nineteenth century, radicalism emphasized the need for positivist reforms. Doctors such as A. Combes and G. Clemenceau, professors such as C. Renouvier, F. Buisson, J. Simon, lawyers such as L. Gambetta preached the faith in science and reason. Radicals adopted Proudhon's saying that "democracy means teachocracy." [2] School reform, together with the separation of church and state, became the major points in the Radical program. Significant of the radical thinking of the time was A. Targé's statement that "all men, instructed in the same things, thinking the same, will respect one another and will at last treat one another on a footing of equality, as in America." [3]

At a meeting in Belleville in 1869, Gambetta endorsed a program which remained for years the charter of radicalism. It called for universal suffrage in local as well as national elections, for legal guarantees of civil rights, for complete freedom of the press, for the trial of political crimes by jury, for complete freedom of reunion and association, for the separation of church and state, for compulsory and free primary public schools, for the election of civil servants, for the disbanding of professional and permanent armies, and for the abolition of monopolies. Later, the progressive income tax was added to that basic program. From the fall of the Empire in 1870 to the beginning of the twentieth century, Radicals were returned to parliament in increasing number. In 1901 the two major Radical groups, the Republican Radicals and the Socialist Radicals fused to form the "Radical-Republican and Radical-Socialist" party, thus becoming the largest parliamentary group—a group dominating French politics until the First World War, and to a lesser extent until the Second World War. In 1902 the Radicals obtained 26 per cent of the votes; 28.5 per cent in 1906; 38 per cent in 1910; 33 per cent in 1914. Already before 1914 the Radical party had seen most of its program turned into laws by governments they had either supported or led. A law of 1881 had abolished censorship and formal authorization for newspapers, laws of 1881 and 1907 guaranteed the right to assemble freely, a law of 1884 authorized the formation of trade unions and associations, one of 1901 extended the unrestricted right to form associations to all groups except financial undertakings and religious orders which required specific legal authorizations. Church and state were separated in 1905. Laws of 1881 and 1882 rendered education compulsory for children between the ages of six and thirteen and made primary public schools free of charge.[4] The progressive income tax was introduced in the early twentieth century. Hostile to the military, Radicals had at first opposed colonial expansion. On becoming a governmental party they changed their outlook; they abandoned the program for abolition of standing armies and established the French protectorate over Morocco. Abandoned also were the proposals for electing judges and civil servants. Before the First World War the Radical party had already become conservative.

After the Boulanger episode, the party had lost ground in the cities, particularly in the Paris area, and had gained support in the provinces. Radical parliamentarians tended to become country and small-town delegates sent to Paris to control the government and to resist the powers that be, governmental as well as economic. After the First World War the Radicals began to decline, their share of the votes fell below 20 per cent.[5] The efforts made at strengthening the cohesion of the Radical parliamentary group before the two wars met with little success. In 1924 E. Herriot failed to obtain the expulsion of some Right-wingers like P. Strauss and A. Sarrault. The question of taxes on capital supported by Herriot but opposed by Caillaux divided the party as well as the caucus. E. Daladier leading the Young Radicals gained the party leadership in 1928 but failed to streamline the organization and to impose discipline. Like P. Mendès-France thirty years later, Daladier became the prisoner of local bosses controlling the party machine.

The Center position of Radicals in parliament made them necessary to the formation of coalition governments. Having to please the Socialists through whose support most Radicals were elected, but having also to satisfy the Right-wing parties whose votes were required for a government to remain in power, the Radicals gave the impression of not knowing their minds, of fluctuating between Left and Right. They were tempted not to act in order to avoid criticism. The crisis of 1934 for a while removed the Radicals from their dilemmas. The belief that parliamentary institutions were in danger provoked alignment with the Left to defend the Republic. Radicals, Socialists, and Communists formed the Popular Front which won 57 per cent of the votes and 64 per cent of the seats in 1936. However, the Popular Front victory was not a Radical victory. With only 14.6 per cent of the votes, the Radicals came behind the Socialists' 20 per cent, and even the Communists' 15.4 per cent. The decline in number was not compensated by increased party cohesion—Radical senators contributed to the fall of the Popular Front governments led by L. Blum. Revealing the Radical's problems, in the last parliament of the Third Republic, although elected on Left-wing coalition tickets, at the outbreak of the war Radicals formed a government led by Daladier in which neither the Communists nor the Socialists were represented. Elected on the Left but governing on the Right, the Radical party had become symbolic of the Third Republic, of its perverted and absurd system of parliamentary government. For this identification the party suffered during and after the war.

Although Radical leaders such as Daladier, Herriot, and J. Zay had to suffer from the Vichy regime, although Radicals such as P. Mendès-France, J. Moulin, and H. Queuille rallied early to General de Gaulle, the Radical party, as a whole, did not contribute to the Resistance as much as did Communists, Socialists, and Christian Democrats. A great majority of Radicals, small-town and village councilors in particular, followed their natural inclination to abide by the legal authorities, and the legal authorities happened to be in Vichy not in London.

The First World War had weakened the Radical party; the Second almost destroyed it. The parties that controlled most Resistance organizations, Communists, Socialists, and MRP, agreed with de Gaulle's plan to start anew, to discard the institutions of 1875. In the referendum of 1945 which asked whether the people wanted a new constitution, the Radical party was almost alone in campaigning for a return to the prewar system. Only one of twenty-six voters thought like the Radicals who in the following election to the Constituent Assembly obtained only 10 per cent of the votes and seats.

The constitutional history of the Fourth Republic represents a gradual return to the Third. In keeping with this evolution, the Radicals gradually increased their influence between 1946 and 1958. As long as the MRP, the Socialists, and the Communists governed together, the Radical party failed to play its former role of Center party necessary to the formation of governmental coalitions, but when the Tripartite government broke down in 1947, the Radicals reëntered the field in their traditional role of ideal mediator. By 1958 they had succeeded again in identifying themselves with the regime, in being the governmental party *par excellence.*

During their opposition period, in the years following the liberation, the Radicals had had ample time to redefine their positions. The major question was whether they should align themselves with their former Popular Front allies or whether they should assume the role of an opposition to the new version of Popular Front known as Tripartism, in which the MRP had replaced the Radicals. The party's extreme Left, following P. Cot, wanted close collaboration with the Communists; more moderate Leftists such as J. Kayser, wanted collaboration with the Socialists. However a majority of Radicals hostile to the government's economic and financial policy preferred positions more toward the Center. Cot was expelled in 1946, and the same year Kayser resigned as administrative secretary. The Nice congress of 1947 concentrated on attacking the government's policy of economic controls resented by the Radical clientele of small businessmen and shopkeepers as an unbearable infringement of their freedom.

Although the Radical party had expelled many of its prewar parliamentarians and local leaders because of their support of Vichy, the party largely remained in the hands of its prewar leaders. The election of Anxionnaz, backed by the younger generation to the position of administrative secretary in 1946 did not obliterate the fact that most local machines were still governed by older politicians and that in the national congresses Herriot and Daladier were adding new acts to the "war of the two Edwards," in all respects similar to their prewar performances.

The creation of the Gaullist Union, then of the RPF, cost the Radical party some younger members and parliamentarians, among them M. Debré and C. Chaban-Delmas. By 1950 however Radicals had reëstablished their electoral machines destroyed by the liberation upheaval and had regained their prewar parliamentary strength. Although their percentage of votes remained below 15, the number of their deputies increased regularly. There were 17 Radicals in the 1945 Assembly; 42 in 1946; 69 in 1951 and 71 in 1956. During the same period their popular vote had increased only from 11 to 13 per cent; but the Socialist and the MRP vote having considerably declined, the Radicals were again, even in terms of electoral support, among the big parties—big by French standards.

In 1958 a sudden reversal reduced the Radical vote to less than 5 per cent, and the Radical deputies to 15. Two crises explain this decline, the first resulting from Mendès-France's attempt to control the party, the second from General de Gaulle's return to power. Mendès-France who had first been elected to parliament before the war and had served in de Gaulle's liberation government, had by 1954 become the leader of the Radical party's Young Turks. Mendès-France planned to modernize France's outdated economic structures through a renovated Radical party. The prestige gained, for a time, from the Indochinese settlement and the help received from aging Herriot who felt the need of crowning a successor, enabled Mendès-France to gain the party presidency in 1954. In attempting to transform an anarchical collection of personal electoral machines into a disciplined, clear-minded national party on the British pattern, Mendès-France damaged his career and nearly destroyed the party. Although the membership doubled, the new members were neither numerous enough nor sufficiently experienced to help their leader break the local machines and discipline the Radical parliamentary group. Notwithstanding a series of expulsions and withdrawals from the party, Mendès-France failed to impose his rule, and the Radical party remained as undisciplined as ever. After he relinquished the leadership of the party in 1957, membership dwindled to 20,000-odd.

The party had not yet recovered from the Mendès-France episode when de Gaulle's return to power further divided it. In 1958, a majority of the party congress having decided to approve the new constitution, a minority led by Mendès-France left the party. The elections of 1958 were a general defeat for the Radicals, even those supporting de Gaulle. In the elector's mind the Radical party was identified with the fallen Republic, maybe more so than were Socialists and the MRP although the Radicals had opposed the constitution of 1946 which Socialists and MRP had made. But if the Radicals had not made the Fourth Republic, more than any other party had they accepted as fit for France a parliamentary system in which the parliament was supreme and in which political parties were not expected to be more than parliamentary clubs. So far as the French trend is toward more powerful executives, the Radicals appear outdated. Reduced in 1958 to the rank of a minor party, they hope to regain their positions by acting as a catalyst in the regrouping of French political liberals. However, the odds against the party are great. The *arrondissement* electoral system for which the Radicals had campaigned may well turn to their disadvantage. Great is the temptation for Radical parliamentarians to care solely for their own constituencies rather than organize their party nationally.

### Organization

Even after 1959, when an effort was made to streamline its organization, the Radical party remained in a state of gentle anarchy. The failure of Mendès-France to control the party once he had acceded to the presidency revealed the lack of hierarchical connection between the national organization and the local units. Like American parties, the Radical party is composed of autonomous local electoral committees. Radicals still take pride in their lack of organization; their concept of representative democracy is that deputies should be answerable only to their conscience and to their constituents. The party, to them, is no more than a club of like-minded professional politicians. A sincere attachment to Republican institutions, an instinctive distrust of *les pouvoirs,* and a traditional hostility to the church accused of enslaving men's minds, bring the Radicals together, but this communion of feelings is to them no justification for discipline. Not rarely do Radical parliamentarians help to the overthrow of a Radical government. In 1932, twenty Radicals contributed to the downfall of Herriot's government; in 1955 R. Mayer followed by twenty other Radicals joined the opposition to Mendès-France; a year later Mendès-France, on the eve of a general election, entered into open conflict with E. Faure, then prime minister; in 1958 fourteen Radicals voted the overthrow of F. Gaillard's cabinet.

Their national congresses also indicate the little importance Radicals attach to having a common policy and to forming a united front. Thesis and antithesis are often vigorously applauded by the same persons and are eventually embodied into so-called "negro-white" motions, mixtures of contradictory statements in which the membership finds no line of action but an indication of tolerance and broadmindedness.

The reforms of 1955 and 1959 fell short disciplining the Radical party but introduced at least some improvements. The establishment of a national file of party members for the first time gave national headquarters the possible control of allocating voting mandates to federation delegates. Also, the regulation of voting procedures should prevent voting from becoming a caricature of democratic practices. When Herriot had the chair at an important party meeting he tipped the scale in favor of Mendès-France by giving this astonishing ruling in order to justify a vote by a show of hands: "those who want the vote count to be according to the mandate system seem to have the rules on their side, but those who want the vote to be by a show of hands have the ease of counting votes on their side." [6]

The party local organizations comprise district committees and specialized groups. The first have a territorial basis which may be a group of city blocks (*quartiers*), a commune, a canton, or an electoral district. The specialized organizations are women, youth, and civil-servant groups among others and also, a peculiarity of the Radical party, newspapers. The district committees and the specialized organizations must be affiliated to a federation, each *département* having its own. All such federations are directly affiliated with national headquarters; however, departmental federations may group themselves into regional federations. The Southwest under the leadership of Sarrault and then Baylet had tended to form a party within the party. In addition to being affiliated with a departmental federation, the specialized groups may be authorized to form national organizations, and come under the direct control of the party national bureau. The federations played an important role in the selection of candidates to parliamentary seats when the *département* was the basic electoral district. The return to small constituencies in 1958 increased the importance of local committees and reduced in proportion the powers of departmental federations. The latter hold congresses composed of delegates from the local committees and affiliated groups. Such congresses elect a federation executive and appoint delegates to the national congress; in fact, these choices are usually made by coöptation.

The national congress meets every year in a city selected by the previous congress. The delegates with voting rights are the members of the national executive committee, the federations and local organizations' delegates on the basis of one delegate per hundred members, and the editors of the newspapers affiliated to the party. Extraordinary meetings of the congress may be called by either the executive committee, the bureau, or by thirty federations. The congress agenda is determined by the bureau which also appoints *rapporteurs*. The draft report must theoretically be sent to the federations a month before the congress. A committee on motions, selected by the bureau and approved by the congress, studies amendments and countermotions with a view to presenting to the delegates a single text which can obtain the support of as large a majority as possible. The motions are supposed to be the party's platform but generally signify little since no one considers them as binding. In addition to passing motions, the congress selects part of the party's executive organs. The regular voting procedure is by a show of hands, but the chairman may, when in doubt, ask that the vote be taken by remaining seated or standing. Furthermore the bureau or ten federation presidents may request that the vote be according to the mandate system. In such case the delegates of a federation have as many votes as the federation has hundred members. Finally secret ballot is compulsory for the selection of officers and for disciplinary matters.

The major national executive organs are the president, the bureau, and the executive committee.

The executive committee which until 1959 was an unwieldy assembly of some six hundred members is now composed of about two hundred members of the bureau, Radical parliamentarians, and federation chairmen. The latter vote according to the mandate system, one vote for three hundred members,[7] and can thus dominate the committee. When voting is done by mandates, the federation chairmen may split votes to represent proportionally the various factions within their *départements*. Introduced in 1959, this rule was intended to increase the control of grass-root organizations over the national leadership. The committee which meets at least six times a year acts as the party's supreme organ between congresses. In 1959 the executive committee inherited the powers formerly given to a joint committee of parliamentarians and party delegates, the Cadillac committee, the powers in particular to decide whether Radical parliamentarians should participate in a government. The executive committee divides itself into subcommittees to study proposed legislation and prepare the reports submitted to the congresses.

The bureau is selected by the executive committee from among its members. Election is for two years, half the members being renewed each year. Of thirty-three bureau members, six must be deputies and six senators. The majority is thus given to the militants or more precisely to the local party bosses. The bureau meets every week. Its role is to help the president in governing and administering the party. The bureau has also the theoretically important role of investing candidates for parliament, subject to appeal before the executive committee. The bureau, except on rare occasions, simply endorses the local organization nominees.

The president is elected for two years by the congress and may be reëlected only once. This restriction introduced in 1959 was intended to prevent the Radicals from indulging in their own version of the cult of personality, that is maintaining their leaders in office but following them ever less as they respect them ever more.

In administering the party, the president is assisted not only by the bureau but also by the conference of federation presidents and secretaries general which must meet before congresses and executive committees and must be consulted on the agendas of these two bodies as well as on eventual changes in the party rules.

The lack of formal channels between the party machine and the caucus, and the lack of caucus discipline, have the result that the entire Radical organization often works in a vacuum. The Radical party is foremost a party of parliamentarians not attached to their electorates and to their electoral committees through the party organization; the link is direct. The major problem with the Radical party organization, as with many other French parties, is not so much with the party machine as with the parliamentary group, and with respect to the Radicals one may even question whether at the parliamentary level such a thing as a Radical party exists.

### Doctrine

There are three basic tenets to the philosophy of French radicalism: political liberalism, anticlericalism, and economic featherbedding of small business.

Alain, the self-appointed philosopher of Radicalism, defined it as essentially negative.[8] According to him, to be a Radical was to oppose the state, the church, and generally all groups that tried to restrict the individual's freedom of choice. The radical is to be a law-abiding citizen but however respectful of the legal authorities, he should distrust them. Let your body obey, Alain used to say, but never your mind. The individual should never renounce his right to criticize and should even at all times use it for fear that it may lose its sharpness and effectiveness. In order to maintain the state in a position of useful tameness, the government should be not only watched but continually weakened. The true Radical is the very opposite to a fascist. Never applaud, said Alain, because your applause will come back to you and seize your heart.[9] In order to maintain governments in a state of subordination Radicals trust the parliamentary system and the power of reason—to criticize and to vote "against."

Their unquestioned liking for republican institutions and their distrust of all monarchical structures classify Radicals as Leftists. It was not mere chance that of all the parties which decided to vote for the constitution of 1958, the Radicals did so with the least liking. The political system preferred by Radicals is still that of 1875, a system in which parliament is supreme, the government being a mere committee of the legislature, answerable to it at all times. Radicals are ill at ease in the twentieth century; they refuse to acknowledge that the fight against the groups endangering individual freedom requires the adoption of techniques of collective and organized action. The rebellion against Mendès-France who wanted no more than to organize his party on the British model was evidence of the refusal to adopt modern techniques of political pressure. In turn Mendès-France's objections to the constitution of 1958 showed his fundamental hostility to cabinet government as it is practiced in Great Britain.

The belief that parliamentary government is the best possible is qualified by the restriction that such a system can work effectively only in an educated society, only among rational beings. Education is consequently of prime concern to the Radical party. Education should be provided and used by the state not to obtain passive subjects but to mold citizens emancipated from all ideologies which do not propose man's own reason as his sole guide for action. The conflict with the Catholic church, the "great debate" of the late nineteenth and early twentieth centuries, is still remembered by Radicals, although less vividly since the war. The party is no longer virulantly anticlerical; some Catholics or Catholic sympathizers like B. Lafay and R. Billères have made careers among Radicals, and many leaders would prefer that the school question—the granting of public subsidies to Catholic schools—be not reopened. However when forced to take a stand, Radical parliamentarians, except for a very small minority, show their hostility to the church and to confessional schools.

The Radical party has had and still has among its leaders some "big" businessmen and industrialists but A. Sigfried's observation that Radicals had a natural sympathy for anything "little" from the little farmer and the little businessman to the little tax evader remains true.[10] When, at the end of the nineteenth century, it lost ground in large cities and in northern France but grew in southern rural France, the party fell prisoner to an economically decadent part of the country. The Radicals became the first Poujadists of France. They used the political process to delay an economic evolution which tended to destroy those who could not or would not adapt themselves to a modernized economy. Mendès-France's failure to give sufficiently strong new roots to the Radical party in northern and urban France explains in part his failure to change the Radical's outlook on economic problems.

Still somewhat unified in their traditional ideology, Radicals are divided on the concrete problems of the day. One could not define a Radical position on Algeria nor on the integration of western Europe. If R. Mayer and H. Queuille refuse to see France's claim to sovereignty over Algeria questioned, others such as E. Faure or F. Gaillard do not exclude autonomy or even independence. If E. Daladier objects to abandonments of sovereignty in favor of European institutions, M. Faure is among the most European of French politicians. These divisions are not peculiar to the Radicals. Except for the Communists, no French party has a totally unified front on any of the major contemporary problems, but of all, the Radicals are the most divided.

Their parliamentary caucuses are unpredictable groupings of ever-changing coalitions. Whether because of internal divisions or because of natural conservatism, Radicals, except in rare occasions, tend to favor the status quo. Internationally, in agreement with Herriot rather than de Gaulle, they have accepted a France reduced to the rank of a second-rate power and try to make the best of it, leaving to the United States the leadership of the free world.

### Leadership

"Mon cher Président" is a common form of greeting among Radicals. The Radicals are a party of presidents and chairmen; any meeting of Radical leaders shows an unusual density of present or former premiers, assembly speakers, parliamentary group or party leaders, and local council chairmen. Among such groups any man finds difficulty in rising to a position of supremacy; one can be at best first among equals. Herriot, during his lifetime the party's grand old man, was more a figurehead than an actual leader. The Radical flag passes from hand to hand and has a tendency toward multiplication.

With the expulsion of E. Faure in 1956, the resignation of A. Morice the same year, Herriot's death in 1957, Mendès-France's back-door departure in 1958, and J. Baylet's death in 1959, the Radical party suffered heavy losses among its leaders. A new generation is coming to the fore, one which entered politics after the war and which contains men like M. Faure, and Gaillard who became the party president in 1958. The Radicals having, for almost a generation, attracted few young men, those who joined the party find the avenues to prominence less encumbered. The Radicals are an aging party with young leaders.

### Members and Electors

With a membership of about 20,000 in 1959, the Radical party is a typical example of what M. Duverger calls a "cadre party." The majority of party members and practically all active members are nationally or locally elected representatives. The party's mainstays are mayors and municipal councilors of small communities. In 1951, of 5,000 Radical mayors, only 40 belonged to communities of more than 10,000 inhabitants. Small independent farmers, artisans and businessmen, country doctors and lawyers, are also commonly found among party members. The long association of the Radical party with the government of France and the lesser importance of ideological requirements for entering the party have resulted in the Radicals attracting would-be professional politicians without clear political principles other than a general acceptance of the rules of parliamentary government. A Radical background is not an obstacle to promotion within other non-Communist parties except the MRP. Progressive P. Cot and Gaullist Debré started their careers as Radicals. As the Radicals become less ideological, they take more of the features of "road of access" parties.

The *Institut Français d'Opinion Publique* poll of 1952 shows that the Radicals like the Communists have fewer women among their electorates than other parties. The largest single group of Radical electors were independent farmers with 31 per cent, followed by retired people with 14 per cent. These two groups, together with the shopkeepers (7 per cent) had a higher ratio within the Radical electorate than within the electorate at large. Other groups were about proportionally represented, such as civil servants (5 per cent), managerial class (4 per cent), liberal professions (1 per cent); or largely underrepresented in comparison with their share of the total electorate, such as industrial and farm workers, and white collar employees in private businesses. Salaried people who made 38 per cent of the total electorate had only 21 per cent of the Radical electorate. On the contrary for profit makers other than farmers the figures were respectively 25 and 42 per cent. Since this poll was taken, the Radical electorate has dropped by more than one-half. First, the Radicals lost many of their shopkeepers and artisans to the Poujadists, then lost to the UNR without recovering the votes which had gone to Poujade. The losses to the UNR occurred mostly in the cities and in northern France where the Radical party was already weak. In this increased identification with agricultural southern France lies the Radicals' greatest weakness.

# 6 *The MRP*

The *Rerum Novarum* encyclical of 1891 and the lifting after the First World War of the interdict by the Holy See forbidding Italian Catholics to seek election unless by special permission, invited Catholics throughout the world to renounce their widespread opposition to democracy and to make the best of the parliamentary institutions which had during the nineteenth century replaced in Europe the traditional forms of monarchical governments. Unlike German, Swiss, or Belgian Catholics who had organized themselves into political parties even before *Rerum Novarum*, unlike Italian Catholics who formed one of Italy's largest parties after the First World War, French Catholics waited until after the Second World War to give mass support to a party of their own. However slow in organizing themselves politically, French Catholics had produced many of the early philosophers of Christian democracy.

The first significant attempt by a group of Catholic thinkers to reconcile Christian values and political freedom was made by

J. B. Lacordaire, C. de Montalembert, and F. de Lamennais. A few months before the revolution of 1830, they founded the newspaper *L'Avenir* in which they criticized as inhuman a system of economic liberalism causing social injustices, and in which they denounced as oppressive the conservative and clerical government of Charles X. The failure of the 1830 revolution to instal a democratic system, but most of all the condemnation of Lamennais by the Holy See for unorthodoxy ended the first Christian democratic movement in France. A second attempt was made after the revolution of 1848 by Lacordaire, A. Ozanam, and A. de Melun who wanted to give a Christian as well as democratic orientation to the newly founded Republic. *L'Ere Nouvelle* tried to continue the work of *L'Avenir* but met with little response. Following the workers' uprising of June 1849 Catholics supported conservative groups more than ever. The few isolated Christian democrats thought of themselves as battling on two fronts, against atheism and socialism on their Left and against clericalism and conservatism on their Right. In the last decade of the nineteenth century a few "democratic" priests were elected to parliament; publications such as the newspaper *Ouest-Eclair* and the review *La Quinzaine* expressed Christian democratic points of view, and the first French Christian democratic movement to have long-lasting effects and to reach the masses, the *Sillon*, was founded by M. Sangnier. The *Sillon* was not properly speaking a political party but rather a philosophical society not unlike the Fabians, doctrine kept apart. The *Sillon* propagated a Christian ideal of brotherhood, fraternity, and respect for individual freedoms. Sangnier was not only an articulate speaker, he was also a shrewd organizer, using slogans and poster campaigns most effectively. Like Lamennais, Sangnier made the mistake of wanting to commit the church to a particular form of government, and the *Sillon* was condemned by the Holy See in 1910. Sangnier submitted to the pope's orders but did not cease political activity. In 1912 he founded a political party, the *Jeune République*, but failed to group around himself more than a few deputies. The majority of the forty-odd so-called Social Catholics elected in 1919 under various tickets remained outside the *Jeune République*. In 1924 thirteen deputies founded the Popular Democratic party (PDP), a Christian-democratic group more oriented to the Right on socioeconomic questions than were the *Jeune République*. Among the founders of this new party were A. Bour, A. Champetier de Ribes, R. Lecourt, G. Peyrolles, and G. Poinso-Chapuis who after the war played an important part in the launching of the MRP. Before the Second World War, the influence of Christian-democratic deputies remained weak: the PDP never had more than fifteen deputies. In order to bring together the Christian democrats of various allegiances, F. Gay founded in 1932 the newspaper *l'Aube*, and the *Nouvelles Equipes Françaises*, Christian-democratic clubs appealing mostly to young people dissatisfied with both the atheistic Left-wing parties and the "heartless" conservative and Center groups.

Between the two World Wars, Catholic trade unions and youth organizations made significant progress and formed the future cadres of the MRP. The *Confédération Française des Travailleurs Chrétiens* (CFTC) founded in 1919 soon grouped over 150,000 adherents. The *Jeunesse Ouvrière Chrétienne* and the *Jeunesse Agricole Chrétienne* also developed successfully and became nation-wide organizations.

During the occupation of 1940–1944, Christian democrats participated actively in the Resistance or rallied to de Gaulle. In London, M. Schumann became the spokesman for *Fighting France;* in Beyrouth, A. Colin encouraged French troops to disregard the armistice and to continue the fight; in France, F. de Menthon and P. H. Teitgen organized underground movements. In 1943, G. Bidault became president of the National Resistance Council (CNR). Resistance activities brought together the various Christian-democratic factions, in particular the *Jeune République* and the Popular Democratic party, and linked together political and some nonpolitical Catholic organizations. The *Association Catholique de la Jeunesse Française* in particular provided many of the cadres and troops required by the underground. Men like A. Colin, P. Bacon, R. Simmonet, F. Bouxom, R. l'Huillier, R. Plantade who became MRP parliamentarians or party officials had not before joining the Resistance engaged in political activities.

In 1943, G. Dru, J. Gilibert, F. Gay, G. Bidault, and A. Colin decided to accept Dru's proposal to draw into a single political movement all Christian-democratic groups engaged in the Resistance. Colin was entrusted with the preliminary organizational work. In the summer of 1944 he and Simmonet drafted a manifesto which served as a doctrinal foundation for the proposed party tentatively named *Mouvement Républicain de Liberation,* and which drew on the political program of the National Resistance Council.

In order to free the nation from domination by private financial interests, the program called for the nationalization of banks and companies producing energy. A state system of social security and a vague proposal that workers be associated with management and share the profits of the industries for which they worked were also included in the manifesto.

In October 1944 the first congress of the new party, finally named *Mouvement Républicain Populaire* (MRP) was held in Paris. Schumann was elected president. Most members of the PDP joined the MRP. The *Jeune République* was at first more reluctant. Sangnier and Schumann were among the first to join but most members of the executive committee waited two years before making a similar decision.

Following the liberation the MRP won unexpected electoral successes. Rightly or wrongly people believed that de Gaulle's sympathies went to that party which, unlike the Communists, the Socialists, and the Radicals, was not marked by the Third Republic. The MRP did nothing to dispel this belief, but on the contrary called itself the "parti de la fidélité," ready to follow de Gaulle. With the Center and Right-wing parties having emerged from the war discredited and disorganized, the moderate electorate found no better alternative to Marxian parties than the MRP. The latter's social and economic program was to many electors as objectionable as that of the Socialists, but the movement's Christian principles were reassuring.

Three MRP entered the first de Gaulle government, G. Bidault as minister for foreign affairs, F. de Menthon as justice minister, and P. H. Teitgen as information minister. In the elections to the first Constituent Assembly of 1945, the party gained 25 per cent of the votes and 27 per cent of the seats. The MRP further demonstrated its hold on the electorate by having the first draft constitution devised by Communists and Socialists rejected by the people. By so doing, the MRP further identified itself with de Gaulle who had left the government because of his disapproval of the draft constitution. The elections of 1946 to the second Constituent Assembly made the MRP the largest parliamentary group, with 30 per cent of the seats for 28 per cent of the votes. The Movement claimed to have then more than 150,000 members. It felt strong enough to go its own way and refuse to follow de Gaulle when the general asked the people to vote against the second draft constitution.[1] The break with de Gaulle caused a few MRP parliamentarians like J. P. Giraudoux and L. Terrenoire to leave the Movement for the newly founded Gaullist Union. In the elections of November, 1946, the MRP maintained its position with 27 per cent of the votes and 29 per cent of the seats. The Communists had regained the lead with 28.6 per cent of the votes and 30 per cent of the seats, but the MRP could still claim to be the largest "national" party since the Socialists and the Radicals came far behind with 18 per cent and 14 per cent of the votes. The MRP could still reasonably hope to grow and, like its Italian counterpart, to conquer a majority in parliament. The disorganization of Right-wing groups and of the Radicals rendered possible a two-party system's emergence in France. Working toward this goal, the Movement emphasized its nonclerical character, its attachment to the principles of 1789, and its basic acceptance of the principle of separation of church and state.[2]

But if Christian democrats wanted to expand, they did not all want to expand in the same direction. The party's Left wing, strong in the Paris area, wanted to continue collaborating with Socialists and Communists; the Right wing, strong in western France, would have preferred a "Bidault without Thorez" type of government. The formation of the *Rassemblement du*

*Peuple Français* by de Gaulle in 1947 ended the MRP's hopes of expansion. In the municipal elections of 1947 more than half the MRP electorate went to the Gaullist party. In October, 1948, the MRP senatorial caucus dropped from 63 to 20 members. The MRP then conceived of itself as the backbone of a coalition of Center parties, the Third Force, which would defend the regime against the attacks of both the Communists and the Gaullists. The MRP gave less and less attention to problems of economic reforms, concentrating its action and propaganda on a social problem, the protection of the family, and to a political problem, the unification of Europe. In 1950 Bidault succeeded Schumann to the party presidency notwithstanding the reluctance of some local organizations, in particular those of Seine and Seine-et-Oise, to vote for the former president of the CNR thought to have become too conservative. Colin, a Bidault supporter, was elected secretary-general with only 341 of the 596 votes. As among Socialists, a rank and file oriented to the Left was reluctant to accept the party's alignment with a more conservative electorate. In 1951, the MRP recovered somewhat from its 1947 and 1948 electoral defeats but could do no more than obtain 12.5 per cent of the total votes. The Movement had fallen behind the Communists, the Socialists, the Gaullists, and the Conservatives; it had fallen almost to the rank of the Radicals. Notwithstanding its evolution to the Right, the party had lost mainly from its conservative electorate. In an effort to regain this lost electorate, the Movement continued its evolution toward the Right. The expulsion of A. Denis and A. Bouret, the resignations of Abbé Pierre and L. Hamon marked this evolution. In 1951 the MRP supported A. Pinay's policies of economic liberalism, and was brought closer than ever to the Independents by the vote on the Barangé law. In the first postwar parliament, the Movement had shunned raising the school question in order to avoid a choice. But when the Independents decided in 1951 to introduce a bill calling for some state financial support to private schools, the MRP could no longer dodge the issue. Although many of its leaders would have preferred the status quo, the parliamentary group was compelled to follow the wishes of its electorate and thus break the Third Force alliance with Socialists and Radicals. In protest, some members of the MRP's Left wing went to the *Jeune République;* however most Left-wing Christian democrats preferred, like F. Gay, to stay within the Movement, hoping that eventually they could gain the leadership and swing the party's course if and after proof had been made that the MRP could not regain the conservative electors who had abandoned it.

Already severed from the Socialists and the Radicals by the vote on the Barangé law—the law granting state subsidies to private schools—the MRP was further separated from the Radicals by Mendès-France's alleged "killing" of the European Defense Community treaty. However, the MRP could not bring itself to join the opposition. Never more valid than in the last years of the Fourth Republic was the saying that the MRP has the soul of an opponent but the body of a joiner. For participating in practically all the governments of the 1951–1956 legislature, the MRP paid the usual price of parties not allowing themselves "opposition holidays." The elections of 1956 gave only 11.1 per cent of the votes to the MRP which had fallen behind the Radicals and even the Poujadists. In the last years of the Fourth Republic, the MRP found a unifying principle in European integration but the Algerian war provoked serious tensions within the party and eventually split the leadership. Bidault's uncompromising stand on the question of maintaining French sovereignty over Algeria conflicted with Pflimlin's desire to seek liberal solutions to the Algerian conflict. When, during the last ministerial crisis of the Fourth Republic, Bidault tried to form a government, he was turned down by a majority of the MRP joint party executive and caucus committee. After de Gaulle's return to power, Bidault tried to regroup conservative Christian democrats in a new party, the *Démocratie Chrétienne.* This splinter group ran its own candidates in 1958 and caused the MRP vote to drop from 11 to 9 per cent. However the new electoral system enabled the MRP to elect 44 deputies while the Socialists returned only 40 and the Radicals 15. Bidault refused to join the MRP caucus but could not prevent some of the deputies elected under the *Démocratie Chrétienne* ticket from doing so.

The weakening of Socialists and Radicals and the near elimination of Communists from the 1958 National Assembly, placed the MRP farthest to the Left yet; its deputies sat on former Communist and Socialist benches. The MRP was no longer necessary for the formation of Center coalition governments. The Movement could have joined the Socialists in opposition to the Debré government, but preferred to remain on the de Gaulle bandwagon. The elections of 1959 confirmed the Christian democratic leaders in their belief that their advantage was in remaining associated with the UNR and the Independents. In the municipal elections of 1959 the MRP resisted UNR and Independent progress better than did the Socialists and the Radicals. The Movement lost about 3,600 seats compared to 6,000 for the Socialists and 9,000 for the Radicals.[3] The senatorial elections of 1959 were a success for the MRP which for the first time since 1947 increased its parliamentary representation; the number of its senators rose from 21 to 29.

At its 1959 congress the MRP could look with some confidence toward the future. Neither the Bidault split nor the UNR landslide had seriously weakened the party. However the Movement's hopes are more limited than in the early years of the Fourth Republic. French Christian democrats can no longer expect to become as powerful as their German or Italian counterparts in the near future, but can reasonably hope to have put an end to their electoral decline and, by maintaining a Center position, to remain at the crossroads of French politics. From this privileged position the MRP can try to orient French policies on the roads of its choice; that is, as far as internal matters are concerned, a New Deal-type of free enterprise which would avoid the ill effects of both collectivism and individualism and, as far as international affairs are concerned, the construction of a United Europe which would meet the challenge of the U.S.S.R. and of the United States.

### Organization

Whether a parliamentarian should be responsible primarily to his party or primarily to his electors is a question not answered clearly in the minds of French political organizers, Communists excepted. The SFIO, which had at first based its organization on the principle of the subordination of the elected representatives to the party machine, has abandoned this extreme solution. The MRP which, on the contrary, had first instituted the domination of the party by the parliamentarians has been obliged, under the pressure of grass-root organizations, to give more say to party members. Coming from opposite directions, SFIO and MRP are moving toward a common party structure where leadership is in fact in the hands of the elected representatives but where militants are not altogether powerless. However, even after the reforms of 1959, the MRP's internal structure was still less democratic than that of the SFIO.

The MRP in 1945 adopted the classical French party organization with local sections, regional federations, and national congress and executive. The sections are organized territorially, generally on the basis of the commune, in some cases however the canton is the primary unit. A section must have at least ten members and an executive which is in theory elected by the members. In fact, except in a few large sections, election is a mere formality, the selection being made by coöptation or by the upper echelon. The MRP, no more than other French parties, the Communists excepted, has found ways of preventing the hardening of its local arteries. Sections often remain in the hands of once dynamic or at least once active members who have ceased to devote enough time to party activities. Most sections are dormant between elections and some never waken.

The sections of a given *département* form a federation. In order to be affiliated with the Movement, a federation must have at least five sections and a total of at least one hundred members. In fact, some federations like Corse and Creuse fell below the required minimum without losing their status as federations; however they did lose representation in the national congress.

The party rules leave each federation free to write its own constitution provided it follows a common general pattern. A federation must have a federal congress where the sections are represented and an executive committee, one member of which must be a woman. According to national rules, members over eighteen are given the right to vote. Voting is compulsory in a federal congress when at least 10 per cent of the delegates request a vote. Finally, the election of officers must be by secret ballot. These rules are often ignored. As in the sections, the choice of officers or delegates is usually made by coöptation. Only the largest federations use the secret-ballot procedure. In such cases elections are by a majority on the first ballot and by a plurality on the second ballot. Unlike the SFIO, the MRP is not at the regional level usually divided into majority and minority pressing for a vote on all possible occasions. However, in the few federations where the Left-wing *Rénovation Démocratique* has either made serious progress or obtained control of the federation executive, the opposition between factions has produced a more active political life and given increased significance to the selection of regional officers.

In addition to stimulating and controlling the sections, the federation is also supposed to create and activate a number of specialized groups such as women's, youth, workers, rural, and professional groups. Their organization is facilitated by an abundant and usually well-done series of publications issued by national headquarters. However, few are the specialized groups which show any sustained activity; more important to the MRP than its own satellite groups are such nonpolitical Catholic organizations as *Action Catholique*, *Confédération Française des Travailleurs Chrétiens*, *Jeunesse Ouvrière Chrétienne*, *Jeunesse Agricole Chrétienne*, and *Jeunesse Etudiante Catholique*. Although not affiliated to the Movement, they are sources of party members and leaders.

Few federations can afford full-time party officials. In 1958 the largest federations had a yearly budget of about $3,000.[4] The federations' financial resources come from the selling of membership cards and from occasional contributions to campaign funds. Membership in the MRP is through affiliation to a federation; the latter collects the money derived from membership fees and then returns part of it to the sections and to national headquarters. The yearly stamps which establish membership are bought by the federations from national headquarters at a fixed price but sold to members at a price determined by the federation itself. In 1957, for example, the Seine federation bought the stamps at 50 francs and sold them at 600 francs, 250 of which accrued to the section.

The Movement's national organization is complex, with two "legislative organs," the national congress and the national committee, and with four executive organs, the president, the secretary-general, the executive commission, and the bureau.

The national congress which meets at least once a year is the party's supreme decision-making body. Extraordinary congresses may be called at the request of the national committee or at the request of one-quarter of the federations.

Federations are represented in the congresses according to a sliding scale. Each federation may have one delegate for each fifty members up to 200, one for each one hundred members from 201 to 5,000, and one for each two hundred members over 5,000. The delegates are theoretically chosen by secret ballot. In addition to federation delegates, members of the national committee and MRP parliamentarians attend congresses with full voting privileges.

The function of a congress is to determine the party's doctrine and program and to elect some of the party leaders.

The motions before a congress may have been submitted by any member in good standing. In order to prevent loss of time on unimportant matters, the noncontroversial motions are posted for twenty-four hours and are considered passed if not opposed. Before and during the congress a committee on motions attempts to reach compromise between conflicting motions. The debates center on the reports presented to the congress by the various *rapporteurs* designated by the party leadership.

The national congress also selects part of the party's executive organs. The president and the secretary-general are elected by secret ballot, and such elections are rarely contested. In 1950 however A. Colin was elected secretary-general with only 341 votes; the Left-wing candidate J. Dumas had 224. Generally, opponents of the nominee either abstain or vote for persons who are not officially candidates.

The national committee, supposedly subordinated to the congress, is another version of it, but the committee membership is such as to give greater weight to parliamentarians and national headquarters. The national committee is composed of four types of members: ex-officio members, parliamentary delegates, federation delegates, and coöpted members. The ex-officio members are the president, the secretary-general, the MRP cabinet ministers,[5] the chairmen of Senate and National Assembly if they are MRP, the chairmen of the MRP caucuses and all the members of the party executive committee. The parliamentarians select delegates from among themselves, up to one-third of the membership of the committee. The federations are entitled to one representative for every 1,000 members, each federation having at least one representative. The coöpted members include ten militants at large and fourteen representatives of the party's specialized groups like those of women, youth or local councilors. Less unwieldy a body than the congress,[6] better controlled by the leadership, the committee may be summoned between congresses to make urgent decisions like whether to participate in a government.

The party executive is shared by a president, a secretary-general, a national executive commission and a bureau. The division of responsibilities between president and secretary-general is clear-cut only in theory. The president is entrusted with the leadership of the party in political matters, the secretary-general concentrates on matters of organization. There is overlapping, especially if the president was a former secretary-general and thus opiniated on problems of party internal organization. An early party rule that president and secretary-general could not combine their functions with those of ministers was abandoned, thus enabling Bidault, then Pflimlin, to be cabinet ministers while remaining party presidents. But, in order that the party president be more free to criticize the government the original rule was reintroduced in 1959. Unlike the presidents who cannot be reëlected more than three times, the secretary-generals are usually maintained in office for long periods of time; A. Colin was secretary-general from 1945 to 1955 and A. Simmonet who succeeded him, still held the post in 1960. The president and the secretary-general are theoretically subordinated to an executive commission and to a lesser extent to a bureau.

Between meetings of the national committee, the executive commission has the responsibility of making all urgent decisions. The commission includes ex officio and elected members. In the first group are the president, the secretary general, the treasurer, the chairmen of the Senate and of the National Assembly, if they happen to be MRP, and the MRP members of the government in office.[7] The elected members are selected by the national committee: twelve of them have to be parliamentarians chosen from the members, eighteen must be federation representatives selected from the nonparliamentarian members, and five must be ordinary members chosen from inside or outside the committee. The number of ex-officio members and ministers may not exceed one-fourth the total executive-commission membership. This rule maintains about equal balance between parliamentarians and nonparliamentarians. The former cannot have more than one-half the seats on the commission and usually have a few less. However, the selection of the executive commission by the national committee and not by the congress guarantees that the extreme points of view be either not represented or much underrepresented. The executive commission has on the whole been sympathetic to the parliamentarians' point of view. No serious conflicts have arisen between parliamentary group and national executive in any way comparable to those which occurred in the SFIO. The commission which could impose bloc-voting on the parliamentarians has never done so against the wish of the caucus.

Until 1959 the bureau played a very minor role. Elected by the executive commission from among its members, the bureau was an intermediary between the secretary general and the commission. In 1959 under pressure from rank-and-file elements wanting to democratize the party organization, the rules were modified. The bureau like the executive commission is now partly elected by the national committee. As a further step in the liberalizing of party structures, it has been suggested that the bureau be elected by the national congress itself. In its present form the bureau is composed of five ex-officio members—the party president, the secretary-general, the treasurer, and the chairmen of the Senate and National Assembly caucuses—and eight members elected by the national committee. Of these eight, three at least must be nonparliamentarians.

The secretary-general administers a national headquarters which, according to party figures, operates on a budget of about $40,000 a year; more than half is spent on salaries. The secretary-general is helped by four vice-secretaries-general who are full-time party officials and who are each in charge of one of four fields—political affairs, overseas affairs, propaganda, and party organization. The secretariat organizes and supervises the activities of a number of specialized organizations federated nationally outside the regular party structures, women, youth, and worker groups among others. For the study of doctrine and legislation a number of study groups composed of parliamentarians and nonparliamentarians have been arranged. The nonparliamentarian members are appointed by the national secretariat.

The MRP parliamentarians who are theoretically bound by the congress's and party executives' doctrinal and tactical positions are in fact largely autonomous. Bloc voting is the rule but may be waived by the parliamentary group unless it is prevented from doing so by the executive commission. In the beginning of the Fourth Republic, the MRP caucus used to enforce voting discipline, but does no longer. The attempts at democratizing the party structure may eventually be frustrated by the refusal of the caucus to submit to the party machine if it ever happens that the executive be no longer controlled by the parliamentarians themselves. The case of the MRP even more than that of the SFIO shows that French party organizations are not adapted to the necessities of a parliamentary system. In theory the party organization is based on the assumption that the leaders are responsible to the members while in fact they cannot but be responsible to the electors. When, as in the MRP, membership and electorate do not have the same political orientation, one being more conservative than the other, the party organization cannot give an accurate representation of the membership without risking alienation of the electorate.

### The MRP and Christian Nonparty Organizations

Helpful to the MRP are a number of religious or lay organizations supporting the principles of Christian democracy. The role of the Catholic church is difficult to assess. Officially there are no links between the Catholic Church and the Movement. French bishops do not instruct their priests to ask their parishioners to vote for a particular party or candidate. Catholics are simply recommended to vote for candidates who defend Christian principles, but are left free to decide by themselves who such candidates are. However, the priest in his capacity as a citizen often lets it be known who his preferred candidate is. In the areas where Catholics are also often anticlerical, the priest's taking a particular stand may not result in many parishioners taking a similar one, but in regions like the West, especially in small communities, where the priest has remained a social and political leader, his political opinions carry great weight. Undoubtedly the support given the MRP by the clergy in the East and in the West has greatly helped the MRP. Even in these areas however not all priests vote MRP; far from it.

The Movement is also sometimes helped by church lay organizations. *Catholic Action*, far less powerful in France than in Italy, tends to back the MRP's Right wing. More oriented to the Left are such youth organizations as the boy scouts, the *Union Nationale des Etudiants de France*, *Jeunesse Ouvrière Chrétienne*, and *Jeunesse Agricole Chrétienne*. They are particularly useful to the MRP in helping at election time and in being a pool of future party leaders. The Movement maintains close contacts with some professional associations like the *Ordre des Médecins*, the doctors' corporation, and the ACAF grouping family organizations. The relations with the Christian-democratic union *Confédération Français des travailleurs Chrétiens* are no longer as close as in the early years of the Fourth Republic. The union now concentrates on the defense of its members' economic interests. A growing minority within the CFTC, the Reconstruction group composed mainly of industrial workers, is driven from the MRP by its middle-of-the-road economic policy and by the fact that the MRP is forever "in" the government against which the workers claims are directed.[8]

Paradoxically, the MRP benefits from the existence of some Christian-democratic clubs or *societés de pensée* which often take anti-MRP positions. The *Esprit* and *Témoignage Chrétien* group are examples. Far more to the Left than the MRP, often close to the Communists, they attract young people who might have otherwise gone to the Socialists or to the Progressives, or more likely would have remained politically inactive. After having satisfied their desire for self-affirmation in nonconformist groups, such people often join the ranks of the MRP, especially through the channel of the MRP's own Left-wing faction, Democratic Renovation.

### Ideology and Program

Twice since the last war the French Christian democrats forming the MRP have refused to call their party "Christian Democratic." The first time was when the party's name was chosen in 1944; a second time in 1959 when the Movement refused to follow Bidault's advice. By so doing the MRP would have been simply respecting a tradition which makes French political organizations hide themselves behind titles which are puzzling and obscure when not totally meaningless. The refusal to adopt the term Christian Democratic was however due to more serious reasons. Although Christian democrats do take christianity and democracy as their terms of reference, although, as in the nineteenth century, they still seek to find a pass between the two, their political sense as well as their religious convictions make them hesitate to associate the terms too closely; their political sense, so far as they wish to avoid any association with clericalism, their religious convictions so far as they do not want to associate the church with secular politics. The promotion of some of the few Protestants who belong to the MRP to such important positions as the presidency of the parliamentary group may have served to emphasize that the MRP was in no way subordinated to the Catholic church. The MRP is thereby distinguishable from the Italian Christian Democrats whose association with the church is far more intimate. Notable also is that unlike the Belgian Catholic party, the MRP has avoided as far as possible raising the school issue. But while accepting the system of separation of church and state, the MRP proposes a political doctrine based on Christian ideals. At the root of this doctrine one finds not economic or political, but moral premises. Rejecting the liberal theories of individualism as egoistic and rejecting the totalitarian theories of group supremacy as inhuman, the MRP seeks to protect the individual's autonomy of thought while favoring voluntary group action. Democracy, so far as it supposes collective action but implies free and voluntary cooperation, appears to Christian democrats as the best form of government for the "good life."

Assigning the state a charitable duty to the community, the MRP favors social reforms which correct social distortions and alleviate the sufferings caused by free competition. Unlike the Socialists, the MRP never proposed to transfer all or even most powers of economic decision from the individuals to the community. Nationalization of banks and of some key industries, and redistribution of income through family allowances or social security schemes gained the MRP's support, but a systematic program of transfer of private property into collective ownership would not. In its economic and social thinking, the MRP is closer to new dealism than to socialism.

While in religious matters the Christian democrat accept unquestioned the authority of the church, he refuses or at least thinks he can refuse to translate such an attitude into secular terms. Political authorities must be questioned and held responsible. In political matters the Christian democrat is in a sense a Protestant; he must avoid Luther's two mistakes of having been a "Protestant" in religion and a "Catholic" in politics.

The MRP program which at first gave primary emphasis to social and economic reform now concentrates on two major points: the protection of the family and the unification of Europe.

The family is viewed as the most basic natural group, that which is necessary to the normal expansion of the individual's personality, that which gives stability to a society, and that which is better able to resist the pressures of totalitarianism. The policies of family allowances, of tax deduction for family obligations, of subsidizing married women who stay at home rather than work outside, the campaigns against alcoholism and prostitution considered as destructive of harmonious family life, all receive MRP support.

The MRP has been one of the parties most constantly associated with the building of a United Europe. The Movement does not consider the recent decline of Western Europe in the economic and military fields as fatal but as caused by national divisions which should and can be transcended. While giving its full support to the Atlantic Alliance, the MRP would like to see Europe less dependent on the United States for military security. One of the most frequent conditions the MRP places on its participation in coalition cabinets has been that the government would have a European policy. The European Defense Community treaty which proposed a military integration of Little Europe [9] was defeated by one of the few coalition governments in which the MRP was not represented. MRP leaders do not agree on the ultimate terms of European integration. From the activists following H. Teitgen to the conservatives following Bidault, opinions vary on the future structure of Europe—loose confederation or true federation. But most find compromise possible on Robert Schuman's program of economic integration first, leaving open the type of political integration to follow.

On matters other than the protection of the family or the integration of Europe, the position of the MRP is not always as clear or as systematic.

The party favors a modernization of French economic structures, but its electoral strength in farming areas often obliges it to speak for the small farmer. On the school question the Movement would prefer to make no choice and to support the status quo. However when other parties force the issue, MRP parliamentarians are compelled to defend private schools and cannot refuse to vote public subsidies to such institutions. A different attitude would be certain to reduce the Movement to a handful of deputies. On the Algerian question as on overseas problems in general, the MRP has had no consistent policy. While some of its leaders accepted concessions to local nationalisms, others wanted to maintain firmly the French Empire. The deposition of the sultan of Morocco, the accession of Tunisia to independence, then the May 13 crisis, obliged the MRP to take definite stands. Bidault took an uncompromising attitude. In coöperation with leaders of Right-wing parties, such as A. Morice, R. Duchet, and J. Soustelle, he campaigned for a French Algeria and contributed to the May, 1958, army rebellion. Pflimlin, R. Schuman and a majority of the leadership took more liberal positions. Placed in the minority, Bidault left the MRP in 1959. Following this split, the Movement was more unified on overseas problems. The Movement agrees with de Gaulle's policy to let the Algerians themselves choose their own future but to refuse that such choice be made by arms rather than by the ballot box. As to what they would prefer the future status of Algeria to be, the MRP is still not clear-minded. The Movement would not, of their own accord, offer independence to the overseas territories but when General de Gaulle did so in 1958, they posed no objections. Convinced that France's future is in Europe not in Africa, the MRP has not evolved a coherent African policy; the party remains open to suggestions, and finally is quite willing to accept the *faits accomplis* whoever accomplishes them.

### Party Leadership

Unlike the Communists and the Socialists but like the Radicals and the Independents, the MRP is not a party behind a leader.

In the years following the war, Bidault played the role of Number One, but the rule preventing the continuous reëlection to the party presidency, as well as the party's social structure, resulted in Bidault's being slowly pulled back into the ranks, to the point that when he left the MRP, he did so without causing a major disturbance. Among the group of prominent MRP politicians, there is no longer even a *primus inter pares*. Pflimlin often served in the cabinets of the Fourth Republic as agriculture or finance minister and during the May, 1958, crisis established a reputation of loyalty to republican institutions which may enhance his future career. Robert Schuman, whose sitting on various European organizations has often prevented his taking an active part in French politics, remains one of the most respected of French politicians. Maurice Schumann, who belongs to the group of Gaullists who did not leave the MRP for the RPF, is more influential within the party than within the parliamentary group; like R. Schuman he devotes himself mostly to foreign affairs. P. Coste-Floret and R. Lecourt have established a reputation on constitutional matters. A Colin and R. Simmonet have directed most of their attention to party organization. P. H. Teitgen and J. Teitgen make themselves the spokesmen for a more rapid unification of Europe. P. Bacon, a former trade-union organizer and B. Buron who was once expelled for his Mendecian sympathies, represent the party's Left. Both Bacon and Buron were ministers in the Debré government of 1959, thus giving the MRP's Left a privileged position in governmental circles. One should also mention a future MRP grand old man, F. Gay, who has always been on the fringes of Christian-democratic movements and now supports the *Rénovation Démocratique* group, an MRP version of Mendecism, an attempt at rejuvenating and orienting more to the Left a party thought to be glued in its conservatism and rigged by bossism.

A large number of MRP leaders come from Catholic youth organizations; for example, Colin and Simmonet, president and secretary-general in 1959.

Most leaders—Bacon is an exception—have a middle-class origin; many of them are lawyers or law professors. In 1959, in an attempt to give representation to other social groups, it was proposed that half the seats in the party's ruling bodies be reserved for workers and farmers.[10] If the rule were ever implemented, farmers more than workers would benefit. In 1954, farmers who accounted for 12.5 per cent of militants had only 3.2 per cent of federation leaders and 5 per cent of the national committee members.

### Membership and Electorate

A study made in 1954 by Professor Pépy, bearing on about one-fifth of the total MRP membership showed the following distribution of members: [11]

TABLE 4

Distribution of MRP Membership
(In per cent)

| | |
|---|---|
| Without profession or non-recorded profession | 25.1 |
| Students | 0.3 |
| Pensioners, retired people | 5.4 |
| Liberal professions | 5.1 |
| Industrialists and management | 11.0 |
| Civil servants | 13.2 |
| Artisans, shopkeepers | 10.9 |
| Farmers | 12.8 |
| Workers (private industry) | 5.2 |
| State workers and white collars | 9.0 |
| Total | 98.6 |

The MRP appears as a party of salaried middle-class people which has made inroads among farmers, shopkeepers, and artisans but has failed to attract workers.

For a short time after the liberation, with about 150,000 members the MRP could claim to be, together with the SFIO, second only to the Communists in terms of membership. By 1950, following the creation of the RPF, the MRP had lost more than half its original members. In 1958, the total membership was

46,000 members.[12] Seven federations only had more than 1,000 members: Nord with slightly more than 4,000, Bas-Rhin and Seine with more than 3,000, Haut-Rhin and Pas-de-Calais with more than 2,000, and Moselle and Seine-et-Oise with more than 1,000. Seventy-three federations had less than 500 members. Notwithstanding its attempt at mass membership the MRP has, like the SFIO and even more so, become a party of municipal councilors. However, unlike the Radicals and the Socialists, the MRP has been able to maintain a relatively large number of young people within the party. Although no statistics are available for accurate comparison, the average age of party members seems much lower in the MRP than in other non-Communist parties.

### The Electorate

The MRP started in 1945 with 24.9 per cent of the total vote. In the following June, 1946, election to the Constituent Assembly this percentage increased to 28, but later declined constantly until 1958; it was 26.3 in November 1946; 12.5 in 1951; 11.1 in 1956; and only 9.6 in 1958.[13] The municipal and senatorial elections of 1959 indicated a slight recovery. The Movement seems to have stabilized its voting strength around 10 per cent of the electorate. The MRP has two major areas of electoral strength: west of a line Nantes-le Havre and the *départements* on the German border.[14] Outside these two areas the party is weak except in scattered *départements* such as Ardennes, Marne, Haute-Savoie, and Aveyron. In the agricultural West the MRP electorate is conservative and most likely goes to the MRP for confessional reasons. In the more industrial East the electorate is oriented to the Left of Center and is more open to international and domestic problems of a nonconfessional nature.[15]

Most striking is the weakness of the MRP in urban areas except in the East. In 1958 the Movement did not elect a single representative in the seven largest French cities—Paris, Marseilles, Lyon, Nice, Bordeaux, Tolouse, and Lille.

The 1952 poll by the *Institut Français d'Opinion Publique* showed the MRP to have, after the Communists, the youngest electorate; 66 per cent of its electors were under fifty. Contrary to what is generally thought, the Movement attracted proportionally as many men as women. It is of all parties that which had the least unbalance between sexes, 47 per cent men and 53 per cent women, as compared with a national average of 48 and 52 per cent. Of the MRP electors 67 per cent lived in communities of less than 20,000 inhabitants; a percentage higher than that of any of the other major parties. The socioeconomic groups overrepresented in the MRP electorate were white-collar employees, farmers, liberal professions, and shopkeepers. Industrial and farm workers, civil servants, and managers were underrepresented; retired people and nonworking women were equally represented.

Practically all MRP electors are Catholics. The little Protestant support given to the Movement does not come from areas like Alsace and Cévennes where the Protestants still have some traits of a religious minority. Unlike the German Christian democracy, the MRP has not gained any significant support from non-Catholic Christians or what is more important in France from the agnostics. If the Catholic church were to take an anti-MRP stand, the Movement could not survive. The fact that the MRP attracts many of its electors for religious more than for political reasons is a possible source of weakness but has some immediate advantages. There is between the MRP electorate and the party a *quid pro quo*, a basic *malentendu*. Many MRP representatives especially in the West are elected on issues not of primary importance to the party, for instance the support of private schools. Many voters cast their ballot for a Catholic party which takes pains not to appear as Catholic. The result for the MRP is a certain feeling of insecurity, due to the always present possibility that the Church would revise its attitude on secular matters. What if the Church were again to condemn freedom of the press as she did in the nineteenth century? What if the Church were to ask French Catholics not to seek election to parliament as she asked Italian Catholics in the nineteenth century? These are of course remote possibilities but possibilities nevertheless. While a source of insecurity, this *quid pro quo* has, however, definite advantages for the MRP representatives in parliament. They do not have any binding contract on many secular problems with their electorate. The representative elected because of his religion may be freer in his socioeconomic policies; on such matters as the unification of Europe, the granting of independence to former colonies, and the liberalization of economic structures, the MRP may have a greater leeway than other parties, prisoners of a more clearly opiniated electorate.

# *7 The Independents*

Maurice Barrès used to say that in the course of one's political career the time always comes when one has to cease fighting one's Right-wing opponents in order to turn back and club one's Left-wing followers. This, he added, was to become moderate, a French word for conservative. Today's French moderates are the heirs of former Center or Left of Center groups which have ceased fighting monarchists for lack of such enemies and now concentrate their attacks on Socialists and Communists.

A feature of the Third and to a lesser extent of the Fourth Republic was that the death rate of political parties was much greater on the Right than on the Left. None of the parties now occupying the Right benches in the National Assembly existed before the war. Attempts at organizing and disciplining conservatives in order to meet the challenge of monolithic Left-wing parties were not successful. Neither Waldeck-Rousseau who founded the *Alliance Démocratique* in 1901 nor R. Poincaré,

A. Tardieu, L. Marin nor Colonel de la Rocque after the First World War could overcome the personal conflicts dividing the Right. In the last parliament before the Second World War, the moderates had one hundred and eighty representatives in the Chamber of Deputies, divided between six major parliamentary groups: the Republican Federation led by Marin, E. Temple, and F. Dupont; the Democratic Alliance, the most prominent members of which were P. Flandin, P. Reynaud, J. Laniel, and L. Jacquinot; the Independent Republican and Agrarian group with E. Pébellier, P. Antier and M. Fauchon; the Independents for Popular Action led by M. Walter and the Democratic Left with M. Petsche and L. de Chappedelaine. The Republican Federation with sixty deputies and the Democratic Alliance with forty-four deputies were much larger than the other groups but could not even claim 60 per cent of all moderates. The division would have been even greater had elections been held in 1939 when most likely the newly formed PSF of Colonel de la Rocque would have obtained the support of about one-third of the conservative electorate. Prewar moderates lacked a well-organized party, an outstanding leader, and a well-formulated program. They stood mostly for resistance to communism and socialism. They further distinguished themselves from the Left by their willingness to support clerical claims, and by their frequent criticism of the parliamentary system operating under the Third Republic.

The moderates emerged much weakened from the war. Some of their leaders took an active part in the Resistance, J. Laniel and L. Marin for example, or had to suffer deportation by the Germans, such as P. Reynaud, or even death, like G. Mandel, but the moderates' participation in the Resistance was unorganized, most of them maintaining a "wait and see" attitude. Furthermore the moderates, like the Radicals, were associated in the public mind with the defeat. The war had started under a Radical, E. Daladier, it had ended in disaster under a moderate, Reynaud. That Reynaud himself had warned the French of the oncoming disaster, that he had been among the few politicians to adhere to de Gaulle's strategic concepts was easily forgotten;

but some of Reynaud's unfortunate wartime morale boosters were remembered as examples of fateful self-confidence—for instance Reynaud's statement a few weeks before the routing of the French armies that "we shall win because we are the strongest." Like Daladier, Reynaud had become a symbol of a satisfied and inefficient parliamentary system.

The dissastisfaction of conservatives with their traditional parties could have benefited Colonel de la Rocque's PSF but it was disserved by the fact that many of its supporters had rallied to Pétain at least during the early months of the Vichy regime.[1] That de la Rocque was still in German concentration camps after the liberation of Paris did not help either but most of all there now was a more brilliant charismatic leader than de la Rocque; de Gaulle himself who was thought then to be in closer sympathies with the MRP than with any other political party.

In 1936, the National Front, a coalition of Right-wing parties had obtained 42 per cent of the votes and 36 per cent of the seats. In 1945 Rightist candidates obtained only 13.3 per cent of the votes and 11.9 per cent of the seats. In the elections of June and November, 1946, their percentage of votes fell to 12.8. In the constituent assemblies and in the first parliaments of the Fourth Republic the moderates formed three parliamentary groups: the Farmers' group which comprised Antier, Bardoux, and Laurens among others; the Independent Republicans which included Coty, Canon Kir, Médecin, and Roclore; and the Republican Unity group, the largest of the three with forty-odd members grouped around Audibert, Clémenceau, Frédéric-Dupont, Laniel, Marin, and Mutter.

Between 1946 and 1958 the moderates regained the ground lost after the war and sought again to organize themselves. They did so with more success than before the war.

Striking is the difference between the 1946 and the 1958 parliaments. While the 1946 assemblies were dominated by three large parties of the Left, the Communists, the Socialists, and the MRP, the 1958 Assembly was controlled by two Right-wing parties, the UNR and the Independents. The benches to their left are occupied by six political groups, the largest of which, the MRP, has three times fewer seats than the smaller of the two Right-wing groups. The crystalization of the moderates into large parliamentary formations and their electoral gains at each of the elections following 1946, are among the most important developments in contemporary French party politics. The "natural" flow of French politics which seemed to be from the Left to the Right until the Second World War may have been reversed.

Notwithstanding the efforts of Louis Marin, the Republican Federation, the largest of the prewar moderate groups, could not be revitalized after the liberation. An attempt at regrouping moderates in a new organization was made by Clémenceau and Laniel who founded the Parti Républicain de la Liberté (PRL) before the elections of November, 1946. The new party campaigned against the nationalizations and other socialistic policies of the postwar governments, and accused MRP and Socialists of betraying the national interest by their alliance with the Communists. Although better organized and more dynamic than other moderate parties, the PRL failed to provoke a regrouping of conservatives, who remained divided into six parliamentary groups.[2]

In 1947, R. Duchet, a senator, proposed to federate all moderate parties in order to answer the challenge not only of well organized Left-wing parties but also and foremost of the newly launched Gaullist RPF. The idea required two years to materialize. In 1949 the National Center of Independents and Farmers (CNIP) was founded by Duchet, Coty, and J. Boivin-Champeaux to prepare for the forthcoming elections. The CNIP sought first of all to regroup at the local and at the regional level all economic liberals except those affiliated to the RPF, the Radicals, and the MRP. Whenever a promise to collaborate could be obtained from a sufficient number of local politicians, *département* centers were founded. They grouped municipal and *département* councilors together with the presidents of professional, industrial, or agricultural groups. These centers were clubs of politicians wishing either to regain the seats they had lost to the RPF in the municipal elections of 1947, or to preserve the seats they still had but which, they feared, could be lost if they did not agree among themselves on tactics and candidates. After local committees had been established, national headquarters tried to assert their authority by playing the role of an umpire in the many personal conflicts within local organizations. For the national election of 1951 the CNIP gave its endorsement, in each district, to the moderate candidates of its choice. National headquarters usually followed the advice given by the *département* centers. The lists of candidates presented by the CNIP obtained 7 per cent of the total vote. Another 7 per cent went to conservative candidates, a large number of whom had campaigned on coalition tickets supported by the CNIP as well as other parties. The CNIP could claim 76 of the approximately 110 moderates elected to the National Assembly. With 14 per cent of the total vote, the moderates had increased over 1946 by only 2 per cent but, significantly, they were, with the RPF, the only groups to increase their electoral support.

Moderates had been excluded from the postwar tripartite governments. Expulsion of his Communist ministers by Ramadier in 1947 obliged MRP and Socialists to seek allies on the Right. Independent M. Roclore had entered the reshuffled Ramadier government of October, 1947, as minister of agriculture; R. Coty served as minister for reconstruction in the R. Schuman government of 1947; P. Reynaud obtained the ministry of finance in the A. Marie government of 1948 and was vice-premier in the second Marie government of 1950.[3] The first Independent to form a government was A. Pinay who, unexpectedly, obtained the Assembly's investiture after part of the Gaullist group voted for him notwithstanding party orders.

The Pinay ministry marked a turn in the history of postwar France. For the first time since 1939 a moderate had obtained the premiership. Economic liberalism, seemingly utterly defeated at the time of the liberation, had made a comeback. Socialists were now on the defensive. The split provoked by Pinay within the RPF group caused de Gaulle to end the RPF experiment.[4] The CNIP could hope that it would inherit the RPF electorate and thus realize the great French conservative party which was Duchet's desire. This hope was frustrated in the following two elections, first by Poujade's UFF in 1956, then by the UNR in 1958.

The moderates obtained 14 per cent of the votes in the election of 1956. Most of those elected to parliament had been endorsed by the CNIP. The RPF dwindled from 21 to 4.3 per cent of the votes. However the Independents had not benefited from the RPF losses as much as they had hoped. The Poujadists by obtaining 12 per cent of the votes and 9.6 per cent of the seats had prevented the Independents from becoming the largest French party; with eighty representatives in the National Assembly, the CNIP had only the third-largest parliamentary group, coming after the Communists (144) and the Socialists (94).

After 1956 the CNIP tried to rally all "nationals" and all economic liberals. Although they participated in the governments of the last legislature of the Fourth Republic, these groups became increasingly hostile to the Left-wing and Center governments, criticizing either their economic or their Algerian policies. By repeatedly using the *coup de frein* tactic, by their repeated sudden braking, they brought down the Mollet, the Bourgès-Manoury, and the Gaillard governments, thus contributing to the fall of the Fourth Republic and creating circumstances favorable to de Gaulle's return to power. The Independents succeeded in doing in the 1956 legislature what the Gaullists had wanted but failed to do in 1951, that is, to jam the parliamentary mechanism. The election of 1958 gave 19.9 per cent of the votes to the moderates on the first ballot, putting them ahead of other groups. But the UNR which had obtained only 17.6 per cent of the votes on the first ballot rose to 26.4 on the second ballot, as compared to 23.6 for the moderates. The Gaullists elected 189 deputies, the Independents, 120. As in 1956, the CNIP failed in 1958 to integrate all conservative forces, but again the party can hope to inherit one day the Gaullist electorate and thus become *the* conservative party. However, the day still seems far away when French conservatives can boast the strength and the discipline of their English, Canadian, or Australian counterparts.

### Organization

The CNIP has few written rules; its organization is mostly customary. The basic unit is the *département* center grouping the parliamentarians, the general councilors, and some of the municipal councilors elected under the CNIP ticket, together with some of the most prominent among defeated candidates and some local personalities not seeking election for themselves. There are more than seventy such *département* centers. Their creation was prompted by the Paris headquarters, and their major function is to select candidates for elections. In theory the *département* center does no more than propose candidates to the Paris headquarters, but in fact the national organization intervenes only when the *département* center cannot agree on a candidate and seeks arbitration from Paris.[5] Electoral alliances are determined at the local, not at the national, level. The national headquarters has been either unwilling or, when trying, unsuccessful in imposing a national pattern of alliances with other parties. In a 1957 Marseille by-election R. Duchet was unable to persuade the local candidate, de Fraissinet, to withdraw from a hopeless contest so as to prevent the election of a communist. A year later, de Frayssinet was elected to parliament and was welcomed to the Independent parliamentary group. Duchet's attempt at intervening in the politics of local organizations has met with much resistance from parliamentarians and in particular from Reynaud and Pinay.

Each *département* center has a secretary maintaining contact with the national level. The *département* centers recruit exclusively by coöptation. There is no formal membership, no party card. The number of people participating actively in the life of the party is, for the whole of France, probably less than one thousand. They are surrounded by at the most 20,000 people, usually municipal councilors, who become active only at election time.

At the national level, the CNIP's major organs are the congress, the executive committee, the parliamentary group, and the secretariat.

Congresses meet at irregular intervals. They bring together the parliamentarians, the delegates from *département* centers and a few nonpoliticians invited personally by the party secretariat.[6] The congress meets to hear and to discuss privately; they avoid public debates and votes. The national council, which brings together the parliamentarians and the secretaries-general as well as the presidents of the approximately eighty federations, meets from time to time between congresses to discuss informally the major problems of the day. The council has no power of decision.

The executive committee has no fixed membership. It comprises CNIP parliamentarians chosen by the caucuses of both houses, and nonparliamentarians selected by coöptation. In 1960 there were twenty-one deputies, seventeen senators, and ten nonparliamentarians on the committee. Among the nonparliamentarians were a representative of the largest farmers union, the FNSEA, and a representative of the PME, a trade association of small businessmen. The committee meets usually once a week. Between these meetings the committee's parliamentarians sometimes meet in the absence of the nonparliamentarians. They then take the name of executive commission. The functions of the executive committee and of the executive commission are not clearly defined. The executive committee is, in theory, the supreme executive body. The executive committee endorses the candidates selected by the *département* centers and selects such candidates when the *département* centers are unable to do so. The executive committee may also expel departmental centers from the party. On questions of participation in a government the executive committee may decide by a majority vote that the CNIP's position will be determined by a joint caucus of deputies and senators. If the caucus reaches a decision by a two-thirds majority, those not abiding by such decisions are, in theory, automatically excluded from the CNIP. In practice the party excludes only those willing to leave.

The parliamentary groups may be said to be the supreme CNIP's organs. They are club-like organizations discussing major parliamentary problems but not enforcing voting discipline. Independents rarely vote as a bloc; like the Radicals they usually split into three factions, the yeas, the noes, and the abstentions. Among the rare issues which found the Independents unified were the Barangé law of 1951 providing for public funds to private schools, and the Pinay fiscal amnesty of April 1952.

The Secretary-general, R. Duchet, is the keystone of the CNIP machine. His talent as an organizer and his awareness that the disciplining of French conservatives can be done but very slowly have enabled him to retain the position of secretary-general since the party's creation. He controls personally the CNIP's official publication *France-Indépendante*, a small but well-made weekly, sent to about 20,000 persons. *France-Indépendante* propagates the doctrine of economic liberalism and tries to make French conservatives realize that their strength is in unity and discipline.

The CNIP remains at present much akin to American political parties with their lack of party discipline in Congress and with their local machines more powerful than national headquarters. But the hope of Duchet is to model the CNIP on British not on American parties. In order that he may succeed, the CNIP must first build its prestige to the point that endorsement by party national headquarters will be so much more significant than support by local electoral committees as to render possible the disciplining of the parliamentary group.

### Ideology and Program

Two words often appear in the CNIP's electoral manifestos: liberal and national.

The Independents are liberal in wanting the economic system to allow individuals to make economic decisions. Free economic initiative and a market economy are believed by Independents not only to be beneficial to the individual but also beneficial to the country as a whole. German economic recovery under Ludwig Erhard strengthened the French liberals' confidence in free enterprise. However, the Independents claim not to be the prisoners of ideologies, but rather prefer to be thought of as empiricists. In the name of free enterprise they do not propose to denationalize the banks nor even the key industries for they realize the advantages in the state's directing if not controlling private economic initiative; monetary controls may be used to maintain the conditions of free enterprise. Instead of proposing that the socializing done after the Second World War be reconsidered, the Independents propose that the state use its acquired means of economic control to maintain a free market economy, to break monopolies, to favor the dynamic and internationally competitive industries instead of featherbedding the inadapted ones, and to prevent inflation instead of using it as a means of financing economic expansion. The state should be strong economically as well as politically, although its strength should not be used to enforce equality, but rather to maintain freedom of action and of decision. To be a conservative, French moderates claim, means no longer to fight rear-guard battles. Their wanting to make a liberal "revolution" in a sclerotic economy, their assertion that the economic revolution of 1789 has to be refought, puts them on the offensive. The Socialists now appear to be preserving the established order. Whether this appearance is the result of a temporary reversal or of a change in the evolution cannot be said; undoubtedly French economic liberals are now confident of molding the future rather than of saving as much as possible from the past. Professor Jacques Rueff, the economic advisor to A. Pinay, believes that after a departure from soundness into socialistic experiments the nations of Western Europe will reestablish their economies on the principles of economic liberalism. Just as for the Radicals no freedom exists without political liberalism, for the Independents no freedom exists without economic liberalism. As political liberals want to free men from arbitrary government, economic liberals want to free men from economic controls unduly restrictive of the individual's freedom of choice. In France they wish also to free man from the fears of inflation. For more than seventy years Frenchmen have not known periods of monetary stability lasting more than four years. On the basis of 100 in 1911, the cost of living index was at 500 in 1935, 3,000 in 1945, and close to 20,000 in 1958. Independents think that inflation is as dangerous to security and freedom as arbitrary government. One of the first duties of a government should be to maintain the value of the currency. The two Pinay experiments, that of 1952 and that of 1958, attempted to stabilize the franc in order to restore confidence in it.

From their desire to free the economy and to stabilize the currency, as well as from their fear that anything approaching direct democracy would lead to anarchy, Independents derive a preference for strong and stable executives. In 1953, seeking the investiture from the National Assembly, Reynaud made his forming a government conditional to a constitutional reform which would have resulted in the automatic dissolution of the Assembly overthrowing a government. Notwithstanding their lack of sympathies for Gaullist parties, Independents have supported de Gaulle since 1958. Their liking for strong governments may, in times of crisis, make them prefer undemocratic governments. Many conservatives, among them Pinay, were in 1940 sympathetic to the Vichy regime, however the Independents do not, on the whole, question the democratic order.

Independents often refer to themselves and to the parties closest to themselves as the "national forces"; they see themselves at the forefront of a battle against ideologies and policies foreign or treacherous to France. They have repeatedly asked that the Communist party be outlawed, generally opposed all policies tending to the abandonment of sovereignty over oversears possessions, and are resolutely hostile to concessions in Algeria. Toward de Gaulle's and the UNR Algerian policy they maintain a position of wait and see, ready to raise a flag of nationalism if any serious concessions be made to the Moslem rebellion.

The position of the Independents on the issue of European integration is not too nationalistic. Although hostile to any abandonment of sovereignty on the part of France, most Independents have become convinced that France cannot by herself meet the economic and political challenge of the U.S.A. and of the U.S.S.R. While favorable to the Atlantic Alliance, the Independents wish France to maintain her autonomy in international affairs. This desire reinforces their conviction that, thanks to the wealth of her African territories and thanks to economic and political collaboration with her European neighbors, France will regain a position of international prominence.

### Leadership

Even more than the Radical, the CNIP is a party of personalities. In a sense it has nothing but leaders. R. Duchet, the party's secretary-general directs most of his attention to questions of organization and propaganda but has also taken some definite political stands classifying him as one of the most intransigent defenders of French sovereignty over Algeria. Pinay, probably the most popular of Independents, represents, for the conservative middle class, the little man without phrases or complicated theories who has come to parliament from his province and his small enterprise, in order that the voice of common sense be heard in Paris. Pinay is the embodiment of a golden age, of a time when business was free and when prices were stable. Reynaud like Pinay is an advocate of "sound" economic and financial policies; that is, of a balanced budget and light taxation. But he is still marked in the public mind by his association with the defeat of France in 1940. One of the most effective parliamentary debaters, Reynaud does not have as much influence in his own party as his talent and past political experience might suggest. Among the up and coming young politicians, one at least should be mentioned, V. Giscard d'Estaing who, in the best conservative tradition, makes a parliamentary and governmental career as a specialist on financial questions. Other types of CNIP personalities are C. Laurens, the spokesman for farming interests, Canon F. Kir, mayor of Dijon, J. Isorni, Marshall Pétain's lawyer, and J. Laniel, leader in the Resistance movement. Independent leaders are recruited from the middle class, in particular from lawyers, industrialists, and wealthy farmers. In the 1956 parliament, Independents, of all parties, had the highest ratio of farmers and industrial managers.

### Electorate

The public opinion poll of 1952 although studying all moderates as a single group may nevertheless be used as indicative of the Independents' electorate. Four groups were proportionally underrepresented in that electorate: industrial and farm workers, white-collar employees other than civil servants, and nonemployed women. On the other hand, management, shopkeepers, and farmers were much overrepresented, with about twice their national average. Civil servants, professional people, and pensioners were either equally or slightly overrepresented. The moderate electorate was the wealthiest of all. Forty-three per cent owned a car and 31 per cent had domestic servants; that is, about twice the national average. Moderates were particularly strong in small and large communities, but below the national average for cities between 5,000 and 100,000 inhabitants.

The CNIP has its major strongholds in the East, in the West and on the southeast border of the Center Plateau. It is particularly weak in the Southern Alps and in the Eastern Pyrenees. While remaining strong in agricultural areas, especially in the Catholic West, the moderates, unlike the Radicals, have not lost ground in the cities and industrial areas.

Not being too closely identified with any particular region, having maintained an agricultural as well as an industrial support, appealing to agnostics as well as to practicing Catholics, the Independents seem in a good position to rally all French moderates and to succeed finally in forming the large conservative party which thus far has failed to materialize. But the CNIP finds now a serious competitor in the UNR which has the advantage of making its way behind a prestigious leader. It remains to be seen whether French conservatives will succeed in integrating their forces and if they so succeed who will rally them, de Gaulle or Pinay.

# 8 *The UNR*

The history of Gaullism to 1958 was first that of a leader who could not maintain power without a party to support him, then of a party which after a sudden growth could not prevent decline without its leader in office. In 1958 at last both de Gaulle and a Gaullist party made a simultaneous "conquest" of the government. However, the future of Gaullism as a political force remained uncertain; de Gaulle had now ceased to consider himself as leader of any party, while the Gaullist party acknowledged no other *raison d'être* than de Gaulle himself.

A monarchist at heart, de Gaulle lives in a time when monarchies no longer prosper, and because dictatorships—these perverted forms of monarchical rule—are abhorrent to him, he tries to fit himself into a democratic system as well as fit democracy to himself. The result is the quasi-presidential system of 1958, where the president, being above party politics, is able to impose arbitrations based on his interpretation of the national interest. To de Gaulle a political party is at best a means among others of gaining access to power. His uneasiness in the role of party leader during the RPF experience and his refusal to allow any political party to campaign in 1958 under the name of Gaullism, show on de Gaulle's part either a lack of understanding of the functions of political parties in a parliamentary system, or a fundamental, if repressed, hostility to the system of representative government.

The UNR is, in relation to de Gaulle, somewhat like the MRP in relation to the Church, but more precariously so. While able to break the MRP, the church did not create it. If the MRP wants to translate Christian ideals into political programs it does not have to act as a spokesman for the religious authorities. Between Church and party there is a division of responsibilities, but both de Gaulle and the UNR act in the same secular and political field.

The first Gaullist party, the Gaullist Union, was founded in 1946 by R. Capitant, L. Vallon, and J. de Lipkoski. A few months before, de Gaulle had unexpectedly resigned from office because of the Constituent Assembly's unwillingness to draft a constitution with a strong executive. In a speech at Bayeux, the general had openly criticized the second constitutional draft about to be submitted to the peoples' approval and he had outlined the governmental structure of his preference, which included a system of double arbitration of conflicts between the legislative and the executive—by the president of the Republic on the one hand and by the people on the other hand. Neither endorsed nor disavowed by the general, the Gaullist Union campaigned against the constitutional draft but could not prevent its being passed. The Union ran candidates in the elections to the first parliament of the newly founded republic. The hope of rallying those who had voted against the constitution to these candidates did not materialize: the *Union Gaulliste* obtained less than 2 per cent of the total vote and less than 1 per cent of the seats in the National Assembly. The Union had suffered from not being publicly endorsed by the general and from being oriented too much to the left.[1] This was the first of a series of unsuccessful attempts at creating a Leftist, neo-Socialist Gaullist party.

In 1947, in a speech at Strasbourg, de Gaulle proposed that all Frenchmen who wanted to strengthen the state by reforming the constitution rally above the old parties. J. Soustelle, A. Malraux, and G. Palewski were entrusted with the organization of the Rally, which was an immediate success. The hastily organized RPF headquarters were crowded with people who, in an atmosphere of mobilization, wished the privilege of joining the new movement early.

Unlike the Gaullist Union, the RPF drew members from all political parties. Socialists, Radicals, and even Communists as well as MRP and conservatives joined the new organization.[2] According to Soustelle the Rally soon had one million adherents and eventually reached a peak with another half million.[3] Less optimistic and probably more reliable figures propose 400,000 as the peak membership.[4] Even on the basis of this last figure, the RPF appeared a year after its creation as the strongest of all non-Communist parties, and as better able to resist the Communist attempts at disrupting the economic and the political life of the nation after Communists had been expelled from the government. The municipal elections of 1947 were, by French standards, a triumph for the Rally. When the candidates endorsed by the RPF polled close to 40 per cent of the total vote, de Gaulle could reasonably hope that the parliament elected the year before would not stand the pressure of public opinion; and that following a dissolution, the Rally would gain a majority in the parliament or at least obtain such a high percentage of the seats that de Gaulle would have to be called back to power and given the authority to revise the constitution.

But the old parties resisted well. The RPF parliamentary club (*intergroupe*) attracted only eighty-odd deputies and when the club turned itself into a caucus requiring the discipline of vote, twelve members resigned. Having failed to paralyze the National Assembly from within, having failed to rouse public opinion to the point where the Assembly could not but dissolve itself, the RPF tried to jam the new institutions by gaining control of the upper house. The senatorial elections of 1948 were a severe setback to the Rally. Only sixty of the three hundred twenty senators joined the RPF parliamentary group; many of those elected with RPF endorsement preferred to remain with their traditional groups. In 1949 after the Queille ministry had lasted more than a year it became evident that the RPF would not benefit from the psychological shock of a dissolution imposed from outside parliament and that Gaullists would have to wait for the National Assembly to complete its five-year term.

The founding of the RPF in 1947, at a date far removed from a general election, would have turned to de Gaulle's advantage had the National Assembly agreed to a dissolution, but the deputies had successfully resisted the extraparliamentary pressure, and this early founding became a tactical mistake. The RPF could not maintain enthusiasm and devotion among its adherents and parliamentarians for four years. The Rally could not prevent its supporters being split by disagreements on other than constitutional problems, in particular on the school question. The first RPF congress, that of 1948, was unable to resolve the opposition between the "clericals" whose point of view was defended by Bishop Heinki, and the "neutrals" represented by Capitant. As a majority of the RPF leadership and membership were inclined to support the "clericals," many former Radicals and Socialists left the Rally. By 1951 the RPF could no longer hope to win the coming general election in a Fourteenth-of-July atmosphere but on the other hand the Rally had had ample time to organize its electoral machines and to test the loyalty of its followers. The RPF could not expect to gain a majority nor even a near majority, but could hope to obtain a sufficient number of deputies in the Assembly to paralyze the regime.

For this eventuality the RPF had adopted a structure based on the principle of the strict subordination to the higher echelon, General de Gaulle himself. A special effort had been made to develop specialized organizations, in particular veterans, students, youth and sports organizations. Actual direction of the party was entrusted to a secretariat of thirteen,[5] chosen by de Gaulle from his collaborators who were in London during the Free French period and from leaders in underground wartime organizations. All important decisions were taken by the General himself. A national congress where national and local leaders as well as parliamentarians were represented, and a national council the members of which were de Gaulle appointees had purely advisory functions.

This early RPF organization was remarkable because it reduced the parliamentarians to a very minor role. None sat on the first RPF national council, and up to 1949 they were not allowed to be members of the national secretariat. In 1949 a reform of the party rules gave to the congress the right to choose a fraction of members of the national council, and parliamentarians became ex-officio members of such a council; four deputies and three senators were added to the national secretariat bringing its membership to twenty. Even then parliamentarians remained the minority in the RPF's leadership. Their subordination served to emphasize that the Rally was not created to work within the "system" as de Gaulle used to call the Fourth Republic, but to destroy it. After 1951 de Gaulle's failure to return to power resulted in a growing tension between parliamentarians and the national machine.

The general election of 1951 gave only 21.7 per cent of the votes and 19.6 per cent of the seats to the RPF. The *apparentement* electoral law had worked to the advantage of the Center parties by giving them 62 per cent of the seats with only 51 per cent of the votes. By reducing the Communist representation to 17.8 per cent of the seats, with 25.9 per cent of the votes, the electoral system had indirectly hurt the RPF, the support of which was not necessary to the formation of governmental coalitions. De Gaulle's hope that the Center parties having no other alternative than allying themselves with either the Communists or the RPF would of course choose the latter and thus bring the Gaullists back to power, failed to materialize. Instead, the RPF parliamentary group split over the investiture of Pinay in 1952. Ordered by de Gaulle to vote against the Independent leader, twenty-seven RPF deputies rebelled. In the following months the Rally was unable to reassert authority over the dissidents. The latter even increased to about fifty who refused to sign a pledge to abide by the rule of bloc voting and formed the splinter *Action Républicaine et Sociale* which eventually merged with the Independents. The loss of economic liberals who preferred Pinay to de Gaulle resulted in greater unity within the Rally on economic problems. Capitant and Malraux pressed their idea of reforming the capitalist system by associating labor and management in profit-sharing schemes. De Gaulle adopted such ideas and proposed an attack on the privileges of both parliament and the capitalist class. This appeal to the Right on political questions and to the Left on economic and social issues later served de Gaulle by his not having associated himself clearly with either side but in the short run caused him the loss of much support, especially among his more conservative followers. In May, 1953, de Gaulle dissolved the RPF parliamentary group which formed the *Union des Républicains et d'Action Sociale* (URAS) and eventually, after further splits, became the Social Republican group (SR). Making de Gaulle's return to power and the reform of the constitution their major objective, the Gaullist deputies however did not object to participating in the "system" and served in many of the ministries. De Gaulle ceased public political action. The Rally stopped recruiting members, its local organizations were brought to a standstill, and national headquarters slowed to a dormant life. However, de Gaulle did not preoccupy himself only with writing his memoirs. Either in his country house in Colombey-les-Deux-Églises or in Paris, where he used to go about once a week, he maintained contact with the many Gaullist and non-Gaullist politicians who would consult with him. In incarnating the national consciousness he served his own myth better than by leading a party. Freed from the paraphernalia of mass meetings and of party conclaves tending to pull him into the common political arena, he could again emerge as the respected war leader, as the nation's supreme recourse. Convinced that the regime would falter at the first serious crisis de Gaulle waited, avoided compromising himself by taking sides in the political problems of the time. In the meantime the Gaullist deputies, profiting from the freedom given them by the general, took definite positions. Under the influence of Soustelle now converted to a policy of complete integration after serving as governor general in Algeria, the Gaullist parliamentarians defended the maintenance of total French sovereignty over Algeria. Most of the Gaullist senators and deputies also followed Debré in refusing any abandonment of French sovereignty in favor of European institutions. Severed from de Gaulle, the Gaullist parliamentarians suffered heavy electoral losses. In 1956 they obtained only 4.3 per cent of the votes in elections to the National Assembly and in 1958, a month before the May, 1958, rebellion, they obtained only 3.5 per cent in the cantonal elections. But the Gaullists in parliament had given proof of "republicanism"; they had participated in governments headed by Radicals and even by Socialists; they were no longer feared as dangerous to democratic institutions. Thus it happened that the participation of Gaullists in the governments of the Fourth Republic eventually served de Gaulle and rendered his return to power in 1958 easier for Radicals, Socialists, and MRP's to accept.

After his return to power, de Gaulle did not recreate the RPF, but although refusing to lend his name to any political party he privately encouraged or at least let develop freely two movements aimed at rallying Gaullist forces. One attempt, oriented to the Left was a failure; the other oriented to the Right produced the UNR, the leading party in the first parliament of the Fifth Republic.

The attempt at launching a Left-wing Gaullist movement was made by a group of personalities including J. de Lipkowski, among the founders of the unsuccessful Gaullist Union of 1946, P. Alduy and G. Juskiewenski, from the Socialist party, P. Clostermann and P. Naudet, Mendecian Radicals. Vague as the program of Left-wing Gaullists was, it tended to appeal to the "labor" electorate by emphasizing free association between France and the overseas territories as well as a type of nondoctrinaire socialism. Left-wing Gaullists were completely defeated in the elections of 1958, polling less than 1 per cent of the votes. They undoubtedly suffered from de Gaulle's not having given them any seat in his cabinet, preferring to rely on Right-wing Gaullists and on Socialists.

The other attempt, that at forming a Gaullist party with its axis on the Right, was immediately successful, although not as much as the RPF of 1947. The *Union pour la Nouvelle République* obtained close to 20 per cent of the votes in the 1958 elections to the National Assembly. With more than 35 per cent of the seats in the National Assembly the UNR found itself in a commanding position in the first parliament of the Fifth Republic; the prime minister, six out of sixteen ministers, the chairman of the National Assembly, and three of the six chairmen of the Assembly's standing committees belonged to the UNR in 1959.

Created in October, 1958, less than two months before the elections to the lower house, the UNR was in some respects a relaunching of the RPF under a new name. Usually the former local RPF organizations were reactivated, and in their recruiting of members and selecting of local leaders, UNR headquarters made use of the RPF files. However, at the top level the UNR was not a simple continuation of the RPF or Social Republican leaderships. The Union was formed as a result of a fusion between "old" Gaullist machines and new movements issuing from the May 13 events.

Three major Gaullist groups merged to form the UNR. The *Union Civique pour le Référendum* led by J. Chaban-Delmas, R. Triboulet, and L. Terrenoire represented the moderate parliamentary tradition. The *Convention Républicaine*, founded in September, 1958, by L. Delbecque, and the *Union pour le Renouveau Français*, founded by Soustelle in July, 1958, represented the Gaullist groups most active in preparing and channeling the May 13 rebellion. Other organizations were of lesser importance; Biaggi's extreme Rightist league and Ali Mallem's group of Algerian leaders favorable to de Gaulle merged within or affiliated themselves to the UNR.

At the time of the merger the most prominent UNR leader

was Soustelle, but the objections of moderate Gaullists as well as de Gaulle's personal veto, prevented the former governor general of Algeria from becoming president of the new party. Instead, the leadership of the UNR was given to a directorate of fifteen members composed of representatives of the founding parties and groups. Such collective leadership also served to show that the true leader of the UNR was General de Gaulle, notwithstanding his refusal to lend his official support to any political party.

By 1960 the more extreme nationalists among the UNR leadership had either resigned from the UNR—J. B. Biaggi and J. Thomazo for example; had been suspended, like Delbecque; or had, like Soustelle, been expelled. However, the UNR congress of November, 1959, had shown that if the liberals—liberals on overseas affairs—were able to impose their leadership, thanks to de Gaulle's full support, the Rightists had widespread sympathies among the party. Like the MRP at one time, the UNR appeared as a party with a leadership much to the Left of the rank and file.

### Organization

According to the party rules of 1959 the basic units are electoral district organizations grouped into *département* unions. These unions elect their own executive committee which then selects its secretary-general and its treasurer. The *département* unions also select delegates to the national council and to the national congress. Dominated by its executive, itself often controlled by the *département's* UNR parliamentarians, the major function of the *département's* organization is to activate the district committees, to select candidates for local elections, and to propose candidates for national elections to the Paris headquarters.

At the national level the party organs, as those of most other parties, comprise a national congress, a national council, a central committee, a political committee, and a secretariat.

The national congress, called Assizes, is composed of the members of the central committee and of the national council on the one hand, and of delegates from the *département* unions on the other. The ex-officio members each have one vote while the union delegates have a number of votes fixed by the central committee on the basis of the membership of each union in the *département*. The agenda of the congress is determined by the central committee at least six weeks beforehand. The *rapporteurs* are appointed by the committee and reports must be sent to the unions at least one month before the congress.

The congress which meets at least once a year acts as the party's supreme legislative body by defining doctrine and program. The congress also elects an arbitration committee, a credentials committee, and most members of the central committee. Decisions are taken by a majority vote. Mandate voting is compulsory for all questions on the agenda and whenever requested by one-fifth of the *département* unions. In all other cases the personal vote which reduces the influence of *département*-union delegates may be used.

The national council is intermediate between the national congress and the central committee and has executive as well as legislative functions. Theoretically, the council controls the central committee and sees to it that the congress's decisions are respected. Between congresses the council may also be asked to decide on matters of program or policy. The national council is composed of an equal number of parliamentarians and nonparliamentarians. The nonparliamentarians include the *département* unions' secretaries-general and an additional number of ordinary members necessary to maintain parity between parliamentarians and nonparliamentarians. The national council meets yearly, but extraordinary meetings may be called either by the central committee or by twenty unions. The national council is assisted by standing commissions which study political, professional, social, and party problems.

In theory the central committee is the party's supreme executive organ. It controls the secretary-general, makes decisions which cannot wait for a national council, endorses candidates for national elections, may veto the choices of *département* unions for local elections, arbitrates in final resort on drop-off agreements or withdrawal of candidates after the first ballot, and more generally has disciplinary powers over unions as well as individual members.

The central committee is composed of ex-officio and of elected members. The latter are twenty-five parliamentarians (nineteen deputies and six senators) and twenty-five militants elected by the national congress, the former are the UNR cabinet ministers, parliamentary assembly and caucus chairmen, the party secretary-general and the treasurer. In addition the central committee recruits by coöptation two representatives of youth organizations. The central committee may ask the chairmen of the national council's standing commissions to participate in the meetings in an advisory capacity. The central committee, which meets only monthly, delegates its powers to the political committee.

In 1960, the political committee comprised twenty members: the UNR cabinet ministers, parliamentary assembly chairmen, the parliamentary caucus chairmen, the secretary-general, the treasurer together with three parliamentarians, and five non-parliamentarians elected by the central committee.[6]

The composition of this committee shows a concentration of powers into the hands of cabinet ministers and parliamentarians. Like the MRP in its early days and for the same reasons the UNR leadership does not trust a membership recruited too rapidly. Notable is that through its political committee the UNR will in fact be led by its cabinet ministers as long as the latter are in sufficient number. The constitutional rule which forbids cabinet ministers to hold parliamentary mandates does not prevent them from holding party positions. The necessary contacts between executive and parliamentary groups may thus be established through the party. Under the UNR rules the granting of cabinet positions has for indirect effect promotion to the party leadership. Inversely, loss of a cabinet seat may also mean loss of an important party post. Soustelle's dismissal from the cabinet in February, 1960, deprived him of membership in the political committee.

Unlike the Radicals or the MRP but like the SFIO and the Independents, the UNR has no president. The day-to-day administration is entrusted to a secretary-general elected by the central committee after each national congress. The secretary-general chooses vice-secretaries-general in agreement with the political committee.

In controlling the *département* unions, the political committee and the secretary-general are assisted by the arbitration committee and by the credentials committee. The latter, composed of five members elected by the national congress, advises the central committee on the admission of new members, and controls and validates mandates of *département* unions. The arbitration committee is composed of nine members elected by the national congress from among members having a judicial training, and although its major function is to settle conflicts between *département* unions and the credentials committee, it also advises the political committee of all infringements of party rules by an individual member or by local unions.

This organization of the UNR, devised by the party's provisional directorate in 1959 may be amended by a two-thirds vote in the national congress.

The UNR caucus in the National Assembly elects its own chairman and vice-chairmen.[7] The bills pending parliamentary discussion are debated at caucus meetings, and bloc voting may be imposed by a majority of the caucus. The size of the 1958 caucus rendered necessary its division into smaller study groups. The UNR members of the various parliamentary committees sometimes met separately to define a common position. In order that backbenchers not be too isolated from the caucus leadership, an attempt was made to assign about twenty-five deputies to each of the vice-chairmen. This experiment with nonspecialized subcaucuses seems to have been unsuccessful.

At the end of 1959, after a year of uncertainty when the party machine, the parliamentarians, the ministers, and the militants were not clearly related, the UNR evolved a more coherent organization, following the creation of the political committee. So far as the rank and file and also, to a large extent, the parliamentarians, are excluded from the governing of the party, the UNR resembles the RPF. In its new version the Gaullist party is not ruled directly by de Gaulle, but—like the cabinet —through Prime Minister Debré, who has thus been put in the party as well as in the government, in the position of a chief of staff.

## Ideology and Program

In 1959, Albin Chalandon, then secretary-general of the UNR, analyzing the difficulties and responsibilities of his party said "we must see things as they are. General de Gaulle is our commander in hiding. We are somewhat in the position of secret agents owing total obedience to a military chief, who does not hesitate to disavow his secret agents when things go wrong. Our position is uncomfortable. Let us console ourselves by saying that we are somewhat heroic!" [8]

Chalandon thus placed the UNR parliamentarians on a par with the backbenchers in the British system. In Chalandon's version the party should act as a brain trust trying to influence the leader but not opposing him in any circumstance.

De Gaulle's two major objectives seem to be to give France political stability and to reassert her position as one of the world's major powers. In his various speeches as leader of the RPF or as president of the council, de Gaulle insisted that nineteenth-century parliamentarism was outmoded and dangerous; government by discussion and compromise was no longer adaptable to the present. The crux of power had to be in the executive, not in the parliament.

Whether because of long-time preferences or to avoid taking the path followed by Pétain, de Gaulle did not wish to sacrifice democracy to the necessities of strong government. Parliament should not be rendered powerless; it should remain the main source of law and should have the power to resist the executive. But while acting as a check on the executive, parliament should be deprived of its former privilege of settling all conflicts in its own favor. Such conflicts should ultimately be settled by the people themselves. In de Gaulle's schemes appeal to the electorate plays an important role. The procedures of dissolution and referendum are to be used by the executive to prevent the legislature from being at the same time contestant and umpire. Having a marked hostility to the parliamentary profession, de Gaulle thinks maybe that his feeling is universal among the electorate and that people would naturally side with the executive rather than with their representatives. This assumption, if made, may well be correct, at least for the present. It is unlikely that the electorate would now react as they did in 1876 when after the dissolution of the Chamber of Deputies, they sided with the parliamentarians against the president. The French of 1960 do not react against a former authoritarian government but against the weak and unstable parliamentary systems of the Third and Fourth republics. It remains to be seen what the evolution of de Gaulle's thinking would be if in a conflict between the executive and the legislature the people were to back the parliamentarians. The UNR would probably divide over those who would sacrifice democracy for the sake of stable and efficient government.

De Gaulle thinks that France can be restored to a position of great influence among nations by a strong executive and by her strategic position. De Gaulle is probably aware that France cannot meet the challenge of the continent-size nations without the support of Africa and Western Europe, and hopes for a voluntary but effective association between France and her former African colonies.

While hostile to France's abandoning part of her sovereignty,[9] de Gaulle favors some of the efforts made to integrate Europe. He sees French-German reconciliation as written in the political geography of the twentieth century, but he does not contemplate, like many Socialists and Christian democrats, the creation of a European state. If Western European powers must collaborate they should not subordinate themselves to supernational executives or parliaments. He prefers a reformed Council of Europe where the assembly would be popularly elected but could act only as advisor to a council of ministers selected by the governments of the member states, such council being subjected to the rule of unanimity. If with regard to Africa de Gaulle seemed at first to prefer a French-African union of a federal or at least confederate type, for Europe he has thus far opposed abandonments of sovereignty. In the UNR, hostility to too loose an association between France and her former colonies of Black Africa remains widespread, but de Gaulle's offer of a permanent right of independence to the member states in the Community did not provoke any serious opposition among Gaullist parliamentarians who would not have let the governments of the Fourth Republic make such an offer without claiming it to be national betrayal. The UNR is also generally hostile to European integration. In the Senate of the Fourth Republic, Debré had made himself the champion of French nationalism. But on the question of European integration as on that of French-African union, the UNR is on the whole willing to accept de Gaulle's leadership, even if it means realigning their positions.

In the conflict for power between the U.S.A. and the U.S.S.R., de Gaulle and the UNR have chosen the side of the West. The General thinks however that because of her former internal weaknesses France has become, within the North Atlantic alliance, a mere supporter of the United States, and he endeavors to obtain the status of full-fledged partner for his country.

The Fourth Republic's failure to solve the Algerian problem returned de Gaulle to power, and with him the UNR. It could, therefore, have been expected that it be on the Algerian question that de Gaulle and the Gaullist party be in closer sympathy. This, however, is not the case. Notwithstanding the resignations or expulsions from the party of the more nationalistic among UNR leaders, the party remained, in 1960, divided between those prepared to follow de Gaulle in carrying his policy of self-determination for Algerians and those who thought that the General, by refusing to rule out independence as a possible choice for Moslems, may have seriously damaged France's chances of keeping the whole of Algeria. In the event of some form of independence being actually given to Algeria, the UNR would probably be seriously split.

Gaullism does not have a specific social or economic program. De Gaulle claims credit for the postwar social reforms, for the social-security, family-allowances, and unemployment-benefits schemes. In the 1950's the RPF's Left wing led by Capitant and Vallon tried to commit de Gaulle to a policy of labor-capital coöperation which would have gone further than new dealism. Projects of labor's sharing in the management and in the benefits of enterprises were put in the RPF platform and inherited by the UNR. It is doubtful however that such projects ever lead to any significant reforms of the economic system. On matters of economic policy de Gaulle has tended to rely on his ministers of finance, on Petsche and Pléven after the war, on Pinay and W. Baumgartner after 1958. And when choosing his finance ministers de Gaulle seems to have given little consideration to their economic beliefs. Before appointing liberal Pinay in 1958 de Gaulle had offered the position to Bloch-Lainé, a believer in strict economic planning. It is revealing that the General presided over the liberal "revival" of 1959, he who had presided over the Socialist "conquests" of 1945. On economic questions, the UNR parliamentary group is generally conservative, closer to economic liberalism than to socialism. One can find many shades of such conservatism. Those closer to the Independents supported without restrictions Pinay's policies of financial stabilization and economic liberalization, but others, including A. Chalandon and E. Michelet, would have preferred to place economic development ahead of financial stability and to rely more on state planning.

### Leadership

In the recruiting of its leaders each French party tends to give preference to specific groups: Socialists to anticlerical or agnostic civil servants and teachers; Radicals to anticlerical lawyers and doctors; the MRP to the members of Catholic youth associations; Poujadists to small shopkeepers; Communists to industrial workers turned party officials. The Gaullist parties have recruited their leaderships mostly from the well to do and upper middle class [10] but the criterion for recruiting has been less social than historical. Promotion to the leadership in the UNR as well as in the RPF has been from the wartime Resistance organizations and from the cadres of the Gaullist government in exile.

The UNR ministers in the Debré cabinet in 1959—J. Soustelle, A. Malraux, E. Michelet, R. Triboulet, B. Cornut-Gentille, and R. Frey—had either served de Gaulle during the Second World War or had been active in underground movements favorable to the general.

The most influential members of de Gaulle's personal cabinet, G. de Courcel, R. Brouillet, General G. de Beaufort, and R. Janot among others, had similar war records. The same applies to other members of the UNR leadership not serving in the government, J. Chaban-Delmas, L. Delbecque, A. Chalandon, and J. Fourcade for example.

### Members and Electors

As one moves down from the leadership to the rank and file and to the electorate one finds that Resistance activities are less and less a common denominator.

The membership of the UNR was given as 100,000 by party officials in 1959. This figure seems in excess of the actual membership, which is known to be much lower than that of the RPF. Following the foundation of the UNR, a debate opposed Chalandon and Delbecque on recruiting policies. The former wished the party to remain one of cadres, the latter wanted to turn it into a mass organization. Chalandon may have been rationalizing recruiting difficulties; he may have been afraid also that if the rank and file were to play too great a role in the shaping of the party's course, the leadership would become hindered by too Rightist a following.

The UNR electorate is mostly conservative. True the party seems at times able to attract Left-wing votes, Communists included, but the elections of 1951 indicate that Gaullist gains were made principally at the expense of the MRP, and of the Poujadists and Radicals in 1958.

According to the *Institut Français d'Opinion Publique* poll of 1952 the Gaullist electorate was, according to socioeconomic groups, more like that of the MRP than of any other party. Industrial workers accounted for 18 per cent of the RPF electorate (MRP, 15 per cent); farm workers 4 (MRP, 3); civil servants

2 (MRP, 3); white-collar employees in private business 7 (MRP, 11); management 7 (MRP, 3); shopkeepers 7 (MRP, 5); farmers 18 (MRP, 20); liberal professions 1 (MRP, 1); retired people 4 (MRP, 6); nonworking women 32 (MRP, 30). The only significant differences were that the RPF had fewer white-collar employees and more business executives than the MRP. The RPF electorate was, if ownership of an automobile be taken as a sign of wealth, second only to the Independents —33 per cent and 43 per cent respectively. Of all voters, the RPF's were those most hostile to the Communists and those who gave most emphasis to party leadership. Thirty-five per cent thought that party leadership was more important than doctrine, program, or party cohesion. For other parties the percentage varied between 7 among Socialists and 20 among Radicals. A poll of the 1958 UNR electorate probably would have confirmed that for the Gaullist voter de Gaulle is more important than a particular program or ideology. In this dependence on de Gaulle's personality for support lies the UNR weakness. Assuming that the general succeeds in stabilizing French democracy and in provoking political regroupings leading to a simplified party system, it is not certain that the UNR, rather than the Independents for example, would be the ultimate beneficiary of his success.

# 9 *Minor Parties*

When no single party can hope to gain a majority of the seats in the legislature and when the representative does not depend for reëlection on endorsement by the party's national machine, the temptation is strong to form one's own political party, one's own coterie. The experience of the Third and Fourth republics show the natural tendency of parliamentary groups to split because of doctrinal or personal conflicts, which in a disciplined two-party system would have most likely been resolved without party break. In a multiparty system the founding of a new party may be a quicker way to reach power than by working through a well-established political organization. Multipartism, in France at least, breeds multipartism; it grows cancerously.

Some of France's present-day minor parties are remnants of once major political groups such as the French Reconciliation, the heir to the prewar PSF; others, like B. Lafay's Republican Center and P. Mendès-France's Union of Democratic Forces

(UFD), originated after a split from a larger formation; both were created following cessessions from the Radicals. A third type consists of small parties having had an independent life for so long that they could be assimilated neither to splinter parties nor to remnant parties; to use one of Toynbee's classifications, they are "arrested parties," parties that failed to grow. Such is the case of the anarchists and of the Young Republic.

To minor parties one should perhaps assimilate the *societés de pensée*, the political and philosophical clubs which have a political doctrine and program but do not feel strong enough to turn themselves into election-contesting organizations. Such societies or clubs try sometimes to influence the major parties but more often, in keeping with French political habits, hope to become the nucleus of new political groupings. These potential political parties are generally grouped around a weekly or a monthly, for example J. P. Sartre's *Les Temps Modernes*, Left-wing Catholic *Témoignage Chrétien* and *Esprit*, monarchist *Aspects de la France*, or Petainist *Rivarol*.

Minor political parties may be grouped into six categories: anarchist and Communist, labor, liberal, conservative, extreme Rightist, and monarchist.

### The Anarchist and Communist Groups

At the beginning of the century, anarchists had been influential in the French Socialist movement and had conquered important positions in the trade unions especially in the Southwest. But they are now little more than a philosophical society with hardly any influence on the working class. Grouped around the newspaper, *Le Libertaire*, anarchist leaders attack both the capitalist and the Communist regimes. Following Bakunin they think that liberty without socialism means privilege and injustice, but that socialism without liberty means slavery and brutality. Their enemy is the state, whether capitalistic or Communist. French anarchists propose to substitute for the system of state supremacy a society of freely constituted syndicates not based on a whole profession but on small working groups. Each group would elect for short-terms delegates responsible with administering group affairs. Each would send representatives to coördinating committees and the committees to a supreme council which would replace the government and would substitute counseling and coördinating for commanding and oppressing. Anarchists remain faithful to the First International's ideal of a world revolution made by the workers who, having no fatherland, are fundamentally pacifist. In keeping with the teachings of the Syndicalists, French anarchists think that workers in their efforts to destroy the state should not make use of political parties, but should rather use the working class's natural weapon, the trade union. Anarchists consequently tried to infiltrate all workers' unions, but obtained some limited successes only within the Socialist CGT-FO, more particularly in the printers' unions. Although condemning parliamentary action as inefficient, anarchists sometimes run candidates in selected districts in order to propagandize. Their electoral strength is insignificant.

The International Communist party (PCI), more commonly known as the Trotskyist party, claims to be the true heir of Marx and Lenin. It refuses to submit to Moscow, but it thinks that the U.S.S.R., the first proletarian state, must be defended against the attacks of international capitalism. Trotskyists criticize Stalinists for the role they assign to the Communist party. According to the PCI, the party should take the leadership in spontaneous strikes and insurrectional movements but should not artificially impose on the working class actions for which it is not ready, and not impose a bureaucratic dictatorship after the revolution.

In 1946 when Communists were in the cabinet and supporting an austerity program, the PCI contested seventeen consituencies against the "Stalinists." By splitting the vote they caused the PCF to lose a few seats, but failed to gain representation for themselves. Since the return of Communists to the opposition in 1947, Trotskyists have practically disappeared from the electoral scene. Like the anarchists but with a little more success, they have concentrated on trade-union activities. They try to reach the general public through their weekly *La Vérité*.

Former members of the Communist party have tried at times

to launch French versions of a Titoist party. In 1951 D. le Corre founded the French Communist Movement; in 1956, A. Lecoeur, former secretary of the PCF, founded *La Nation Socialiste* to propagate his version of democratic and national communism.[1] Both attempts ended in complete failure and the two former deputies did not even save their own seats.

Unlike anarchists, Trotskyists, and national Communists who oppose it, Progressives support the PCF and for this support have been rewarded with parliamentary representation. The Progressives originated as a parliamentary group founded by former Radicals like P. Cot, Christian democrats of the extreme Left like G. de Chambrun, and even members of traditionally royalist families like E. d'Astier de la Vigerie. This group of personalities, because of their past, could not have made a career in the Communist party itself. In 1950 the Progressive parliamentary group gained a more solid party basis by fusing three pro-Communist organizations, the *Parti-Socialiste Unitaire*, the *Union Républicaine et Résistante*, and the *Union des Chrétiens Progressistes* into the Progressive Union which organized local federations in a few *départements* and published a small quarterly, the *Cahiers du Progressisme*. The Progressive Union did not reach many more than a thousand members and never succeeded in creating a party machine which could obtain the election of its own candidates without Communist support. In the election of 1951, a group of Progressives campaigned independently on neutralist tickets, committed neither to the West nor to the East but all were defeated. Only those Progressives who were on Communist lists were reëlected. The Progressives disappeared from parliament in 1958 but continue to serve Communist propaganda, mostly through d'Astier de la Vigerie's newspaper *Libération* which is geared to the shifting electorate of temporary Communist sympathizers.

### Labor Groups

The hope of French laborites is to be able to insert themselves between Communists and Socialists and to attract the electorates of both parties. Laborites think that the SFIO, dominated as it is by civil servants and school teachers, lacks the dynamism necessary to reconquer the working class from the Communists. Watered-down reformism cannot be a substitute for revolutionism. With that in mind laborites advocate further transfers of property from private to public ownership, policies of emancipation in favor of former colonies including Algeria, and attitudes of greater independence from the United States in the cold war. Various groups agreeing with most if not with all that basic program tried to federate themselves before the elections of 1956. In February, 1955, the *Union Démocratique du Travail* was founded, grouping Gaullists such as R. Capitant and I. de Lipkowski, members of the Young Republic, including its sole parliamentarian, A. Denis, extreme Left-wing Catholics belonging to the *Témoignage Chrétien* group, ex-MRP's such as L. Hamon, and personalities close to the Progressives such as P. Rivet and J. Cassou. Later in the year, C. Bourdet and G. Martinet, editors of *France-Observateur*, founded the New Left, an organization more oriented to the Left than was the UDT. The New Left attracted a few expellees from the SFIO as well as from the Communist party. In 1957 further efforts made to regroup labor forces resulted in the launching of the *Union de la Gauche Socialiste* (UGS) which brought together five small parties: the New Left led by Bourdet; the *Mouvement de Libération du Peuple*, a Christian movement close to Marxism in its economic and political conceptions; two splinter Socialist groups —the *Action Socialiste* and the *Unité-Socialiste;* and dissident members of the Christian-democratic Young Republic.[2] Taking P. Nenni's Socialist party as a model, the UGS, while refusing to ally itself with the Communists on all questions, accepted collaboration with Marxist parties on a common program. Publishing a weekly, *Tribune du Peuple* and organizing federations in about seventy *départements*, the UGS claimed to have about 10,000 members. In 1958 a challenger appeared when dissident and expelled members of the SFIO founded the Autonomous Socialist party (PSA) with a program, like that of the UGS, calling for a more active socialism, for internal democracy within the party organization, for peace in Algeria, and for the nonsupport of confessional schools by the state.

Notwithstanding an electoral alliance, the elections of 1958 were a severe defeat for both groups which failed to elect any representative to parliament and which only obtained substantial electoral support in the sole districts where the Communist party abstained in their favor. In 1959 the larger of the two labor groups, the PSA, was joined by Mendès-France.

In 1960 some clarification resulted from the fusion of the UGS, the PSA and the *Tribune du Communisme*, a small Marxist group. They formed the *Parti Socialiste Unifié* which, in trying to appeal to liberals as well as Socialists, found itself in the same position as the UDSR after 1945: that of expecting to reunify the French Left in the ruins of the SFIO, the Radicals, and the Communist party. The secretary-general of the PSU is E. Depreux, a former SFIO leader. The better-known of the PSU members, P. Mendès-France, preferred not to share executive responsibilities and to continue in temporary political retirement. Notwithstanding its claim of offering a rejuvenated form of socialism, the PSU does not appear as basically different from the SFIO, except however in their systematical opposition to de Gaulle's rule, judged undemocratic.

### Liberal Groups

As splinter Labor groups hope to force their way between Socialists and Communists, splinter liberal groups hope to reconcile either Socialists and Radicals or Radicals and moderates. The leadership of most of these splinter liberal parties has come from the Radicals.

The belief that the Radical party was dying and that more dynamic groups should fill the void led, after the war, to the creation of the UDSR which hoped to become a big liberal-labor party but found neither its Lloyd George nor a sufficiently large membership. In 1956, following their expulsion from the Radical party, E. Faure and J. P. David sought to transform the RGR parliamentary group into another Radical party, one which could attract all those opposed to Mendès-France's politics and leadership. In the late 1950's two other former Radicals, B. Lafay and A. Morice, tried first separately then together to regroup the Center forces outside the Radical party; before the elections of 1958 they formed the Republican Center which polled almost as many votes as the Radical party itself.

### The UDSR

The only French party born of the Resistance organizations, *Union Démocratique et Sociale de la Résistance*, never succeeded in attracting a mass following but instead remained a group of parliamentarians dependent on their own political machines for elections. Among the founders of the UDSR are some of the better known among postwar politicians: E. Claudius-Petit, R. Pléven, R. Bourdan, F. Mitterand, E. Bonnefous, J. Soustelle, and R. Capitant. The UDSR's original program was socialistic—"on the ruins of capitalism we shall found a classless society," proposed a 1945 party manifesto.[3] The UDSR sought the support of all those who accepted the principles of a lay state, whether Christian or not; all those who believed in socialism and in democracy; and those who wanted to organize the French Union on the basis of a free association of free peoples. The foundation of the Union Gaulliste, then of the RPF, caused Capitant, Soustelle, J. Nocher and others to leave. Under the leadership of Pleven, the UDSR modified its early course, parallel to that of the SFIO, to come closer to the Radicals. The refusal of a majority of UDSR leaders to link their fate with that of the RPF cost the party twelve of its twenty-six deputies. In 1953 Mitterand succeeded in gaining the party presidency, because the defeat of the EDC treaty had seriously weakened Pleven whose great design was the constitution of a united Europe. Under Mitterand's leadership the UDSR formed a close alliance with an African party, the RDA, led by F. Houphouët-Boigny who had become converted to the idea of a French-African federation. The events of May, 1958, and the decision taken by the UDSR national congress to ask their followers to vote against de Gaulle's constitution broke the party and separated the RDA from the UDSR. Houphouët-Boigny and other members of the RDA approved the 1958 constitution and consequently severed their alliance with the UDSR; for the same reason Claudius-Petit and Pléven resigned. In the 1958 elections for the National Assembly, the UDSR lost all its seats; in 1959, however, Mitterand was elected to the Senate. Reduced to the rank of a remnant party with only occasional representatives in parliament, the UDSR, born with the Fourth Republic, may well be considered as having died with it.

### The Rebublican Center

Founded by B. Lafay in the 1950's and recruiting at first almost exclusively in the Paris area, the Republican Center benefited in 1958 by the adhesion of a group of former Radicals led by A. Morice who had left the Radical party because of their hostility to Mendès-France's leadership. The Republican Center can be classified as being to the Right of orthodox Radicals on such matters as the school question and the Algerian problem, but on the whole the differences between the Republican Center and the Radicals are more personal than ideological. Former Radicals who left or were expelled from the Radical party still remember the "betrayal" they suffered from colleagues who, if for only a short time, followed Mendès-France. In 1958 the Republican Center with nearly 4 per cent of the electoral vote and fourteen deputies fared almost as well as the party itself.

Personal resentments also explain the survival of the *Rassemblement des Gauches Républicaines* (RGR) which had originated under the Fourth Republic as a parliamentary group composed of Radicals and other parties like the UDSR, the Democratic Socialist party of P. Faure, and the *Réconciliation Française*, and which had been turned later into a political party separate from the Radicals, following Mendès-France's expulsion of E. Faure from the Radical party. Under the leadership of J. P. David, the RGR hopes to be the embryo of a French liberal party which would regroup Radicals and like-minded Center parties.

French liberals find difficulty in adapting to the necessities of twentieth-century politics. Their unwillingness to accept any amount of party discipline while wanting to expand and broaden their electoral basis leads to disintegration.

### Conservative Groups

In the course of its expansion the CNIP has absorbed most small conservative groups, although some of them maintained a precarious autonomy or independence.

More a club of survivors than an actual party, *Réconciliation Française*, led by P. de Léotard, is heir to de la Rocque's PSF. Most of the latter's prewar followers have gone to other parties—Independents, UNR, or Radicals. While closer to the Independents in their outlook, especially on the school question, the *Réconciliation Française* joined the RGR under the Fourth Republic. Following the elections of 1958, party representation was reduced to four deputies who joined the Independent's parliamentary group.

The farmers' party groups conservative parliamentarians from rural districts, mostly in central France; they are ever engaged in a process of secessions and reconciliations. In the 1950's C. Laurens led a faction of the farmers' group into the CNIP where they retained a certain autonomy; another group led by P. Antier remained outside. In 1957 the party split again after Antier had tried to launch a new farmers' party oriented to the extreme Right in coöperation with agricultural syndicalist and politician H. Dorgère and with P. Poujade.[4] Following the elections of 1958, the farmers disappeared from the National Assembly as a separate group. Some of Laurens's followers were reëlected on CNIP tickets, but Laurens himself was defeated. In the Senate, supporters of Antier as well as of Laurens have maintained their positions better; they form a group of about twenty senators.

The name of the farmers' party changes from time to time, following splits or regroupings. In 1960 the farmers called themselves Movement for Agricultural and Social Union. In the Senate, however, they took the name of Republican Center for Rural and Social Action.

### The Algerian Group

E. Herriot's description of the constitution of 1946 as the Moslem constitution of France was more amusing than substantiated. The few Algerian deputies represented in the constituent assemblies had occasionally been able to swing votes, but could not properly be said to have held the balance of power. Nor did the overseas representatives, whether the IOM group close to the MRP, or the RDA close to the UDSR, or the Algerians themselves, ever play a significant role in the parliaments of the Fourth Republic. The constitution and the electoral law of 1958 eliminated the representation of the overseas states, but significantly increased the representation of Algeria. Overseas now elects 16 per cent of the National Assembly, and nearly 9 per cent of the deputies are Moslems as compared with 13 per cent and 2.4 per cent under the preceding Fourth Republic. Although the overseas areas represented have diminished, the influence of the overseas has increased and in particular the influence of Algerian Moslems.

When the first parliament of the Fifth Republic met in 1959, Algerian deputies were confronted with the alternative of affiliating themselves with metropolitan groups or of forming their own parliamentary group. Ten Algerians joined the existing parties, nine went to the UNR, and one to the SFIO; the remaining sixty-one deputies preferred to form a group of their own. At first they called their parliamentary caucus a temporary administrative group, in order to emphasize that they did not consider themselves a separate political party, an idea which might have been interpreted as contradicting the claim that Algeria was part of France. The group was not unified and early divided into three major factions. A minority of Moslems supported by a few European Algerians expected that de Gaulle's policy would lead to the granting of a certain administrative and political autonomy to Algeria within the French fold. This group was led by Ali Bendjelida and supported by the *Echo d'Oran*. A second group comprising European activists and a few Moslems wanted complete integration with France without delay. This group was led by P. Lagaillarde, P. Vignau and R. Vinceguerra who had much in common with the Poujadists and accepted democratic procedures only so far as they did not weaken the economic, political, and social positions of the European settlers in Algeria. The third and largest faction followed M. Lauriol and P. Marcais in wanting a double integration, that of Algeria with France and that of Moslem and European in Algeria. During the first parliamentary session of 1959 the Algerian group lost its Left-wing and Right-wing factions. Nine Moslems, following Bendjelida, went their own way criticizing their former colleagues for not having liberal enough plans for Algeria. On the opposite side, Lagaillarde and Vignau seceded from an Algerian group which they thought was not determined enough in its policies of territorial integration. Reduced to forty-five members in January, 1960, the Algerian group was more unified behind the moderate integrationists, who wanted that Algeria be turned step by step into just another French province like Alsace or Brittany. It seemed doubtful, however, that Lauriol could prevent a further weakening of the Algerian group, and whether he could reverse the trend which led Algerian Moslems to join the UNR, and European Algerians to join the Independents.

### Extreme Rightist Groups

Of all extreme Rightist movements the Poujadists are the only ones to have achieved any electoral success since the war. The Poujadist movement started in 1953 as a pressure group fighting for the defense of small businesses squeezed out of existence by economic changes. Concentrating on the demand for repeal of the many financial controls which plague French small storekeepers and businessmen and which are, because of the nature of small family undertakings, resented as invasions of one's privacy, Poujade advocated refusing to pay taxes and to submit to financial controls. He succeeded in arousing a social group most difficult to organize. The *Union de Défense des Commerçants et Artisans* (UDCA) was at first not committed to any political party. By harassing the Mendès-France and then the Faure governments, the Poujadists obtained some success when financial controls were somewhat relaxed. Either on his own initiative or on the advice of the North African lobby which had early tried to give the UDCA a political slant, Poujade decided in 1955 to turn his pressure group into a party. Running under a *Union et Fraternité Française* ticket (UFF), Poujadist candidates obtained 2,500,000 votes and 52 seats in 1956. A social group up to that time practically unrepresented in French parliaments entered the National Assembly; a group of *brave gens* with innocent political ideas, a group of small artisans and shopkeepers who had always thought of the powers that be as "they," and of the parliamentarians as traffickers and robbers. With neither a doctrine nor even a program but aware of their intellectual limitations, the Poujadist deputies could not for long resist feeling the dignity and importance of their new functions once they discovered that not all parliamentarians were what they had been thought, and UFF deputies became restive under the tutelage of their leader who had not lowered himself to run for election. Like the RPF representatives a few years earlier, the Poujadist parliamentarians, refusing to make a systematic opposition, began collaborating with other parties. In order to regain control over "his" deputies, and in order also to give new vitality to a party on the decline, Poujade contested a Paris by-election in 1957. Not only did he fail to win the seat but he polled only half as many votes as the UFF candidate the previous year. Trying to use a defeat attributed to the lightheadedness of Parisians, Poujade toured the provinces, concentrating on two themes, the defense of small business and the protection of France and the French empire against all that was "non-French or un-French," all American, Russian, German, and Jewish influences. Poujadists played an active role in the formation of the Committees of Public Safety during the May 13, 1958, rebellion in Algiers; but Poujade, who had played the nationalist card, was easily outwitted by the Gaullists. Poujade's refusal to grant emergency powers to de Gaulle's cabinet in June, 1958, provoked a split between UFF parliamentarians and the party machine. In 1958 the Poujadist vote dropped from 12 to 3 per cent; all but one

Poujadist candidate, including Poujade himself, were defeated. However, he did not reconvert his movement into any ordinary pressure group. Depicting de Gaulle as a traitor ready to give Algeria to foreigners and ready to abandon France herself to the domination of both the trusts and the Socialists, Poujade tries to rally the extreme nationalists. He bases his nationalist and antiparliamentarian movement on a group of discontented artisans and shopkeepers, while other extreme nationalists seek to recruit from "disgusted" veterans and "angry young men."

A number of small parties and groups propose to save Algeria for France, even if the saving means the destruction of a "decadent" parliamentary system. In the last years of the Fourth Republic, two former Poujadists, J. M. le Pen and J. Demarquet founded the *Front National des Combattants*, and a former Gaullist, J. B. Biaggi, created the *Parti Patriote Révolutionnaire.*[5] If Biaggi and le Pen have no fundamental love for the republican system, they are not systematically hostile to it; they propose to judge democracy on its ability to maintain French sovereignty over Algeria. On the contrary, *Jeune Nation* led by the Sidos brothers, the *Rivarol* group, the adherents to G. Sauge's theories of national catholicism, and the followers of General Chassin and Robert Martel, are fundamentally opposed to democracy. These small fascist groups succeed occasionally in staging street demonstrations, such as the attack on Communist headquarters following the Hungarian insurrection, but their electoral influence is nil. Notwithstanding the French army's being at war for the past twenty years, veterans' leagues have not assumed the political importance of the 'thirties. A continuation of the Algerian conflict might, however, create a new situation, if only by increasing the number of veterans once actively engaged in a war.

In Algeria, the Moslem insurrection has occasioned the rise of quasi-military leagues among the European settlers, particularly in Algiers. Determined to maintain Algeria French, if necessary by illegal action, these groups usually question the democratic system for its "inherent weakness" and for its equalitarian implications. The more influential of such leagues include the

*Front National Français* led by J. Ortiz; the *Mouvement Populaire du 13 Mai* led by R. Martel; the corporatist movement of Dr. Lefèvre, and the students' and former students' groups which recognize P. Lagaillarde as their leader.

Some of these leagues have tried to establish branches in metropolitan France but have not been too successful, except in the Southwest where a relatively high proportion of former *colons*, repatriated from Tunisia and Morocco, have resettled. The Algerian leagues maintain close contacts with the extreme Rightist movements of metropolitan France, such as the Poujadists, the *Front National des Combattants*, and *Jeune Nation.*

### Monarchist Groups

Although there is now only one contender to the throne, French monarchists are not united. The Count of Paris refuses to associate himself with the extreme Right monarchists grouped around publications like *Aspects de la France* and *La Nation Française.* In 1950, the Count of Paris returned to France when the exile laws forbidding his family to live on the territory of metropolitan France were repealed. Since then most laws restricting the political rights of members of families that reigned over France have been repealed, and the Count of Paris could legally run for the presidency. In normal times his electoral chances would be negligible, but in the event of a national crisis, if the country happened to be short of other charismatic leaders, the Count's coming to power should not be taken as an impossibility. Rather than trying to organize his small number of followers, the Count of Paris wishes to remain free from political entanglements. In an essay published in 1948, he outlined a draft constitution [6] maintaining the basic feature of a parliamentary system, the responsibility of the cabinet before an elected assembly. He suggested the creation of a "great council" and of people's delegates. This council would be selected by the king, the Assembly, the great corporations (including unions), and the universities. In case of conflict between cabinet and Assembly, the council would decide whether to consult peoples' delegates through a referendum. These peoples' delegates, elected for a term, would never meet together but would be consulted all at one time to decide by a majority vote the problem submitted to them. The Count invited the French to rally around Pétain in 1940 and approved de Gaulle's return to power in 1958. Although not anti-European, the Count objects to integration plans which would restrict French sovereignty; he favors an economic program of moderate socialism and generally approves de Gaulle's liberal policies for the overseas.

After the war the remnants of C. Maurras' *Action Française* grouped themselves around two weekly publications, *Aspects de la France* and *La Nation Française*. Closer to the old *Action Française*, *Aspects de la France* diffuses the writings of G. Gaudy, X. Vallat, J. de la Varende, and H. Massis who in the best Maurassian tradition wish to strangle the Republic as the source of all French evils and wish to reëstablish a strong and respected monarchy. *Nation Française*, issued from a split within *Aspects de la France*, brought together monarchists and Pétainists who wish to channel a nationalist upsurge toward a monarchical solution and, strangely enough if one considers Pétain's and Maurras' records, who endeavor to exploit anti-German feelings in order to oppose the move toward European unification. Both groups hope to bring the Count of Paris back to power and make him the authoritarian king that he claims he does not wish to be. Although reaching from twenty to thirty thousand readers, *Aspects de la France* and *La Nation Française* have no electoral influence of any significance.

Notwithstanding its deep-rooted individualism and its dislike of monolithic political structures, the French electorate prefers large and well-established parties. New parties find difficulty in growing other than by amalgamating with existing political groups. There is one exception. Antiparliamentary parties may develop rapidly by directing to their profit an ever-possible antiparliamentary outburst. In this event the new party does not grow in opposition to some specific parties but in opposition to all parties. There lies the weakness of such antiparliamentary parties. Once in parliament they appear to be like other parties and disappoint their followers who return to their old ways of voting. The French electorate is fundamentally conservative. This conservatism more than any anarchistic trait in the national character renders difficult the discarding of the present multiparty system in favor of a simplified one.

# 10 *Parties and Pressure Groups*

Most Frenchmen consider the party they vote for as only one of the groups which represent them and not necessarily the one which represents them best, even politically. To many, voting is a means of recording ideological preferences, more than a means of choosing a delegate. In normal times the citizenry aligns itself with political groupings identified with traditional political philosophies; in times of crisis the voters often desert the parties for such groups as the army, the Catholic church or the trade unions. In 1958 the electorate first voted overwhelmingly for parties hostile to de Gaulle, then looked with indifference at their representatives being forced to vote de Gaulle into power, and finally voted again, at least most of them, for the same parties as before. Unlike Anglo-Saxon nations, the French have not completely accepted the principle of the delegation of rights and powers as implicit in the act of voting. Professor C. Morazé rightly observed that Frenchmen make excellent subjects but bad citizens,[1] the good subject being always ready to oppose and to resist.

Noncommitment to political parties enhances the power of other groups. Four types stand out—the army, the Catholic church, the trade unions, and the trade associations. The army has played an important role in the political evolution of France either by active participation or more often by remaining passive. Without army support the Bonapartes could not have staged their coups d'état; had the army intervened, the revolutions of 1830 and 1848, the Boulanger affair, and the 1934 street riots might have taken different turns; without the army rebellion of 1958 de Gaulle would probably not have returned to power. In times of insecurity, prominent military figures come to the fore: Cavaignac in 1849, Lyautey in 1934, Pétain and Weygand in 1940, de Gaulle in 1958. The *Appel au Soldat* is but one of the consequences of the military's prestige and power. However, during the Third Republic the army remained aloof from politics and promoted neither Boulanger in 1889, nor Pétain in 1940. This tradition was broken in 1958 when the army took sides between de Gaulle and Pflimlin. Having experienced the ease with which a regime can be toppled and having no bloodshed on its conscience, the army may be tempted to intervene again. In February, 1960, it took the officers corps in Algiers a week to decide on obeying the government and putting an end to the settlers' insurrection. It is yet too soon to determine whether the French military will want to substitute the soldier-citizen for the soldier-instrument. As long as the Algerian problem remains unsolved and as long as Communist subversion from inside remains a danger, the army will probably be a major extrapolitical force in France, one around which disappointed or defeated conservatives and nationalists may regroup—a Maginot line of conservatism.

Veterans' organizations may, when the army remains neutral, try to capitalize on military prestige. French veterans' groups are of three types: those with purely social purposes and not directly concerned with politics except on questions of pensions and other such benefits; those created by and closely subordinated to political parties such as the Communist *Association Républicaine des Anciens Combattants;* and those not affiliated to any political party but taking political stands on the major problems of the day. The *Union Nationale des Combattants* for instance favors the unification of Europe and wants to maintain French sovereignty over Algeria.

Among this last group of politically oriented veterans' associations the antiparliamentary groups invite special attention. They appeal to the *brave gens* and *gens braves* as opposed to the "weakminded" and "dishonest" politicians and they assume that those once ready to die for the fatherland should again unite in the spirit of battleground comradeship in order to "throw the rascals out," and restore national greatness and decency. Powerful under the Third Republic when a veterans' organization like the *Croix de Feu*[2] could become the political party with the largest membership, the antiparliamentary veterans' organizations have played only a minor role since the Second World War. The number of French war veterans was of course more limited under the Fourth Republic than in the era after the Second World War. In the 1950's some antiparliamentary veterans' groups staged a few street disturbances, but these were in no way comparable to those of 1934. The continuation of war in Algeria might nevertheless provide material and cause for powerful antiparliamentary leagues in metropolitan France.

The Catholic church avoids supporting any political party officially, and because the bishops depend directly from Rome no religious authority can speak for France as a whole. After the liberation many bishops and priests seemed to support the MRP but such solid backing no longer exists; Independents and Gaullists now benefit as much as Christian democrats from church influence over the electorate. The MRP's desire to collaborate with Socialists on social and economic reforms, and its wish to create a united Europe led to the Movement's early refusal to raise the school question. By taking more clerical positions, the RPF, then the Independents, weakened the MRP, especially in areas where public support of private schools is the foremost political issue. Normally, the church can help political parties but is in no position to dominate them. In that respect France is more akin to Germany than to Italy. In exchange for its support the church expects relatively little from "acceptable" candidates: the freedom to found private schools, some limited state support for such schools, and legislation protecting the family and restricting divorce. In 1958 some religious leaders believed that the new draft constitution was unacceptable to Catholics because it defined the Republic as a lay state, but the assembly of French cardinals agreed that this was insufficient reason for rejecting the proposed text.[3]

The campaigning for state support to private schools is not done directly by the Catholic church but by the *Association des Parents d'Elèves des Ecoles Libres* (APEL). The parliamentarians committed to support the APEL's claims form a parliamentary association (*intergroupe*) which, in 1959, included the Independents, the MRP, and about two-thirds of the UNR representatives, and thus had a majority of votes in the National Assembly.

Churches other than the Catholic play no significant role in French political life. Protestants and Jews have contributed greatly to France's economic and political history, proportionally more, in recent times, than Catholics who took some time to overcome their original reluctance to capitalism and parliamentary democracy. But such contributions were made individually, not from the pressures of Protestants and Jews acting as religious groups.

In the late nineteenth century, philosophical and political associations like Freemasonry and the League of the Rights of Man assumed great political importance. Their opposition to clericalism and their desire to protect the individual against group tyranny led these two associations to form a close-working alliance with the Radicals. Since the Second World War Freemasonry and the League have lost both members and political influence. Freemasonry remains close to the Radicals but the League is now, because of changes in leadership, closer to the Socialists.

The major trade unions, the *Confédération Générale du Travail* (CGT), the *Confédération Générale du Travail-Force Ouvrière* (CGT-FO) and the *Confédération Française des Travailleurs Chrétiens* (CFTC) have probably between 1,800,000 and 2,000,000 members.[4] With 800,000–1,000,000 members, the CGT is by far the largest of the three major unions. The CFTC has probably a few more than 300,000 members and CGT-FO a few less. The other significant unions are the Autonomous Teachers Union with about 200,000 members, and the *Confédération Générale des Cadres,* for middle management, with approximately 100,000. The CGT recruits mainly among industrial workers, the CFTC among white-collar employees in private undertakings, and the CGT-FO among civil servants and workers employed by the state. France, if compared to Great Britain, Germany, Belgium and Switzerland, has a relatively low degree of trade-union membership. Roughly 80 per cent of the teachers and 40 to 50 per cent of the state employees and civil servants are unionized, but less than 10 per cent of salaried people in the private sector. Low as percentage in trade-union membership is, it is much higher than political-party affiliation. About one voter in sixty is a party member, but one in fifteen is a trade unionist. The CGT has more members than all political parties together.

French trade unions still adhere to the theory proposed by early twentieth-century syndicalists that unions should not be affiliated with political parties, and that workers should act primarily through their trade organizations and not through parliament. Political parties are considered *bourgeois* in their nature, while trade unions are the working class's best organs of representation and the strike their major weapon. Although such theories are still used to block official affiliation with political parties, they have become myth without reality. Since 1947 the major union, the CGT, is totally controlled by the Communist party, and its leaders serve on the highest party organs. Since the split of 1947, non-Communist rank-and-file members of the CGT are excluded from significant positions, or are carefully kept in the minority and used to advertise the union's broad appeal. CFTC is closer to the MRP than to other parties, and CGT-FO closer to the Socialists; however, neither is dominated by the closest political party. In many cases the local unions of CFTC or CGT-FO support candidates other than those of either the MRP or the SFIO. A minority within the two non-Communist unions support dissident Socialists and Radicals, in particular Depreux and Mendès-France, in their attempt to launch a new party, the PSU, broad enough to appeal to Socialists and Left-wing liberals, Catholics and non-Catholics.

No French trade unions have the advantages which English unions derive from close association with a political party, nor do French trade unions have the advantages which American unions obtain from their political independence. Their own divisions weaken French syndicalists less than does Communist control of the CGT on the one hand and the lack of realism of non-Communist unions on the other. The old myths of class warfare, working-class united action and revolutionary general strikes are not the proper guiding principles or tools for pressure-group action within a representative system of government.

Unlike the workers' unions, the trade and farmers' associations have remained freer from political entanglements. Following the liberation, Socialist F. Tanguy-Prigent tried to form a large farmers syndicate politically oriented toward the SFIO, but failed after some initial success. The Left-wing *Confédération Générale de l'Agriculture* was soon overshadowed by the *Fédération National des Syndicats d'Exploitants Agricoles* which is not connected with any party and which avoids taking positions on questions not directly affecting agricultural interests. The transformation of the Poujadist *Union de Défense des Commercants et Artisans* into the *Union et Fraternité Française* marked another attempt at establishing a close association between a pressure group and a political party. After the electoral defeat of Poujade and his candidates in 1957 and 1958 many members of the UDCA returned to organizations less politically engaged.

Trade associations are grouped into various organizations, the most representative of which are the *Petites et Moyennes Entreprises* (PME) for artisans and small businessmen, and the *Conseil National du Patronat Français* which, although open to small business, is dominated by big business and usually recognized as its spokesman. Poujade speaks for the small and depressed shopkeepers. M. Gimgembre, secretary-general of the PME, speaks for small business, and P. Villiers, president of the CNPF, speaks for big business. In France, as in the United States, the various trade associations make a common front only on such broad issues as opposition to socialism. Each association defends its own interests separately. Therefore not infrequently the various trade associations back different candidates in an electoral district. CNPF leadership prefers the Independents and the Gaullists, and is perhaps biased toward the Independents who are weakly organized and thus likely to allow more control over the representative by the pressure groups which helped in his election. Among the sources of trade associations' disagreements are the liberalization of internal economic structures, and the question of European integration. Industries and businesses surviving only because of tax privileges, price supports, or subventions oppose freer competition. When R. Schuman proposed a treaty of economic integration between France, Germany, and other European countries in 1950, he met with the general hostility of the CNPF as well as of the PME. The major industries, in particular iron and chemicals, have revised their attitudes and, trusting that they can meet German competition, now favor European economic integration. However, most French industrialists are still protectionists, either within a purely French or within a "little European" context.

A variety of legal structures have been devised which enable pressure groups to advise the government and the parliament on policies, or to help the executive administer social and economic schemes. Farmers elect chambers of agriculture, businessmen elect chambers of commerce, artisans elect artisans chambers.

Trade unions and associations collaborate to administer unemployment-insurance schemes. Trade unions and family associations run candidates for elections to the social-security administrating boards. Trade unions and trade associations have representatives on the price-index committee. Economic, social, and cultural groups are represented on the Economic and Social Council. Bypassing this latter body, the government often sets up special advisory committees. In the 1950's more than four thousand committees had been created and were still officially alive. Such committees are usually composed of civil servants and representatives of the private interests concerned. Usually the government is free to seek the committee's advice or not, but the executive is sometimes obliged by law to consult a particular committee before passing certain types of decrees. Other nonofficial influence by pressure groups on the parliament or government comes from various forms of lobbying.

That French parliamentary committees make little use of hearings may account for the formation of parliamentary associations known as intergroups—groupings of parliamentarians for the defense of specific and usually private interests and for that reason cutting across the regular caucuses. Powerful under the Third Republic, the intergroups have been forbidden since 1946 but have tended to reappear under the name of study groups. Intergroups act like pressure groups within parliament. Most are no better disciplined than other parliamentary groups and try not to impose any voting discipline on their members. But such groups as the intergroup formed before the Second World War by members of the League of the Rights of Man or the postwar one for the support of private schools have, because of their cohesion, much influence on parliament and on the government—often more than the regular parliamentary groups themselves.

Many pressure groups send questionnaires to candidates before an election and ask them to sign pledges. Some parliamentarians refuse in principle to make any written commitment but others, especially candidates not subject to a party authority have no objection to written promises. Before the election of

1951, the PME had obtained a pledge from many deputies to refuse a tax increase, and during the parliamentary debate on the budget, the PME contact men acted as effectual reminders.

If the one-member district system reintroduced in 1958 is maintained for a sufficiently long period of time, pressure groups should normally gain in influence over parliamentarians, but on the other hand, if the executive proves to be more stable than before, pressure groups will lose their influence over the government. These two tendencies, increased influence of pressure groups over the legislature and greater independence of the executive from such pressures, would make the French system of government even more similar to the American.

Because of their greater electoral support in certain regions or because of the social and economic characteristics of their membership and electorate, French parties although founded on an ideological basis must also act as representatives of special interests not necessarily connected with their ideology. The Socialist party is also the party of civil servants, school teachers, and wine growers; the MRP is also a spokesman for agricultural interests; the Radicals also represent the Southwest; the Independents, at least those following Legendre, also speak for the beet growers.

The geographical distribution of the 1958 deputies shows most parties to be concentrated in specific areas. The Socialists represent the mining North and the wine-growing South; the MRP, the Catholic East and West; the Radicals, the economically depressed Southwest; the Independents, northern France, Brittany's south coast, and the Lyon area.

The poll taken in 1952 by the *Institut Français d'Opinion Publique* [5] also gives an approximate idea of the electorate's behavior according to socioeconomic groups. Industrial workers prefer the Communists and the Gaullists; agricultural workers, the Communists, Socialists, and Gaullists; civil servants, the Communists and Socialists; white-collar employees in private industry, the Communists, MRP and Gaullists; the managerial class, the Conservatives and Gaullists; shopkeepers, the Conservatives and Gaullists; farmers, the Radicals, Conservatives, and

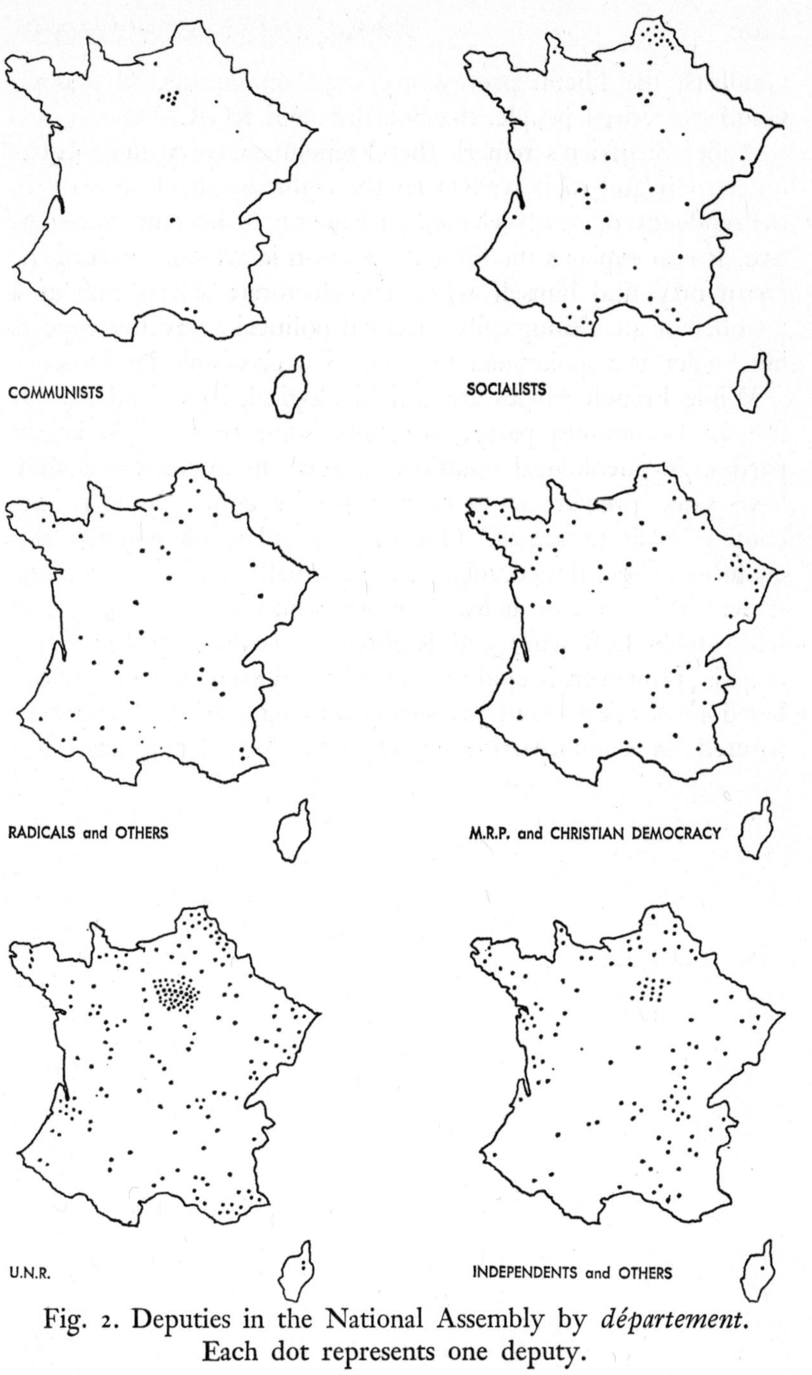


Fig. 2. Deputies in the National Assembly by *département*.
Each dot represents one deputy.

Gaullists; the liberal professions, the Communists, MRP, and Gaullists; retired people, the Socialists and RGR.

André Siegfried's remark that Frenchmen carry their hearts on the left and their wallets on the right was made to explain the tendency of newly elected parliaments to become conservative. It also explains the difficult position in which a parliamentarian may find himself when the electorate selects him as a member of an ideologically oriented political party but expects him to act as a spokesman for particular economic interests.

While French parties are still ideological, they tend, except for the Communist party, to assume some traits of American parties. As ideological conflicts decrease in intensity—as they have since prewar days—French parties come closer to becoming roads of access.[6] One may speculate on whether this evolution, if continued, might not eventually create a two-party system in France, or at least a more concentrated party system with stable Left-wing and Right-wing coalitions as in Scandinavia. However, it could well lead to an extreme multipartism based on sectional and pressure-group oppositions being substituted for a multipartism based on ideological conflicts.

# II *The Drafting of the 1958 Constitution*

Since the revolution of 1789 France has been seeking an institutional framework, a constitutional formula, which could satisfy her desire for freedom and her need for authority and stability. The revolutionary shock of the late eighteenth century was followed by a period of frequent sweeping constitutional changes. Republics, monarchies, and dictatorships alternated between 1789 and 1875. Following the founding of the Third Republic the pendulum-like movement between authoritarian and democratic solutions was much reduced in its amplitude; Republican forces seemed to have definitely won. However, the events of May, 1877, the Boulanger affair, the *Action Française* agitation, the Millerand attempt at strengthening the presidency, the riots of February, 1934, showed that the movements for constitutional changes, if they had lost strength, had not lost all vitality. Broadly speaking, the Left defended the status quo, while the Right wanted to strengthen the executive. The Right-wing opposition to the constitution was divided into antiparliamentarians and democratic conservatives. The *Action Française*, the Déat and Doriot fascist groups belonged to the first category, the so-called neo-liberals to the second. The term neo-liberal does not describe a coherent, easily identified political grouping, but rather a state of mind, a general philosophy of government the main tenet of which was that the best means of guaranteeing freedom was not to oppose the government constantly and weaken it, but rather to strengthen it within a democratic system. Law professors such as Carré de Malberg and J. Barthélémy, politicians such as A. Millerand, J. Bardoux, and A. Tardieu found arguments in the British and American constitutions as well as in Montesquieu, to show that the French representative system, instead of maintaining the necessary balance of power between branches of government, had resulted in legislative supremacy and that the weakening of the executive had had the effect to render the Republic incapable of defending the national interest, and of preserving the public liberties against the attacks of fascism and communism. In order to strengthen the executive while preserving the parliamentary system, neo-liberals proposed various devices, the most frequently advocated being the unconditional right of the government to dissolve parliament, the election of the president of the Republic by a large electoral college so that he may have greater authority over parliament, the separation of an executive-order field from the legislative field, the choice of the prime minister by the president of the Republic without further endorsement by parliament, and finally the shortening of parliamentary sessions. The military defeat of 1940, the establishment of Marshall Pétain's temporary dictatorship, the hazards of history, divided the neo-liberals into two camps, the Gaullists and the Vichyists. Joseph Barthélémy and Raphaël Alibert supported Pétain; R. Capitant and his disciple M. Debré joined the Resistance. In 1943, Debré published a draft constitutional-reform project giving increased powers to the executive, and in particular to the presidency, while maintaining the parliament's legislative and political supremacy. The reforms proposed by Debré were by no means original; they were patterned on those suggested by Tardieu, Barthélémy, and Capitant before the war. Debré proposed that parliament be composed of two houses, a national assembly of four hundred and fifty to five hundred members and a senate of two hundred to two hundred and fifty members; the first elected directly, the second indirectly. He rejected the idea of a corporatist senate proposed by some of his Christian-democratic associates in the Resistance organizations. The parliament would meet for two short sessions of three months each. The legislative power of the assemblies was limited firstly by a separation of the executive-orders field and the legislative field and secondly by the provision that if the budget had not been voted by a certain date, the governmental project would automatically become law. The domain reserved to parliament included civil rights, constitutional reform, treaties, and the most important social and economic questions; other matters could have been regulated solely by executive orders. The executive was to be divided between a premier responsible before parliament and a president whose major duties would have been to appoint the premier and to arbitrate conflicts between the government and the parliament, thanks to an unconditional right to dissolve the lower house. All these provisions eventually found their way into the constitution of 1958. On other points the early Debré proposal of 1943 differ from the constitution of the Fifth Republic. The president of the Republic, whom Debré calls a "republican monarch," was to be elected for twelve years; [1] the government could have been overthrown only once a year after an "interpellation" debate. Finally Debré had proposed to render the judiciary freer from executive control and to include in the constitution a charter of the press which would have guaranteed its independence.

In 1943, Debré was not alone in proposing such reforms. In the General Studies Committee (CGE) created by the Resistance National Council (CNR) Debré was surrounded by men such as P. Bastid, F. de Menthon, and P. Teitgen who had proposed reforms basically similar to his. In 1944, the members of the committee suggested to General de Gaulle that he make use of the constitution of the Third Republic after it had been properly amended. De Gaulle apparently had first agreed to this project but later changed his mind and preferred discarding the constitutional laws of 1875 altogether and calling a national convention to draft an entirely new constitution. Whether from lack of political realism or because of a distaste for being assimilated to politicians, after the liberation de Gaulle failed to obtain the strengthening of the executive which he and his advisors wanted. Had he taken the leadership of a political party, he might have rallied the conservative and Christian-democratic forces and so transformed French party politics in order to obtain a cabinet type of government on the British model. He could have also, as proposed to him by de Menthon, submitted to the people's approval, a constitution of his own making. Instead, de Gaulle chose to leave an elected Assembly to devise a new constitution. Controlled by the Socialists and the Communists, the first Constituent Assembly refused any serious strengthening of the executive. As before the war, Left-wing parties were opposed to any basic amendment to the parliamentary system evolved by the Third Republic. De Gaulle's sudden resignation, his speeches against the draft constitutions proposed by the first then by the second constituent assemblies could not reverse a trend away from authoritarianism which he had failed to channel to his profit. Left-wing parties gave to France a constitution much like that of 1875, and Gaullism became the heir of the prewar neoliberal opposition to legislative supremacy. The Debré proposals of 1943 were adopted by de Gaulle and by the RPF. Debré and Capitant, later joined by Habib Deloncle and M. Blocq-Mascart proposed to transform the French Union into a federation.

While orthodox Gaullists insisted that to strengthen the executive a revision of the constitution was an urgent necessity, Center and Left of Center parties revised their positions. The MRP first, then the Socialists after the downfall of G. Mollet's government in 1957, admitted that a curtailing of the parliament's powers was the price to pay for an increased stability of the executive.[2]

While the revisionists gained ground in metropolitan France, overseas the African movements for autonomy or independence also pushed toward constitutional reform. In 1957, the Bamako Congress of the African Democratic Rally (RDA) approved a French-African federation project which would have given increased autonomous powers to the African territories. Early in 1958 the *Parti du Regroupement Africain* went one step further. The party's most prominent leader, L. Senghor, proposed the creation of an occidental African state linked to France by a treaty ever subject to denunciation. Among French parliamentarians some had supported the RDA's proposals, Mitterand and Defferre in particular, but no influential non-Communist parliamentarian had gone as far as Senghor in proposing that France should offer her former African colonies a permanent choice between independence and free association.

If the constitution of 1958, although drafted in record time, had been thought of long beforehand with regard to metropolitan institutions, it was suddenly improvised under the pressure of the overseas with regard to the former French Empire.

The constitution went through various committees and was amended many times to maintain agreement within the cabinet. If, after all this, it can be said to be the work of any one person, it is Debré's constitution with regard to metropolitan France and Senghor's with regard to the overseas community. But as neither Debré nor Senghor could have obtained on their own authority the reforms they thought necessary, the constitution may also properly be considered as de Gaulle's. The choices made by de Gaulle among the solutions offered to him give to the constitution of 1958 a libertarian-authoritarian flavor unmistakably his. He recognized that similar political dogmas could not be used to solve the problems of France and the problems of the French Union. For metropolitan France, de Gaulle sided with the Right-wing neo-liberals, for the French Union he went even further to the Left than the Socialists and Mendecists.

One of de Gaulle's conditions for coming back to power was that his government would be given authority to draft a new constitution and to submit it directly to the people. Before seeking the investiture he held meetings with the leaders of all parties except the Communists who had refused the invitation, and outlined some aspects of his projected constitution. He stressed the necessity of stabilizing the executive by increasing the powers of the president of the Republic while maintaining a parliamentary system, and outlined some specific reforms such as making executive posts and parliamentary mandates incompatible.

The submitting of a draft constitution directly to the people without preliminary approval by the parliament required an amendment to Article 90 of the constitution of 1946. Such an amendment was passed in the National Assembly by 350 to 163, and in the Senate by 256 to 30. The same constitutional amendment, while delegating constitutional power to de Gaulle's government, set certain limits to this power. The constitutional law of June 3, 1958, defined five principles on which the new constitution would have to be based.

1. Universal suffrage is the only source of power. Legislative and executive powers are derived from universal suffrage or from its elected bodies.

2. The legislative and the executive must be effectively separated in order that the parliament and the government assume all their functions separately and under their own responsibilities.

3. The government must be responsible before parliament.

4. The judiciary must remain separate in order to be able to guarantee the respect of essential freedoms such as defined by the preamble of the constitution of 1946 and by the Declaration of the Rights of Man.

5. The constitution must render possible the organization of relationships between the Republic and the people associated to it.

These restrictions were far from clear. Clauses 2 and 3 in particular, if taken literally, are contradictory. The first describes a system of separation of powers, the second a parliamentary system. Clause 5 is pure verbalism. Anyway, in the absence of judicial control of the constitutionality of the laws, no political nor judicial body could have declared the future constitution in violation of the constitutional law of June, 1958.

More important were the provisions calling for a referendum

and creating an advisory constitutional committee, the function of which was to give an opinion on the draft constitution.

Work on a draft constitution began in the second week of June. A committee of ten "technicians," drawn from among junior members of the Council of State was entrusted with submitting proposed drafts to a committee of politicians composed of G. Mollet, P. Pflimlin, F. Houphouët-Boigny, P. Jacquinot, M. Debré, all members of de Gaulle's cabinet together with R. Cassin, vice-president of the Council of State and R. Janot, juridical advisor to de Gaulle. The committee of technicians worked under the leadership of Debré and Janot. According to Mollet, General de Gaulle had first outlined his constitutional preferences before the ministerial committee and asked Debré to work along those lines with his technical assistants. De Gaulle's outline was familiar to Debré, because in many respects it followed the Debré proposals of 1943. One must rely on yet incomplete data to reconstruct de Gaulle's original scheme. According to Mollet's speech [3] before the SFIO national conference of July, 1958, de Gaulle's outline concerned both the French Union and France. The idea proposed by the Social Republican party's congress of 1957, to organize immediately a French-African federation, was not retained. Agreeing with Houphouët-Boigny, de Gaulle ruled out a true French-African federation for the present, on the ground that a federal system could not work properly between communities whose degree of evolution was vastly different. However, his preferences went to a system which would enable a gradual evolution toward such a federal structure. Each overseas territory was to have a prime minister who, while nominated by the governor general, would be responsible before the territory's elected assembly. France was to retain control of all matters not of local interest. The French parliament would be divided between two houses: A lower house elected by universal suffrage and a senate to be divided into at least two sections, one for metropolitan France and one for the French Union—a thought early abandoned by de Gaulle would have made the Economic Council a third section of the Senate.

Executive power, still according to de Gaulle's original proposals, was to be shared by the president of the Republic and the cabinet. The president would be given the power to choose the prime minister, to call for a referendum on certain issues, to dissolve parliament on his own accord; he would also be given the powers necessary to enable him to rally the nation in the event of a crisis like an international conflict. The president would be elected by a college including the members of the local and national elected bodies. The prime minister, entrusted with the day-to-day government of the nation, would be responsible before parliament.

On other points de Gaulle remained vague; means were to be found for preventing the parliament from assuming the role of an executive; a separate executive-order field would be defined and the members of the cabinet would not be allowed to hold seats in the assemblies.

That the presidency was the keystone of de Gaulle's proposed new constitution appears clearly in the early outlines. The other organs of parliament were to be organized and their relationships defined according to the role assigned to the president, that of an umpire not interfering with the political contest as long as no deadlocks or serious crises occur. From the start de Gaulle had refused to devise a classical parliamentary system of the British type or a classical presidential system of the American type. On all matters concerning the presidency de Gaulle resisted the pressures within his cabinet which would have brought his schemes closer to either the American or British models. He refused to concentrate executive power in the hands of a prime minister responsible to parliament; he refused also to entertain a project making the prime minister and the cabinet responsible before the president.

The committee of experts under the leadership of Debré, worked on a sketchy outline of the new institutions grouped under main headings: presidency, government, parliament. The twelve members of the committee then formed small subcommittees of two to three members who worked on a more elaborate drafting of the chapter or section of a chapter assigned to them. When completed by a subcommittee, a draft would then be submitted to the ministers' committee, meeting under de Gaulle's chairmanship. The discussions in this committee progressed so slowly that in mid-July the procedure was changed. De Gaulle asked Debré to prepare a complete draft of the constitution during the Fourteenth-of-July holidays and to submit it to the ministers' committee on July 16. In the second half of July the draft project was discussed by the ministers at a series of meetings. De Gaulle agreed only to minor changes, such as increasing the number of parliamentary standing committees and deleting the articles which required political parties to file their statutes and their yearly statements of financial resources with the Constitutional Council. De Gaulle also agreed to introduce the various devices proposed by Pflimlin to render more difficult the overthrow of the government by a vote of non-confidence and to prevent parliament's forcing the government from office by refusing to legislate.

The draft project of the new constitution as approved by de Gaulle's ministers was made public on July 29, 1958, and submitted to the Advisory Constitutional Committee. This committee was composed of thirty-nine members: sixteen were elected by the Committee on Universal Suffrage of the National Assembly, ten by the corresponding committee of the Senate, the remaining thirteen appointed by the government.[4]

The committee which met under the chairmanship of Paul Reynaud had the choice between proposing amendments to the project or rejecting it altogether and writing their own draft constitution. They decided on the first course well aware that because of the then prevailing antiparliamentarism any counter-project of their own held no chance of support from public opinion. On August 14, Paul Reynaud sent to the government the observations of the committee together with a series of proposed amendments. The report was adopted by thirty of thirty-nine members, six members abstained, two others were absent. The abstentions were those of three of the four Socialists, of the two Radicals, and of L. Senghor (PRA). The committee's suggestions concerned primarily the presidency, the relations between the parliament and the government, the judiciary, and the association with the former overseas territories.

With regard to the presidency, the Advisory Committee's proposals would have prevented the election of a president by a mere plurality of the electoral college. Taking the United States constitution as a model, the committee proposed that if after two ballots no candidate had obtained a majority, election would be made by a smaller electoral college composed of the members of parliament, the presidents of the departmental councils, and the presidents of the overseas territories. The committee took strong exception to the president's emergency powers and proposed that the assumption of all governing powers by the president in the event of a national crisis be made subject to a decision of a constitutional committee. Both amendments, on the election and on the emergency powers, were turned down by de Gaulle.

The committee sought to amend the provision that members of parliament named to the cabinet would have to resign from their seats and proposed instead that the parliamentarians elevated to the position of a minister be on a temporary leave of absence and be thus able to regain their Assembly or Senate seats, following resignation from the cabinet or following the cabinet's overthrow. This amendment met with no more success.

On the relations between government and parliament the committee proposed to increase the restricted list of legislative matters defined by the draft project and in particular to give to parliament the organization of the armed forces, the control of public finances, and the control of the budget. The committee was given satisfaction on this point. The constitution finally gave the parliament not only the specific powers requested by the committee but also the power to add to the list of legislative matters by means of an organic law.

The committee proposed that one-half of the Council of the Judiciary be composed of ex-officio members drawn from the judiciary. The government maintained its original proposal, giving to the executive the power to appoint all members of this council.

The major difference between the original daft and the final text of the constitution lies in the organization of the association between France and the former overseas territories. The pressure of a minority of the Advisory Committee on the government to substitute confederal for a federal structure was largely successful.

The draft project called for the creation of an association which, although called "federation," was only a more liberal version of the French Union. The president of the French Republic would have been ex-officio president of the federation. There would have been a federal executive and a federal arbitration court. The overseas territories party to the federation would have been represented in the Senate which would have been divided into two sections, a French section and an overseas section, meeting separately on matters of either purely French or purely overseas interests and, apparently, meeting jointly on matters of common interest. The federal matters which, for all practical purposes, would have been reserved not to the federal but to the French executive and parliament, were: foreign affairs, defense, money, financial and economic policy, the use of strategic raw materials, the control of the judiciary, and university education.

The Advisory Committee split into two groups, federalists and confederalists. The major point of contention was the right of secession. For the confederalists, led by Senghor, the units party to the association should have been given a permanent right to secede; for the federalists such right was out of the question. At the height of the controversy, on August 10, de Gaulle went before the committee and in an unexpected move announced that the territories which would vote against the constitution would have, by so doing, chosen to secede from France and would become independent.[5] But he refused to contemplate a confederal association. In other words, the former colonies had to decide, once and for all, whether they wanted independence or not. This declaration was favorably received by the overseas representatives G. Lisette and P. Tsiranana, but left Senghor unsatisfied. He indicated that, if a confederation had been ruled out, the choice had not been made in favor of a true federation, which remained an ideal for the future. He argued that one could not properly choose between independence and a future federal scheme which was not only left vague but without guarantee that it would be implemented.

After de Gaulle's intervention, the committee rallied to a solution which had the government's support. The proposed federation was renamed "community," and the overseas territories were given internal autonomy. The committee further proposed that instead of representation in the Senate, the territories be given representation in an Assembly of the Community composed of delegates from the French parliament and the overseas assemblies, and that the Community executive be composed of the ministers of the French cabinet entrusted with the administration of Community matters together with the prime ministers of the overseas territories. These proposals were retained by de Gaulle. Other suggestions were discarded, such as giving to the Assembly of the Community, the power of regulating the use of common resources and of deciding on the applicability of French laws to the rest of the Community.

In his Brazzaville speech of August 23, 1958, de Gaulle in a second surprise move rallied to Senghor's proposals and announced that the French Community would be an "open" one, that the states party to it could withdraw and achieve independence at any time of their choice. Finally the government accepted a committee's proposal to offer the overseas territories the possibility of integrating themselves to France and becoming French *départements* if they wanted to cancel their options on autonomy as well as on independence.

After the Advisory Committee had handed in its report on August 14, 1958 and after de Gaulle had returned from his African tour, the government began working on a new draft which was submitted to the Council of State for legal advice on August 30.

In addition to suggestions for stylistic improvements, the Council of State singled out two articles for criticism. The first was an article introduced by the government at the request of the

Advisory Constitutional Committee to the effect that political parties should respect the rules of democracy. The Council of State thought that such a provision might lead to arbitrary measures in the absence of any constitutional definition of the sanctions which would be imposed on "undemocratic parties" and in the absence also of any allocation of the sanction power to any organ of government in particular. The suggestion made by the Council of State that the article be either dropped altogether or at least made more precise was not retained by the government. On the second point the Council of State obtained satisfaction. They had requested that the article defining the matters falling within the legislative field be defined more specifically [6] and that the article be eventually completed by an organic law. This last concession rendered less significant the constitutional division between a legislative and an executive-orders field, since the parliament was given the possibility of increasing the matters subject to its control.

The final constitutional draft, after being approved by the Council of Ministers was made public on September 4, anniversary of the proclamation of the Third Republic in 1870.

During the drafting of the constitution, political parties which had not yet recovered from the shock of May 13, remained prostrate. They set up committees which were supposed to watch over constitutional developments and express party recommendations, but these committees did little useful work. The knowledge that de Gaulle could have written practically any constitution of his choice and have had it approved by the people was not favorable to partisan activities.

The publication of the draft constitution was followed by a rebirth of political activity. The parties determined their position for the referendum of September 28. A decision to vote Yes was matter of course for the Independents, the Social Republicans, the RGR, and the Republican Center (dissident Radicals). The national committee of the MRP favored the constitution by a 90 per cent majority (121 to 12, and one abstention). The Socialists held an extraordinary congress which approved the constitution by 70 per cent. The leaders of the Socialist opposition, including E. Depreux and D. Mayer, split from the party and formed the Autonomous Socialist party which campaigned for a No vote. In the Radical party congress the majority in favor of a Yes obtained only 57 per cent of the votes, and the minority, led by Mendès-France, did not rally to the majority and campaigned against the constitution. The executive committee of the UDSR by a 38 to 15 vote decided to campaign against it. The minority led by R. Pléven left the party. The Poujadist movement was split between its parliamentarians (most of whom rallied to the constitution) and the party machine controlled by Poujade who had grown hostile to de Gaulle.

The referendum was held on September 28, throughout France and the overseas *départements* and territories. Each voter was offered a choice between two ballots, one with the answer Yes, the other the answer No to this question: "Do you approve the constitution submitted to you by the government of the Republic?"

There were 47 million voters on the electoral rolls; 26.6 million in metropolitan France, 15 in the overseas territories, 4.2 in Algeria, 0.4 in the overseas departments and 0.4 in the French consulates in foreign countries. The results were as follows:

TABLE 5

REFERENDUM, SEPTEMBER 28, 1958
(In per cent)

| Area | Abstentions | Yes votes: Per cent of registered votes | Yes votes: Per cent of valid votes cast |
|---|---|---|---|
| Metropolitan France | 15.1 | 66.4 | 79.2 |
| Overseas *départements* | 33.8 | 58.4 | 89.7 |
| Algeria | 20.4 | 76.1 | 96.5 |
| Sahara | 16.3 | 82.2 | 98.6 |
| Frenchmen abroad | — | — | 95.8 |
| Overseas territories | 30 | 65.1 | 93.5 |
| Total (excluding Guinée) | 19.6 | 67.7 | 85.1 |

Approved by more than 80 per cent of the voters, the constitution took effect on the day of its printing in the *Journal Officiel*, October 4, 1958. The only territory to have voted No, Guinée, became automatically independent.

# 12 *The Executive*

Whether because of the constitution or the party system, democracy has, in England and in the United States as well as in other Anglo-Saxon countries, evolved monarchical structures; supreme executive power rests with one man, president or premier. Every four years in the United States, at less regular intervals in England, the people are in fact if not in law called upon to elect a leader. In continental Europe where presidential systems have left bad memories and where, if one excepts Austria and possibly Western Germany, two-party systems have not emerged, democracy has traditionally adopted oligarchical structures. Ruling the nation is done by coalition cabinets when not by the parliaments themselves. The multi-leader governments of continental Europe are not so well adapted to modern conditions as the one-leader governments of Anglo-Saxon countries. The latter are on the whole more efficient administrative and political machines. They also satisfy better the people's need to feel secure.

With the constitution of 1958, France comes closer to the

Anglo-Saxon model, but does so, as it were, reluctantly, and preserves some of the features of her previous oligarchical structures. The powers of the executive are divided between a president who, like the American president, is not responsible before parliament and a prime minister who being responsible before the National Assembly might remain the prisoner of the various parties and groups making his governmental coalition, at least so long as no single party controls the majority of the seats in this Assembly.

### Elections to the Presidency. The Electoral College

The president is elected for seven years by an electoral college composed of three categories of members—the national, the local, and the overseas representatives. The total membership fluctuates around 80,000.

The national representatives are the 465 deputies and the 230 senators.

The local representatives, by far the largest group, included in 1958: 31,401 mayors, 3,149 general councilors, 32,524 vice-mayors and municipal councilors from the middle-size and large communes, and 8,541 additional delegates for the larger communes. The vice-mayors, municipal councilors, and additional delegates are selected as follows: In addition to the mayor, the ex-officio members of the electoral college are: the first vice-mayor in the communes with 1,001 to 2,000 inhabitants; the first vice-mayor and the senior municipal councilor in the communes with 2,001 to 2,500; the two vice-mayors in the communes with 2,501 to 3,000; the two vice-mayors and the first three senior municipal councilors in the communes with 3,001 to 6,000; the two vice-mayors and the first six senior councilors for the communes with 6,001 to 9,000 inhabitants; all the vice-mayors and municipal councilors in the communes with more than 9,000 inhabitants.[1] The municipal councils of communes of more than 30,000 inhabitants elect additional delegates by proportional representation, according to the d'Hondt system (list system) and the highest remainder rule. Each commune has one additional delegate each 1,000 inhabitants over 30,000.

The overseas representatives include all members of the local assemblies of the overseas territories (in 1958: Comores, 31; New Caledonia, 69; Polynesia, 58; Saint Pierre and Miquelon, 22; Somaliland, 34) and the senators, territorial or provincial councilors, municipal councilors and delegates from the nonindependent states of the Community. In 1958, there were altogether 2,553 delegates from the overseas states, that is, 4 per cent of the presidential college. It was unlikely that their vote would be of great weight in selecting a president, but hostility of the overseas states to the president would have seriously weakened him in his capacity as head of the French Community. Algeria would be influential if she underwent a municipal reform that would put her on a par with France. In 1958, because of the war, deputies and senators were the only Algerian members of the electoral college, thus giving Algeria only 76 votes. The first municipal elections in Algeria, under the Fifth Republic, were held in 1959 after the presidential elections. About 16,000 municipal councilors were elected for a population of 10,000,000. The ratio of municipal councilors to the total population is thus still much lower than that of France which has close to 450,000 councilors for 43,000,000 inhabitants.

The presidential college favors French small towns and rural areas. The communes with less than 1,000 inhabitants control 38 per cent of the college, the communes with 1,000 to 9,000, an additional 50 per cent. The Paris area (Seine *département*) with about one-eighth of the total population of France has only 7 per cent of the votes. Such a college also favors the traditional and Center parties, rather than the newly created or extremist parties which have always found more difficulty in making gains in the small cities and villages than in large urban areas. The election of de Gaulle in 1958 is not illustrative of the politics of the electoral college in a time of normalcy. De Gaulle was elected less by the will of a college of electors than by the force of circumstances. The dominance of rural France among presidential electors has troubled political analysts such as M. Duverger and G. Vedel [2] who fear that in normal times the president would be not only imposed by rural France over industrial France, but would be imposed by the most backward rural France; as Vedel puts it, not by the France of wheat and corn but by the France of chestnut and barley. It may indeed be questioned whether the electoral college is adapted to the role expected from the president, that of a supreme umpire who, because of his authority and prestige, can arbitrate serious political conflicts and restore order in a time of crisis. Would a man elected by the France of the nineteenth if not of the eighteenth century be acceptable to modern France in other than a figurative capacity? The objective of the constituents, and in particular of de Gaulle, was to devise the electoral college in such a way as to make it sufficiently broad for the president to have enough authority vis à vis the government and vis à vis the parliament, but sufficiently conservative to prevent any Boulanger from gaining access to the presidency. The safeguards against that danger may eventually negate the benefits expected from a large electoral college. Short of a reform which would give France a truly presidential system, it is likely that under de Gaulle's successor the president would, because of his mode of election, become a figurehead not unlike the governor-general in Canada. The constitution of 1958 was obviously made for de Gaulle but obviously not for another de Gaulle. The composition of the presidential college gives one of the keys to the constitution of 1958. There are in fact two constitutions in one text. The one for de Gaulle's time, when the powers given to the presidency are fully used by the president and one for the era after de Gaulle when the president's powers would most likely fall into disuse or be inherited by other organs of government, most likely the premier and the cabinet.

### The Candidates

There are no specific constitutional or legal restrictions to candidacies for the presidency, other than the requirement of endorsement by fifty members of the presidential college. This nomination procedure is intended to prevent crackbrained candidates such as Ferdinand Lop, the favorite of the Latin Quarter, from running for office as they never failed to do under the

Third and Fourth republics. The barring of members of families having reigned over France has disappeared from the constitution. Heirs to the Crown or descendants of the Bonapartes could now run for the presidency, for the first time since 1884.

### The Campaign

The electoral campaign is by law restricted to the electoral college. The candidates may send propaganda material or speak before presidential electors, but the general public is not supposed to be brought into the campaign. The candidates are not allowed to make use of radio, television, or even billboards. The certainty of de Gaulle's election in December, 1958, added to the quietness of the preëlection period. De Gaulle himself did no campaigning at all. Most political parties had held meetings of their executive bodies to determine their position on the election and had informed their supporters of the party's decision. Had de Gaulle not been a candidate the election would of course have been far more lively. The parties and the candidates might have sought to enter drop-off agreements for the second ballot, and political parties would have put special pressure on the many mayors of small cities and villages who are often without clear party affiliation and who would have formed the bulk of the uncommitted electorate on which the campaign would have been concentrated.

### The Election

The presidential electors vote in the capital cities (prefectures) of their *départements*, or in selected cities of the overseas states. The votes are centralized in Paris. The elector who performed his duty receives an expense allowance; he who fails to vote is subject to a fine amounting to the equivalent of six dollars.

On the first ballot an absolute majority of the valid votes cast is required. If such a majority is not obtained, a second ballot is held a week later. A plurality is then sufficient. No new candidate may enter the contest after the first ballot unless he be a compromise candidate presented by at least two contestants withdrawing after the first ballot.

THE ELECTION OF DECEMBER, 1958

Of the 81,761 registered voters, 81,290 went to the polls and 79,471 cast valid ballots. De Gaulle obtained 77 per cent of the votes; Marrane, 13 per cent and Chatelet 8 per cent.

Broken down by areas the vote was as follows:

TABLE 6

ELECTION, DECEMBER, 1958

| Area | De Gaulle Votes | Marrane Votes | Chatelet Votes |
|---|---|---|---|
| France | 57,649 | 10,125 | 6,617 |
| Overseas *départements* | 937 | 176 | 38 |
| Algeria | 65 | 0 | 0 |
| Sahara | 214 | 2 | 3 |
| Overseas territories | 204 | 0 | 4 |
| Overseas states | 3,325 | 51 | 60 |
| Total | 62,394 | 10,354 | 6,722 |

Marrane was supported by the Communist party, Chatelet by Mendès-France's UFD, dissident Socialists, and various splinter Left-wing groups of Socialist leanings. All other parties supported de Gaulle except the Poujadists who were hostile to his candidacy but did not run a candidate of their own, mostly to avoid showing how little the opposition against de Gaulle was accepted by the Poujadist rank and file.

The election also illustrated how parties which had been at odds for long, such as the Socialists and the Independents not to mention the UNR, could easily agree in support of a common candidate. True the parties themselves had little choice. It might have been suicide for the Socialists or the MRP to propose their own candidates to the electorate against de Gaulle, but interesting nevertheless is the large majority polled by de Gaulle from an electorate where those favorable to a Gaullist party did not account for more than 20 per cent. As in the United States, the presidential election had the effect of bringing together groups which go their own ways at the parliamentary level. Because of the particular circumstances of 1958 such a coalition was realized on the first ballot; in more normal times it would probably have taken place on the second ballot.

### Powers of the President

The president of the Republic has powers of his own and powers which he shares with the premier. Article 19 makes a clear distinction between the acts which the president can take under his sole signature and those requiring the prime minister's countersignature.

The exclusive powers of the president are to choose the prime minister, to dissolve the National Assembly, to veto a referendum asked either by the government or the parliament, to address public messages to the two houses, to appoint three members of the Constitutional Council, to request such council to pass on the constitutionality of a bill or of an international agreement and, finally, to assume emergency powers under Article 16.

### Choosing a Prime Minister

The designation of the prime minister was the only important political power reserved to the presidents of the Third and Fourth republics. Under the constitution of 1875, the president would choose a premier (*Président du Conseil*) who would form a cabinet and would remain in office as long as he had parliament's confidence. The constitution of 1946 amended the practice of the Third Republic. The candidate the president of the Republic selected for the premiership had to present his program to the National Assembly. A special majority of all members of the Assembly and not only of those present was required for endorsement. If voted in, the prime minister would then form his cabinet. The procedure was amended in 1954. The prime minister-designate would form his cabinet before seeking the Assembly's approval and a simple majority was sufficient for the investiture. The constitution of 1958 further returns to the practice of the Third Republic. As in 1875 the prime minister is appointed by the president, and no special procedure is devised for an investiture by the parliament, although the ambiguous Article 49, which will be examined later, might be construed as obliging the prime minister to engage the responsibility of his newly formed government before the National Assembly. But whether the prime minister intends to seek the investiture or not, the president has to keep in mind when selecting a candidate that the cabinet is collectively responsible before the Assembly. The president is thus not free to choose whoever he wishes; but, as long as France has a multiparty system and as long as most parties are not well disciplined, the president will have much leeway in making his selection.

Under the Fourth Republic the president had to negotiate the choice of candidate with the leaders of the various parties. He would even sometimes delegate the negotiation to one influential member of parliament entrusted with a *mission d'information.* René Pléven was asked to perform this role by both President Auriol and President Coty. The president of the Fifth Republic is in a much better position to conduct the negotiations for the formation of a cabinet himself. He can even, if public opinion backs him, threaten the National Assembly with dissolution in order to force his candidate for the premiership on them.

### The Power of Dissolution

Under the constitution of 1875, in order to dissolve the Chamber of Deputies the president had to have the approval of the Senate and of the prime minister. The right of dissolution was used only once, by MacMahon in 1877. The elections following were a defeat for the presidency; the right of dissolution then fell into disuse. The constitution of 1946 revived the right of dissolution and transferred it to the premier, but limited it by such restrictions as to make its usage infrequent. The National Assembly could not be dissolved during the first eighteen months and then was subject to dissolution only after at least two cabinets had been formerly overthrown. Dissolution was used only once, by Edgar Faure in 1955. Although this last dissolution, unlike that of 1877, was generally popular and thus washed off, as it were, an undemocratic stigma, it was most inconclusive in its results. Dissolution had not been made on any single issue which could help the electorate in making their choice.

It has indeed been questioned whether dissolution is adapted to the French parliamentary system. Multipartism and its corollary, coalition cabinet, render difficult the use of dissolution in order to ask the people to settle a conflict between executive and legislative, and might only result in adding parliamentary to governmental instability. But contrary arguments have been presented to the effect that without the right of dissolution a two-party system might not have emerged in Great Britain, and that even if not frequently used, such right can act as a deterrent on parliament and prevent it from overthrowing cabinets too frequently.

The constitution of 1958 again like that of 1875 gives the right of dissolution to the president but with two major differences. Firstly, dissolution can be called by the president under his sole authority, while under the system of 1875 he had to have a minister's countersignature. Secondly the consent of the Senate is not required. The only two restrictions are that, following a dissolution, the National Assembly cannot be dissolved again for a year and that in a time of emergency under Article 16, the Assembly is not subject to dissolution. The right of dissolution can be used by the president not only to end a conflict between the Assembly and the cabinet, but also eventually to settle a conflict between himself and a prime minister backed by the Assembly. In so doing the president would revive the centuries-old tactic of the kings of France to call the people to their help against the barons.

### Addressing of Messages to Parliament

The constitutions of 1875 and 1946 gave the president the right to address messages to parliament. Use of this right was made by presidents to express their views on political problems only in very exceptional circumstances. President Coty used it in May, 1958, to warn parliament that he would resign if General de Gaulle were not invested as prime minister; President Auriol had contemplated using the same procedure to warn the representatives and the nation of the fateful consequences of governmental instability but he refrained from doing so, fearing that his act might be interpreted as a sign of tension between the presidency and the legislature. The messages addressed by the president no longer have to be countersigned by a minister.

When the president assumes emergency powers under Article 16 he addresses the nation directly to inform them of his actions and motives. From this provision one can infer *a contrario* that in a time of normalcy the president cannot communicate directly with the nation unless he obtains the prime minister's approval. He cannot, for example, without the latter's consent, address the nation through radio or television or send political *communiqués* to the press.

### The President and the Constitutional Council

The president selects three of the nine appointed members of the Constitutional Council, including the chairman who casts the deciding vote in the event of a tie. The president, before ratification, may ask the Constitutional Council to pass on the constitutionality of a bill or of an international commitment.

### The Emergency Powers: Article 16

The most controversial article of the constitution of 1958 is undoubtedly article 16 which gives the president the right to assume emergency powers. The article reads:

> When the institutions of the Republic, the independence of the nation, the integrity of its territory or the fulfillment of its international commitments are gravely and immediately threatened and when the regular working of the constitutional public authorities is interrupted, the President of the Republic takes the measures required by these circumstances after official consultation with the Prime Minister, and the chairmen of the assemblies as well as with the Constitutional Council.
>
> He informs the nation by a message.
>
> The measures must be prompted by the will to ensure to the con-

stitutional public authorities, in the shortest possible time, the means of accomplishing their mission. The Constitutional Council is consulted regarding these measures.

Parliament meets as of right.

The National Assembly may not be dissolved during the exercise of the emergency powers.

In wishing this provision in the constitution, de Gaulle was certainly influenced by recent events. He is said to have been impressed by the fact that in 1940, as well as in 1958, the president of the Republic was prevented by the negative features of the constitution from rallying the nation in a time of emergency. He may also have been influenced by the old Roman practice of appointing "dictators" in times of danger.

Article 16 gives the president the right to declare an emergency at any time of his choosing, although if he were to do so in a time of normalcy he could certainly be violating the spirit of the constitution. In proclaiming the emergency the president assumes all the executive, legislative, and constitutional powers he deems necessary in order to meet the challenge of circumstances. Unlike in ancient Rome the period of emergency is not limited in time.

The prime minister, the chairmen of the two houses and the Constitutional Council must be consulted by the president on his emergency measures, but he need not follow their advice or recommendations. The National Assembly sits during the whole time of the emergency, and is not subject to dissolution, but the function of the Assembly may be modified according to the emergency measures taken by the president. He may, for example, deprive it of its legislative and political powers.

The only legal check on the president during an emergency would be his being declared incapacitated by the Constitutional Council or his being tried for high treason by the High Court of Justice after the Senate and the National Assembly had accused him of such a crime. But these checks were not meant to restrain the president in the exercise of the emergency powers; in the event that the president would violate the spirit if not the letter of the constitution, it is doubtful that these legal checks would be of much use. The problem would be one of plain power politics.

The major restraint on the president is that imposed by the administrative machinery and by public opinion. The president who in normal times does not control the police or the army could not assume extraordinary powers unless with the consent of either the army or the police and probably both. Such support would be likely only if backed by a large section of the electorate. Furthermore election by a college of local and national representatives is a safeguard that the presidency would not fall into the hands of politicians likely to misuse its powers. The presidential electoral college thus performs the role given to the Roman consuls—that of selecting the absolute ruler for a time of national danger. It remains that the president's power to change at will the role of major organs of government is abhorent to democratic practice. The proposal made by the Advisory Constitutional Committee that the emergency be declared by the Constitutional Council would have made Article 16 more in keeping with republican traditions whether those of ancient Rome or modern France.

## The President's Powers as Head of State

All acts of the president other than those previously analyzed have to be countersigned by the prime minister and eventually by the ministers concerned. The powers of the president as head of state may be classified under three categories: the right to preside and counsel, the right to act subject to the prime minister's approval, the power to validate documents.

### *The right to preside and counsel*

The president presides over the Council of Ministers, the Superior Council and committees of National Defense, the Superior Council of the Judiciary, and the Executive Council of the Community.

The most important of these presidencies is that of the Council of Ministers. At this point the difference between a cabinet council and the Council of Ministers should be made clear: the former meets under the chairmanship of the premier, the latter under the chairmanship of the president. According to the constitution certain matters, such as the appointment of ambassadors, have to be determined by the Council of Ministers. Ordinances, formerly called decree-laws, must also be passed in the Council of Ministers. Prior to engaging the responsibility of his government before the National Assembly, the prime minister must debate the question at a meeting of such a council. The Council of Ministers which, normally, meets once a week is a more solemn meeting than the cabinet councils. Important decisions, even when there is no constitutional requirement, are usually taken here. As head of state, the French president can thus have far more influence than the queen of England. He not only has the right to be informed and to advise but he may in addition influence the making of decisions at the time they are made.

His presiding over the Superior Council of the Judiciary and over the Superior Council of National Defense also fulfills the purpose of keeping him informed and of giving him an opportunity to voice his opinions before those entrusted with deciding the policies of the nation or the community. A further reason for his presiding over the Superior Council of the Judiciary is that, according to the constitution, he is the warrantor of the Judiciary's independence.

*Power to act subject to the Government's approval*

The constitution specifically gives to the president the right of pardon, the right to negotiate treaties, and the right to designate the members of the Superior Council of the Judiciary. These acts have to be countersigned by the prime minister and eventually the ministers concerned; for example the minister of justice countersigns a pardon. Furthermore, although not specifically mentioned in the constitution, the president is called upon, as head of state of France, to make public declarations on political matters. Such declarations must receive the prime minister's assent.

### *The Power to Validate*

The president's signature is required on the laws, ordinances, treaties, and certain types of decrees before they come into force. He signs the laws within fifteen days of their transmission to the government by the parliament. He may ask that parliament proceed to a new reading and to a new vote on the bill. This demand which cannot be rejected by parliament has to be countersigned by the prime minister. The same provision existed in the constitution of 1946, and was used in rare cases for bills badly drafted and sent back to the legislature for stylistic improvements.

The president signs the decrees which have been passed in the Council of Ministers. The constitution further provides that the council appoints certain civilian or military functionaries. These are the councilors of state, ambassadors and extraordinary envoys, master counselors of the Accounting Court, prefects, government's representatives in the overseas territories, general officers, rectors of academies, directors of central administrations, and the grand chancellor of the Legion of Honor. Nominations to other civilian or military positions may be made by a cabinet council but, under the constitutional provision that the president appoints to all state civilian and military posts, the president must sign to validate the appointment decree.

The president may delegate his appointment power and thus be relieved from signing unimportant commissions. He could not delegate his power to sign the laws and treaties.

Nothing in the constitution prevents the president of the Republic from using his "power to validate" as a veto power. The constitution of 1946 specified that if the laws were not signed within fifteen days, they would automatically come into force. No such provision exists in that of 1958. But if the "power to validate" were systematically used as a veto, the spirit as well as the working of the constitution would be profoundly changed.

THE PRIME MINISTER AND THE GOVERNMENT

Chosen by the president, the prime minister selects the members of his government which is collectively responsible before the National Assembly. The government determines and carries out the nation's policy; it controls the administration and the armed forces.

The members of the cabinet, including the prime minister, cannot combine their ministerial positions with functions of parliamentary or professional representation, nor with any public employment or professional activity. Such mandates, positions, or activities must be abandoned within a month of the minister's appointment. If he is a member of parliament, he must resign his parliamentary seat which is then filled by his alternate. Upon resigning from the cabinet, the former government member cannot regain his parliamentary mandate, unless it be at a general or at a by-election. The intended purpose of this provision, borrowed from the Second Empire, is to render government positions less attractive than before, to free cabinet members from caucus and party control, and thus to reduce governmental instability by limiting the number of parliamentarians anxious to have a turn at the wheel. It was thought also that the incompatibility would emphasize more clearly in the minds of the parliamentarians and the people the separation between the executive and legislative branches of government. However, an unwanted effect of the incompatibility may be, under certain circumstances, to increase the bargaining position of a minister within the cabinet. A minister, formerly a parliamentarian, may threaten to withdraw from the cabinet and to have his alternate resign from parliament so as to force a by-election. The by-election would then take added political significance. An unfavorable by-election would weaken a cabinet more than the sole resignation of a minister. A measure intended, in part, to free ministers from party politics may in fact have the opposite effect.

The formation of a ministry is a delicate task. Describing the ideal way of choosing one's colleagues, Léon Blum wrote: "My recipe [is] to lock oneself up at home, keep one's door strictly shut and think. No conversation with key aids, with anyone, all deliberations with one's self." [3] Needless to say, this recipe was never used, not even by Blum himself. The formation of a ministry under the Third Republic and even more so under the Fourth was a time of negotiations between political parties and groups for defining a program and allocating ministerial posts. Political parties had their preferred ministries. The Radicals had a traditional claim on the Interior, the Socialists on Labor, the MRP on Public Health. The prime minister had lost most of his power of free selection of ministers; the selection was in fact made by the political parties themselves. Only in extraordinary circumstances, such as at the time of the formation of Mendès-France's government in 1954, was a prime minister in a position to impose his own choices for the key ministries. The constitution of 1958 by maintaining cabinet responsibility did not free the prime minister from parliamentary groups, and even added a further obstacle to his freedom of choice. In addition to political parties, the prime minister must now satisfy the president of the Republic. The fact that he can refuse to sign the decree appointing a minister, but most of all the authority which he derives from his reserved powers give to the president the possibility of influencing the prime minister in the selection of the cabinet. Under the Third and Fourth republics the presidents had sometimes advised premiers on the choice of ministers but had not tried to impose their preferences. The selection of the first cabinet of the Fifth Republic in January, 1959, was made more by the president than by the premier. However, the circumstances were exceptional and need not be a precedent. The spirit of the constitution as well as tradition would call for noninterference by the presidency in the selection of ministers; but General de Gaulle may well put an end to old practices and establish new constitutional customs.

The number of ministers is not fixed; it varies according to the requirements of coalition governments and may be increased or reduced for the sake of maintaining or changing the balance between political parties. When Paul Ramadier reshuffled his cabinet after the municipal elections of 1947, eight ministries were either combined with others or abolished altogether. The combining of ministries formerly separated, or vice versa, may also result from certain changes of policies. Political liberals such as A. Pinay want to see Economic Affairs attached and subordinated to the Ministry of Finance; Socialists would rather see the two separated, in order that the nation's economic policy be not determined by the bureaus of the Finance Ministry, thought to be too conservative.

The size of the cabinets under the Fourth Republic varied from twelve to twenty-six if only ministers are included and, if the undersecretaries are added, reached a total of forty with the Faure cabinet of 1952. Two types of ministers are usually found —ministers with portfolio and those without portfolio. The ministers of state and the ministers attached to the presidency of the Council are without portfolio. The former are usually in the position of vice-premiers. They may, as in the de Gaulle ministry of June, 1958, form an inner cabinet. The ministers attached to the presidency of the council were, before 1959, in a more subordinate position. The appointment of Jacques Soustelle to such a position in the Debré cabinet gave lustre to the office.[4] The ministers without portfolio are usually given responsibility for particular problems. In the Debré cabinet of January, 1959, Louis Jacquinot was entrusted with scientific research, Robert Lecourt with Community Affairs, André Malraux with cultural questions, J. Soustelle with overseas *départements* and territories and with Saharan affairs.

Ministers with portfolio have the responsibility for a particular administration; the most important are Finance, Interior, Foreign Affairs, and Defense. Other ministries of significance include Justice, Education, Public Works and Transport, Construction, Health, Labor, and Veterans. Often but not always found in the cabinet are Economic Affairs, Industry, Posts and Telegraphs, Agriculture, and Information.

In 1959 positions of advisory ministers were created. Such ministers do not normally sit at the meetings of the cabinet or the Council of Ministers but they may be invited to do so. They are ministers without portfolio. The four advisory ministers selected in 1959, Houphouët-Boigny, Senghor, Lisette, and Tsiranana were already premier or president of a state associated to France within the Community. The major function of advisory ministers is to facilitate communications between France and the overseas. It is doubtful however, that they play a significant role. Appointments to the position of advisory minister were probably made to satisfy personal ambitions and to give special recognition to the leaders of Black Africa and Madagascar.

Undersecretaries (*Secrétaires d'État* and *Sous secrétaires d'État*) are under the authority of a ministry. Their number varies; the smaller the number of ministers, the higher the number of secretaries. Sometimes they are chosen to balance a particular ministry. For example, in the Schuman cabinet of 1947 the Ministry of the Armed Forces was held by an MRP, and undersecretaries for War, Sea, and Air belonged to the MRP, the SFIO, and the Radicals. Frequently the ministers and the corresponding undersecretaries belong to the same party, as is normal in Finance and Economic Affairs.

Somewhat subordinate to undersecretaries are the high commissars, found in some ministries, but their functions are for all practical purposes similar to those of undersecretaries. In De Gaulle's cabinet of 1958, there was a high commissar for National Economy; in the Debré cabinet of 1959, a high commissar for Youth was created for Maurice Hertzog.

Under the Third and Fourth republics, ministers were almost exclusively drawn from parliament, principally from the lower house. The first ministry of the Fifth Republic gave a larger share of seats to nonparliamentarians—ten out of twenty-seven. This is due less to the rule which obliges ministers to resign their parliamentary seats than to de Gaulle's desire to avoid giving crucial ministries to politicians.

Each minister appoints a varying number of advisors, rarely more than ten, who form, within a given ministry, a minister's personal cabinet, (*cabinet ministériel*). These advisors are usually drawn from the civil service—Council of State, Inspectorate of Finance, prefect corps among others. Serving a few years on such cabinets is usually a means of obtaining faster promotion, rather than a means of shifting to a political career.

### The Investiture

The investiture is governed more by tradition than by legal prescription. Article 49 of the constitution stipulates that the prime minister, after a Council of Ministers' debate, engages the responsibility of his government on his program of action. If the Assembly disapproves this program, the prime minister must submit his resignation to the president. The difficulty raised is that this article does not clearly oblige a newly formed government to seek approval of the Assembly. The theory that the government is indeed not compelled to seek the investiture is reinforced by the fact that the constitution does not provide for the compulsory calling of an extraordinary meeting of parliament if a new government were formed during a legal parliamentary recess. A government formed in July might thus not have to meet the Assembly before the following October. The presentation of a program to the Assembly would by that time be superfluous. However, it is likely that the new prime minister will seek endorsement by the National Assembly, even if that means calling an extraordinary session. Michel Debré followed such a procedure in January 1959. The difference between the premier's asking for a vote of confidence on his governmental program and the premier's waiting for the Assembly to move nonconfidence, is that the majority required for overthrowing the government is not the same in both cases. In the first case a majority of those voting is sufficient, in the second a majority of those elected to the Assembly is required.

### The Government's Powers

The government's powers are given by the constitution either specifically to the prime minister or to the government in general. The prime minister is the only member of the executive to have legislative initiative and is personally entrusted with National Defense and the execution of the laws. He alone of the Executive can call extraordinary sessions of parliament. He must countersign acts of the president not falling within the "reserved powers." He alone can engage the responsibility of the government before the Assembly. He may ask the Constitutional Council to pass on the constitutionality of a bill or on an international agreement. He may initiate a revision of the constitution. The Council of Ministers, as a body, may proclaim an *état de siège* of up to twelve days.

Some of the acts of the premier can be taken only after consultation with the Council of Ministers or have to be taken "in council." He must consult the council on his engaging the government's responsibility and, as already stated, he has to make the most important appointments to the civil service and to the armed forces "in council." In its relations with the parliament, the government is given certain rights intended to facilitate its political and legislative leadership. Government bills are given preferential treatment since, unlike private bills, they cannot be amended in committee. The members of the government have not only the right to follow parliamentary debates from the seats reserved to them, but they must also be heard at their request by the assemblies and have the right to move amendments. The government may shorten a debate, and may prevent the using of pork-barrel techniques by compelling the houses to accept or reject by a single vote the whole or part of a bill under discussion together with acceptable amendments.

### Constitutional Devices Used to Strengthen the Government

There was general agreement in the last parliament of the Fourth Republic that the technique of government by crisis was disastrous. Too short-lived governments could not act with authority nor plan over-all and long-range policies. Members agreed that the tutelage exercised by the legislative over the executive branch was aberrant. But there was no consensus on any of the proposed cures. The techniques more often suggested to strengthen the executive were the unconditional right of dissolution, the election of a cabinet for a set term of office, and the substitution of the notion of plurality for that of majority in the passing of bills. Notwithstanding the impending crisis, the parliamentarians of the Fourth Republic had failed to agree among themselves on any significant constitutional reform. Having agreed on the diagnosis, they let the patient die while debating the merits of their various prescriptions.

The constitution of 1958 uses direct and indirect techniques to strengthen the cabinet. The indirect technique, prohibiting the cumulation of ministerial and parliamentary functions, has already been examined. It is doubtful that this technique will be effective and might well be one of the first constitutional provisions amended when the wave of antiparliamentarism which accompanied the fall of the Fourth Republic has abated.

The direct techniques are the right of dissolution and the special majority required for overthrowing a government. True, the right of dissolution is not given to the cabinet and could even be used by the president against the premier to force the latter's resignation, but more likely the right of dissolution will be used to keep the parliament in line and prevent it from overthrowing a government without accepting the risk of being sent back to the electorate. The right of dissolution might be useful in preventing the disintegration of a parliamentary majority; the example of Great Britain would point to that effect, but the example of Weimar Germany would show that the repeated use of dissolution may actually weaken and discredit a parliamentary system rather than strengthen it.

The overthrow of a cabinet may result from the Assembly's refusal to endorse a program of action or a declaration of general policy. In that event an ordinary majority is sufficient for the overthrow. Except in these two instances where the initiative of asking for a vote of confidence rests with the prime minister, the overthrow of a government is rendered more difficult under the new constitution than under those of 1875 and 1946.

The National Assembly alone can overthrow the cabinet. The Senate has no such right. The government's responsibility is engaged by a motion of censure which must be signed by at least one-tenth of the members of the Assembly, that is, 56 members. In the parliament of 1958 only four groups had more than

56 members: the Independents, the UNR, the Christian democrats, and the Algerians. None of the parties in the opposition to the Debré government of 1959 had independently the minimum membership required for tabling a motion of censure. Small parliamentary groups, unless finding allies willing to support them, thus have difficulty in using the motion of censure. The Communists in particular, with only ten deputies, are practically barred from using it. If the motion is defeated, the signataries cannot during the same session move a second similar motion. For a motion of censure to pass, it must obtain a majority not only of those voting but of the total membership. Under the Fourth Republic the government was not obliged to resign if the same special majority of the house membership had not been obtained, but in practice governments supported only by a minority of those voting felt obliged to withdraw. To prevent the "majority of the membership" rules from becoming a dead letter, the constitution of 1958 introduced a new voting procedure for motions of censure. On such a motion only the Yes votes are recorded, and the motion is passed only if these number the required majority of the total membership. Not recording the Nos means that the Nos and the abstentions cannot be separated. It is thus assumed that all those who would have liked to abstain actually supported the government. This new voting procedure itself would be of little avail if the parliament, while unable to formally overthrow a cabinet, could still force it to resign by refusing to pass legislation. This the parliament can no longer do because the government can attach a motion of confidence to a bill. In such a situation, the National Assembly must use the motion of censure to kill the bill. As a result, a government with the active support of only a minority of those voting, not only is not obliged to withdraw but can have legislation passed as long as the active opposition has not mustered a majority of the total membership. Thus, in order to remain in office and in order to have its bills passed, the government can forcibly enlist, as it were, the support of those who, absent, had not delegated their votes, and of those who wanted to abstain. This may seem unethical, but much has to be said also against abstention. As ab-

stentions are in fact counted either for or against the government, why not count them in its favor? The mode of voting on the motion of confidence gives effect to the rule that the government needs only a plurality to govern but the opposition needs a majority to overthrow the government or prevent it from putting a legislative program into effect. In the French context, this procedure is sound.

### The Executive in Practice

Power may be derived from constitutional or from extraconstitutional sources. If the United States had disciplined parties of the British type and if the leader of the party in control of the Congress was in the White House, the president would enjoy not only the powers specifically given to him by the Constitution but also powers derived from his controlling the party with a majority in the legislature. In the Fifth Republic, the powers actually exercised by the two branches of the executive are not, of course, solely determined by the constitution but also by the authority derived by either of these two branches from support in and out of parliament. Three facts must be kept in mind when the working of the constitution of the Fifth Republic in its first years of existence is analyzed. Firstly, de Gaulle found moral and political authority in having been the choice not only of the sole presidential college but of the people as a whole when in June, 1958, the nation accepted the delegating of all executive powers to him and when the electorate approved the new constitution by a near 80-per cent majority. By contrast, M. Debré, the prime minister, selected by the president and approved by the National Assembly, was, in fact, further removed from universal suffrage. Secondly, the largest party in the National Assembly, the UNR, without which no stable government could be formed, had de Gaulle for its leader. True, the general refused to be associated with any party but, if de Gaulle was not necessarily "UNR oriented," the UNR was necessarily "de Gaulle directed." The situation was therefore as though the leader of the dominant party in parliament were also president of the Republic. Thirdly, de Gaulle came back to power in 1958 to prevent a likely *coup d'état* and a possible civil war. As the only possible umpire between the army and that part of the nation not willing to accept political leadership from the military, de Gaulle derived great political strength.

For these various reasons, whatever the letter or even the spirit of the constitution, executive leadership normally came from the presidency, not from the premier or from the cabinet. The constitution had devised a number of checks and counter-checks between the president and the prime minister which could turn to the advantage of either. For example, the president can refuse to appoint the ministers or the top civil servants nominated by the premier; inversely, the president cannot make political pronouncements without the prime minister's approval except through messages read before parliament. In the first year of the Fifth Republic, the checks on the president remained ineffective; not so for the checks on the prime minister. A few examples may serve to illustrate the dominant role played by the presidency. A couple of weeks before the official announcement that de Gaulle had selected Debré as prime minister, Debré had been unofficially approached by the president and asked to proceed to the usual consultations which were carried at the top party level between members of the de Gaulle cabinet. When Debré was officially asked to form the government, the cabinet was in fact already selected and had been approved by the president. During negotiations de Gaulle had expressed his wishes and vetoed certain suggestions, such as giving the Ministry of the Interior to J. Soustelle. The president had used his validation power as a veto power. The text of the communiqué issued by the presidency after the appointment of Debré as prime minister is worth quoting in its entirety; it describes well the relative position of prime minister and president and also emphasizes that the president had finally appointed the premier only after the latter had submitted the list of his ministers to the president's approval.

General de Gaulle, President of the Republic, convoked Mr. Michel Debré, Keeper of the Seals, Minister of Justice for 4 P.M. He discussed with him the whole of the country's affairs.

At the conclusion of the meeting, General de Gaulle entrusted Mr. Michel Debré with submitting to him proposals regarding the eventual composition of the government.

At 19:30 Mr. Michel Debré was again received at the Elysée Palace. He submitted for General de Gaulle's approval his conceptions concerning general policy and the names of the notabilities who would eventually become his collaborators in the government.

The President of the Republic appointed Mr. Michel Debré as Prime Minister.

On the basis of the Prime Minister's proposals, he appointed the members of the government.[5]

The press conference of February, 1959, is another example of the subordination of the government, expressed in de Gaulle's "grand" style, which to an Anglo-Saxon public may well appear as bordering on the ridiculous but which must be viewed in the French context of 1959 when no universally accepted hierarchy between the various constitutional organs of government existed and when the necessity of expressing such hierarchies visually may have been felt. The entire cabinet was lined up before a podium from where the general talked to the journalists and answered their questions. It was thus emphasized that the government was subordinate to the presidency not only in matters of formal hierarchy but also in the determining of the nation's policy. In answering questions on matters of vital interest to the nation, without having first to check his answer with his prime minister, as would have been the case under the Third and Fourth republics, de Gaulle wanted to signify that he himself was leading the nation and that the ministers' countersignatures and other constitutional checks were not to be interpreted as hindrances to his power of decision. It may also be noted that as soon as a summit meeting seemed likely in 1959, de Gaulle announced that he would attend such a meeting, thus putting himself on a par with the American president, and thus relegating the French premier to a far more subordinate role than that of England's prime minister.

Not only with regard to the cabinet but also with regard to parliament did de Gaulle make full use of the powers at his disposal. In March, 1960, as a result of pressure from organizations of farmers opposed to the government's agricultural policy, a majority of deputies requested an extraordinary meeting of parliament. By refusing to issue the order necessary for the opening of the extraordinary session, the president in fact vetoed the deputies' move to recall the assemblies. Thus was set a precedent which, if followed, would give the presidency a large power of veto not clearly granted by the constitution. (See p. 195.)

De Gaulle's main concern with external and military affairs resulted in a certain division of fields of action between the presidency and the government. In the Debré cabinet of 1958, as in the de Gaulle cabinet of transition, Foreign Affairs and National Defense were given to former civil servants. The president probably thought that he might find greater ease in imposing his ideas on a "technician" rather than on a politician who might be answerable before party caucuses and headquarters. From the beginning de Gaulle reserved to himself all important decisions concerning Algeria, the Sahara, the Community, Foreign Affairs, and Defense. It might have been expected that the premier would have brought under his control the fields for which the president showed only secondary interest. However, this did not happen. Up to January, 1960, when he was dismissed for political and personal disagreements with the president, Pinay was the cabinet's most influential minister. But even after that date, the prime minister's role remained limited to that of an intermediary between the presidency on the one hand, parliament and political parties on the other. Within the narrow field of initiative left to him, Debré endeavoured to make the constitutional system, which he had devised, become accepted practice, especially as far as relations between the parliament and the executive were concerned. In fashioning the new parliamentary institutions the prime minister played an important role, but one inferior to that given him by the constitution itself.

The governing coalition's large majority in the National Assembly; the constitutional devices restricting the use of votes of nonconfidence; de Gaulle's announcement that the cabinet had been appointed for a five-year term and that if the government were to be overthrown, the Assembly would be dissolved; and the veiled threat of having the constitution amended in order to establish a truly presidential system—all these have freed the first government of the Fifth Republic from the wars of exhaustion waged against its predecessors by the parliaments of the Third and Fourth republics. From being supreme emperor, the legislature found itself demoted to the position of humble servant. This situation is a little as though the American Senate had suddenly been turned into a House of Lords and the House of Representatives into a House of Commons. After almost a century of constant frustration the French executive suddenly enjoyed exhilarating freedom of action. Like the English cabinets, although to a lesser extent, the French executive became the major source of legislation.

The bills and ordinances are prepared by the bureaus of a particular ministry and submitted to the other ministries with a possible interest in the matter. Joint meetings may be held between various ministers and their advisors to iron out differences. Arbitration may be asked from the premier or, on matters of greater significance, from the president of the Republic. Important bills and ordinances are submitted to the Council of Ministers chaired by the president. Usually no vote is taken. If there is disagreement, the opinion of the president prevails.

The new role of the presidency has given significance to the president's personal secretariat, composed of about fifty members divided into four sections: the general secretariat, the civil cabinet, the military cabinet, and the secretariat general for the Community. The first-mentioned, the general secretariat, maintains contacts with the ministries and the administrations; its most important section is that which deals with diplomatic affairs. The civil cabinet plays the role of a public-relations bureau in contact with the private sector. The military cabinet has its functions described by its name. The secretariat general of the Community is in a special position. In all but name it is a ministry for the Community—but a ministry coming directly and solely under the authority of the president of the Republic in his capacity as president of the Community. The president of the Republic is thus surrounded by three different "cabinets"; his personal Elysée Palace cabinet, the Community secretariat-general, and the regular Council of Ministers.

Not only has the constitutional cabinet been weakened by the setting up of presidential personal cabinets but also by the creation of *ad hoc* committees bringing together the prime minister, specific ministers, and civil servants under the president's chairmanship. In 1960 there were four such specialized committees—Community, Defense, Foreign Affairs, and Algeria. The latter was particularly important in that, following the settlers' insurrection of 1960, it was given authority to take measures required for the solution of the Algerian problem. The splitting of the ministry into specialized subcommittees comprising civil servants was evidence of de Gaulle's attempt to "de-politicize" the cabinet and to divide it in order to rule it better.

# 13 *Parliament and the Legislative Field*

English constitutional theory was used by de Gaulle's opponents to point out that France, under the constitution of 1958, had ceased to have a true parliamentary system; English constitutional practice was used by defenders of the new constitution to demonstrate that the French National Assembly was yet more powerful than the House of Commons. Theoretically the French legislature has powers lesser than those of their English and American counterparts. The constitution drastically limits the field of legislative action by making the executive the normal source of legislation in all matters not specifically reserved to parliament. The constitution further prevents members of parliament from initiating legislation which would result in a lowering of state revenues or in an increase of state expenditures. As R. Pléven put it, the legislative branch could not even abolish the death penalty if the executive took the position that the keeping of prisoners alive would result in increased expenditures. The constitution also restricts the powers of the legislature in the selection of prime ministers and in the overthrowing of governments and if it be added that the president of the Republic has according to the letter of the constitution a possible right of veto over legislation, the French parliament which, among Western democracies, was before 1958 one of the more powerful and certainly the most eager to display its strength, has now been subjected to such restrictions that it seems condemned to fall into subservience to the executive. However, as long as executive and legislature are not integrated by a disciplined party gaining a majority of the seats in the lower house, as long as France maintains her traditional multiparty system and as long as parliament has the right to overthrow the cabinet and to pass the budget, the legislature cannot but remain powerful. The curtailment of the legislature's powers by the constitution of 1958 was an attempt at obtaining by constitutional means results obtained in Great Britain by the emergence of a disciplined two-party system. The evolution of the Fifth Republic may well show that a party system is more important than constitutional structures in determining the workings of a parliamentary system.

### The Legislature

Parliament comprises two houses, the National Assembly and the Senate. The constitution provides that the National Assembly is elected directly, the Senate indirectly and that in both cases voting is universal, equal, and secret. The electoral system is determined by the National Assembly. The lower house is meant to represent the people at large, the Senate to represent local communities and Frenchmen living abroad. Unlike under the Third and Fourth republics, the former colonies are no longer represented in either house, unless they have the status of overseas *départements* or overseas territories.[1]

### Parliamentary Sessions

Parliament meets twice a year in regular sessions. Extraordinary sessions may be called subject to certain restrictions. The regular sessions are compulsory; they are being called automatically and thus do not depend upon either the executive or the parliamentarians. The first yearly session begins the first Tuesday of October and ends the third Friday in December. The second session begins the last Tuesday of April, and ends when the assemblies decide to adjourn but cannot last more than three months. The first session is intended to be the budget session, the second the legislative session; however, laws other than the budget can be put on the assemblies' agendas during the first session as well. The regular yearly sessions of parliament cannot thus last more than six months. During intervals the parliamentary committees may meet and debate proposed legislation but no meetings of the whole house may be held. The short session system was intended to free the government from parliamentary nibbling and to oblige parliamentarians to concentrate on the most important pieces of legislation. The constituents had much reason to believe that unless obliged to stop, a legislative machinery always finds material to grind. Furthermore the legislature having been deprived of the regulating of many matters which now fall within the executive-orders field,[2] it was thought that parliament could do its legislative work in six months' time. However, the short session system is not rigid. Extraordinary sessions of parliament can be called either by the prime minister or by a majority of the members elected to the National Assembly. Extraordinary sessions must be called on a specific agenda which may not be modified by parliament after reconvening. When the session is requested by the premier, the time is not limited; when called by the deputies, a session may not last more than twelve days. Finally, extraordinary sessions, unlike the regular ones, do not convene automatically once called by the prime minister or the deputies. Such sessions must be opened as well as closed by a presidential decree. The president of the Republic may thus, by refusing to sign the decree, veto extraordinary sessions.

The debates of both houses are public; they are printed in the *Journal Officiel*. At the request of the prime minister or of one-tenth of its members, a particular house may hold closed-door meetings.

### The Control of Credentials

Under the Fourth Republic, deputies and senators were the sole judges of the eligibility of their peers. As might have been expected, this system led to the abuse by the assemblies of their validation power for political reasons. In 1951 the National Assembly gave opposite rulings on the interpretation of the electoral law for the Seine-Inferieure and Haut-Rhin districts for entirely political reasons. In 1951 a strict but unfair interpretation of the electoral law resulted in the unseating of about one-fifth of the Poujadists. Since by-elections were then held under a majority system while general elections under a PR system, the unseating of ten-odd Poujadists had for effect to deprive their party of the benefits of proportional representation. The regrettable effect of such partisan decisions on public opinion and on parliament itself led the constituents of 1958 to make the Constitutional Council the sole judge of parliamentary credentials.

The council sees that the representatives meet the legal requirements of age and citizenship and are not barred by any of the incapacities set by law. The council also hears of all complaints of violation of the electoral code. If the council is of the opinion that the campaign has been distorted by unlawful practices, they may quash the election. The present system of validation of credentials by a nonparliamentary body and the fact that by-elections are held under the same electoral system as general elections, result in a definite improvement over former practices.

### The Parliamentary Profession

However regretted, politics tends to be a full and life-time profession. During sessions, the representative is expected to be present at all debates; his absence is recognized by a cut in his salary, unless he be excused for cause. Between sessions the parliamentarian, often member of a local council, has to attend to the affairs of his commune, or of his *département* and to nurse his district. If he wishes to keep informed and to further his political career, he must also attend the between-session meetings of his parliamentary committee. However, the parliamentary profession being most insecure, parliamentarians often maintain some outside activity. The insecurity of the profession favors the recruiting of parliamentarians from certain professions, such as lawyers, party officials, civil servants, and to a lesser extent independent landlords and businessmen.

The practice of doubling the parliamentary profession with an outside interest led the constituents of 1958 to list a number of activities forbidden to members of parliament. They may not hold any nonelective public post; [3] in other words they may be mayors, or local councilors but not civil servants, judges, or members of the military. If they occupied such positions before their election to parliament they must either resign or ask for temporary and unlimited leaves of absence. Certain private activities are also forbidden to parliamentarians. They may not hold controlling positions, specifically described by an organic law,[4] in the directorates of banks and of undertakings working for or under the control of the state or receiving directly state subsidies. Members of parliament who are lawyers may not, either personally or through their associates, participate in criminal cases affecting the state, nor in press trials, nor in the trial of crimes against credit and public savings (*le crédit et l'épargne*). Parliamentarians are also forbidden to mention their parliamentary position after their names on the advertisements of any financial, commercial, or industrial undertakings.

The salary of parliamentarians is indexed to that of the highest-paid civil servants. In addition, deputies and senators receive a special indemnity equal at most to one-quarter of their regular salary. Altogether a parliamentarian was paid approximately eight hundred dollars a month in 1960.[5] Both houses have a retirement plan for the benefit of their members.

### Parliamentary Immunities

Three basic rules govern parliamentary immunities. The first is that members of parliament may not be the object of any judicial action for opinions or votes expressed in the exercise of their functions. The second that during sessions a member of parliament may not be prosecuted, detained, or tried for crimes or misdemeanors without the authorization of his house, except in cases of flagrant violations of the law (*flagrante delicto*). The third, that the prosecution or detention of a parliamentarian arrested for *flagrante delicto* must be suspended if his house so requests. Between sessions the same rules apply except that prosecution may be started even in cases other than *flagrante delicto*. However the member of parliament so prosecuted may not be detained without specific authorization by the bureau of his house.

### The Legislative Field

In the constitutions of the Third and Fourth republics, the hierarchy between legislative and executive rule-making was clear. Any *décret* or *arrêté* had to be hooked to a law and could not be in violation of the latter. A law could only be modified by a law or a decree-law. The so-called decree-laws resulted from the legislature giving to the executive the right to amend laws by decrees. Such delegations of powers were not permanent. Parliament could at any time cancel the delegating act or pass laws modifying decree-laws. The legislative field was thus whatever the parliament decided. If parliament had passed a law to the effect that umbrellas were not allowed inside museums and theaters, such a rule could not be changed by a ministerial decree or by an *arrêté* from the local prefect. Because executive orders could not violate laws, while laws could modify or cancel executive orders, the field of legislative action tended to expand continuously. Such an overexpansion combined with the paralysis often seizing a parliament confronted with important pieces of legislation had led to this aberrant situation that parliament, when delegating part of its legislative task to the executive would delegate not only unimportant and time-consuming matters but would delegate also important questions which parliament was unable to resolve because of its internal divisions and because of the slowness of its decision-making process.

The constitution of 1958 introduces an innovation by defining two fields of rule making—one reserved to parliament, the other to the executive. Everything not defined by constitutional texts (constitution and organic laws) as falling within the legislative domain, belongs to the regulatory. The residual powers are thus in the executive's hands.

The legislative field is defined by articles 34, 35, 36, 47, and 53 of the constitution.

Article 53 specifies that treaties of peace or commerce, treaties or agreements concerning international organizations, treaties involving state finances, treaties modifying a law, treaties concerning personal status, and treaties resulting in abandonment, exchange, or addition of territory may not be ratified or approved without parliamentary authorization. Executive agreements or treaties which do not fall within the categories described do not require parliament's sanction—such as a treaty of friendship or a convention on import quotas.

In order to avoid the difficulties which would result from putting treaties and laws on a par, the constitution specifies that treaties are superior to internal laws with the restriction that in order to have such privileged status over municipal law, a treaty must be implemented by the contracting parties. The constitution does not specify who determines whether a treaty is implemented or not. Should the judge resolve a conflict between a treaty and an ordinary law? Should the government? In keeping with the French tradition that ordinary judges do not have the control of the constitutionality of the laws, and since Constitutional Court judges would lack the means of appreciating whether a treaty is respected by a foreign state, it would seem that the power of appreciation rests with the French executive.

In the event of abandonment, exchange, or addition of territory, the consent of the affected populations is required by the constitution. If this requirement is not met, the Constitutional Council, when asked to render a verdict, could rule a treaty unconstitutional.

Article 47 reserves to parliament the right to pass the budget, subject to two major restrictions. Firstly, members of parliament may not amend the budget proposed by the executive unless to reduce expenses, to increase revenues, or to insure the control of public expenses. Secondly, if parliament has not voted the budget seventy days after it was submitted to them, the budget may be executed through ordinances.[6]

Articles 34, 35, and 36 define the matters which, other than treaties, belong to the legislative field. Article 36 stipulates that a state of siege of more than twelve days has to be authorized by parliament. Article 35 specifies that declarations of war have to be approved by parliament. Finally Article 34, certainly the most complex and one of the worst drafted, attempts to define the legislative field. The article makes a distinction between two types of laws, those setting rules and those setting fundamental principles.

To the first type belong the laws concerning eight categories of subject matter.

Civil rights and their guarantees; public freedoms; demands made by national defense on the citizen's persons and goods.

Nationality; status and legal capacity of persons; matrimonial laws; inheritance and gifts.

Definition of crimes and misdemeanors, determination of penalties; criminal procedure; amnesty; creation of new types of jurisdictions; status of the magistracy.

Incidence, scale, and method of collection of taxes of all kinds; the system of emission of money.

The electoral system of local and parliamentary assemblies.

Creation of categories of public corporate bodies.

Fundamental guarantees granted to civil servants and military personnel.

Nationalization of undertakings; transfer of ownership of undertakings from the public to the private sector.

The second category of laws sets only fundamental principles, leaving the executive to work out the actual rules on the basis of such principles. Such laws come under five headings:

Organization of national defense.

Free administration of local collectivities, their functions and their resources.

Education.

Property system, property rights (*droits réels*), civil and commercial obligations.

Labor law, trade-union law, and social security.

Such a separation of the rule-making power between the legislative and the executive creates many difficulties of application and interpretation. The status of the magistracy and the creation of new types of jurisdiction which belong to the legislative domain may not be separated easily from the setting of rules of procedure and of competence which belongs to the regulatory domain. With regard to property rights and property systems, what is fundamental principle and consequently within the parliament's powers may not be separated easily from what is rule of application and consequently reserved to the executive. To decide whether a treaty modifies solely internal rules belonging to the regulatory field, in which case the treaty need not be submitted to parliament, or whether such treaty modifies laws falling within the legislative domain, in which case the treaty must be submitted to parliament, may be difficult to decide. Crimes and misdemeanors being defined by parliament while *contraventions* (minor offenses) are regulated by decrees, the executive and the legislative may try to define either as misdemeanors or as contraventions the same types of offenses. Not evident is whether the control over the systems of circulation of money gives parliament the right to legislate concerning bank money as well as legal tender.

To separate absolutely a regulatory from a legislative field is indeed impossible. It is thus to be expected that because of the vagueness of the constitution, the executive will try to invade the legislative field by way of its regulatory power, and that the legislature will try to reduce the regulatory domain by way of its legislative power. In such events two attitudes are possible. The invaded party will either accept or resist the invasion. In the first alternative, two hypotheses have to be contemplated according to whether the invasion has been by the executive over the legislative or vice versa. If the executive invades the legislative without the latter's opposition, the rule thus put on the books is nevertheless subject to being declared *ultra vires* by administrative courts. The *Conseil d'État* and the prefectural courts are thus made the defenders of the parliament's legislative privileges even in the absence of parliamentary objections. If on the other hand the legislature invades the regulatory domain without the executive objecting, the law, once passed cannot be declared invalid by any court, not even by the Constitutional Council.

If instead of passivity the invaded party shows active opposition, the procedure is different according to whether the invader is the legislative or the regulatory power. If the executive thinks a bill or even a law violates the separation of powers, the president of the Republic or the premier may ask the Constitutional Council to pass on the constitutionality of such text. The council's decision is without appeal. If on the contrary the legislature thinks that the executive is infringing on their legislative rights, parliament cannot appeal against the contested ordinances, decrees or *arrêtés*. The only parliamentary recourse is to pass a law over the same matter and thus oblige the executive to appeal to the Constitutional Council or risk its regulations being declared *ultra vires* by administrative courts.

The Constitutional Council may be called to play a crucial role in drawing the separation between regulatory and legislative fields. The obscurities of the constitution as much as the mode of selection of councilors makes the Constitutional Council less an impartial judicial tribunal than a political organ which by siding either with the legislature or with the executive may contribute to the evolution of the Fifth Republic either toward a presidential or toward a classical parliamentary system.

The separation between legislative and regulatory fields is not legally immutable. The legislature may delegate to the executive some of its legislative powers; it may grant the government the right to take ordinances (decree-laws) for a limited period of time on matters normally within the legislative domain. Such ordinances are taken by the Council of Ministers after advice from the Council of State. Ordinances have the force of law; they could be declared *ultra vires* by administrative courts only for violation of the delegation law.[7] Ordinances must be tabled before parliament within a period of time specified in the delegation law. Failing such tabling, ordinances cease to be valid. During the period of time for which the delegation has been granted, ordinances may be amended or abrogated by other ordinances. At the expiration of the delegation time, ordinances may be modified only by laws.

If the parliament may choose to deprive itself of some of the legislative powers specifically given it by the constitution, it may also increase such powers by organic laws amending Article 34 of the constitution. After enumerating the matters on which parliament exercises its legislative powers, Article 34 specifies that "the dispositions of this article may be elaborated and completed by an organic law." Although the word "completed" is far from clear and might eventually have to be interpreted by the Constitutional Council, the general understanding is that parliament may increase the legislative domain by an organic law. Again it appears that the council may have to play a decisive role in controlling the evolution of the relationships between the executive and the parliament.

# 14 *Elections to the National Assembly*

France changed electoral systems even more often than she changed constitutions. In the past hundred years, either the type of constituency, the number of ballots or the method of allocating seats were modified fifteen times. The longest-existing electoral system, that of 1889, lasted only thirty years. From 1945 to 1959 elections were fought under three basically different sets of electoral rules.

Tampering with the electoral machinery destroys the public confidence in the representative character of parliamentary institutions. Only if the electorate has become universally dissatisfied with the electoral system, should the system be changed. But in France the discarding of electoral systems has rarely been done for reasons of greater justice. True the shifts to proportional representation (PR) in 1919 and in 1945 were in part the result of campaigns conducted, since the beginning of the twentieth century, against majority systems considered as oppressive of minority opinions. Both reforms were made after a world war, when political parties, which had collaborated while the existence of the nation was questioned, agreed to share the benefits of parliamentary representation in proportion to their electoral strength. It happened also that an electoral system which had proved defective, was discarded by general agreement, as in 1927 when the erratic quasi PR introduced in 1919 was abandoned. On the whole, however, electoral reform has been a means to a partisan end. In 1873 a monarchist majority substituted a two-ballot for a one-ballot system in order to prevent Republicans and Bonapartists from benefiting from the split in the monarchist camp; in 1875 the monarchists abolished multimember in favor of single-member districts in order to resist better an expected Republican landslide in the cities. In 1885, after the Republicans had gained control of parliament, the list system was reintroduced over opposition of the conservatives. In 1889 the Republicans switched back to single-member districts for fear that multimember districts would produce a Boulangist majority. Even in 1945, prominent among the reasons for the adoption of PR was the common belief of Christian democrats, Socialists, and Communists that they would fare better under such a system than under the old *scrutin d'arrondissement* which, they thought, would have been advantageous to the Radicals and the moderates with their long established local machines. In 1951, the system of *apparentement* was introduced in order to reduce the parliamentary representation of Communists and Gaullists. In 1958, finally, the single-member district with two-ballot system was resurrected by preference to other systems in order to cause a drop in Communist representation and to prevent a UNR landslide.

### France's Experiment with Electoral Systems

Among the various electoral systems used by France since the introduction of parliamentary elections in 1791, three types stand out: the one-ballot plurality system, the two-ballot majority system, and proportional representation.

*The one-ballot plurality system*

This system was used under the Second Republic in 1848 and 1849 and for the Third Republic's first election in 1871. Contrary to Anglo-Saxon practice, the system was not used in connection with single-member but with multimember districts, except in the *département* of Guyane, which was given a single-ballot one-member-district system after the electoral reform of 1951. It is often claimed that the one-ballot plurality system would reduce the number of French political parties. Undoubtedly it would reduce the number of parties contesting each seat, but would not necessarily reduce the number of parties represented in parliament. In each district the competition would tend to be between two parties, but not the same two parties in all districts.

*The two-ballot majority system*

This system has been the most often used since 1875. It was in effect throughout the Third Republic except in 1871 and except from 1919 to 1927. Discarded in 1945, it was reintroduced under the Fifth Republic in 1958. It has been used in connection with single-member and multimember districts. On the first ballot the candidate or the list of candidates obtaining a majority of votes is elected. If no such majority is obtained, a second ballot takes place, at which time a plurality is sufficient for election. The runoff was never limited to the top candidates as in some American primary elections. In France candidates are left free to withdraw from or remain in the contest for the second ballot. Under the Third Republic new candidates were even allowed to enter the race after the first ballot.

The two-ballot majority system is usually called *scrutin d'arrondissement* after the name of the administrative unit which served as electoral district before the Second World War.

*Proportional Representation*

The system of strict proportional representation introduced in 1945 was of a classical type. Elections were in multimember constituencies for lists of candidates. The larger parties were slightly overrepresented but the seats gained by these parties were shared among themselves on a proportional basis. The MRP with 24.9 per cent of the votes obtained 27 per cent of the seats; the Socialists with 23.8 per cent of the votes, 25.7 per cent of the seats; the Communists with 26.1 per cent of the votes, 28.4 per cent of the seats. Right-wing parties and independent candidates obtained 11.9 per cent of the seats with 13.3 per cent of the votes, while the Radicals with 11.7 per cent of the votes had only 6.7 per cent of the seats. The elections of June and November, 1946, were fought under the same system.

From this short experiment with unqualified proportional representation a few conclusions may be drawn. The system favored the large and well-organized parties such as the MRP, Socialists, and Communists and worked to the disadvantage of small parties relying on local machines rather than on a national organization. The dependence of a representative on party headquarters rather than on a personal machine produced better disciplined parliamentary groups. This last effect may be counted as an advantage, but PR also had disadvantages. Parliament tended to reproduce the divisions of the electorate instead of giving representation to its dominant elements. A parliament mirroring the electorate may not be objectionable in Switzerland or Sweden where the same fundamental rules of government are accepted by all major parties, but one may question whether proportional representation should be used in France where a large section of the electorate supports parties favoring the overthrow of the present system of government. On the surface the argument that when Communists have 25 per cent of the votes, they should have 25 per cent of the seats may seem only just. It is, in fact, no more valid than to say that if they have 25 per cent of the seats in parliament, they should have 25 per cent of cabinet posts. Proportional representation favors pluralism; to extend the benefits of such a system to those who do not accept pluralism is to invite governmental difficulties.

De Gaulle's creation of the RPF in 1947 led to the abandonment of strict proportional representation. The parties in power feared that if Communists and Gaullists were represented on a proportional basis, no government majority could emerge from parliament. To prevent a deadlock, the system of *apparentement* was introduced. Elections continued to be contested by lists of candidates in multimember constituencies but any party or coalition of parties obtaining a majority of the votes, obtained all the district seats. The coalitions of parties had to be official alliances (*apparentement*) registered with the authorities before the election. The benefit of *apparentement* was reserved to the parties presenting lists in at least thirty *départements*. The type of coalitions entered into by a party could vary from district to district. If a majority of the votes had been obtained by such a coalition in a district, all seats of that district were distributed, on the basis of proportional representation, to the parties having formed the coalition. If no party or no coalition of parties had obtained a majority of the votes, the seats were allocated among all parties according to proportional representation. As an exception the two *départements* of Seine and Seine-et-Oise, where the Third Force had little prospect of forming coalitions able to get a majority of the votes, remained under the strict PR system of 1946.

For the election of 1951, the Center parties formed electoral alliances in 76 of the 95 districts where the *apparentement* was in use. Although the system had been divised against the RPF rather than against the Communists, no single coalition was formed with the Communists, while Center parties formed alliances with the RPF in thirteen districts because of local considerations.

In one constituency a single list won an absolute majority; in thirty-eight, a coalition obtained a majority of the votes. In all other districts the seats were allocated according to proportional representation among all parties. The Center parties' coalitions had obtained the majority in a sufficient number of districts to keep a majority in the National Assembly. But the Center parties, notwithstanding the danger they thought was menacing them, had failed to unite and reap all the benefits of the system they had devised for their own sake. Among the misleading clichés concerning the French Republic should be added the saying: "If the Republic governs badly, she defends herself well." With 21.7 per cent of the votes, the RPF received 19.6 per cent of the seats; and the Communists, with 25.9 per cent of the votes, received 17.8 per cent. Even more revealing was the election of 1956. The Center parties divided themselves into competing coalitions. Alliances won all the seats in only eleven constituencies. As a result, the number of seats won by the major parties was almost proportional to their votes. The *apparentement* system would have made sense had the democratic parties used it to exclude their nondemocratic opponents from parliamentary representation. But partisan and petty rivalries had blinded the governmental parties of the Fourth Republic to what they had in common and to what menaced their existence.

### The Electoral System of October, 1958

The question of electoral reform had seriously divided the last parliament of the Fourth Republic, contributing to the rift between Mendès-France and Edgar Faure, and delaying attempts at reforming the constitution under the Bourgès-Maunoury and Gaillard governments. Practically all parties had become dissatisfied with the system of proportional representation with *apparentement* but they could not agree on an alternative. Most Radicals and a majority of the Independents favored a return to the *scrutin d'arrondissement.* The Socialists preferred a modified version of the German system of proportional representation combined with single-member districts as used for elections to the Bundestag, or a form of alternative voting patterned after that used in Australia for elections to the Senate, but were willing to rally to the *scrutin d'arrondissement.* Communists, Christian democrats, Poujadists, and a minority of Independents wanted some form of proportional representation. The Social Republicans supported a multimember constituency majority system. In February, 1958, the National Assembly by 297 against 263 refused to take into consideration a motion to discuss the *scrutin d'arrondissement.*

After the new constitution had been approved by the people in September, 1958, de Gaulle asked the members of his cabinet to state their preferences regarding an electoral system and required that the system should be simple, without gimmicks puzzling the electorate, and identical in all districts of metropolitan France. The cabinet divided into three groups.[1] Nine ministers supported a proposal by Justice Minister M. Debré and Information Minister J. Soustelle, that elections be by a majority system in multimember constituencies of four to five deputies each. Nine other ministers favored a Radical and Socialist proposal that the *scrutin d'arrondissement* be reintroduced. Finally the four MRP ministers and Independent A. Pinay favored proportional representation with *apparentement*. De Gaulle followed the opinion of the majority after the MRP ministers had rallied to the *scrutin d'arrondissement* as a lesser evil.[2] The decision was important as the different systems were expected to produce different results. It was thought that the Debré system would be most harmful to the parties closely associated with the governments of the Fourth Republic, especially to the Radicals, Socialists, and MRP, and most favorable to the "neo-Gaullist" party, the UNR. It was thought that the single-member district system would prevent a "Gaullist" landslide, the traditional parties being better able to resist the pressure from the UNR in small constituencies where the locally influential personalities would channel better the electorate into its traditional patterns. Either the Debré or the *arrondissement* system were expected to reduce sizably Communist and Poujadist representation.

As an exception, Algeria was not given a *scrutin d'arrondissement* but instead a single-ballot list system used to guarantee that two-thirds of the Algerian seats would go to Moslems and to oblige the two communities, Moslems and Europeans, to an electoral collaboration.

The two systems, that for metropolitan France and that for Algeria, will be analyzed separately.

## Elections in Metropolitan France

### *The districts*

France is divided into 465 districts, all within the boundaries of one of the 93 *départements*, but often cut across communes and cantons. Notwithstanding the rule that the districts should be as nearly equal as possible in population, wide differences exist. In the Rhône *département*, the Villeurbane district has 137,000 inhabitants, while Tarare district has only 70,000. In the city of Lille the fourth district has 62,000 inhabitants, while the eighth has 117,000. In Paris, the eighth district has a population of 123,000, the twenty-fourth only 70,000. Glaring as they be, these inequalities are not as great as under the Third Republic when each administrative *arrondissement* had at least one deputy irrespective of its population. In 1928, the smallest constituency had 22,338 inhabitants, the largest 137,718. In the 1880's, northern France, with 55 per cent of the total population, had only 44 per cent of the deputies.[3] Although the new districting is still advantageous to southern and rural France, the advantage is not as great as it was. Northern France with 44.6 per cent of the population has 43.4 per cent of the seats in the National Assembly.[4]

The redistricting of 1958 was done by the Ministry of the Interior under cabinet supervision. There were some obvious cases of gerrymandering, such as in Lozère and Creuse where geography and history were violated in order to dissolve Left-wing into conservative votes.[5] Throughout France districts were so drawn as to favor the major non-Communist leaders of the Fourth Republic, those who had supported neither de Gaulle nor the constitution, as well as those who had. Mendès-France and Mollet were equally favored, and in the Nièvre, where a tentative districting of the Morvan along north-south lines would have been harmful to Mitterand, the personal intervention of de Gaulle resulted in an east-west division. Except in isolated districts there were, before the elections, few complaints of grossly biased redistricting. Considering the speed with which the districting was done—less than fifteen days—it can be considered as generally fair.

The ten districts of the overseas *départements* are similar to those of France. Guadeloupe, Martinique, and Réunion are each divided into three constituencies. Guyane constitutes a single one.

*The candidate*

At the latest twenty-one days before the first ballot candidates must send a formal application to the local authorities, giving names, dates and places of birth, residences, and occupations. The candidate must deposit 100,000 francs (about $200), be at least twenty-three years old, and not be subject to any of the incapacities defined by law. Prevented from running for parliament are persons condemned for certain crimes and misdemeanors, foreigners, naturalized citizens of less than ten years' standing, and the descendants of families which reigned over France.[6] This last provision precludes the Count of Paris and the members of his family from seeking election. Members of the armed forces and civil servants are eligible. If elected they are given leaves of absence. Few military men have sought election but each parliament has had some. The first parliament of the Fifth Republic has among its military parliamentarians, Colonel J. Thomazo who played an important role in the army rebellion of May 13, 1958.

There are no residence requirements except that certain categories of civil servants such as prefects and members of the judiciary cannot run in a district which was under their authority unless there has been a lapse of time which varies from six months to three years, according to the positions. In other words, the only residence requirement is that in certain cases the candidate must be resident of a district other than that in which he runs.

If a candidacy is thought to be in violation of the law, the prefect brings the matter before the local administrative court which must render a decision within three days. The court's decision can be appealed to the Constitutional Council but only after the election.

A candidate may not run in more than one district. In the early years of the Third Republic multiple candidacies were allowed. In 1873, Thiers had been elected in twenty-six *départements*.[7] In 1889, for fear that General Boulanger might turn the election into a plebiscite, the rule was introduced that a candidate could run in only one constituency.

### *The substitute*

The constitutional provision that a member of parliament appointed to a cabinet position has to resign his seat and the desire to avoid too many by-elections led to the institution of a substitute, whose name must appear on the ballot of any candidate. The substitute must satisfy the same general requirements as the candidate. A substitute called to fill the seat left vacant by his team leader, after the latter's appointment to the cabinet for example, cannot run in the following election against his team leader if the latter decides to stand again.

### *The elector*

All Frenchmen over twenty-one are eligible to vote. The other rules governing electoral capacity are the same as those governing eligibility for candidacy, except that a naturalized Frenchman may vote five years after his naturalization and that the members of the families having reigned over France are enfranchised. As an exception to the age regulation, persons having been awarded some civil or military distinctions, such as the *légion d'honneur* or the *médaille militaire* may vote when they are eighteen. No serious campaigning has been done to lower the age requirement. Such reform would favor the extremist or nonconformist parties, Communists and UNR for example. Electors are registered on permanent electoral rolls.[8] Registration is made by the municipal authorities on the basis of their lists of residents. Each year the rolls are open for a limited period of time to enable checking by anyone concerned. The percentage of potential electors not registered at the time of an election is relatively low, usually about 10 per cent.[9]

### *The regulation of election campaigns*

The law strictly regulates written as well as radio and television propaganda. In each district a certain number of small wooden bill boards planted side by side are allotted to each candidate. Election posters, the number and size of which are also regulated (the biggest are three by two feet) have to be placed on these panels. The type and number of folders or pamphlets the candidate may send to each elector is also set by law. The literature of all the district's candidates is sent under a single envelope in order to reduce expenses. The distribution of all such literature is done by a special committee composed of local officials.

The state radio and television which has a broadcasting monopoly allocates free time to the parties recognized as national, that is, to those presenting candidates in at least seventy-five districts. In 1958, twelve parties qualified as such.[10] They were given three five-minute broadcasts at dinner time, around 8 P.M., one on the national radio network, one the national television network and one on a regional network. Each broadcast took place on different days between November 12 and November 20.

While the state bears the cost of television and radio propaganda, and pays for the expenses of distributing electoral literature, the candidate must pay the cost of printing his own voting ballots, posters, and pamphlets. If the candidate polls more than 5 per cent of the votes on the first ballot, such expenses are refunded. Before 1958 the candidate was reimbursed for gasoline expenses up to a maximum set for each district on the basis of population and geography, but since the adoption of single-member districts all traveling costs must be borne by the candidate.

Violation of the rules concerning electoral propaganda may result in the unseating of a candidate by the Constitutional Council and he may also be punished in criminal courts by a fine of $600 to $1,600 and imprisonment from fifteen days to three months. Two deputies were unseated by the Constitutional Council following the election of 1958. The council which studied more than two hundred cases ruled that violation of the electoral propaganda code was not sufficient for cancelation of the election; required was the belief on the part of the council that the result of the election would have been different had the violation not occurred.

Notwithstanding many loopholes, the law is effective in controlling radio and television propaganda and in limiting the cost of a competition which, otherwise, might be too heavy to bear not only for independent candidates but even for some political parties.

The $200 deposited by each candidate is refunded if the candidate obtains more than 5 per cent of the votes. Spurious candidates are a limited source of income to the state; they help to cover part of the cost of mailing electoral propaganda. In 1958, on the first ballot 435 candidates, that is 14 per cent of all candidates, lost their deposits.

### *Voting*

As a rule voting is personal. The vote by mail is limited to certain categories of invalids and to salesmen, newspapermen, agricultural or industrial workers momentarily displaced, and to some categories of transport employees among others. A wider use is made of voting by proxy. It applies to French citizens in foreign countries and to members of the armed forces outside metropolitan France.

Voting takes place on a Sunday in public places such as town halls or public schools. It is illustrative of a French conception of the state and of the separation of public and private matters that the setting up of polling stations in private homes, as done in the United States, would be shocking to a Frenchman. The electoral code describes with some precision the material organization of the vote, the type of ballot box to be used, the kind of slot it should have; it tells how there should be two locks, how the keys should be held one by the president, the other by the older member of the polling committee, and what should be done if the two keys cannot be produced when the time comes to open the ballot box.

From the voter's point of view, voting is a simple operation. From a table where each candidate has deposited a pile of ballots, the voter picks his preferred ballot plus, if he wants to preserve the secrecy of his vote, a number of ballots from other piles; he isolates himself in an electoral booth, puts the ballot of his choice in an envelope, then drops this envelope in the ballot box. Voting machines have never been used nor even contemplated. The voting ceremonial is simple. Among discarded ballots which accumulate on the floor, people wait their turn to enter the *isoloirs* which are made to look like modified versions of church confessionals, and after each vote has been cast, the president, to comply with the law, says "has voted."

### *The allotment of seats*

On the first ballot, a majority of the valid votes cast insures election. Relatively few are the candidates elected on this first run: in 1936 only 185 of 618 and in 1958, only 39 of 465. In the constituencies where no candidate has been elected a run off takes place the following Sunday. Candidates with less than 5 per cent of the votes must withdraw from the race. No new candidacy may be introduced. The candidate with the highest vote is elected.

## The Politics of Elections to the National Assembly

The dynamics of elections can be studied from two different points of view: that of the candidate and that of the voter.

The French electoral system with its small districts and low deposits induces any would-be politician to run for office. In 1958 about 7 per cent of the total vote went to candidates not associated with any nationally known party. But such candidates finally had less than 2 per cent of the seats. It is therefore wise on the part of a candidate to seek endorsement by one of the regular parties if he expects more from elections than the peculiar pleasure of offering oneself to public sarcasm or indifference. The politics of nomination vary from one party to the next. In some parties, especially Left-wing parties, endorsement for election to the National Assembly is given in recognition of a party career; in other parties, especially Right-wing parties, endorsement may be obtained sooner by prospective candidates provided they be well-known local personalities. One might say with some exaggeration that on the Left, the party makes the candidates while on the Right the candidates make the party.

In safe districts nomination is of course more difficult to obtain. When proportional representation was in use, the party list gave a formal aspect to the rank held by the various party candidates. Such listing of candidates had the advantage of regulating promotion. A candidate in, for example, a fourth position on the party list at a previous election was expected to move to a more favorable number if there were suitable openings on the list because of death or other reasons. The party problem of choosing new candidates was thus simplified. But this system had great disadvantages. It resulted in the hardening of party structures and in the aging of a party's representation in Parliament. The return to a single-member district system made political parties better able to rejuvenate themselves; it should normally reduce the duration of a prospective candidate's purgatory.

One of the surest ways of obtaining nomination for national elections is to demonstrate vote-getting ability at the local level. The importance of local elective positions is so great that many politicians even among the better known keep their local offices after they have been elected to parliament. E. Herriot remained mayor of Lyon; P. Mendès-France, mayor of Evreux; G. Mollet, mayor of Arras, even after they had become prime ministers. The citizens of an American city whose mayor would spend most of his time in the national or even in the state capital would probably feel deserted and would reject the deserter at the polls, but the citizens of a French city whose mayor sits in the National Assembly or the Senate and, even better, has a cabinet seat, feel flattered, represented, and closer to the springs of power and wealth. If a deputy in the National Assembly were to relinquish a local mayoralty he would in effect ask his betrayed city to choose his successor in parliament.

The obvious purpose of the candidate once nominated is to be elected if not on the first at least on the second ballot and to that effect to have as few competitors as possible appealing to his electorate and as many opponents as possible competing for electorates not transferable to him. A Right-wing candidate will want as few conservative competitors as possible but as many Left-wing opponents as possible. In order to split the opposite camp a candidate may fan the issues dividing it. For example a Communist candidate, in order to prevent a Socialist-MRP coalition or at least the abstention of one of these two parties from the race may choose to maintain the school question alive in his district.

Before the first ballot, candidates and parties often pass "drop-off" agreements (*désistements*). According to these bilateral or multilateral agreements only the candidate with the highest vote will contest the second ballot. These agreements are easier to conclude between well-disciplined parties having sufficient control over their candidates than between loosely organized parties.

Campaigning consists primarily in touring the constituency, talking to influential persons, and holding public meetings, usually at night in the public schools which are always available free of charge. These meetings are badly attended. Their major defect is that they are too long and that they attract almost exclusively the voters who have already made up their minds and who have come either to heckle or to give the speaker an audience. Matters of national interest are discussed but the candidate prefers to concentrate on local problems because such questions have often greater appeal to the public and because with an eye on the second ballot he must think of rallying the electorates of other parties.

Regional newspapers, dailies and weeklies, play an important role in the campaign. A candidate sometimes may have to buy space to have his *communiqués* printed, but independent newspapers do little advertising of candidates, and opinion papers support, of course, the candidates of their own choice. Before the war, the control of many local papers by the Radicals was an element of their strength in the provinces. The control of a large number by the Communist party since the Second World War contributed to the electoral gains they made outside urban centers. Some newspapers are controlled by prominent politicians; the *Dépèche de Toulouse* by Radical J. Baylet; the *Méri-*

*dional* by UNR J. Fraissinet; F. Mitterand publishes a small weekly, the *Courrier de la Niévre* and R. Pléven, the *Petit Bleu des Côtes du Nord*. Without having actual control of the publication, other politicians are supported by local newspapers devoted to their cause. A good case study of the importance of a weekly in building up a candidate could be made of *Eure Eclair* which for three years promoted R. Montagne before he defeated Mendès-France in 1958.

Most candidates agree that an "American" type of campaigning would not be rewarding. It is generally thought that a candidate must give the impression that he is like a reliable lawyer, that he does not wish to sell himself like a product, that he does not throw money lavishly into the campaign, that he is simple but not folksy. Speaking proper French is not a disadvantage, but the knowledge of local *patois* may be helpful. The candidate usually avoids forcing the campaign into the intimacy of the home. Relatively little use is made of canvassing.

The campaigns *à l'américaine* waged in 1956 by R. Hersant in Seine-et-Oise and P. Clostermann in Paris make one wonder whether the candidate's general hostility to an advertising kind of propaganda is not a rationalization of their lack of financial means more than a true appreciation of the electorate's maturity. The use of free movies with Miss Lollobrigida by Hersant (a professional publicity man) and sky writing by Clostermann seem not only to have pleased their constituents but also to have been effective. The dislike for canvassing may also be unjustified. Provided the canvasser knows how to present himself, canvassing can be and has indeed been used quite successfully in some districts.

In 1958, Hersant used another technique, reminiscent of the food baskets of nineteenth-century American bosses. Together with Strauss, a candidate in a neighboring district, Hersant had the following announcement distributed throughout his constituency:

> We wish to know our friends. After our election, we shall have many friends. We wish now to know those who desire our victory on November 23.

With this in mind we have decided to found the "Robert Hersant—Robert Strauss club" for the purpose of grouping our friends of the first hour!

Each member will receive a membership card. He will have a free subscription to the club's newspaper. He will be entitled to the use of the legal service of the club which will defend his interests free of charge. He will receive a buying card entitling him to between 5 per cent and 10 per cent reduction at a great number of the area's businesses, themselves members of the club. In a time of need, (old age, sickness) he will receive the help of the club's social service.[11]

But such advertising techniques are rarely used.

Increasingly, organized debates between competing candidates enliven campaigns and draw better attendances to public meetings. However, the great number of parties contesting elections would render difficult the systematic use of panel discussion campaigns of the Swedish model.

If the first ballot is inconclusive, candidates and parties have to make one of three choices: to remain in the race, to withdraw from the race, to withdraw in favor of another candidate. A candidate's course of action may be determined by a drop-off agreement, but such an agreement does not have legal authority.

Negotiations for withdrawing candidates are usually conducted by party headquarters on a *département* and sometimes on a national basis. Ideologically close to party *B*, party *A* will ask its own candidates to withdraw when they are less favored than *B*'s candidates and vice versa. Complications arise in practice. District seven of Bouches-du-Rhône, in 1958, may illustrate the difficulty. On the first ballot the votes were distributed as follows: [12]

| | |
|---|---|
| Communist | 12,848 |
| Socialist | 9,570 |
| UNR | 7,716 |
| Left-wing Gaullist | 4,468 |
| Poujadist | 592 |

All non-Communist candidates agreed that the objective was to prevent the Communist from coming on top on the second ballot. The Socialist took the position that since he, himself, was the most favored of all non-Communist candidates, he should have the privilege of fighting the Communist on the second ballot. But the UNR objected that although personally having 2,000 votes less than the Socialist, he was more likely to obtain on the second ballot the support of the 592 Poujadists and of the 4,400 Left-wing Gaullists. Consequently, he refused to withdraw hoping that some Socialist voters would realize that he had a better chance of winning than the Socialist candidate. On the second ballot the Communist was elected.

The candidate who on the first ballot obtains a number of votes which excludes his victory on the second ballot may in certain cases play the kingmakers. Assuming that he has a faithful electorate ready to follow his advice, he may ask his voters to support on the second ballot the candidate of his choice. If he suspects that his electors have already made up their minds on their second choice and if he, the candidate, does not agree with his voters on this point, he may try to neutralize his own electorate by remaining in the race. In the second district of Côte d'Or (1958) two candidates had come ahead and had a chance of winning the seat, an Independent (12,000 votes) and a UNR (10,000 votes). With no chance of winning, a Socialist (6,000) could take one of two steps. Knowing his electorate he could first of all withdraw from the competition, with the effect that the UNR would be elected; or, he could run on the second ballot for the sole purpose of preventing his votes being transferred to the UNR and thus insure the victory of the Independent. The Socialist took this latter course; the Independent was elected. More generally in 1958 the Communist party, had they wanted, could have caused a Socialist victory had they withdrawn their candidates in the districts where they themselves held no prospect of gaining seats. Communist leaders knew that left to itself the Communist electorate, in the absence of a Communist candidate, would turn to a Socialist, as it did for example in the third district of Nord. Communist leaders preferred to have a conservative rather than a Socialist parliament. Acceptance of such tactics by the Communist electorate is perfectly logical.

MONEY, AND ELECTIONS TO THE NATIONAL ASSEMBLY

In the absence of any reliable information on party finances, any estimate of election costs must be taken with reservation. Under the system of proportional representation campaigns were probably much more expensive than under the present single-member district system, but even then the cost of elections was relatively low. The most expensive campaign in 1956 was probably that arranged by Hersant who is said to have spent fifty million francs (about $100,000). However, this is exceptional. An average campaign in the same election must have cost one or two millions per district, that is to say, between one hundred and two hundred million francs nationally ($200,000 to $400,000) to be borne either by the candidates or the party organizations. National Headquarters contribute more or less to the campaign according to the parties concerned. Their main help is in the sending of party propaganda and in the financing of local campaign chests. It is estimated that for the 1956 campaign, the Radical national organization had an election budget of $400,000 which is double the yearly budget required to maintain the national headquarters. Political parties and candidates may indirectly benefit from the financing of newspapers favorable to the party. Before the campaign of 1956, the weekly *L'Express* was turned into a daily at an estimated cost of about forty million francs ($80,000).[13] For the same election, as well as in 1958, the Poujadists with the daily *Fraternité Matin* also incurred heavy expenses.

The sources of financial support are kept secret. The parties and candidates are under no legal obligation to publish the source or amount of funds spent for the types of propaganda not regulated by law, in fact practically any means of propaganda other than the candidate's personal posters and pamphlets. There are no legal limits to the contributions made either by trade unions or professional organizations. The bulk of the money for parties other than the Communists, comes probably from the CNPF (*Conseil National du Patronat Français*) and its affiliated professional unions. It often subsidizes more than one party, preferably Right-wing and Center parties but also, sometimes, Socialist candidates when the latter happen to be in a better position to defeat a Communist.

## Elections from the Voter's Standpoint

For a voter confronted by a number of candidates which is rarely under five and sometimes over ten, the two-ballot system has definite advantages. On the basis of the results of the first ballot, the voter may reconsider and transfer his support from his originally preferred candidate to another in a better position to win. Voting in the thirty-third district of Seine in 1958 may be taken as an example:

TABLE 7

Voting in Thirty-third District of Seine, 1958

| Party | 1st ballot | 2d ballot |
|---|---|---|
| Communist | 18,492 | 19,798 |
| UNR | 12,487 | 21,921, elected |
| Socialist | 8,296 | 4,942 |
| MRP | 4,334 | withdrew |
| Radical | 2,201 | withdrew |
| Others | 962 | withdrew |
| Total | 46,772 | 46,661 |

Not only the Radical and the MRP voters but also a fraction of the Socialist electorate transferred their support to the UNR after the first ballot had proved (and probably only because such proof had been made) that their own candidates could not expect to beat the Communist. The two-ballot system has thus the advantage of enabling the voter to choose the candidate he likes best on the first ballot without its resulting in the election of the candidate he likes least as might happen if there were only one ballot. True, if there had been only one ballot the voting pattern probably would have been different. Maybe neither the Radical nor the MRP would have contested the election, and even if they had, their electoral support might have been less. But whatever be the case, the voter would not have been able to determine his vote on the basis of the political preferences of the whole constituency as well as on the basis of his own preferences. The two-ballot system renders easier for the electorate a meaningful and rational choice. The voter has two basic elements on which to make a choice: his own political preferences and those of his neighbors. The example already given indicates how the regrouping of votes takes place after the first ballot. A further example can be taken from the fifty-third district of Seine.

TABLE 8

VOTING IN FIFTY-THIRD DISTRICT OF SEINE, 1958

| Party | 1st ballot | 2d ballot |
|---|---|---|
| Communist | 13,216 | 16,231 |
| Left Center (CR) | 7,877 | 8,220 |
| UNR | 7,797 | 22,435, elected |
| Independent | 6,636 | withdrew |
| Independent Socialist | 5,165 | 489 |
| Socialist | 4,171 | 3,893 |
| MRP | 3,120 | withdrew |
| Left-wing Gaullist | 1,429 | withdrew |
| Diverse | 2,169 | withdrew |

The candidate finally elected had come only in third position on the first ballot but was in fact preferred as an alternative choice by most voters who, on the basis of the first ballot, decided to change their preference. Had the runoff been limited to the first two candidates as in some American primaries, the candidate preferred by a plurality of the district could not have been elected.

This last example, however, can also be used to illustrate that if after the first ballot the electorate is offered too many alternatives, the purpose of the two-ballot system may be defeated. It is remarkable that only one of the most-favored non-Communist candidates on the first ballot gained any significant number of votes on the second ballot. Had the transferred votes been more evenly split between the Left Center and the UNR candidates, the Communist might have been elected. This happened in the seventh district of Bouches du Rhône:

TABLE 9

VOTING IN SEVENTH DISTRICT OF BOUCHES-DU-RHÔNE, 1958

| Party | 1st ballot | 2d ballot |
|---|---|---|
| Communist | 12,348 | 14,266, elected |
| Socialist | 9,570 | 12,177 |
| UNR | 7,716 | 10,887 |
| Left Center | 4,468 | withdrew |
| Poujadist | 592 | withdrew |

The second ballot reduces the chances of election of one of the district's least-favored candidates but does not eliminate this possibility altogether. To do that, one would have to hold as many ballots as necessary until a candidate would have a majority after elimination of the least-preferred candidates. A three-ballot system limiting the third ballot to the two candidates coming on top might produce almost similar results.

## ELECTIONS TO THE NATIONAL ASSEMBLY: AN EVALUATION

Hindrances to the effectual working of French parliamentary institutions since the Second World War have been many. The faults lay with the constitution, with the party system, but also with the electoral system. Instead of producing coherent majorities, elections have increased political divisions. Instead of strengthening the democratic process they corroded it. After an election, the French electorate is usually seized with this hopeless disappointment which must have been that of Sisyphus. It is not surprising then that this electorate is tempted to give itself a holiday from political responsibilities. One of the reasons for the electorate's feeling dissatisfied with its task is that the voter was rarely given the possibility of fulfilling his task intelligently. The voter should be in a position to judge governments on their records. Under the system of coalition cabinets and changing majorities this voter could not clearly decide either for or against the government. The responsibility for this state lay of course mainly in a faulty constitutional structure and in a multiparty system. But one may also ask whether the electoral system was used as effectively as possible to improve the working of the parliamentary system. Both proportional representation and the *scrutin d'arrondissement* have the advantage of enabling the voter to make a clear and rational choice. But the nation does not necessarily find its interests in the facilitating of the voters' choice. Proportional representation is dangerous when parties may take advantage of the system and obtain representation in parliament for the sole sake of destroying parliamentary institutions. Germany is wise in combining proportional representation with a constitution calling for the dissolution of parties opposed to democracy. In France, in the absence of any legal interdiction against nondemocratic parties, proportional representation gave a large share of the seats in the National Assembly to the Communists. Proportional representation with *apparentement* would have been better adapted to the needs of France if the Center parties had shown greater desire to collaborate together. But even the *apparentement* could not have led to the forming of stable parliamentary majorities. Whatever the merits of proportional representation it was not suitable for France.

The *scrutin d'arrondissement* does not have as PR, the disadvantage of enabling undemocratic minority candidates to gain any sizable share of parliamentary seats. But notwithstanding this and other advantages such as enabling the voter to make a better-reasoned choice, the *scrutin d'arrondissement* has had a disastrous effect on the parliaments of the Third Republic and may well have the same effect under the Fifth Republic. It weakens national parties and strengthens local machine and pressure groups. In the opinion of A. Pinay as well as J. Jaures, under the *scrutin d'arrondissement* the representative becomes his constituency's lackey; he becomes the servant of a multiplicity of local pressure groups. On the other hand, in a small district the representative is better able to build his own electoral machine. Less dependent on his party for reëndorsement he may more easily ignore his party's caucus's instructions, thus adding to parliamentary confusion.

### Electoral Reform

Among the systems proposed as alternatives either to classical proportional representation and the *scrutin d'arrondissement*, the Debré, the Barrachin, and the Coty systems should be mentioned.

Before the electoral reform in 1958, M. Debré proposed a two-ballot majority system in multimember constituencies. It was not retained because of opposition from a majority of de Gaulle's cabinet and because de Gaulle himself would have preferred to see a parliament more evenly balanced between Left-wing and Right-wing parties rather than a parliament controlled by the UNR which, of all parties, was expected to have benefited most from such a system. The main advantage of Debré's proposal is in the use of large-scale constituencies (*départements*). It would reduce the influence of local pressure groups and strengthen national party organizations but might not necessarily reduce the number of political parties. A potential disadvantage would be to increase the sectional character of each major party; the Socialists might become the party of the Northwest and the South; the Radicals the party of the Southwest; the MRP the party of Alsace-Lorraine and the West; the UNR the party of the Paris area.

The Coty system of 1948 is a combination of the Debré system and proportional representation with *apparentement*. Each *département* would elect a number of representatives determined by population. Each voter would have as many votes as there would be seats; he could dispose of his votes as he liked but could not give more than one to a candidate. Candidates obtaining a majority on the first ballot would be elected. A runoff would be required if seats remained unfilled. On the second ballot parties and candidates could form coalition tickets. Candidates obtaining a majority would be elected. The remaining seats, if any, would be allocated among the lists according to proportional representation. The advantage of the Coty system over that of Debré is the broadening of the geographical basis of party representation; but the problem of multipartism would still be unsolved.

The Barrachin proposal was in the form of an amendment to the present *scrutin d'arrondissement*, to the effect that on the first ballot a plurality of 40 per cent would have been enough for election. Such percentage could have been lowered eventually. Barrachin's purpose is to incorporate some advantages of a one-ballot system without some of its drawbacks; he expects that political parties and candidates would compromise before the first ballot in order to prevent the election of political opponents, and that, consequently, the number of parties contesting the first ballot would be reduced. By maintaining the percentage required for election on the first ballot relatively high, say 30 per cent to 40 per cent, one would prevent the winner being a candidate with little support in the constituency. But the Barrachin proposal falls short of avoiding the major defects of *scrutin d'arrondissement.* It would not free the representative from local interests, and while reducing the number of candidates in each district, would not necessarily reduce the number of parliamentary groups.

Other proposals put forward at various times include the one-ballot plurality single-member district on the British and American models, the single transferable vote on the Irish model, the alternative vote as used for elections to the Australian Senate until 1949, and the combination of proportional representation and single-member districts as in Germany.

From what has been said it would appear that an electoral system in France should be designed to avoid representing non-democratic parties, to limit and strengthen political parties in order to produce more coherent and stable majorities in the parliament, and to give the representative as much of a national and as little of a local outlook as possible.

Theoretically such results can be obtained by law. One might compel the electorate to give a parliamentary majority to a single party, for example by asking the electorate to designate by transferable vote in a nation-wide primary the two parties preferred by most voters and then limiting the electoral contest to these two parties.

But France like other democracies is not prepared to consider the regulation of her party system as much a matter of public law as the organization of the legislative, of the executive or of the judiciary. Even if she were prepared to do so, it is unlikely that any device limiting drastically the number of political parties, disciplining them, and substituting a national to a local outlook among representatives, would be acceptable to a nation used for so long to multipartism, parliamentary freedom of vote, and sectionalism. France would rather seek governmental stability by revising her constitutional structures instead of her party system. If she were offered the choice between the British and the American types of government, she would probably choose that of the United States where governmental stability does not result from the domination of the legislature by a well-disciplined party but from the existence of an independent executive.

### Elections in Algeria and Sahara

To dispose of an oddity, one may mention the district of La Saoura in Sahara. Only in this constituency is there an electoral system similar to that of Great Britain and the United States. Students of electoral behavior may regret that one of the rare experiments made by France with a single-member district one-ballot plurality system be relegated to the African desert.

The other eighteen districts of Algeria and the Sahara have a one-ballot plurality list system. All seats go to the list of candidates at the top. Each list has to be composed of members of the two communities known as common-law and local-law communities but usually referred to as the European and the Moslem communities, although a small number of Moslems belong to the first group. Each district must elect a set number of Europeans and Moslems; Algiers-town for example must elect two Europeans and two Moslems; Tizi-Ouzou, one European and three Moslems; Oran-town, two Europeans and one Moslem. For the whole of Algeria twenty-one representatives must belong to the European group, forty-five to the Moslem group. For Sahara, the figures are one and three. A Moslem with common-law status may, as an exception, choose to run either as a European or as a Moslem. Lists without the required number of candidates from either groups are not valid. The Algerian electoral system obliges the two communities to form electoral teams and prevents the creation of purely communal parties. The system is also used to give the numerically inferior European community a reserved number of seats higher than the number to which the group would be entitled on a strictly proportional basis. Although they account for about 13 per cent of the total Algerian population, they have 30 per cent of the seats. On the other hand, one could argue that if the representation of each community had not been made compulsory, the Moslems, because of the conditions of insecurity created by the war and because of a lesser political awareness, might have allowed the European community to monopolize parliamentary representation even in purely Moslem areas. It remains that the legal ratio between the two groups might have been made less favorable to the Europeans and thus more in keeping with the promises of equality between Moslems and non-Moslems. Also, the representation of Algeria and Sahara is proportionally inferior to that of metropolitan France. On a strict population basis Algeria should have 17 per cent of the seats in the National Assembly, that is to say ninety seats instead of its present seventy. But if only the population of voting age is taken into account, Algeria is about proportionally represented.

### *The politics of elections in Algeria*

So short has been the experience of Algeria with universal suffrage of men and women, with a single electoral college, and with untampered electoral returns, that no clear picture of electioneering on that side of the Mediterranean emerges.

In the cities and in the coastal areas where they are settled in large numbers, Algerians of European stock have the political initiative. As long as the Algerian conflict is not settled Moslems are unlikely to withdraw from their electoral passivity. Administrative pressure is usually required before they run as candidates or turn out at the polls in large numbers. Outside the cities, the purpose of elections remains obscure to a population still largely illiterate.

The system of "official candidacies" is widely used in Algeria. Even if the army or the civil administration wanted to remain aloof from politics, they could not do so, because their neutrality would be interpreted as hostility toward a given candidate. Official candidacies, as under the Second Empire in France, are now used in Algeria; firstly to select a new political elite and give it some prestige, secondly to introduce universal suffrage in a population not yet ready for it.

If peace is restored to Algeria, if a Moslem intelligentsia accepts a policy of integration, if in other words Moslem leaders decide to draw all the advantages from their French citizenship, the yet apathetic mass of Moslems might turn to Moslem leaders for guidance rather than to the administration. France, in the past so divided in politics, was unified in culture. A minority problem would be new to her. It is yet too early to forecast how the Moslem community would act politically. Algeria is in more than one respect the unknown of French politics.

# 15 *Organization, Powers, and Functions of the National Assembly*

## Membership

The National Assembly is composed of 552 members elected for five years. Metropolitan France elects 465 deputies, Algeria 67, the Sahara 4, the overseas *départements* (Guadeloupe, Guyane, Martinique, and Réunion) 10, and the overseas territories (Saint Pierre and Miquelon, Somaliland, Comores, New Caledonia, Polynesia) 6.

Although lower than under the Fourth Republic, the number of deputies remains high.[1] The example of the American Senate might have led the constituents of 1958 to think that a large number of parliamentarians is not necessary either for the sake of committee work or for the sake of increasing the statistical chances of obtaining statesmen of high caliber. A small Assembly of a hundred members where each deputy could employ four to five legislative assistants would probably be preferable and no more expensive for the quality of debates and of legislation than an Assembly of five hundred representatives. But such an Assembly would also through its small membership gain in power and prestige. The constituents of 1958 although claiming that they wanted to increase the prestige of parliament were primarily concerned with weakening the legislative branch in favor of the executive. A small National Assembly would have been in contradiction with such a goal. The Assembly remains an unwieldy and slow moving organ of legislation.

On a population basis, metropolitan France is overrepresented in the Assembly as compared to overseas France; but not to such a point as to deny influence to the latter. With 78.1 per cent of the total population, France has 82.2 per cent of the seats, Algeria and the Sahara 18.2 and 12.9; the overseas *départements* 1.5 and 1.8; the overseas territories 0.7 and 1.1.

## Organization

The National Assembly elects its own chairman who, according to constitutional requirements, is elected for the whole legislature, five years, except in the event of dissolution. The Assembly's standing orders require that the chairman obtain an absolute majority on the first two ballots, a plurality being sufficient on the third. Election to the chairmanship is important because of the powers and prestige attached to the office, and also because such election is the first important vote of a legislature—a vote which clarifies the balance of power in a new assembly following a general election. Since the chairman is selected by secret ballot, the degree of cohesion of the various parliamentary groups is tested. In 1958 the election to the chairmanship of the first National Assembly of the Fifth Republic served to establish which of the UNR and the Independents (CNIP) was the parliament's controlling party. The UNR was the larger of the two groups but did not have enough votes to obtain an absolute majority. The CNIP tried to contest with the

UNR the role of Center group able to rally the Algerian and MRP votes. Four candidates contested the election: J. Chaban-Delmas for the UNR, P. Reynaud for the Independents, M. Lejeune for the Socialists, and F. Grenier for the Communists. The first ballot gave the following results:

| | |
|---|---|
| Chaban-Delmas (UNR) | 259 |
| Reynaud (Independent) | 168 |
| Lejeune (Socialist) | 89 |
| Grenier (Communist | 12 |
| Others | 13 |

The UNR had obtained about fifty more votes than the total membership of their parliamentary group; the Independents about sixty more. The CNIP had failed in its bid to rally sufficient support in order to challenge seriously a UNR leadership. Rather than face certain defeat on the third ballot, Reynaud withdrew from the contest, thus enabling Chaban-Delmas to be elected by an absolute majority of 355 votes on the second ballot; however, this second ballot showed that a large minority of Independents had preferred to vote for the Socialist candidate rather than for Chaban-Delmas. Lejeune obtained 132 votes, Grenier 16, and various other candidates 13. Such a split in the Independent's vote could be interpreted as a warning to the UNR, that the CNIP was not prepared to support them unconditionally and in particular that they did not quite trust Gaullist Algerian policy.[2] But above all the election established the UNR as the leader of the parliamentary majority.

The major duty of the National Assembly chairman is to administer the standing orders. With regard to debates, the powers of the French chairman are in no way comparable to the powers of the speaker in British or American practice. The debates are organized beforehand by the chairmen's conference which is controlled by the government and the caucus leaders. Furthermore the National Assembly standing orders give little leeway to the chairman for exercising influence through rulings from the chair. But unlike his English counterpart, by the constitution the French chairman is given powers unconnected with the coördination of parliamentary debates. The chairman of the National Assembly selects three members of the nine-man Constitutional Council and shares with the chairman of the Senate, the premier and the president, the right of appeal before this council. For administering the rules, the chairman is assisted by two committees of great importance, the bureau and the chairmen's conference.

The bureau is composed of six vice-chairmen, three *questeurs* and fourteen secretaries. Under the Fourth Republic the members of the bureau were elected on the basis of proportional representation of all parliamentary groups. The principle is now a majority election but is not strictly adhered to. In 1958 the National Assembly reverted to the system of the Third Republic which was to obtain representation corresponding to the size of each parliamentary group. Before the election of the bureau by the whole house, the National Assembly chairman called a meeting of parliamentary group chairmen. The committee thus formed agreed to the following distribution of seats: vice-chairmen: one UNR, two Independents, one MRP, one Algerian, one Socialist; questors: one UNR, one Independent, one MRP; secretaries: five UNR, two Algerians, and one each for the other groups including the Communists. Each group proceeded to designate its candidates. The members so designated were then formally elected to the Assembly. The agreement reached was broken only with respect to the Communist candidate. The Algerians, having put forward three candidates instead of two, obtained the election of three secretaries thus depriving the Communists of representation on the bureau.

The members of the bureau have specific duties. The vice-chairmen take the chair in the absence of the chairman, the *questeurs* watch over administrative matters and are the Assembly's bursars, the secretaries help keep the agendas, tabulating and recording the votes and drafting the minutes. The most significant powers of the bureau are exercised as a body. The bureau rules on the receivability of private members' bills. If the bureau rules that the text submitted to them is in violation of the constitutional rule that parliamentarians may not reduce revenues or increase expenditures, the text is not received. This power to scotch legislation may remain a dead letter if the majority of the bureau favors expansion of parliamentary powers; it may on the contrary be used to maintain parliamentary initiative within constitutional bounds or even restrict it further if the bureau is controlled by a majority sympathetic to the executive. Between sessions the bureau is the Assembly's representative in protecting parliamentary immunities. A deputy may not be arrested without the bureau's consent, except *flagrante delicto.*

The chairmen's conference is composed of the chairman and the vice-chairmen of the Assembly, the chairmen of the standing committees, the *rapporteur* general of the finance committee, and the chairmen of parliamentary groups. The government, which has to be kept informed of the conference meetings, may send a representative. The meetings are held weekly to establish the Assembly's agenda. The government representative may request that government bills be put on the agenda on the dates of his choice. After priority has been given to the government, the conference is free to draw the agenda as it wishes. Decisions are taken by a majority vote, each parliamentary group chairman having as many votes as he has members in his group who are not already on the committee. The conference is thus dominated by the caucus chairmen. The agenda prepared by the chairmen's conference has to be submitted to the Assembly for approval. The Assembly may not amend that part of the agenda which was requested by the government but is free to modify the rest. However, the Assembly practically never does change the proposed agenda.

The bureau is in a sense the administrative head of the Assembly, the chairmen's conference is its political head. This division at the top is paralleled by the division of parliamentarians into legislative committees and parliamentary groups.

### *Legislative committees*

The constitution provides for two types of committees, the ad hoc committees and the standing committees limited to six.

The reason for restricting the number of standing committees was a desire to reduce their importance in the law-making process. Some of the constituents thought that by making the standing committees large unwieldy bodies one would give a premium to temporary ad hoc committees and thus reduce the political importance of standing committees which had become a source of constant annoyance for the ministers. Another reason was to avoid too great a specialization and prevent committees from acting as representatives for private interests, and thus forming pressure groups within parliament, such as the committee on pensions or the committee on beverages and alcoholic drinks.

The constitution restricts the standing committees to six, but leaves the Assembly free to define the area of specialization of each.

In 1959 the Assembly's standing orders created the following:

The Committee on Cultural, Family, and Social Affairs, the jurisdiction of which extends to education, arts, sport, youth, culture; population, family, public health, civil and military pensions, social security, and information;

The Committee on Foreign Affairs;

The Committee on National Defense and the Armed Forces;

The Committee on Finance, Economics, and Economic Planning;

The Committee on the Constitution, Legislation and General Administration, which covers: constitutional, organic, and electoral laws; standing orders; the judiciary; civil, administrative, and criminal legislation; petitions; general administration of the Republic and of local collectivities;

The Committee on Production and Trade, which covers agriculture, fisheries, commerce, industry and energy, labor, means of communication, tourism, public works and equipment, planning, urbanism, housing, and construction.

The first and the last mentioned each have 120 members; the committee on the constitution and the committee on national defense have ninety members; the two remaining, the most important, the foreign-affairs committee and the finance committee, have only 60 members.

The members of standing committees are selected by the parliamentary groups which are allocated a number of seats proportional to their size. A group accounting for 20 per cent of the Assembly's total membership receives 20 per cent of the seats on all of the standing committees.[3] Trading of seats between groups may lead to the overrepresentation of certain parties on certain committees and to their underrepresentation on others, but such exchanges, frequent under the Fourth Republic, are now less likely, the committees having a broad scope of competence. The proportional distribution of seats is made solely between the political formations which qualify as parliamentary groups; that is, those with at least thirty members. In 1959, after the proportional allocation of seats to the various parliamentary groups, twelve committee seats were still vacant. Such seats go to "isolated" deputies, elected by a majority vote of the whole assembly. These individual elections may take on a particular significance when influential parliamentarians happen not to be affiliated to any parliamentary group. In 1959, the election of G. Bidault to the foreign affairs committee by 434 out of 435 votes was a personal success for the former president of the MRP.

Each standing committee elects a chairman, from three to four vice-chairmen and from two to four secretaries, depending on the size of the committee. In addition the finance committee elects a *rapporteur* general. Intracommittee elections are by majority vote but, as in the elections to the bureau, the committees satisfy the agreements passed by the various parliamentary groups. In 1959, negotiations between leaders of the major parliamentary groups led to an agreement giving Cultural Affairs, Constitutional Laws and Production to the UNR, National Defense and Finance to the Independents, and Foreign Affairs to the MRP.

Membership in a standing committee is no longer a deputy's right; there are only 540 committee seats for 552 members. The Communist deputies who had only ten deputies in 1958 did not obtain representation.

During parliamentary sessions, Tuesday, Wednesday, Thursday, and Friday mornings are set aside for committee meetings.

During as well as between sessions, committee meetings are convened at the request of either the government, the committee chairman, or of a majority of committee members. The committeemen who fail, without excuse, to come to three consecutive meetings, are automatically expelled from the committee and may not be replaced until the following year. Furthermore the absentee's salary is cut by about one-tenth until the following October session. When excused, a member may delegate his right to vote to one of his colleagues but no member may hold more than one proxy vote.

The large membership of standing committees tends to render their debates less informal than under the two preceding constitutions. The committee chairman may have to limit drastically the time allotted for the discussion. A committee such as that on production and trade has more members than the American or the Dutch Senate. The main advantage of discussion in committees as opposed to discussion in the house is that, first, standing orders do not govern the debates and, secondly, that the debates are not public. Discussion can be organized more freely and outside the pressure of public opinion.[4] Decisions are taken by a majority vote. Unlike in the United States, the committee chairman is only *primus inter pares;* he could not stand in the way of the committee's majority. Among the committees, one—the finance committee—has grown to a position of greater influence and prestige. The bureau of the finance committee may, for example, on its own initiative, kill a private member's bill, thought in violation of the rule that deputies may not reduce revenues or increase expenditures, even after such bill had been considered acceptable by the bureau of the Assembly.

The drafters of the constitution intended that on important questions, and especially on those requiring speedy solution, use would be made of ad hoc committees. The government and the Assembly are privileged to decide that a bill or resolution should be studied by such a committee. When the request is made by the government, the Assembly has to comply. Ad hoc committees have no fixed membership: they are elected by a majority vote of the whole house. As in standing committees, the number of seats reserved to each parliamentary group is decided beforehand on the basis of an agreement between group chairmen. The first ad hoc committee under the new constitution—the committee on standing orders—comprised thirty members and thirty alternates selected on the same proportional basis as the standing committees. Ad hoc committees are not necessarily selected from the membership of the corresponding standing committees. Only six of the thirty members of the committee on standing orders belonged to the committee on the constitution.

### The Parliamentary Groups

Not all parties represented in the National Assembly qualify as parliamentary groups, because a group must have at least thirty members.

In the 1959 National Assembly there were six parliamentary groups: the Socialists, the MRP, the UNR, the Algerians, the Independents, and the Democratic Entente, a group of Center and Right of Center deputies belonging mostly to the Radical and Center Republican parties. The privileges of parliamentary groups in selecting committee members, in the selection of the bureau, in the control of the agenda, in the selection of representatives to international bodies such as the European Assembly or to other French constitutional organs such as the Senate of the Community are such as to give a definite advantage to the member of a parliamentary group over those who by force or by choice remain isolated.[5] The rise of parliamentary groups in the last fifty years has been constant. Under the Third Republic they played such a minor role that members of parliament were allowed to belong to more than one. The Fourth and Fifth republics forbade multiparliamentary group membership and recognized such groups as part of the regular legislative machinery, giving them an importance almost as great as that of the committees.

Parliamentary groups are required to select a chairman, to register their list of members with the bureau of the Assembly, and to publish a declaration of political principles. In all other respects the parliamentary groups are free to organize themselves as they wish. Some, such as the UNR or the SFIO, correspond to a caucus, others are loose confederations of caucuses such as the Democratic Entente. Finally there are caucuses not affiliated with any parliamentary group; the Communists after 1958 for example.

Caucuses and consequently parliamentary groups belong either to the rubber-stamp, the club-like, or the parliament type.

An example of the first category is provided by the Communist caucus. It has little initiative; its actions are controlled by the party secretariat; its votes, its legislative or political moves are determined by the party's headquarters. The Communist rank-and-file deputy has no autonomy of action; he reads prepared speeches approved by the party leadership; impromptu interventions are restricted to caucus leaders. This lack of freedom makes the Communist one of the dullest of parliamentarians. Few are the Communists who like Duclos are at ease in the house and succeed in gaining the attention of their colleagues.

Classical examples of club-like caucuses are the Radicals. They do not attempt to enforce any voting discipline in the house. However, they organize caucus meetings with debates and votes for the sole purpose of informing their members; they give them a chance to discuss issues of common interest and to influence their colleagues. In 1957 Mendès-France made an attempt to discipline the Radical parliamentary group and obtained a promise from Radical parliamentarians that on important questions they would submit to caucus orders except that a representative could always choose to abstain. The effect of such an agreement was that if the majority of the caucus had decided a positive vote, the Radical deputy could abstain but not vote negatively. At the first serious test the agreement was broken. Having failed to have his party employ sanctions against those who had violated the agreement, Mendès-France soon afterward, for that and other reasons, abandoned the party leadership. The Radicals and the Independents who also form a club-like caucus adhere to the Burkean theory of representation that the deputy is the sole master of his votes.

The parliament type of caucus, of which the Socialists and to a lesser extent the UNR and the MRP are examples, is based on a different theory of representation, according to which the representative is the sole master of his vote in the caucus but in parliament acts according to the orders, not of his conscience, but of his party.

The leadership of the Socialist caucus, for example, is shared by a bureau and an executive committee (*Délégation éxécutive*). The bureau comprises a chairman, four vice-chairmen, a legislative secretary, a secretary-general and a treasurer. Together with the chairmen or senior Socialist members of the Assembly's standing committees, the bureau forms the executive committee. This committee decides on important matters; the bureau is entrusted with day-to-day caucus administration. The caucus chairman is usually selected informally by the most prominent parliamentary leaders; election by the caucus is a mere endorsement of the leaders' choice. Other bureau posts are often contested. The chairman, whose functions are mostly political, speaks for the parliamentary group in its relations with the government, with other parties and with the party machine. The vice-chairmen help him to carry out his political duties and assume also such chores as taking turns on the floor of the house to follow the proceedings. The secretary-general supervises a small caucus secretariat (three full-time employees in 1959). The secretarial facilities are used mostly by the caucus leaders and only occasionally by the rank and file. The legislative secretary coördinates the group's legislative work; he supervises the drafting of bills or amendments submitted by the Socialist parliamentary group and follows their progress through the various legislative stages.

Leadership positions in the caucus always go to influential party politicians, but the dominant personalities in the parliamentary group are not necessarily in the caucus executive which is in no way comparable to the British shadow cabinet. In order to prevent too great a concentration of powers and honors, a party may be unwilling to choose as caucus chairman a deputy already holding an important position in the party hierarchy. Such a deputy may also be unwilling to assume the time-consuming task of caucus leader. Guy Mollet, who became secretary-general of the SFIO in 1946, never sought the chairmanship of the Socialist parliamentary group and when he became prime minister in 1956 agreed to having such chairmanship given to one of his most vocal critics, R. Verdier. This was somewhat as though A. Bevan, left out of a Labour cabinet, had been made floor leader. The caucus chairmanship is only one among the positions which must be allocated to members of the party oligarchy. In the balancing of government, party machine, and caucus positions, the leadership of the parliamentary group may fall to a fraction supported only by a minority of the caucus.

The Socialist parliamentary group is organized to carry out the threefold function assigned to it: elective, legislative, and political.

The group's major elective role is the assigning of its members to the various committees. At the beginning of each parliament, the caucus secretariat draws a list of vacancies and asks new deputies and returning deputies who wish to change committee to state their preferences. The caucus leaders try to settle conflicting claims on a friendly basis, then submit the list of committee assignments to the caucus which has to approve or reject the whole list. A similar procedure is used for the selection of ad hoc committees and for the selection of representatives in the Senate of the Community, in the Assembly of the Council of Europe and in the Assembly of the Common Market organization.

To perform its legislative function the Socialist caucus operates as a parliament. All motions, bills, and amendments originating with a member of the group must first be sent to the caucus legislative secretary. He may either give his approval if the proposal is neither controversial nor important, or refer the matter either to the caucus bureau or to the caucus executive committee, which have then to make a series of decisions: first whether to give approval; secondly, if approved, whether to have the proposal introduced in the Assembly with the sole signature of its authors or to seek endorsement by the whole parliamentary group. The refusal to approve or the decision to seek caucus endorsement starts a deliberative process. If the members of the caucus executive disagree on a particular proposal or feel that they are not sufficiently informed, they often send the controversial proposal to one of the party's study groups (*sections d'études*), each of which is composed of parliamentarians and nonparliamentarians and is under the dual chairmanship of one of both types of member. The study group can only advise the caucus, but such advice carries much weight. To report on the proposal submitted to them or to defend their own proposals, the study groups may either ask their parliamentary chairman to report their conclusions to the caucus or they may choose to send their own *rapporteur*, not necessarily a parliamentarian, to speak before the caucus. The latter may either endorse without change or amend the texts submitted to them by the party study groups or by the caucus executive. Decisions are taken by a majority vote.

Socialists require bloc voting in parliament. Any member of the group who does not vote according to caucus orders or who does not show up for the vote without being excused by the caucus executive is automatically suspended for one month from all positions to which he had been elected by the caucus, such as caucus executive or Assembly committee assignments. He is also deprived of the right to vote in the caucus for the same length of time. In addition, the party executive may impose on the rebel a number of sanctions ranking from a reprimand to expulsion.

Rebellions against party orders have been frequent since the war. Fifty-three deputies refused to vote the EDC treaty in 1954, eighteen refused to vote the London and Paris agreements of 1954, nineteen did not vote extarordinary powers to the government in 1957. As a result the party is often obliged to expel rebels or to accept, as for the investiture of de Gaulle in 1958, that the deputies be not bound by bloc-voting rule. The degree of party cohesion then is high, usually over 90 per cent; rebels, rather than vote against their colleagues, usually choose to abstain.

For the most important political decisions, such as participation to a ministry and voting of confidence or nonconfidence in the government, the National Assembly caucus, the Senate caucus and the party executive committee meet jointly. Senators and nonparliamentarians are thus called to share in decisions expressly reserved to the deputies by the constitution. As there are only twenty-five nonparliamentarians on the party executive committee, parliamentarians can normally be expected to have a large majority on the joint committee, usually well over 80 per cent, but the rule that failing a two-thirds majority in the joint committee, the decision is taken by the party executive committee, invites the parliamentarians to settle their differences beforehand if they do not want the decision-making authority to be transferred from the caucus to the party machine. It may happen, as it indeed happened in 1958, that there are more Socialist senators than deputies.[6] The paradoxical effect of holding joint meetings of Senate and National Assembly caucuses is then, if the joint-meeting decisions are obeyed by the deputies, that the Socialist senators may be more powerful than the deputies in settling questions not within the Senate's powers, such as the overthrow of a government.

Other disciplined caucuses, such as the UNR and the MRP, have organizations basically similar to that of the SFIO, but with the major difference that, in the case of the UNR, the caucus, although theoretically autonomous, is in fact directed by the UNR ministers through the party's political committee; and with the other difference that, in the case of the MRP, bloc voting instead of being the rule, as it used to be in the early years of the Fourth Republic, has now become the exception.

## Functions and Powers of the National Assembly

The National Assembly has three major functions, elective, controlling, and legislative.

The Assembly selects from its members one-half the French representatives of the Senate of the Community, one-half the judges of the High Court of Justice, and one-half the French representatives in the European assemblies. Although selection is by majority vote, the Assembly usually does nothing more than endorse the choices made by the major parliamentary groups on a more or less proportional basis. Finally the Assembly's chairman selects three of the nine members of the Constitutional Council. Thus the Assembly, as under the Fourth Republic, still shares in the selection of some of the constitutional organs of government, but has lost the power it previously had of electing the prime minister. While under the Third and Fourth republics the president's nominee had to be endorsed by the National Assembly, the prime minister may now take office without the Assembly's endorsement and may retain his post as long as the Assembly has not overthrown him.

To control the government the Assembly may make use of various techniques. It may subject the government to questions and criticisms during legislative debates and more particularly during the examination of the budget. In addition, the Assembly may use its committees and the question period to obtain information on governmental or administrative activities.

The Assembly's legislative standing or ad hoc committees may request that a minister speak before them on a particular question and submit himself to the committee's queries. The minister's interview may turn into criticism of government policy. In 1959 one of the first acts of the foreign-affairs committee, after selecting a chairman, was to ask the foreign minister to appear before them. The ministers are under no obligation to comply, but would be unwise to delay too long their appearance before the committee. During the period of transition between the Fourth and Fifth republic, de Gaulle had forbidden his ministers to subject themselves to such questioning. This interdict was made possible because of the emergency powers delegated to the government. In normal times the premier could not ask his ministers to answer negatively the committees' calls without inviting serious reprisals.

The Assembly or its regular committees may set up special

committees of enquiry. Important as they may be for the information of deputies, such committees have never achieved in France the importance they have in the United States. One reason may be that the deputies had, and still have to a lesser extent, the use of more effective techniques to control the executive and to draw public attention to themselves. A motion of censure is more effective and more dramatic than the setting up of an investigating committee.

M. Debré who, while a senator, had made a most effective use of the question period, raised it to the rank of major device of parliamentary control in the constitution of 1958. Three types of questions are permissible: the written question, the oral question without debate, and the oral question with debate.

The written question is sent by a deputy to a minister and published in the *Journal Officiel.* The minister is expected to answer within a month but may simply say that public interest forbids him to answer, or he may ask that an additional month be allowed him to gather the information required. When a written question has not been answered on time, the author of the question is asked by the chairman of the Assembly whether the written question should be converted into an oral question. The minister's written answers are published in the *Journal Officiel.* Following are random types of written questions and answers.

*Question No. 1366 (1959).* Mr. Mainguy brings to the attention of the Minister for Education that the three young men interviewed on the French television network on June 5, 1959 . . . showed a remarkable ignorance. The questions asked bore on the major events of the last world war, the list of victors, and the existence of persons as well known as Hitler and Mussolini. He (the author of the question) asks whether French youth could not possibly be given some rudimentary information on this period which although recent is nonetheless of considerable historical importance and still conditions our whole existence.

*Answer:* The weakness in historical knowledge of three young men interviewed on television should not involve public education because we ignore the conditions of selection of the persons interviewed, their intellectual and school background; we do not even know whether they went through the public-education system. As for teaching the history of the last war, it is part of the school program at the primary as well as at the secondary level. It has an important part in the program of the graduating classes and in the program of the second baccalaureat.[7]

*Question No. 1323 (1959)*. Mr. Trémolet de Villers brings to the attention of the Minister of Finance the following case: An undertaking . . . made a profit of 3,532,000 francs between June 1, 1949 and May 31, 1950; and lost 5,123,000 francs between June 1, 1950 and December 31, 1950. The profit made during the term ending May 31, 1950, was used to redeem previous losses so that this particular term, while showing a profit from an accounting point of view, shows a deficit from a tax point of view. He (the author of the question) asks whether the administration is entitled, five years later, to limit the transferable profit for the term ending December 31, 1950, to the difference between the profits made from June 1, 1949, to May 31, 1950, and the losses of the last seven months of the year 1950.

*Answer:* Since the benefits for the term ending May 31, 1950, was totally absorbed by previous transferable losses, the undertaking concerned is entitled to report, until December 31, 1955, the whole of the deficit incurred during the term running from June 1 to December 31, 1950, in accordance with article 44 of the Taxes Code.[8]

Although written questions sometimes raise problems of general policy, they are generally concerned with administrative details brought to a parliamentarian's attention by one of his constituents. The question can be used to obtain free legal advice: it may also be used to redress a wrong interpretation of the law made by a civil servant without having to go through the lengthy and costly procedure of an appeal before an administrative court. The types of questions asked, and the way they are drafted, may also serve to establish a parliamentarian's competence in a particular field, and to gain him the government's as well as his colleagues' attention.

The oral question is theoretically reserved for more important problems. The constitution sets aside one day a week for an oral-question period. Having no control over the questions agenda, the government cannot prevent a particular question from arising. When the question is without debate, only the author of the question and the minister concerned may speak; when the question is with debate, the minister's answer is followed by a general discussion. When drafting their standing orders in 1959, the Senate tried to develop the oral question into a regular "interpellation" by providing that an oral question with debate could be concluded by a vote. Such a vote could have been used as a substitute for the motion of nonconfidence—a motion of nonconfidence not subject to the various constitutional restrictions, an unofficial motion of censure which would not have obliged the government to resign but could have been used by the parliament to weaken a cabinet out of office. The Constitutional Council killed such an attempt by declaring unconstitutional the articles of the draft standing orders giving to the Senate the right to conclude a debate on an oral question by a vote. Whether the assemblies will turn the interdiction remains to be seen. A vote on a procedural question may be used to indicate disapproval for the government's policy. An Assembly cannot be prevented from voting if and when it wishes.

The oral questions with debate, which are reserved to matters of greater political significance, and the questions without debate, are on separate agendas. They are placed on one or the other of the two agendas by the chairman of the National Assembly; the chairmen's conference may send a question from one agenda to the other and may also change the order of priority.

The National Assembly has made little use of the oral question to control the government. The deputies did not make the most of a technique which can be used not only for bringing the executive to account but for dramatizing an issue before the public. Debating without voting seemed pointless to deputies who had lost confidence in the power of the word not accompanied by political sanctions.

Another device to control the government was also little

used during the first two years of the Fifth Republic: the motion of nonconfidence. Such disuse is explained by the majority enjoyed by the Debré cabinet but also by the constitutional restrictions on the Assembly's right to overthrow the government.

To be valid, a motion of nonconfidence must be signed by at least one-tenth of the Assembly, that is, fifty-six deputies. If the motion is defeated, the signatories may not introduce another motion of nonconfidence during the same session. For example, the deputies whose motion of nonconfidence is defeated during the budget session ending in December cannot introduce a new motion until the legislative session beginning at the end of April. Limited to one motion of nonconfidence per session, the deputy hostile to the government normally tends to wait until enough hostility has accumulated against the cabinet before he risks his signature on such a motion. It may also happen that, as a session nears its end, deputies will introduce a motion of censure for the sole sake of not allowing their right to remain unused.

Further restricting the motion of nonconfidence is the provision that it must be passed by a majority of the total Assembly's membership. Under the Fourth Republic many governments were overthrown by negative majorities, by the addition of oppositions which could not be turned into a governing coalition. Without going as far as the Bonn constitution which requires that a successor to the chancellor be elected before he can be overthrown, the French constitution of 1958 requires at least that the coalition which forces a government out of office be composed not only of a majority of those present or of those voting but of those elected to the Assembly. The requirements that debates must be suspended after a motion of nonconfidence has been introduced and that forty-eight hours must lapse between the introduction of the motion and the vote, are intended to prevent the deputies from making a hasty decision in the heat of a debate.

The requirement of a special majority to overthrow a government could be nullified and was indeed nullified under the Fourth Republic by the parliament's refusal to pass legislation.

In order to prevent this occurrence the constitution of 1958 provides that the government may attach a question of confidence to a bill. In such an event the bill is considered passed unless the Assembly counteracts by introducing a motion of nonconfidence and succeeds in passing it. The effect of this provision is to give the government the right to legislate subject to veto by half the Assembly's members. The government needs only a plurality to govern; the Assembly needs a majority to overthrow.

A further check on the use of the motion of nonconfidence is the threat of dissolution. If the president warns, as de Gaulle did when he took office, that he will dissolve the Assembly if the government is overthrown, and if the custom becomes established that dissolution follows automatically the passing by the Assembly of a motion of nonconfidence, then the threat of dissolution may act as a deterrent on the Assembly—more powerful probably than any of the devices restricting the use of the motion of nonconfidence.

In addition to its elective and to its controlling functions, the National Assembly has a legislative function which, although now restricted, remains its major *raison d'être*. The National Assembly together with the Senate pass the ordinary laws and the budget law. To this dual legislative activity correspond the two parliamentary sessions, the April legislative session and the October budget session.[9] Because the procedure is different for ordinary and for budget laws, the two will be analyzed separately.

There are two major types of bills, the government bills (*projets de loi*) and the private members bills (*propositions de loi*). The first receive privileged treatment; they have priority over the second on the Assembly's agenda at the government's request. The Assembly has no recourse against the government's pushing its bills ahead of private members' bills; as there is no separate agenda for private members' bills, theoretically the government could prevent any private members' bill from reaching the floor of the house. However, private members' bills remain more important as a source of law than in Great Britain or

Canada. So long as a single party does not control both the executive and the legislature, a French government could not systematically prevent private members' bills introduced by one of the major non-Communist parties from coming to a debate.

Government bills have another privilege over private members' bills: they cannot be amended by the committees, but must be reported to the Assembly in their original text. The private members' bills may be sent to the Assembly as amended by the committee. As a result the author often fails to recognize his proposal and must suggest amendments to the bill in order to restore the original. In this humiliating situation the government also found itself under the Third and Fourth republics. It was a clear symbol of the parliament's supremacy that the government bills could be amended by the committees.

Expected to act as leader of the Assembly, the government is given specific powers which may be best studied in following the normal process of a bill through parliament.

Legislative initiative belongs to the parliamentarians and to the prime minister. The latter has the choice of introducing a bill in either the Senate or the National Assembly, except for money bills which must go first before the lower house. Before their introduction in parliament, government bills must go before the Council of State for legal advice and then be discussed in the Council of Ministers. The requirements insure that the bill is properly drafted and that the president of the Republic is informed of the government's legislative proposals. Private members' bills are not subject to any pretabling procedure. The representative may either draft the bill himself or seek the help of the legal advisors attached to the various committees. All bills are sent to the bureau of the Assembly. With regard to private members' bills, the bureau has an important decision to make; it must decide whether the bill is acceptable under Article 40 of the constitution which stipulates that members of parliament may not introduce texts which would, if they were passed, increase expenditures or decrease revenues. The bureau's decision is subject to appeal to the house as far as the parliamentarians are concerned; the government could appeal to the Constitutional

Council if the bureau had accepted a bill which, in the government's opinion, violated the constitution. The government, when submitting a bill to the bureau may demand that it be sent to a special committee. Deputies may make such a request but unlike with a government bill the final decision rests with the Assembly itself. It may choose to send the bill to the qualified standing committee. Other committees may ask that the bill be submitted to them for advice. After the bill has been received by the bureau and sent to the committee, members of the house concerned may submit amendments which have to be accepted by the bureau. The author of an amendment may participate without voting privilege in the committee's debates even if he is not a member of the committee. Representatives barred from certain committees and those not assigned to any committee may submit amendments for the sole purpose of participating in committee's debates. When a committee is ready to report a particular bill, a *rapporteur* is elected by a majority vote.

As a matter of principle bills come only once before the house; however, in the course of the debates, the *rapporteur*, the government, or the house itself may decide to return the bill to the committee for additional information. The president of the Republic may also return a bill to parliament for re-reading. Debate begins by the *rapporteur*'s analysis of the bill and his presentation of the Committee's opinion. General discussion is then open, and the government and the parliamentarians discuss the bill as a whole. The time assigned by the chairmen's conference for the discussion is shared by the various parliamentary groups on a basis proportional to their numerical importance. If for example, four hours have been allocated for the debate and if a given parliamentary group has 20 per cent of the house membership, the group's speaking time will be forty-eight minutes. The members of the group must agree among themselves as to who should speak and for how long within the maximum forty-eight minutes reserved to them. After the general discussion each article of the bill and its amendments are debated and voted separately. A vote on the bill as a whole is then taken after all amendments and articles of the bill have been voted on. The government may hasten this process by obliging the Assembly to take a single vote on all or part of the bill discussed, together with the amendments proposed or accepted by the government. This power can be used to prevent an Assembly from amending a government bill beyond recognition or from attaching unwanted riders.

When passed by the National Assembly, a bill is sent to the Senate, and vice versa. As in the United States, a bill in order to become law must be approved in identical terms by both houses. However, the government may decide to waive this requirement and ask the National Assembly to cast the deciding vote. If, after a bill has gone twice [10] before each house, no agreement has been reached, the prime minister may call a joint committee of senators and deputies. If the committee succeeds in reaching agreement, the government may ask both houses to vote on the text agreed on by the joint committee. If the text is not passed or if the joint committee fails to reach an agreement, the government may, after the bill has been once again debated by both houses, ask the National Assembly to cast the deciding vote. In this event the National Assembly may choose to pass either the joint committee's text or the last text approved by the deputies as modified by the Senate amendments acceptable to the deputies. Thus the Senate and the National Assembly have equal legislative powers if the government remains neutral, but if the government sides with the lower house the Senate is deprived of its right of veto. The government may not side with the Senate against the National Assembly.

### Budget and Finance Laws

Three major rules determine the respective powers of government and parliament in the passing of the budget: all taxations and expenditures must be authorized annually by law; the budget is voted by ministry; parliamentarians may not increase expenditures or reduce revenues.

The rule of yearly budgets (January 1 to December 31) protects parliament's right to control the purse, but renders more difficult long-term financial and economic planning. When the state is no longer solely responsible for the maintenance of the public peace and the military protection of the nation but intervenes directly in the economic field, the guarantee of certain revenues and the assurance that the pattern of expenditures will not be fundamentally modified by parliament from year to year may become a necessity for effective government. To alleviate the disadvantages of yearly budgets, the government is authorized to submit to parliament so-called "program laws" committing the legislature to a certain plan of expenditures extending over more than a year. The program laws while not giving a detailed account of expenses set the general principles which will determine the government's action, and evaluate the cost of the plan. These laws are not in any respect substitutes for regular money bills; they are no more than declarations of intention on the part of the executive and promises of support on the part of legislators. The authorization of expenditures outlined in the program laws must be incorporated in the regular budget or in other yearly finance laws to become operative. Program laws are no more than moral commitments. They have the advantage of facilitating long-range planning, but the disadvantage of being submitted to parliament out of context. A particular plan cannot be properly appreciated unless it is part of an over-all program of expenditures.

The constitution of 1958 regulates strictly the budgetary procedure. The budget, divided into two major sections, revenues and expenditures, is prepared by the minister of finance to whom the various ministries submit their requests for the coming year. If no agreement can be reached between a particular minister and the finance minister, arbitration is sought from the premier and eventually from the president.

The draft budget must be sent to the National Assembly on the first Tuesday of October at the latest. The budget is then immediately sent to committee, but debates in the house may not start until fifteen days later. The parliamentarians have thus at least two weeks to study the draft budget. At the latest, the National Assembly must vote on the whole budget forty days after its introduction by the government. If the Assembly has not taken such a vote within the time limit, the government sends the budget to the Senate, either in the original text or together with the amendments passed by the National Assembly and accepted by the government. The Senate must vote within fifteen days. If not, the government again brings the budget before the National Assembly with or without the amendments voted by the Senate and accepted by the government. If the National Assembly still refuses to vote the whole budget, the premier calls a meeting of the joint committee of both houses in order to seek agreement between the Senate and the National Assembly. Failing such an agreement or failing a vote on the whole budget by either of the two houses, the government may ask the National Assembly to cast the final vote.[11] If the Assembly has not complied within seventy days of sending the budget to parliament, the government may effect the draft budget through ordinances. This complicated procedure guarantees that both houses are given an opportunity to study the budget and to reconsider a voting decision on the whole budget. The refusal by the Assembly to pass the budget as a result of a negative vote on the whole text does not entitle the government to legislate the budget by decree. Only nonvoting on the whole budget within the prescribed period gives the government such a right. It may thus happen that on the first of January there is no budget, either because the National Assembly turned the budget down or because the government sent the budget to the Assembly later than required by the constitution. In order to prevent that the executive be left without money, the constitution provides that ten days before the end of the budget session, the government may ask the National Assembly to vote separately on the first section of the budget law, that concerning revenues. If the National Assembly passes it, the draft budget is sent to the Senate in accordance with the emergency procedure. If either house refuses to pass the revenues section, the government may, two days before the end of the session, ask the National Assembly to authorize collection of the existing taxes until the budget is passed. After this authorization is obtained—and it could not be refused without inviting chaos or violation of the constitution—the government may, by decree, allocate money to the various ministries in accordance with that part of the budget already passed by parliament and according to the government draft for that part of the budget not yet approved.

As early as 1713 the British House of Commons denied its members the right to propose new expenditures and to reduce revenues. Such restrictions did not appear in the republican constitutions of France until 1958. The constitution of 1946 had forbidden members of parliament to propose new expenditures during the discussion of the budget, but the rule did not apply to other laws. A decree law of June 9, 1956, deprived parliamentarians of the right to propose amendments to any bill, if such an amendment would increase expenditures or restrict revenues. However, the interdiction extended only to amendments, not to the bills themselves. The constitution of 1958 forbids parliamentarians to increase expenditures or restrict revenues without qualifications. The standing orders of parliament have gone as far as to extend the prohibition to resolutions which are simple petitions without the force of law.

The third and last major rule governing the budget is that expenditures are voted for by ministry. One could conceive of two extreme types of budget; first, a budget limited to a single over-all authorization to spend a certain amount of money; secondly, a budget itemizing every type of expenditure, each item being voted separately. In the Third and Fourth republics, the budget was voted by chapter. The definition of a chapter was flexible but a particular ministry's budget was understood to be divided into titles and into a number of chapters. An increase in the number of chapters was a sign of increased parliamentary intervention in the control of government spending. In 1870 there were 300 chapters; in 1914, 1,500; in 1950, 3,500.[12] Money could not be transferred from one chapter to another at the ministers' discretion. When the vote is by ministry, as requested by the constitution, money may be transferred within a ministry's budget by ministerial decrees. However, an organic law has restricted such transfers by setting the rules that transfers have to be made within the same title of a ministry's budget and that the transfers between chapters be not more than one-tenth of the original appropriation for the chapters concerned.

The Assembly may not debate expenditures before the first part of the budget dealing with revenues has been approved. Expenditures are of two categories, "expenditures already approved" and "new expenditures." The first category comprises the expenditures that the government considers necessary in order to continue the public services approved by parliament the preceding year, and not questioned for the year to come. This category of expenditures is subject to a single vote for the whole. The second category, the new expenditures, calls for as many votes as there are titles and ministries. In the 1960 budget, the new expenditures amounted to about one-fifth of the total.

During the budget year, the government may, through finance laws, request from parliament changes or additions in the original budget.

### Accounting

Government expenditure is controlled by the Ministry of Finance, the National Assembly, and the Accounting Court. The Finance Ministry relies mostly on the *inspecteurs des finances*. A few inspectors are attached to each ministry where they act as agents of the finance minister. The finance committees of the assemblies may also use the inspectors to control government expenditures.

The Finance Ministry has such a tradition of strict monetary control and the finance inspectors such a tradition of integrity and such autonomy, that the parliament relies on them to insure that money be legally and legitimately spent.

However, parliament has other means of controlling the spending of public funds. The government must submit its accounts for the past year to the assemblies to be studied by the finance committees. Furthermore, the Accounting Court, an independent administrative court in which the members do not depend on the executive for promotion, submits to parliament yearly reports presenting findings, criticisms, and suggestions resulting from the auditing of government expenditures. Such reports are sometimes critical of particular ministries; for example, the report of 1948 which was followed by more than a thousand dismissals and prosecutions.[13]

During the nineteenth century and well into the twentieth French parliaments had increased their control over the budget. The delegating of financial powers to the executive in the 1930's, the constitution of 1946, the decree-law of June, 1956, and the constitution of 1958 mark an evolution in the opposite direction, an evolution which is symptomatic of the changing balance of power between parliaments and governments.

# 16 *The Senate*

With powers practically equal to those of the lower house, the Senate of the Third Republic could veto a law indefinitely and could overthrow the cabinet; it had certain privileges not shared by the other Assembly, such as not being subject to dissolution. After the war the drafters of the new constitution remembered the Senate as an obstacle to good and efficient government by its small-town conservatism, its systematic opposition to reforms, and its general delaying of legislation. The first draft constitution submitted to the people in 1946 contained no second chamber. This, however, was too drastic a reform for the MRP and the conservatives, Gaullists included, who feared that a monocameral legislature would be too easily dominated by Left-wing parties. When the first draft constitution was defeated at the polls, Socialists and Communists reluctantly accepted that the second draft constitution include an upper house. While wanting a second chamber which would act as a brake on the National Assembly, the MRP did not wish to recreate the old Senate, the virulent anticlericalism of which was not favorably remembered by the Christian-democratic constituents. The second chamber of the Fourth Republic, as it resulted from a compromise between Communists, Socialists, and MRP, could do little more than delay legislation—two months for ordinary bills, less for the budget and for the bills declared urgent by the lower house. As a symbol of the demotion of the upper house, its name was changed from Senate to Council of the Republic. In the following years the council gained in prestige and power. The councilors succeeded in having their official title changed to that of senator; some prime ministers renewed prewar traditions and H. Queuille even went as far as staking the life of his government before the council. The constitutional revision of 1954 resulted in an increase of the council's powers. The shuttle system according to which bills would go back and forth between the two houses until they agreed on a common wording was restored. But the National Assembly retained the right to cast the deciding vote if no agreement had been found between the two houses after certain time limits which on ordinary bills could be reduced to six months and to shorter periods of time on the budget and urgent laws. The regaining by the upper house of some of its luster was evidenced by the increased number of senators called to the cabinets in the latter years of the Fourth Republic. And while, from 1946 to 1958, all prime ministers had come from the National Assembly, the first premier of the Fifth Republic came from the upper house.

It may seem in contradition to the 1958 constitution's aim of strengthening the executive that the upper house, rebaptized Senate, be given powers much above those of the Council of the Republic. However, not from *esprit de corps* did Senator Debré devise a powerful Senate for the new Republic. The Senate of the Fifth Republic like that of the Third may paralyze the lower house, but unlike its predecessor it cannot paralyze an executive backed by the National Assembly. The Senate can, in certain circumstances, be used by the executive against the National

Assembly, but it cannot without the National Assembly's consent veto legislation wanted by the government.

### Membership and Election

The Senate is composed of 307 members: 255 represent metropolitan France; 32, Algeria; 2, the Sahara; 7, the overseas *départements;* 5, the Overseas territories; and 6, Frenchmen living in foreign countries.

The constitution specifies that senators are indirectly elected by universal suffrage; the actual electoral system is determined by ordinary legislation. The system used for the selection of the Senate of 1959 gave preponderance, as is traditional in French upper houses, to rural and small-town representatives.

Senators must be at least thirty-five years old. They are elected for nine years, one-third being renewed every three years.[1] In fact the number of seats subject to reëlection is normally more than one-third, because the senators who acceded to their posts as a consequence of the death or resignation of the senator originally elected have to go before the electorate at the following senatorial elections.

Election to the Senate is by an electoral college composed of deputies and local representatives. In each *département* the senatorial electors comprise the deputies elected for that *département*, the general councilors, and delegates from the municipal councils in numbers varying according to population. In the communes with less than 9,000 inhabitants the number of delegates varies from one to fifteen according to the number of municipal councilors, a number itself determined by the size of the population. In the communes with more than 9,000 inhabitants and in all the communes of the Seine *département*, all municipal councilors are senatorial electors. In addition, communes with more than 30,000 inhabitants select one additional delegate for each 1,000 inhabitants over 30,000. In the communes with less than 9,000 inhabitants the choice of senatorial electors is made by the municipal councilors on the basis of a three-ballot majority system, a majority required on the first two ballots, a plurality sufficient on the third. Communes with 9,000 to 30,000 inhabitants do not have to select senatorial electors because all municipal councilors of such communes are ex-officio members of the senatorial college. The additional delegates of the communes with more than 30,000 inhabitants are elected by the municipal councilors on the basis of proportional representation.

In the senatorial electoral college, the municipal councilors dominate, at least in number. In 1959, of 108,266 senatorial electors for metropolitan France, there were only 465 deputies and 3,844 general councilors; the municipal councilors were thus more than 100,000. The principle of representation of every commune, however small, gives the preponderance to rural areas and small cities. A village of 800 people has three senatorial electors, while Paris with its three million inhabitants has only 2,791 delegates. More than half of the senatorial electors come from communes with less than 2,500 inhabitants. The senatorial like the presidential college underrepresents modern industrial France. The underrepresentation is lesser however, because the senatorial unlike the presidential college is broken into as many districts as there are *départements* and because the number of senators allocated to each *département* is determined, not by the number of senatorial electors but by the *département's* total population. The thirty-two industrial *départements* electing 55 per cent of the deputies, elect also 50 per cent of the senators. The urban areas are thus at a real disadvantage only in the *départements* where the rural population is much overrepresented in terms of senatorial electors. Even there, specific studies would probably show that in many *départements* the rural and small-town senatorial electors, even though a majority, often follow the city delegates' leadership.

At the same time as they select their senatorial electors, the communal and *département* councils select also a varying number of alternates.

The senatorial electoral campaign is very short and mostly person to person. The candidates make a point of seeing and speaking to as many electors as possible and often succeed in meeting with all. The electoral code forbids public meetings and propaganda. The only campaign meetings allowed are those restricted to senatorial electors. Each candidate or list of candidates is also allowed to send an electoral pamphlet to each senatorial elector. Political parties hardly intensify their general action of propaganda at the time of a senatorial election. The assumption is that most senatorial electors have already made up their minds and that the support of uncommitted electors can be secured only by the candidate's personal contacts.

The senatorial electors of a *département* vote in that *département's* capital city. In the *départements* with a majority two-ballot system, the first ballot is held in the morning, the second in the afternoon.

Four different electoral systems are used for the allocation of seats. In all the overseas *départements* and territories, and in the 83 French *départements* where the population entitles them to no more than four senators, a two-ballot majority system is used. On the first ballot the candidates obtaining a majority of the votes are elected, on the second ballot the seats remaining vacant are allocated to the candidates with the highest votes. The lists are not immutable. The elector may strike out names from a list and write in names of candidates running on another ticket. This explains how on the first ballot some candidates on a given list may be elected while the others fail to obtain the required majority. In 1959, 207 senators were elected by the two-ballot system, akin to that used for the election of deputies. In the Algerian *départements* a two-ballot list system is used. The lists may not be modified. Each list must contain the proportion of Europeans and Moslems specified by law for each district. Twenty-four Moslem and ten European senators are elected for the whole of Algeria and the Sahara. On the first ballot the list obtaining a majority is elected. If no majority is obtained a second balloting takes place, and a plurality is then sufficient. A third system, proportional representation, not used in the elections to the lower house, serves to elect senators in the metropolitan *départements* with at least five senate seats: in 1959, 60 senators for seven *départements*. A classical *d'Hondt* system is used. The lists may not be modified. Each list obtains as many seats as its total vote contains the electoral quotient. Seats which may be left over go to the lists with the highest remainders. Finally, a fourth system is used for the selection of the representatives of Frenchmen in foreign countries: Nominations are made by the Superior Council of Frenchmen in foreign countries; election is made by the Senate. In fact, the Senate only endorses the council's choice since the council nominates no more candidates than there are representatives to be elected. The five senators so selected are in fact chosen by the executive because the Superior Council is composed mostly of government appointees. The council is divided into three sections. In the first section, that for Southeast Asia, eight government appointees and six representatives of associations grouping Frenchmen abroad, select one senator. In the second section, that for Africa, thirty-five government appointees and four associations representatives select three senators. In the third section, that for Europe, the Americas, and the Middle East, thirty-four [2] association representatives elect two senators.

In order to limit the number of by-elections, the law provides that the seat left vacant by a senator elected by PR goes to the next available candidate on the list. In the districts using majority systems, alternates are elected at the same time as senators. By-elections take place only when the alternate is not available.

## Organization

The internal organization of the Senate is basically similar to that of the National Assembly. In the same way as deputies, senators elect a chairman and a bureau, divide themselves into parliamentary groups and committees and entrust a chairman's conference with the organization of their parliamentary activities and legislative work. The smaller membership of the Senate, its greater cohesion (partly because it is composed of older parliamentarians), its atmosphere of lesser political tension make the organization and the conduct of debates in the Senate somewhat more relaxed than in the house. Senate sessions are dependent on those of the National Assembly, and thus normally limited to about six months a year. Being only half as many as the deputies, the senators have more time to debate legislation. Not trusted with the right to overthrow the government, they may with greater freedom of mind concentrate on the study of bills.

### Functions and Powers

Similar to that of the Assembly is the Senate's elective function. The chairman selects three of nine members of the Constitutional Council. The Senate as a whole selects one-half the members of the High Court of Justice, and one-half of the French delegates to the Senate of the Community and to the European assemblies.

The legislative power of the senators is limited. They may not call extraordinary sessions of parliament. They depend for those on the goodwill of the prime minister or of the deputies. Budget and financial laws have to be sent to the National Assembly first, with the result that the Senate may have no more than fifteen days to study and vote on the budget. Finally, and most important, the government may give the National Assembly the power to break a senatorial veto on legislation wanted by the lower house. The first two restrictions—on extraordinary meetings and on financial legislation—are of secondary importance. They would not make the Senate inferior to the National Assembly in law making. The third restriction, however, concerning eventual conflicts between the two chambers, may cripple the Senate. In the event of such conflict two solutions are possible, according to whether the prime minister decides to intervene or not. The difference will be better understood by following a hypothetical process in the Senate.

The texts sent to the bureau of the Senate may be rejected as contrary to the constitution, particularly if they violate the rule forbidding parliamentarians to propose added expenditures and to reduce revenues. If declared acceptable, the texts are sent either to a standing or to a special committee. If the text is a private member's bill originating with a senator or coming from the National Assembly, the committee is free to amend the text and to report it to the Senate as amended. If the text is a government bill, two alternatives are possible. First, the bill may have come directly from the government; the committee must then report the bill in its original wording. Secondly, if a bill comes from the National Assembly, the Senate committee must then report the bill as sent to them by the lower house. Amendments suggested by the committee have to be reported separately. If a bill is passed by the Senate in terms identical to those in which it was passed by the National Assembly, the bill is sent to the president for ratification. If the bill has not yet gone before the lower house or if passed by the Senate in terms different from those approved by the deputies, the bill is sent, or sent back to the National Assembly. Unless the government intervenes, the Senate is under no obligation to vote a nonbudget bill within a required period of time and cannot be forced to compromise with the National Assembly. A bill sent by the National Assembly to the Senate may die there without ever coming to a vote or, if the Senate votes on it but defeats it, the bill may shuttle between the two chambers as long and as often as wanted by both the deputies and the senators. If, on the contrary, the government decides to intervene, the procedure is different. First, the government may compel the Senate, like the Assembly, to put a particular bill on its agenda and to give priority to such a bill. Second, the government may start a compulsory conciliation procedure between Senate and National Assembly. After a bill has gone twice before the two houses, or once if the government has declared the bill to be urgent, the prime minister may call a meeting of a joint committee composed of an equal number of senators and deputies. If the joint committee arrives at a common text by a majority vote, the government may submit such text to both houses. No amendments are then receivable, unless acceptable to the government. If the joint committee fails to reach an agreement or if the text proposed by the committee fails to obtain the support of both houses, in other words if the conciliation procedure has failed, the government may in last resort ask the National Assembly to cast the deciding vote. The

Senate is then, as it were, temporarily excluded from the legislative process.

To perform its function of control of the executive, the Senate like the National Assembly may use legislative and ad hoc investigating committees, may put questions to ministers during the discussion of the budget or of ordinary laws, or may use the more formal written or oral questions procedures. One day a week is reserved for an oral question period, the questions with debates coming first, the questions without debate following. As in the National Assembly, the oral question agenda is outside the government's control. When drafting their standing orders, the Senators had argued that even if the deputies should not be allowed to vote after an oral question, the Senate should be permitted to do so since they did not have the use of the motion of censure. This reasoning was not accepted by the Constitutional Council; senators must, if they wish to respect the constitution, be content with questioning the ministers without concluding the debate by a vote.

Unlike the National Assembly, the Senate does not have the right to overthrow a government. The lower house has the sole use of the motion of nonconfidence and reciprocally only before the Assembly may the government use the motion of confidence. However, the constitution provides that the government may ask the Senate to endorse a declaration of general policy. The refusal by the Senate to give such endorsement has no constitutional sanction. Not giving the use of the motion of nonconfidence to the Senate, cripples it politically; but preventing the government from using the motion of confidence turns to the Senate's advantage. By attaching a motion of confidence to a bill before the National Assembly, the government may succeed in having the bill passed by a mere plurality. Before the Senate, the government may not, through the motion of confidence technique, enlist the support of those who would have liked to abstain. But of course the prime minister may always neutralize the Senate, if he has the support of the National Assembly.

## The Senate in Practice

In 1946, the Council of the Republic had made an unassuming entry on the political scene. The upper chamber knew that they were at most tolerated, not really desired by the government and that there was no strong support for them in the electorate. The Senate of the Fifth Republic, on the contrary, began its career with confidence. The National Assembly elected in November, 1958, was in the main composed of new parliamentarians. But the Senate elected in 1959 had few newly elected representatives.[3] Largely because of the electoral system used, elections to the National Assembly had resulted in a landslide for the Gaullists. The Senate of 1959, because of a different electoral system, favored the traditional parties. The National Assembly was, in a sense, the assembly of the Fifth Republic, the Senate that of the Fourth Republic. Many of the leaders defeated in the elections to the lower house, found a seat in the Senate; Duclos, Daladier, Mitterand, Defferre, Faure, Lafay, Colin, Barrachin, among others. The Senate thus appeared as the opposition chamber, the Assembly as the government chamber. The hazards of electoral systems had also, paradoxically, given to the Senate the claim of being more representative of the electorate than the National Assembly. The UNR with only 19 per cent of the votes on the first ballot of the elections to the Assembly had finally obtained 40 per cent of the seats; in the Senate they obtained 12 per cent. The SFIO with 15 per cent of the votes on the first ballot had obtained only 8 per cent of the seats in the Assembly; in the Senate they obtained 21 per cent. Even if one assumes that the distribution of electoral forces had remained the same between the 1958 elections to the lower house and the 1959 elections to the Senate—a hypothesis favorable to the UNR—the Senate did not have the stigma usually attached to French upper houses, that of misrepresenting the nation. A final advantage of the Senate over the Assembly was that its Algerian members having been elected by a smaller electoral college, less likely to be influenced by techniques of mass propaganda, appeared more representative of

Algerian wishes. The Senate, with a new confidence in itself, took at times a resolute attitude of opposition to the government. Disregarding the prime minister's warning that resolutions requesting increased expenditures were unconstitutional, the Senate passed a few such resolutions. At one point during the 1959 session, the tension between the government and the Senate caused the premier to threaten that ministers would no longer appear before the Senate. The senators however did not wish such a break; they only wanted to emphasize that while deprived of the right to censure the government they intended to make use of all the means at their disposal to control and criticize the executive. It would be ironical if the upper chamber originally devised by French constitutions to guard against the *errements* of universal suffrage become the more representative of the electorate and in the French terminology the more "republican" of the two chambers.

# 17 *The Other French Constitutional Organs*

In addition to the parliament, the presidency, and the government, the constitution created three decision-making bodies of unequal importance—the Constitutional Council, the Superior Council of the Judiciary, and the High Court of Justice; and one advisory organ—the Economic and Social Council. The Constitutional Council is the most important.

## The Constitutional Council

The revolution of 1789 established as a standard of parliamentary republicanism a rule based on both Montesquieu's theory of the separation of powers and Rousseau's theory of the general will, interpreted democratically—the rule that law is supreme, even over the constitution. According to such theory, if either the executive or the judiciary could challenge the law, embodying the people's will, then the system would cease to be truly representative. As French students of public law ceased to turn exclusively to England for an example of a good, working democracy, and drew also on the United States for foreign references, the idea that democracy was compatible with judicial supremacy gained ground. The constitution of 1946 introduced a supreme court of kinds, a Constitutional Committee composed of the president of the Republic, the two assemblies' chairmen, and ten members elected by the National Assembly and by the Council of the Republic; these were entrusted with "guarding" the constitution. However, the procedure for submitting cases to the committee was very restrictive. The committee's function was to judge the constitutionality of bills before they had become laws, but the committee could not initiate cases; it had to wait for them to be started by the president of the Republic and the upper house acting jointly. If the committee had pronounced a bill unconstitutional, it could not become law until the constitution had been modified according to the normal revision procedure. The true purpose of the committee was to protect the Council of the Republic against possible encroachments on its already limited powers by the National Assembly. The council helped in resolving a few minor disputes between the two houses but failed to develop into anything resembling a true constitutional court. There was indeed little *raison d'être* for such a court; the bill of rights included in the constitutional preamble was not considered to be part of the constitution, and the balance of power between the lower and the upper house was so much in favor of the former that conflicts were bound to be of a minor nature. The situation is different under the Fifth Republic. A few public rights have become part of the constitution, and the constitutional division of rule making between the legislature and the executive calls for an arbitrator. As the French constitutional system moves away from the British example and comes closer to the American, as the notion of balance of power replaces that of the supremacy of the law, a true supreme court appears in the French republican system.

The Constitutional Council created by the constitution of

1958 is composed of the former presidents of the Republic and nine members chosen for nine years, three by the president, three by the chairman of the National Assembly, and three by the chairman of the Senate. The councilors other than the former presidents are renewed by one-third every three years; they may not be reappointed. The councilors have a term of office longer than that of the persons nominating them, but the one-term rule and the appointment of three new councilors every three years should normally prevent the council from being completely out of step with the other organs of government. The chairman of the council who carries the vote in the event of a tie is selected by the president of the Republic. Councilors do not have to be selected from among persons learned in the law because, like the United States Supreme Court, the Constitutional Council is primarily a political organ of government. Of the nine members appointed to the council in 1959, two were lawyers, two were magistrates, the others a member of the Council of State, an ambassador, a bank director, a former business executive, and a physician. Five of the councilors belonged or had belonged to either the RPF or the UNR, but none were prominent politicians. The councilors may not combine their office with a position in the executive, the parliament, or other constitutional organs. During their term they may not be appointed to any administrative position or, if they were civil servants before their nomination, may not be promoted in the service unless the promotion is automatic. Councilors are forbidden to make public pronouncements or give advice on matters which may eventually be submitted to them.

The council has four major functions which are to advise the president on an emergency, to pass on a government request declaring the president incapacitated, to act as an electoral court, and—finally and foremost—to pass on the constitutionality of bills, international instruments, organic laws, and parliamentary standing orders.

When under Article 16 of the constitution the president contemplates proclaiming a state of emergency, he must consult the prime minister, the chairmen of both houses, and the Constitutional Council. The president is not bound by their advice, but that their advice has to be sought and rendered public may help the citizens to judge the president's actions and determine whether a state of emergency is justified. The Constitutional Council consulted on an emergency gives an opinion on whether the conditions outlined in Article 16 are met, that is, whether institutions of the Republic, the independence of the nation, the integrity of its territory, or the execution of its international commitments are gravely and immediately menaced. The council's advice has to be motivated and is immediately published in the *Journal Officiel.* The president must also consult the council on measures he intends to take in order to meet the emergency situation.

At the government's request, the council must pass on the question of the president's incapacitation. If the council declares him incapacitated, presidential powers are automatically transferred to the chairman of the Senate.[1] The debate which followed President Eisenhower's illness may have influenced French constituents in devising a procedure for declaring the presidency vacant for reasons other than resignation or death. This procedure was not intended to amount to an impeachment. The president may be removed for political reasons by the High Court of Justice but not by the Constitutional Council. A decision on a president's incapacitation must be reached by the special majority of all members of the council.

As an electoral court, the council supervises the elections to the presidency and the organization of referendums, and decides whether to unseat the parliamentarians accused of having violated the electoral code. No appeals against the council's decisions are possible.

When judging cases against senators and deputies, the council divides itself into three sections selected by lot from each of the three categories of appointed councilors—those appointed by the president, by the chairman of the National Assembly, and by the chairman of the Senate. The number of appeals following a general election obliges the council to seek the assistance of ten so-called vice-*rapporteurs* (*rapporteurs adjoints*) selected each year by the council from the Council of State and from the Accounting Court. Upon receipt of an appeal the council's chairman assigns it to one of the three sections which in turn passes it to a *rapporteur*, either a councilor or a vice-*rapporteur*. The member of parliament whose election is challenged is advised by the council's section preparing the case. The accused is allowed to study the charge and to answer it in writing. The section reports the case to the council, which makes the final decision.

The major role of the council is to act as an umpire between the executive and the legislature by passing on the constitutionality of bills and other texts affecting the balance of power between the two branches of government.

The matters which come before the Constitutional Council are of two kinds—those which have to be and those which may be submitted to it. To the first category belong the standing orders of parliament, the organic laws, and laws that the government wishes to modify by decree on the ground that they cover matters reserved to the regulatory field.

The rule that standing orders and organic laws have to be submitted to the council is intended to prevent the legislature from amending the constitution outside the regular revision process. In its 1959 rulings on the standing orders of the National Assembly and of the Senate, the council pronounced some of the articles of the draft rules to be in violation of the constitution. For each article the council gave its reasons for pronouncing them unconstitutional, thus indicating in what sense they should be modified. The council also made reservations on certain articles without declaring them invalid, thus indicating the sense in which the text should be interpreted.

The decrees modifying previous laws now falling within the regulatory power have, according to Article 37 of the constitution, to be taken after advice from the Council of State. The legislature has no possibility of appeal to the council against such texts, and the council may not bring them before it. As an exception the laws or ordinances passed after October 4, 1958, the date the constitution came into force, may not be modified through decrees unless the Constitutional Council has first declared such texts to be within the regulatory field. In other words, if through a mistake of its own the government has used ordinances to regulate what could have been regulated by simple decrees, or if the government has allowed the parliament to pass a law on what belonged to the field of executive orders, the government is not permanently deprived of powers to regulate over matters which originally belonged to the executive-orders field; the government may recuperate such "lost" powers, but only if and after they have been ruled by the council to be of a regulatory nature.

Unlike the Constitutional Committee of the Fourth Republic, the Constitutional Council has compulsory jurisdiction over certain matters, the most important of which are the parliamentary standing orders and organic laws; however, except on such matters, the council may not act on its own accord, but must wait to be moved from outside. Appeals must come from either the president, the prime minister, the chairman of the National Assembly, or the chairman of the Senate. Such appeals may be made at two stages during a legislative process. Before a bill is voted on, the chairman of the house concerned and the prime minister may appeal to the council, which must render its decision within eight days. After a bill has been passed by parliament, and pending promulgation by the president, an appeal may be made by the chairmen of either house, the prime minister, or the president himself. The council's decision must be rendered within a month or within eight days if the government has declared the bill to be urgent. A text declared unconstitutional may not be promulgated. The council must choose between invalidating a whole bill or invalidating only sections of the bill. In this last case the president has the choice between promulgating the bill minus the articles declared unconstitutional or asking the parliament to reconsider the bill.

The Constitutional Council's decisions are taken by at least seven [2] councilors except *en cas de force majeure*, which apparently would be the presence of less than seven members since no quorum is required. The debates and votes in the council are secret, and minority opinions are not published. The council's rulings are based on the constitution but since there is no appeal against the council's decisions, the constitution is whatever the council chooses it to be. Councilors have in particular to decide whether the preamble which lists civil rights and proclaims the right of self-determination is part of the constitution. Councilors may if they so choose base their rulings on constitutional custom, or on the spirit as well as on the letter of the constitution.

While introducing a constitutional court in its political system, France has not yet gone as far as the United States or even Germany, but she has moved away from her parliamentary traditions. The importance of the Constitutional Council will vary according to whether the constitutional structures of 1958 revert to parliamentary supremacy, evolve into presidential government, or remain as originally planned. The greater the possibilities of rule making conflicts between the executive and the legislature, the greater the role of the council.

### The Superior Council of the Judiciary

A council of the judiciary was first created in 1946 to render the magistracy less dependent on the executive. The judicial system of the Third Republic was based on the principle of the judge's complete independence in interpreting the law; but the authority of the minister of justice over the magistrates was great, if it were only through the power of promotion. The 1946 Superior Council of the Judiciary was composed of 14 members: 6 elected by the National Assembly, 4 by the judges themselves, and 2 chosen by the president of the Republic who together with the minister of justice served ex officio on the council. The role of the council was to advise the president on pardons, to decide on promotions of judges, and to act as the magistracy's disciplinary authority. Although not an unqualified success, the council had nevertheless been a check on the minister of justice. The constitution of 1958, in what is not one of its better features, drastically curtails the powers of the Superior Council.

The council now comprises two ex-officio members: the president of the Republic who is chairman and the minister of justice who is vice-chairman, and nine members appointed by the president for four years. The appointed members must be selected from certain categories of persons defined by an organic law: [3] three must come from the Court of Cassation, three from among other civil and criminal judges, one from the Council of State, and two from outside the magistracy. Except for these last two councilors who may be nominated by him, the president chooses from lists of candidates containing three times the number of positions to be filled. The lists are established by the Court of Cassation for the six civil and criminal judges, and by the Council of State for its own reserved seat. The members of the Superior Council may be reappointed only once. During their term in office they may not be promoted in the judiciary, may not be parliamentarians, and may not exercise the professions of lawyer and attorney.

The Superior Council meets at the request of its chairman or of its vice-chairman. The quorum is five members. The decisions and advice are rendered by a majority of those present.

The council has no power of decision except on matters of discipline. The council advises the president and the minister of justice on appointments, promotions, and pardons. Regarding promotions to the Court of Cassation and to the first presidencies of Appeal courts, the Superior Council submits names of candidates to the president who is free to reject the suggestion. For appointments to all other positions in the judiciary, the Superior Council does not initiate nominations but advises on the nominations proposed by the minister of justice.

When acting as a disciplinary authority for the magistracy, the council meets without the president of the Republic and without the minister of justice under the chairmanship of the first president of the Court of Cassation. The sanctions which may be imposed by the Superior Council rank from a simple warning (*réprimande*) to dismissal without right to a pension. The accused magistrate must be heard by the council after having been given a chance to study the accusation. The council's disciplinary decisions may not be appealed.

There is thus a return to the practice of the Third Republic because the executive regains authority over appointments and promotions and because the disciplinary authority is again in the hands of the magistracy.[4]

The executive's control over promotions is not however without restrictions. An organic law [5] subjects the government and the president to certain specific rules. A magistrate may not be promoted or moved from one court to another without his consent. Promotion in the lower echelons of the judiciary is made by a committee comprising judges, state attorneys, and representatives of the Ministry of Justice.[6] Although the minister of justice is in a position to control such a committee he may not systematically ignore the opinions of the judges sitting on such committee. Promotion to the higher echelons are made directly by the president of the Republic acting on the nominations presented by the minister of justice or, for the higher positions, on the nominations presented by the Superior Council.

Nominations to the magistracy are made by the president of the Republic, subject to the prime minister's countersignature. Most magistrates are recruited on the basis of a competitive examination.

The constitution gives the president of the Republic the specific responsibility of guaranteeing the independence of the judiciary. However such responsibility may agree with de Gaulle's original concept of the presidency as an arbitrator between the various branches of government, the making of an organ of the executive the protector of the judiciary's independence is contradictory.

### The High Court of Justice

The High Court of Justice, a purely political tribunal, is composed of twelve senators and twelve deputies elected by their chambers after each election. The court selects its own chairman and two vice-chairmen. The court may try the president of the Republic for high treason, and the ministers as well as their accomplices for plotting against the state. Cases come before the court only following an impeachment by both chambers of parliament.[7] When judging cases of plotting against the safety of the state, the High Court is bound by the definitions given by the criminal code. Having no legal definition of high treason, the High Court and the assemblies are free to define such a crime and to determine its punishment. High Court judgments, obtained by an absolute majority vote of the total membership, are not subject to appeal. Totally inactive in normal times, the High Court might possibly be called to play a role in the event of a serious conflict between the parliament and a president assuming emergency powers under Article 16.

### The Economic and Social Council

Successor to the Economic Council created by the constitution of 1946, the Economic and Social Council serves both the government and parliament in an advisory capacity. The members of this council are appointed by the government for five years. The councilors are selected to represent the major economic and social groups in the nation. An organic law determines which groups and the number of their representatives.[8] Salaried people have 45 representatives; nationalized undertakings, 6; private undertakings, 9; artisans, 10. The representatives of artisans, private undertakings, and salaried people are chosen by their trade and professional unions. Agricultural organizations select 40 representatives, five from agricultural coöperatives. The government selects 15 members with particular qualifications in the economic, social, or cultural fields. Among the remaining councilors, 15 represent such activities as housing, savings, public health, consumers coöperatives, and family associations; 7 represent coöperatives of production, tourism, exports, regional planning; 2 are designated by "the most representative" of middle-class organizations; 10 are appointed for their knowledge of overseas problems; finally, 20 members represent Algeria and the Sahara, and 10 the overseas *départements* and territories.

The council selected in 1959 divided itself into fifteen committees and fourteen groups which combined political and economic interests. The fourteen political-economic groups were the CFTC (Christian-democratic trade union) with 16 members; CGT (Communist trade union), 14; CGT-FO (Socialist trade union, 15; business executives (*cadres supérieurs*), 6; private industry, 32; nationalized industries, 7; artisans, 11; agriculture, 37; family associations, 10; coöperatives, 12; Overseas *départements* and territories, 9; representatives of the Franc zone, 9; middle-class organizations, 11; various specialists, 15.

In addition to its fifteen standing committees the council may either on its own accord or at the government's request establish temporary committees to study specific questions. When coming from the government the request has to be granted. In addition, the government may designate the members of such ad hoc committees.

The council must be consulted by the government on its "program laws" and on its economic and social plans excluding the budget and other financial laws. The council may be consulted either by the government or by the assemblies on any bill with economic and social implications. More generally the council may be asked either by the parliament or by the government to advise on any economic or social problem. Furthermore the council may on its own initiative call the government's attention to any economic or social problems and make suggestions for their solution. The council may not send draft bills to parliament, but parliamentarians may of course introduce draft texts prepared by the council.

Under the Fourth Republic, the Economic Council did some serious work generally ignored by government and parliament, but nevertheless not entirely in vain. The various pressure groups represented on the council learned of each other's problems and positions, and also learned to compromise.

Not altogether unimportant is the fact that the Economic and Social Council offers a number of patronage possibilities. Defeated members of parliament may wait in the council for an eventual return to the legislature. The councillors draw a salary one-third that of parliamentarians.

## The Revision Process

Constitutional rules are embodied in the basic constitution approved by referendum in September, 1958, and in a series of organic laws.

Numerous articles of the basic constitution specify that organic laws would or might complete the constitution.[9] Between October, 1958, and February, 1959, the government, using the emergency powers delegated to it in June, 1958, and confirmed by the constitution itself, passed twenty-two organic laws, through ordinances. More than twenty times as lengthy as the constitution itself, these organic laws regulated such matters as election to the presidency; appointments to civil and military posts; private and public occupations forbidden to members of the government, parliamentarians, and constitutional councilors; duration of each legislature; parliamentary salaries, vote by proxy in parliament; legislative procedure on financial laws; organization of the Constitutional Council; status of the magistracy; organization of the Superior Council of the Judiciary, of the High Court of Justice, and of the Economic and Social Council; and finally the composition, functions, and powers of the Executive Council, Senate, and Arbitration Court of the Community.

The procedures used to amend organic laws and those used to amend the constitution are different.

The initiative for amending organic laws belongs to the government and to the parliamentarians. The amending bill may come for debate and vote only fifteen days after the bill was introduced. If passed in identical terms by both houses, the organic law need only be approved in each house by a majority of those voting. However, in the event of a conflict between the two houses and assuming that the National Assembly be asked by the government to cast the deciding vote, the majority required is that of the total Assembly membership. Organic laws concerning the Senate have to be passed in identical terms by both chambers; the government could not in that event ask the National Assembly to cast the deciding vote. After being passed by parliament, an organic law must still be submitted to the Constitutional Council which may veto part or the whole of the bill. In order to be constitutionally valid, an organic law would probably have to be hooked to the proper article of the constitution, and to be in agreement with this article as well as with the whole constitution. However the council is privileged to decide on such matters. A badly drafted constitution gives the council greater freedom of choice, and a council's ruling on an organic law extending the field of legislative powers under Article 34 might be crucial for the evolution of the constitution.

Amending the basic constitution is more difficult than amending organic laws. The initiative here belongs to parliamentarians on the one hand and to the president of the Republic and the prime minister acting jointly on the other hand. Neither the president nor the premier may alone start an amending procedure. The draft amendment must be approved by both houses in identical terms, then submitted to a referendum. However, the president of the Republic may choose an alternative procedure. Instead of sending the draft project to one of the two chambers, he may submit it to the two chambers meeting jointly in a congress. In this case, a referendum need not follow approval by the congress, but only provided the amendment was passed by three-fifths of the votes cast.

Any article of the constitution may be amended by one of these two processes; except that the republican form of government is entrenched and thus theoretically unamendable; and except that articles concerning the working of community organs may be amended by laws passed in identical terms by the National Assembly, the French Senate, and the Senate of the Community. Furthermore in order to prevent past history from repeating itself, the constitution of 1958 specifies that no amendment may be made when the integrity of the territory is in danger.

As in ordinary laws, the executive may side with the National Assembly against the Senate even if the revision concerns the powers and organization of the Senate. A curtailment of the Senate's powers which could not be made through organic laws unless the Senate were to give its consent, can be done by a revision of the constitution itself without the Senate's being able to veto such a revision if the National Assembly forms a united front. Assuming that all parliamentarians be present, a three-fifths majority in the Congress is equal to $\frac{(552 + 307) \times 3}{5} = 516.$

With its 552 members, the National Assembly may carry the vote. However, as with ordinary laws, the choice of a procedure more favorable to the deputies does not belong to the National Assembly, but to the executive, in this case the president and the premier acting jointly.

# 18 *The Community*

The terms used to describe French overseas possessions went through an evolution paralleling that which led the British Empire to become first the British Commonwealth and then the Commonwealth. However, if the Community is the heir to the French Union which itself succeeded the French Empire, the Community was not at first intended to be another Commonwealth. In instituting the Community, de Gaulle gambled that the former French colonies would realize that independence and a club-like association would not solve their problems, that in today's world power and prosperity have to be sought in large communities of nations unified at least in their diplomacy, their military defense, and their economic development.

The Community outlined by the constitution of 1958 and organized by subsequent organic laws [1] was based on two principles. The first, that the members of the Community other than France did not have full sovereignty and accepted French leadership. The second, that any member was free to leave the Community. This original scheme did not last two years. In 1960 the constitution was amended in order to enable the Mali federation (Sudan and Senegal), as well as Madagascar, to become sovereign states, while remaining within the Community. The Community then comprised for a time two different institutions under one name; a Community reserved to autonomous states and a Community of independent states. The former fast became an empty shell after all the remaining autonomous states had asked and obtained independence in the second part of 1960. The original Community of 1958 and the "new" Community of 1960 will be examined separately.

## THE ORIGINAL COMMUNITY

The Community defined by the Constitution of 1958 comprises the French Republic on the one hand, the autonomous states on the other.

### *The French Republic*

The French Republic is itself composed of metropolitan France, Algeria, the Sahara and the overseas *départements* and territories.

The twelve *départements* of Algeria, the two of the Sahara, and the four "old" ones of Réunion, Guyane, Guadeloupe, and Martinique are politically assimilated to France. Administratively the degree of assimilation varies; it is almost complete in the "old" overseas *départements* which have basically the same administrative structure as those of metropolitan France and are subject to the laws passed by the French parliament unless specifically stated otherwise by the law itself. As for Algeria, the policy of administrative assimilation pursued by the de Gaulle and Debré governments since 1958 reversed previous trends; administrative assimilation is not, however, as complete as in the "old" *départements*. The various French ministries do not all have the same direct responsibility for the administration of Algeria as for that of France. Most administrations, and services with jurisdiction in Algeria, come under the authority of a secretariat general subordinated to the prime minister.

Article 73 of the constitution stipulates that the administrative organization and the legislative system to which the overseas *départements* are subject may be made to meet specific local conditions. This article seems to restrict eventual attempts at "deassimilating" the overseas *départements* in two ways. First, there cannot be any modification to the principle of political assimilation except with the consent of the populations or through a constitutional revision. Second, short of an abandonment of territory, the administrative and legislative modifications allowed by Article 73 could only be adaptations of the system used for metropolitan France, and because an adaptation cannot contradict a basic principle, such adaptation would have to respect the principle of political assimilation.[2]

The overseas territories are one step further removed from administrative assimilation than are the overseas *départements*. Before 1958 all former colonies which had not become overseas *départements* were classified as overseas territories. Although some of these territories, such as Saint Pierre and Miquelon, were culturally close to France, they were, on the whole, the least assimilable of French colonies. The constitution of 1958 gave the overseas territories a triple choice: status quo, accession to the status of overseas *département*, or adhesion to the community with the status of member state. Most territories chose to become member states, but Saint Pierre and Miquelon, New Caledonia and its dependencies, Tahiti and the Oceania establishments, French Somaliland, and the Comores Islands maintained the status quo. These territories were joined at the end of 1959 by the Wallis and Futuna Islands, two former protectorates. The overseas territories have political institutions of their own with more powers than the metropolitan local governments. As a rule, each territory has an assembly elected by universal suffrage, a government elected by the assembly and, in fact if not in theory, responsible before it. The head of the territory is appointed by the government in Paris. A law of June 23, 1956, defined matters outside the powers of the territorial organs of government. They include foreign affairs, national defense, the courts, labor inspection, the guarantees of civil rights, the protection of the public peace, communications with the outside, currency, credit and foreign exchange, university education, and the creation and control of public and semipublic undertakings. Limited to such matters as local finances, intraterritorial communications, primary and secondary schools, the powers of the territorial governments are nevertheless significant, especially as they extend to the local questions of most interest to the inhabitants of such territories. The territorial assembly's overthrowing its cabinet may also be used as a means of calling the attention of the Paris government to the territory's problems.

*The autonomous member states*

In 1959 there were twelve such states: Ivory Coast, Dahomey, High Volta, Mauritania, Niger, Gabon, Congo, Central African Republic, Tchad, Madagascar, Sudan and Senegal. All the African states adopted republican and parliamentary constitutions of a traditional French type with supreme executive power resting in a cabinet responsible before an assembly elected by universal suffrage. Madagascar gave herself a presidential system akin to that of France. The autonomous states were made entirely free to administer their own affairs; that is, all those not reserved to the Community.

### The Division of Powers

Article 78 of the constitution groups communal matters under two major categories; those of primary importance, reserved to the Community without restrictions, and those of secondary importance, belonging to the Community unless otherwise specified by an agreement between the state and the Community. The first category comprises foreign affairs, defense, currency, Community economic and financial policy, and strategic raw materials policy. The second category includes justice, university education, telecommunications, and interstate transportation.

These classifications are not rigid; powers may be transferred by specific agreements from the states to the community and vice versa.[3]

At various meetings of the Community executive held during 1959, the division of powers between the center and the units was clarified on certain points. The Paris meeting in June established the principle of free movement of goods within the Community, but agreed that within the framework of a general economic policy each state or group of states could set up their own tariffs vis à vis foreign states. The same meeting also decided that judges would be nominated by the governments of the member states and appointed by the president of the Community, and that appeals against the decisions of African courts could be introduced before the French Court of Cassation and the French Council of State. The Tananarive meeting in July confirmed that foreign affairs belonged exclusively to the Community, but agreed that member states could have their own representatives before such international organizations as UNESCO, FAO and ILO.[4]

The constitution created a common citizenship for all members of the Community and set the principle of no discrimination based on origin, race, or religion. The effect of the common citizenship was to give the same political rights to all members of the Community. A Frenchman in the Ivory Coast remained subject to the French civil code but was not politically considered a foreigner; he could vote and run for elections. Likewise, an Ivory Coast citizen could be an electoral candidate in France, or could be appointed to the French civil service.

### Organization

According to the constitutional texts of 1958, the Community is composed of a president, an Executive Council, a Senate, and an Arbitration Court.

The president of the French Republic is ex-officio president of the Community. Although elected by an electoral college including representatives of all the autonomous member states, the president was foremost the choice of France, only secondarily of the French Community. With 56,000,000 inhabitants of 83,-000,000 for the whole Community, that is 67.4 per cent, the French Republic had in 1958, 78,119 presidential electors of 81,754, that is 96.4 per cent.

The powers of the president as head of the Community are hardly outlined in the constitution which states only that he presides over and represents the Community, that he has personal representatives in all member states, that he acts as chairman of the Executive Council, that he summons and closes the Community Senate sessions, and submits to that body economic and financial questions for advice. The organic laws of December, 1958, defined more precisely the president's powers but left much ambiguity over a fundamental question: the restrictions to which the president is subject when acting as head of the Community. The organic law of 1958 gave the president the right to summon the Executive Council either in Paris or in the capital city of any of the member states, the right to determine the council's agenda and to designate those among the ministers of the French cabinet who are given the additional function of "minister in charge of Community affairs" and are thus ex-officio members of the Community executive, the right to ask ministers of any of the member states to participate in the council's discussions, the right to appoint the secretary-general and the personnel of the Community Secretariat, and the right to appoint the seven judges of the Community Arbitration Court. Article 5 of the organic law of December, 1958 (No. 58-1254), states with great lack of clarity that

the President of the Community sees to it that the Constitution, the organic laws of the Community, the Community agreements covered by Articles 78 and 87 of the Constitution, the decisions of the Community Arbitration Court, and the treaties and international agreements that bind the Community, be respected.

He formulates and serves notice of the measures necessary to the direction of common matters; he sees to it that they be implemented.

The relationships between the president and the Community organs are relatively clear. The president is not bound by the advice given him by the Community executive or by the Community Senate, but is bound by the judgments of the Arbitration Court. Not clear is the relationship between the president of the Community and the government and parliament of the French Republic. When acting as president of the Community, the president need not obtain the prime minister's countersignature which he requires when he acts as president of the Republic. It could thus and has indeed been argued that Article 5 of the organic law mentioned had given the president the right to rule under his sole signature on all matters of Community interests, that is, for foreign affairs and economic and financial policy among others.

Such an interpretation does not seem valid. The constitution itself did not give the president the right to rule the Community. Most of all, if as president of the Community the president of the Republic could bypass the whole constitutional system and transfer to himself the powers specifically reserved to French parliaments and governments, the constitution would become a farce. The powers of the president of the Community cannot but be determined in function of the powers of the president of the Republic. It is more in keeping with the spirit of the constitution to think of decisions of the president, as head of the Community, as "executory" solely with regard to the internal organization of the Community, such as the opening or closing of the sessions of the Community Senate or the setting of the agenda of the Executive Council; but with regard to other matters to think of the president's decisions as only "declaratory." Presidential decisions concerning the appointment of Africans to diplomatic positions or France's financial contribution to the economic development of a particular member state have to be endorsed by the proper French authorities, either the government or the parliament, before becoming executory. It remains that the president's power to make such suggestions under his sole signature often brought the governments or legislatures of the Community before a political *fait accompli*. For example, the president's declaration at the Dakar meeting of December, 1959, that Sudan's and Senegal's claims at becoming independent within the Community were valid, created a political situation difficult to reverse.

The Community Executive is composed of ex-officio and of appointed members; the prime minister of the French Republic, the heads of governments of the other member states, and the ministers in charge of Community affairs have a constitutional right to attend meetings. In February, 1959, de Gaulle appointed seven members of the French cabinet as ministers in charge of Community affairs: Couve de Murville for foreign affairs; Guillaumat for defense; Pinay for currency, economic and financial policy; Michelet for justice; Boulloche for education; Buron for interstate transportations, and Cornut-Gentille for telecommunications.

In addition, the president of the Community, who presides at executive meetings, may ask other French and member-state ministers to attend a particular meeting. The council meets at least twice a year during sessions of the Community Senate and as often as the president deems necessary. The council's discussions may be prepared by interministerial meetings bringing together the ministers in charge of Community affairs and the corresponding ministers of the other member states; such meetings are presided over by members of the council selected by the president.

The meetings held in 1959 showed the Executive Council to have a threefold purpose. First, to inform the member states of the French position on international problems and discuss the position. The Tananarive meeting was devoted mostly to hearing Couve de Murville's analysis of the Berlin situation and General Ely's brief on military and strategical problems. Second, to organize the Community by giving advice on appointments and administrative structures contemplated by the president. Third, to debate proposals submitted by the president either on his own initiative or at the request of members of the council. Such proposals fell within the category of communal matters. For example they agreed that the exchange rate between the metropolitan franc and the CFA franc be maintained as it was, that the president determine the list of strategic raw materials, and that a full-fledged university be founded at Tananarive in 1961. Issues possibly raising the constitutional problem of the president of the Community's powers over French affairs were generally avoided. For example, the president of the Community entrusted the French prime minister with the Community's military defense.

Like the Executive Council, the Senate of the Community has purely consultative powers. It is composed of delegates from the French parliament and from the legislatures of the other member states, selected on the basis of one senator for 300,000 inhabitants with a minimum of three senators for each member state.[5] Community senators hold their mandates for a maximum of five years; they must resign their Community seat when up for reëlection in the chamber which appointed them. The Senate of the Community meets at least twice yearly for two month-long sessions. Extraordinary sessions not exceeding ten days may be called by the president. The members of the Executive Council may participate in the debates of the Community Senate and must be heard at their request. Ministers in charge of Community affairs may be questioned by Community senators but only through a written not an oral procedure. At the president's request the Community Senate may give advice on projects concerning the Community's economic and financial policy, on treaties or international agreements binding the Community, on declarations of war, and generally on projects concerning the economic, social, and cultural development of the Community. However, the senators may not initiate debates on those matters; initiative must come from the president. On its own accord the Community Senate may debate and pass recommendations for the harmonizing of legislation among the member states.

The Senate was not intended to be an important organ in the governing of the Community. That the Community Senate was not even assigned a building of its own, but in 1959 had to use the facilities of the French Senate, illustrates the loss of status suffered by the overseas assembly which under the Fourth Republic, had if no more powers, at least proper housing.[6]

### The Arbitration Court

This court is composed of seven judges appointed by the president for six years and may be reappointed. They must be selected from among magistrates who have served on the bench for at least ten years, from university law professors with at least ten years' seniority, or from well-known personalities who by reason of functions exercised for at least twenty years are highly qualified in the law. The court chairman is appointed by the president. The judges may not have political, administrative, or professional activities other than teaching and the magistracy; they may not give legal advice and may not make public their opinions on questions falling within the court's competence. During their term in office the judges appointed from among civil servants may not be promoted, unless automatically. The Court judges may not be prosecuted, detained or judged in criminal matters without the court's consent, and may not be dismissed for violation of their oath except by the court itself.

The function of the court is to arbitrate legal conflicts arising from diverging interpretations of the rules binding the members of the Community, although member states may agree to extend the court's competence to other than constitutional and related matters. The court may grant financial compensations and, at the president's request, acts as an election court for the Senate of the Community and gives advice on the interpretation of the constitutional texts, organic laws, and community agreements. The advice is not made public, but is sent personally to the president. The court's jurisdiction may be invoked either by the member states or by the "Community's representative," apparently the president.

An accused party in a dispute is given the right of answering the arguments presented by the other party. Written documents are the only valid acts on which the court's decisions may be based; however, the parties may present their case orally. The decisions must be rendered by at least five judges but, in the event of a tie, the chairman casts the deciding vote. As before international courts, states may not bring cases of wrongs caused to their nationals unless all possibilities of appeal to municipal jurisdictions have been exhausted. However the court may, exceptionally, agree to hear a case not meeting that requirement.

### The Right of Independence

According to the letter of the constitution, the right of independence is not absolute; the French government or parliament may veto the change of status. Nevertheless, for France to refuse endorsement of a request for independence would be politically difficult. Furthermore the text of the constitution may be interpreted as within the principle of self-determination written in the preamble and most of all within de Gaulle's solemn promises, before and after the passing of the constitution, that France would not prevent an overseas state from becoming independent. The constitution was approved by the overseas states on the basis of that understanding. No objections were raised by France when the autonomous states asked for independence.

Making independence subject to approval by the French parliament may, in fact, have led Madagascar and the African states to claim independence sooner than anticipated, insofar as they may have thought it unwise not to draw on de Gaulle's influence on the first parliament of the Fifth Republic.

### Budget and Secretariat

There are two categories of Community expenses: expenses required for the proper functioning of Community organs such as the Arbitration Court or the Senate, and expenses resulting from the Community's policies. The first may be referred to as the organization budget, the second as the policy budget.

The Community has no right to levy taxes but must rely on the member states for its financial resources. The organization budget is built by contributions from the members as in the United Nations. It was agreed in 1959 that France would contribute two-thirds, the other states one-third.[7] The policy expenses are written in the budgets of the various member states after agreement between the Community and the governments concerned. In fact, all heavy expenses are borne by France, who in addition subsidizes the various member states.

The Community has a Secretariat directly and personally attached to the presidency of the Republic. The Secretariat's personnel is appointed by the president as part of his personal staff. But at first, the Secretariat was more than a body of personal advisors to the president, however; it was a coördinating agency for the whole Community, an agency entrusted with preparing the meetings of the Executive Council and more generally with establishing or facilitating communications between the member states, the French Republic and the presidency. The Secretariat had originally four specialized sections, dealing with economic and financial affairs, telecommunications and transportation, justice and university education, and relations between the Community and international organizations.

A reallocation of jurisdiction between the secretariat and the French Council of Ministers took place in 1960 after some members of the Community Executive Council—in particular Houphouët-Boigny—had criticized the secretariat, viewed as a cumbersome obstacle to direct contacts with the presidency. An under secretary in the French cabinet was entrusted with coordinating political, economic and social policies of the Community. The assigning of these responsibilities to a cabinet member of lower rank was to avoid reviving anything resembling the former ministry for the colonies. The secretariat's task was limited to advising the president and preparing the meetings of the Executive Council.

## Evolution of the Community

The Community was not even born before two basically different interpretations of its nature and future were proposed by African leaders. For Houphouët-Boigny, prime minister of the Ivory Coast, the Community was a federation of unequals where African states recognizing their economic and political backwardness accepted France's leadership as the better means of protection and of improved economic conditions. According to Houphouët-Boigny, the overbalance in favor of France should not have been permanent; [8] the Community should have led to a federation of equals, when African states have reached the proper level of social, economic, and political development. For Senghor, president of the Mali federal assembly, for Mamadou Dia, prime minister of Senegal, and for Modibo Keita, prime minister of Sudan, the Community was a transitional stage which, from the now-abolished colonial status, was to lead African states to complete independence by giving them above all the means of independence, that is, a sound economy and a stable political system.[9] For Senghor and his political friends, the Community opened on a club-like organization, on a French commonwealth bound by language and culture. Senghor's conception finally triumphed; Houphouët-Boigny himself rallied to it in the summer of 1960.

### The "New" Community of Independent States

In June 1960 the Mali federation (Sudan and Senegal) and Madagascar obtained international sovereignty, after an amendment to the constitution had rendered possible independence within the Community. In the following two months all other autonomous states claimed independence. Ivory Coast, Dahomey, Niger, and High Volta insisted on obtaining transfer of all Community powers to themselves as well as admission to the United Nations before negotiating with France a treaty defining their relationships with the Community. Mauritania, Gabon, and the three states party to the contemplated confederation known as Union of the Republics of Central Africa, (Tchad, Congo, and Central African Republic), decided on the contrary to follow the procedure initiated by the Mali and Madagascar and consequently negotiated a treaty of association with the Community before obtaining full sovereignty. But whether the treaty of association with the Community was negotiated before or after independence does not alter the fact that in the new Community of independent states the relationships between members belong to the domain of international, no longer of constitutional law. The agreements between France and Madagascar may serve as an example.

These agreements set forth two principles. The first, that the relations between the two countries were relations of sovereign state to sovereign state; the second, that the two countries formed, along with other states, a community for the purpose of voluntary coöperation.

In application of the first principle, Madagascar was given all the attributes of sovereignty—in particular that of carrying its own diplomatic relations, of organizing and controlling its own army, of negotiating its own trade agreements, and of determining its own policy on imports, exports, and tariffs.

In application of the second principle, Madagascar entered with France a multilateral convention open to other states. This convention called for privileged treatment of the nationals of each country by the other member states. It set the principle that disputes between states should be settled through a procedure of conciliation and that, should this procedure fail, arbitration would be sought from an Arbitration Court, composed of an equal number of members from each state.

Still in application of the principle of free coöperation within the Community, Madagascar agreed to recognize the President of the French Republic as being ex officio president of the Community, agreed to take part in a periodic conference of the chiefs of state and of government chaired by the president of the Community, and to serve on various related committees of ministers and experts. Madagascar was further given the option of sending a delegation to a consultative Community Senate composed of delegates from the parliaments of the member states.

Madagascar and France also agreed to give each other mutual help in the field of defense. To that effect, the strategic base of Diego-Suarez and various other military installations were put at France's disposal. France promised to help the Madagascar republic financially and economically, in particular to guarantee the currency of the new state. On her part, Madagascar agreed to remain within the franc zone and to maintain, with France, a preferential trade system based on the free circulation of goods and commodities.

As the former autonomous states became independent, the Community devised in 1958 had to be modified to meet the new situation. As indicated in the agreements between France, the Mali, and Madagascar, the Executive Council of the Community and the Senate of the Arbitration Court will continue under either their old or new names. But instead of being advisors to the president of the Community they will become international consultative agencies not unlike the Council of Europe with its committee of ministers and its assembly of parliamentarians from various sovereign nations.

Notwithstanding de Gaulle's original hopes, the Community became much like the Commonwealth—a means of facilitating France's granting independence to her former colonies without losing face, while maintaining with them as many cultural, economic, and political ties as possible.

# *Conclusion*

Having resisted and surmounted the pressures which had brought the Fourth Republic to an end, having asserted the authority of the state without suppressing the public liberties, the Fifth Republic seems, in its second year of existence, to have realized the hopes of its founders: to stabilize French democracy by shifting power from the legislature to the executive branch of government. However, the future of the new Republic remains uncertain, not only because of the unresolved Algerian problem but also because so much of the new system of government is dependent on the personality of its first president, rather than on the soundness of the Constitution.

Within a democratic context the strengthening of the executive may come from the constitutional or from the party systems. Under the Third and Fourth Republics it came from neither. Undisciplined political groupings, forming webs of ever changing parliamentary combinations, paralyzed one another in a vain agitation. Wanting in that they had not taken France's anarchical multipartism into account, the constitutions had put the crux of power in parliaments divided against themselves. Instead of being resolved, the oppositions which divided the electorate were magnified.

Following de Gaulle's return to power, the emergence of a large cohesive governmental party appeared to lead the country away from her extreme multipartism. The UNR controlled nearly 40 per cent of the votes in the 1958 National Assembly and, notwithstanding internal dissentions, was sufficiently well disciplined to ensure passage of the laws wanted by the executive. But being still a Bonapartist party, the fate of which is so intimately linked to that of a leader that it might not survive him, the UNR had but a fragile future.

The new constitutional structures contributed to freeing the executive. The unrestricted power of dissolution, the limitations on the use of the motion of nonconfidence, the possibility for the government to have legislation passed by a mere plurality together with the impossibility of overthrowing the cabinet except by a majority of the deputies, the curtailing of the Assemblies' legislative authority, the simplified budget procedure, all such devices contributed to the executive's security in office. But, like for the party system, the gains made remain indefinite. The prime minister is still at all times responsible before a lower house which might easily return to its traditional divisions. The executive itself, separated as it is into president and cabinet, might eventually be weakened or even paralyzed by its duality. To a struggle for power between parliamentary groups and between government and parliament, might be added eventually a struggle between premier and president. The constitutional structures of 1958 are not such as to prevent a *de facto* presidential system from reverting to the traditional French parliamentary regime. De Gaulle's successor, if he will owe the presidency to a college of provincial notables rather than to popularity and prestige among the electorate at large, may find himself losing authority for his greater distance from universal suffrage than the prime minister and thus outside the main stream of power.

Wanting to emphasize that the presidency of the Fifth Republic was unlike that of the Third, de Gaulle is reported to have said that he had no predecessor. It may be that he will not have a successor. Remaining outside the party system and largely also outside the constitutional system he has not identified himself with the institutions. His presidency may well remain an exception rather than create a precedent. If this is so, France may have missed an opportunity of adapting her constitutional to her party system. This lack of adaptation may still invite oscillations between too extreme an authoritarianism and too weak a democracy.

# Appendix

# TABLE I

## Prime Ministers of the Fourth Republic

| Prime minister | Investiture | Resignation |
|---|---|---|
| 1st Parliament | | |
| 1. Ramadier | 21. 1. 1947 | 19. 11. 1947 |
| 2. Schuman | 22. 11. 1947 | 19. 7. 1948 |
| 3. Marie | 25. 7. 1948 | 27. 8. 1948 |
| 4. Schuman (2d) | 31. 8. 1948 | 7. 9. 1948 |
| 5. Queuille | 10. 9. 1948 | 5. 10. 1949 |
| 6. Bidault | 27. 10. 1949 | 24. 6. 1950 |
| 7. Queuille (2d) | 30. 6. 1950 | 4. 7. 1950 |
| 8. Pleven | 11. 7. 1950 | 28. 2. 1951 |
| 9. Queuille (3d) | 9. 3. 1951 | 10. 7. 1951 |
| 2d Parliament | | |
| 10. Pleven (2d) | 8. 8. 1951 | 7. 1. 1952 |
| 11. Faure | 17. 1. 1952 | 29. 2. 1952 |
| 12. Pinay | 6. 3. 1952 | 22. 12. 1952 |
| 13. Mayer | 6. 1. 1953 | 21. 5. 1953 |
| 14. Laniel | 26. 6. 1953 | 12. 6. 1954 |
| 15. Mendès-France | 17. 6. 1954 | 4. 2. 1955 |
| 16. Faure (2d) | 23. 2. 1955 | 29. 11. 1955 |
| 3d Parliament | | |
| 17. Mollet | 31. 1. 1956 | 21. 5. 1957 |
| 18. Bourgès-Maunoury | 12. 6. 1957 | 30. 9. 1957 |
| 19. Gaillard | 5. 11. 1957 | 15. 4. 1958 |
| 20. Pflimlin | 13. 5. 1958 | 31. 5. 1958 |

## TABLE II

ELECTIONS TO THE CONSTITUANT AND NATIONAL ASSEMBLIES IN METROPOLITAN FRANCE, 1946–1958
(In per cent)

| Party | 1945 | June, 1946 | Nov., 1946 | 1951 | 1956 | 1958 1st ballot | 1958 2d ballot |
|---|---|---|---|---|---|---|---|
| Communists | 26.1 | 26.2 | 28.6 | 25.9 | 25.9 | 18.9 | 20.7 |
| Socialists | 23.8 | 21.1 | 17.9 | 14.5 | 15.0 | 15.5 | 13.8 |
| Radicals | 11.1 | 11.5 | 14.0 | 10.0 | 13.5 | 4.8 [a]<br>6.7 [b] | 2.0 [a]<br>5.7 [b] |
| MRP | 24.9 | 28.1 | 26.3 | 12.5 | 11.1 | 9.1 [c]<br>2.5 [d] | 7.5 |
| Independents, conservatives | 13.3 | 12.8 | 12.8 | 14.0 | 14.6 | 19.9 | 23.6 |
| Gaullists | — | — | — | 21.7 | 4.3 | 17.6 | 26.4 |
| Poujadists | — | — | — | — | 12.3 | — | — |
| Others | 0.9 | 0.3 | 0.3 | 1.4 | 3.3 | 4.7 [e] | — |

[a] Radicals.
[b] Republican Center and other splinter center groups.
[c] MRP.
[d] Christian Democracy.
[e] Includes Poujadists and extreme Right, 3.3; and various Leftists, 1.4.

SOURCES: Before 1958: P. Campbell, *French Electoral Systems and Electors, 1789–1957* (London: Faber and Faber, 1958); for 1958: *Le Monde*, Dec. 2, 1958. Because of many coalition tickets, the 1951 and 1956 figures for Socialists, Radicals, MRP, and Independents are subject to reservations.

## TABLE III

SEATS IN THE CONSTITUANT AND NATIONAL ASSEMBLIES IN METROPOLITAN FRANCE, 1946–1958
(In per cent)

| Party | 1945 | June, 1946 | Nov., 1946 | 1951 | 1956 | 1958 |
|---|---|---|---|---|---|---|
| Communists | 28.4 | 28.0 | 30.5 | 17.8 | 26.7 | 2.1 |
| Socialists | 25.7 | 22.0 | 16.6 | 17.3 | 16.2 | 8.6 |

TABLE III (*continued*)

| Party | 1945 | June, 1946 | Nov., 1946 | 1951 | 1956 | 1958 |
|---|---|---|---|---|---|---|
| Radicals | 6.7 | 7.5 | 11.0 | 14.1 | 13.0 | 2.8 [d] <br> 4.7 [b] |
| MRP | 27.0 | 30.6 | 29.0 | 15.1 | 13.0 | 9.4 [c] <br> 2.8 [a] |
| Independents, conservatives | 11.9 | 11.9 | 12.9 | 16.0 | 17.3 | 28.3 |
| Gaullists | — | — | — | 19.6 | 2.9 | 40.6 |
| Poujadists | — | — | — | — | 9.6 | — |
| Others | 0.3 | — | — | — | 1.3 | 0.2 |

[a] Radicals.
[b] Republican Center and other splinter center groups.
[c] MRP.
[d] Christian Democracy.

SOURCES: Before 1958: P. Campbell, *French Electoral Systems and Electors, 1789–1957* (London: Faber and Faber, 1958); for 1958: *Le Monde*, Dec. 2, 1958. Because of many coalition tickets, the 1951 and 1956 figures for Socialists, Radicals, MRP, and Independents are subject to reservations.

TABLE IV

MEMBERSHIPS OF PARLIAMENTARY GROUPS, OCTOBER, 1959

| Groups | National Assembly | Senate |
|---|---|---|
| Communists | 10 | 14 |
| Socialists | 44 | 51 |
| Radicals | 43 | 64 |
| MRP | 56 | 28 |
| Democratic center | | 6 |
| UNR | 218 | 44 |
| Independents | 119 | 74 |
| Farmers | — | 20 |
| Algerians | 46 | — |
| Unclassified | 16 | 6 |
| Totals | 552 | 307 |

The deputies and senators affiliated (*apparentés*) to a parliamentary group are counted as members of that group.

## TABLE V

MAJOR VOTES IN THE NATIONAL ASSEMBLY

| Date | Occasion | Majority of votes cast | For government | Hostile [a] to government | |
|---|---|---|---|---|---|
| Party Strength at Beginning of 1959: | | | | | |
| 1959 Jan. 17 | Approval of Debré cabinet | 255 | 453 | 56 | Ag (Ab |
| Party Strength in July 1959: [c] | | | | | |
| Oct. 17 | De Gaulle's peace proposals for Algeria | 233 | 441 | 23 | Ag (Ab |
| Oct. 30 | Fiscal reform | 198 | 300 | 95 | Ag (Ab |
| Dec. 18 | Budget for 1960 | 187 | 200 | 172 | Ag (Ab |
| Dec. 24 | School reform | 250 | 427 | 71 | Ag (Ab |
| Party Strength at Beginning of 1960: | | | | | |
| 1960 Feb. | Emergency powers on Algeria | 267 | 441 | 75 | Ag (Ab |

[a] The votes hostile to the government are divided into votes against (Ag) and abstentions (Ab); the deputies recorded as having cast an "abstention" vote and the deputies who, while not formally excused, did not take part in the vote, are considered as having abstained.

[b] The members of the Democratic-freedom group founded in October, 1959,

| Against the government by party | | | | | | | | |
|---|---|---|---|---|---|---|---|---|
| Communists | Socialists | Radicals | Neo-Radicals [b] | MRP | UNR | Independents | Algerians | Others |
| 10 | 47 | 15 | 26 | 65 | 204 | 115 | 56 | 29 |
| 10<br>0 | 43<br>3 | 0<br>2 | 0<br>2 | 0<br>11 | 0<br>1 | 1<br>11 | 0<br>1 | 2<br>1) |
| 10 | 44 | 15 | 25 | 56 | 212 | 118 | 50 | 22 |
| 8<br>2 | 0<br>0 | 0<br>2 | 0<br>3 | 0<br>2 | 0<br>2 | 13<br>22 | 0<br>38 | 2<br>8) |
| 10<br>0 | 38<br>4 | 16<br>2 | 10<br>3 | 13<br>0 | 3<br>17 | 2<br>10 | 1<br>13 | 2<br>6) |
| 10<br>0 | 42<br>1 | 33<br>4 | | 1<br>54 | 8<br>21 | 37<br>49 | 35<br>9 | 6<br>22) |
| 10<br>0 | 44<br>0 | 8<br>7 | 0<br>2 | 0<br>3 | 3<br>13 | 2<br>3 | 0<br>15 | 4<br>7) |
| 10 | 44 | 18 | 25 | 57 | 210 | 119 | 45 | 24 |
| 10<br>0 | 2<br>0 | 0<br>1 | 2<br>0 | 3<br>2 | 0<br>3 | 30<br>15 | 21<br>7 | 7<br>7) |

are considered as Neo-Radicals.

[c] The major changes in party strength are due to the fact that the representatives from the former overseas territories, which had become member states of the Community, ceased to be members of the French parliament in July, 1959.

## TABLE VI

### Population over Nineteen Years Old

| Occupation | Millions | Per cent |
|---|---|---|
| Farmers | 4.0 | 14 |
| Farm workers | 1.1 | 4 |
| Industrialists, owners of business | 2.5 | 9 |
| Liberal professions, upper management, upper civil service | 0.6 | 2 |
| Middle management, middle civil service | 1.2 | 4 |
| Lower white-collar workers | 1.9 | 6 |
| Workers | 5.4 | 18 |
| Domestic servants | 1.0 | 3 |
| Miscellaneous | 0.4 | 1 |
| Not in labor force | 11.4 | 38 |
| Total | 29.4 | 99 |

SOURCE: *Annuaire Statistique de la France* (Paris: INSEE, 1957), p. 68.

# *The Constitution of October 4, 1958*

Translations or summaries of selected articles of the organic laws of 1958 and 1959 have been inserted after each relevant article in the constitution. Summarized material has been enclosed in brackets.

## CONSTITUTION

### Preamble

The French people solemnly proclaim their attachment to the Rights of Man and to the principles of national sovereignty as defined by the Declaration of 1789, confirmed and completed by the preamble to the Constitution of 1946.

According to these principles, and to that of the free determination of peoples, the Republic offers to the overseas territories that express the will to adhere to them, new institutions based on the common ideal of liberty, equality, and fraternity and conceived with a view to their democratic evolution.

*Article* 1. The Republic and the people of the overseas territories who, by an act of free determination, adopt the present Constitution, institute a Community.

The Community is based on the equality and the solidarity of the peoples composing it.

### Chapter I

*On Sovereignty*

*Article* 2. France is an indivisible, lay, democratic, and social Republic. It ensures equality of all citizens before the law, without distinction of origin, race, or religion. It respects all beliefs.

The national emblem is the blue, white, and red tricolor flag.

The national anthem is the "Marseillaise."

The motto of the Republic is "Liberty, Equality, Fraternity."

Its principle is: government of the people, by the people, and for the people.

*Article* 3. National sovereignty belongs to the people, who exercise it through their representatives and by way of referendum.

No section of the people, nor any individual, may assume its exercise.

Suffrage may be direct or indirect under the conditions stipulated by the Constitution. It is always universal, equal, and secret.

All French nationals of both sexes who have attained their majority and who have the exercise of their civil and political rights, may vote under conditions set by law.

*Article* 4. Political parties and groups share in the expression of the suffrage. They come into being and pursue their activities freely. They must respect the principles of national sovereignty and of democracy.

### Chapter II

*The President of the Republic*

*Article* 5. The President of the Republic sees to it that the Constitution is respected. He ensures, by his arbitration, the regular functioning of the public authorities, as well as the continuity of the State.

He is the guarantor of national independence, of the integrity of the territory, and of respect for Community agreements and for treaties.

*Article* 6. The President of the Republic is elected for seven years by an electoral college including the members of Parliament, of the General Councils and of the assemblies of the overseas territories, as well as the elected representatives of the municipal councils. These representatives are:

The mayor for communes of fewer than 1,000 inhabitants;

the mayor and the first deputy mayor for communes of 1,000 to 2,000 inhabitants;

the mayor, the first deputy mayor, and one municipal councilor for communes of 2,001 to 2,500 inhabitants.

the mayor, the first two deputy mayors, and three municipal councilors, selected according to seniority in office for communes of 3,001 to 6,000 inhabitants;

the mayor, the first two deputy mayors, and three municipal councilors, selected according to seniority in office, for communes of 6,001 to 9,000 inhabitants;

all the municipal councilors for communes of more than 9,000 inhabitants;

in addition, for communes of more than 30,000 inhabitants, delegates appointed by the municipal council on the basis of one delegate for every 1,000 inhabitants over 30,000.

In the overseas territories of the Republic the elected representatives of the councils of the administrative units are also included in the electoral college as determined by an organic law.

The participation of Member States of the Community in the Presidential electoral college is determined by agreement between the Republic and the Member States of the Community.

An organic law determines the modalities of application of this article.

ORGANIC LAW NO. 58-1064, NOV. 7, 1958

[*Article* 1. The list of candidates is published by the Government at least ten days before the first ballot.

Nominations must be made no later than twelve days before the first ballot, by at least fifty members of the Presidential electoral college. The Constitutional Council checks that the candidates have agreed to their nominations.

*Article* 9. The election of delegates and alternates is by proportional representation (highest-remainder system). The lists of candidates, which need not comprise as many candidates as there are positions, may not be altered by the electors.

*Article* 15. Members of the Presidential college who fail to vote and do not have a valid excuse are fined 3,000 francs.

*Article* 22. The Constitutional Council may quash the election on the ground that serious violations of the electoral process were such as to have distorted the over-all election results.

*Article* 25. The second ballot takes place within eight days of the first ballot. No new candidate may be introduced unless nominated by two candidates withdrawing from the contest after the first ballot.]

*Article* 7. The President of the Republic is elected by an absolute majority on the first ballot. Failing such a majority the President of the Republic is elected on a second ballot by a plurality.

Balloting is opened by a Government convocation.

The election of the new President takes place at least twenty days and at most fifty days before the powers of the President in office come to an end.

Should the presidency of the Republic become vacant, whatever be the cause, or should the Constitutional Council, moved by the Government, establish, by an absolute majority of its members, that the President is incapacitated, the functions of the President of the Republic, except those conferred by Articles 11 and 12 below, are temporarily exercised by the Chairman of the Senate. In case of a vacancy, or when the incapacitation is declared permanent by the Constitutional Council, voting for the election of a new President takes place, except in case of *force majeure* officially established by the Constitutional Council, at least twenty days and at most fifty days after the beginning of the vacancy or after the declaration of the permanent character of the incapacitation.

*Article* 8. The President of the Republic

appoints the Prime Minister. He terminates the functions of the Prime Minister when the latter submits the resignation of the Government.

On the proposal of the Prime Minister he appoints and dismisses the other members of the Government.

*Article* 9. The President of the Republic presides over the Council of Ministers.

*Article* 10. The President of the Republic promulgates the laws within fifteen days after the transmission to the Government of the finally adopted law.

Before this period has come to an end he may ask Parliament to reconsider the law or some of its articles. This reconsideration may not be refused.

*Article* 11. On the proposal of the Government during sessions, or on a joint motion of the two assemblies, published in the *Journal Officiel*, the President of the Republic may submit to a referendum any government bill concerning the organization of public authorities, including approval of a Community agreement, or providing authorization to ratify a treaty which, without being contrary to the Constitution, would affect the working of the institutions.

When the referendum decides in favor of the bill, the President of the Republic promulgates it within the period of time stipulated in the previous article.

*Article* 12. After consulting the Prime Minister and the Chairmen of the assemblies, the President of the Republic may dissolve the National Assembly.

General elections take place at least twenty days and at most forty days after the dissolution.

The National Assembly meets as of right on the second Thursday following its election. If this meeting takes place between the periods provided for ordinary sessions, a session is opened as of right for a fifteen-day period. There may be no further dissolution within the year following these elections.

*Article* 13. The President of the Republic signs the ordinances and decrees considered by the Council of Ministers.

He appoints to state civil and military posts.

Councilors of State, the Grand Chancellor of the Legion of Honor, ambassadors and envoys extraordinary, master councilors of the Audit Court, prefects, representatives of the Government in the overseas territories, officers general, rectors of *academies*, and directors of central administrations are appointed in the Council of Ministers.

An organic law determines the other posts to be filled in the Council of Ministers, as well as the conditions under which the appointment power of the President of the Republic may be delegated and exercised in his name.

ORGANIC LAW NO. 58-1136, NOV. 28, 1958

[*Article* 1. In addition to the positions listed in Article 13, paragraph 3 of the Constitution, the following are filled in the Council of Ministers: the positions of Prosecutor General before the Court of Cassation, Prosecutor General before the Audit Court, Prosecutor General before the Paris Court of Appeal; the positions of management of public establishments and undertakings, and of national corporations when their importance is such as to justify their being placed on a list established by decree taken in the Council of Ministers; the positions for which this procedure is presently prescribed by a specific legal or regulatory provision.

*Article* 2. The President of the Republic appoints by decree: the members of the Council of State and of the Audit Court; the judges; the professors at the university level, the officers of the armed forces of land, sea, and air.

The members of the *corps* normally recruited through the School of National Administration, the members of the prefect corps, the engineers of the technical corps, the recruiting of which is partly determined in function of the Polytechnique School graduation lists, are also appointed by decree of the President of the Republic.

*Article* 3. The appointment powers, other than those listed in Article 13, paragraph 3 of the Constitution, and in Articles 1 and 2 above, may be delegated to the Prime Minister by a Presidential decree in accordance with Articles 13, paragraph 4, and 21 paragraph 1 of the Constitution.]

*Article* 14. The President of the Republic accredits ambassadors and envoys extraordinary to foreign powers; foreign ambassadors and envoys extraordinary are accredited to him.

*Article* 15. The President of the Republic is the head of the armed forces. He presides over the higher councils and committees of National Defense.

*Article* 16. When the institutions of the Republic, the independence of the nation, the integrity of its territory or the fulfillment of its international commitments are gravely and immediately threatened and when the regular working of the constitutional public authorities is interrupted, the President of the Republic takes the measures required by these circumstances, after official consultation with the Prime Minister and the chairmen of the assemblies, as well as with the Constitutional Council.

He informs the nation by a message.

These measures must be prompted by the will to ensure to the constitutional public authorities, in the shortest possible time, the means of accomplishing their mission. The Constitutional Council is consulted regarding these measures.

Parliament meets as of right.

The National Assembly may not be dissolved during the exercise of emergency powers.

*Article* 17. The President of the Republic has the right to pardon.

*Article* 18. The President of the Republic communicates with the two assemblies of Parliament by messages which he instructs to be read, and which are not the object of any debate.

Between sessions, Parliament is convened especially for that purpose.

*Article* 19. Acts of the President of the Republic, other than those provided by Articles 8 (paragraph 1), 11, 12, 16, 18, 54, 56, and 61 are countersigned by the Prime Minister and eventually by the ministers responsible.

## Chapter III

### *The Government*

*Article* 20. The Government determines and conducts the policy of the nation.

It has the administration and the armed forces at its disposal.

It is responsible to Parliament under the conditions and according to the procedures stipulated in Articles 49 and 50.

*Article* 21. The Prime Minister directs the Government's action. He is responsible for National Defense. He ensures the execution of the laws. Subject to the provisions of Article 13, he has the exercise of the regulatory power and appoints to civil and military posts.

He may delegate some of his powers to the ministers.

Eventually he deputizes for the President of the Republic as chairman of the councils and committees provided for by Article 15.

Exceptionally he may deputize for the President as chairman of a council of ministers in persuance of an express delegation and for a specific agenda.

*Article* 22. When appropriate, the acts of the Prime Minister are countersigned by the ministers entrusted with their execution.

*Article* 23. The functions of members of the government are exclusive of the exercise of any parliamentary mandate, of the exercise of any function of professional representation at the national level, and of the exercise of any public position or professional activity.

An organic law determines the rules governing the replacement of the holders of such mandates, functions, or positions.

The replacement of the members of Parliament is made in accordance with the provisions of Article 25.

CHAPTER IV

*The Parliament*

*Article* 24. Parliament consists of the Nation Assembly and the Senate.

The deputies to the National Assembly are elected by direct universal suffrage.

The Senate is elected by indirect suffrage; it ensures the representation of the territorial bodies of the Republic. Frenchmen established outside France are represented in the Senate.

*Article* 25. An organic law determines the term for which each assembly is elected, the number of its members, their emoluments, the conditions of eligibility, and the system of ineligibilities and incompatibilities. The organic law also determines the conditions under which, in case of vacancies, persons are elected to replace deputies or senators until the general or partial renewal of the assembly to which they belonged.

ORGANIC LAW NO. 58-1099, NOV. 17, 1958

[*Article* 2. If an alternate assumes a parliamentary seat when the parliamentarian originally elected to the assembly becomes a member of the Government, this alternate may not run against his former team leader in the next election.]

ORGANIC LAW NO. 58-1065, NOV. 7, 1958, *as amended by organic law No. 59-1605, Nov. 7, 1958*

[*Article* 1. The number of deputies to the National Assembly is: 465 for metropolitan France, 67 for Algeria, 4 for the Sahara, 10 for Guadeloupe, Guyane, Martinique, and Réunion, and 6 for the overseas territories.

*Article* 3. The powers of the National Assembly come to an end at the opening of the regular April session, five years after its election.

*Article* 5. The National Assembly seat which becomes vacant because of the deputy's death, of his joining the Government, of his becoming a member of the Constitutional Council or of his being assigned a governmental mission for over six months is filled by the alternate.

*Article* 6. When an election is quashed, when the provisions of Article 5 are not applicable or when a seat is vacant for reasons other than those outlined in Article 5, a by-election is called within three months. No by-elections take place in the last twelve months of the National Assembly's term.]

### ORGANIC LAW NO. 58-1097, NOV. 15, 1958, *as amended by organic law No. 59-259, Feb. 4, 1959*

[*Article* 1. The number of senate seats is: 255 for metropolitan France, 32 for Algeria, 2 for the Sahara, 7 for Guadeloupe, Guyane, Martinique, and Réunion, 5 for the overseas territories, 6 for Frenchmen residing in foreign countries.

*Articles* 2–3. Senators are elected for nine years. Senate seats belong to one of three series of near equal number, A, B, and C. The Senate is renewed by one-third (one series is renewed at each election).

*Article* 5. The senators elected by a majority system are replaced by their alternates in the event of death, appointment to the Government, appointment to the Constitutional Court, or assignment of a governmental mission for more than six months.

*Article* 6. In the districts where proportional representation is used, the candidate next on the list replaces the senator whose seat has become vacant, whatever be the cause.

*Article* 7. When the election has been quashed, when the seat is vacant for reasons other than those outlined in Article 5, or when the provisions of Article 5 and 6 are not applicable, by-elections are called within three months. No by-elections are called in the year preceding senatorial elections.

*Article* 8. The mandates of persons who become senators in fulfillment of Articles 5, 6, and 7 above, come to an end at the next senatorial election.]

### ORGANIC LAW NO. 58-998, OCT. 24, 1958

[*Article* 2. The minimum age is 23 for deputies, 35 for senators.

*Article* 11. Deputies and senators may not be members of the Economic and Social Council or councilors to the governments of the overseas territories.

*Article* 12. Nonelective public positions may not be combined with parliamentary mandates. This restriction does not apply to certain categories of professors and to the clergy in Alsace-Lorraine.

*Article* 13. A parliamentary mandate may not be combined with important executive positions in national and public undertakings. [The article lists such positions.]

*Article* 15. The same restriction applies to undertakings receiving specific subsidies from the government and to financial corporations holding private savings, as well as to public-works undertakings working principally for the state or local collectivities.

*Article* 18. A parliamentarian who is also an attorney may not, either directly or through his associates, exercise any act of his profession before any court, the High Court of Justice excepted, as far as criminal cases concerning the *res publica*, the press, credit, and public savings are concerned.

*Article* 19. Parliamentarians are forbidden to let their names followed by a mention of their parliamentary mandates be used in any advertisement concerning financial, industrial, or commercial undertakings.

*Article* 20. The parliamentarian in violation of the restrictions listed in this chapter is automatically unseated.]

ORGANIC LAW NO. 58-1210, DEC. 13, 1958

[*Article* 1. Parliamentary salaries are equal to the average salary of the civil servants in the *hors échelle* [above schedule] category.

*Article* 2. In addition, parliamentarians receive a special indemnity equal to one-fourth their regular salary.]

*Article* 26. No member of Parliament may be prosecuted, sought out, arrested, detained, or tried as a result of the opinions or votes expressed by him in the exercise of his functions.

During parliamentary session no member of Parliament may be prosecuted or arrested for crimes or misdemeanors without the authorization of the assembly of which he is a member except in the case of *flagrante delicto*.

Between sessions, no member of Parliament may be arrested without the authorization of the bureau of the assembly of which he is a member, except in the case of *flagrante delicto*, of authorized prosecution or of final conviction.

The detention or the prosecution of a member of Parliament is suspended if the assembly of which he is a member so demands.

*Article* 27. Any binding mandate is void.

The parliamentarian's right to vote is personal.

An organic law may, exceptionally, authorize the vote by proxy. In this case no one may be delegated more than one proxy.

ORGANIC LAW NO. 58-1066, NOV. 7, 1958

[*Article* 1. Members of Parliament are authorized to delegate their right to vote in the following cases: illness, accident, grave family occurrence; temporary governmental mission; service in the armed forces in time of peace or in time of war; participation in the work of international assemblies as a result of appointment by the Senate or by the National Assembly; absence from metropolitan France during extraordinary sessions.]

*Article* 28. Parliament convenes as of right for two ordinary sessions a year.

The first session begins on the first Tuesday of October and ends on the third Friday of December.

The second session opens on the last Tuesday of April; it may not last more than three months.

*Article* 29. Parliament convenes in extraordinary session at the request of the Prime Minister or of the majority of the members of the National Assembly, to consider a specific agenda.

When an extraordinary session is held at the request of the members of the National Assembly, the closure decree takes effect as soon as Parliament has exhausted the agenda for which it was called, and at the latest twelve days after its first meeting.

Only the Prime Minister may ask for a new session before the end of the month following the closure decree.

*Article* 30. Except when Parliament meets as of right, extraordinary sessions are opened and closed by decree of the President of the Republic.

*Article* 31. The members of the government have access to the two Assemblies; they are heard when they so request.

They may be assisted by government commissioners.

*Article* 32. The chairman of the National Assembly is elected for the duration of the legislature. The chairman of the Senate is elected after each senatorial election.

*Article* 33. The meetings of the two assemblies are public. An *in extenso* report of the debates is published in the *Journal Officiel.*

Each assembly may sit in secret committee at the request of the Prime Minister or of one-tenth of its members.

## Chapter V

### *On the relations between Parliament and Government*

*Article* 34. Laws are voted by Parliament.

Laws determine the rules concerning:

Civil rights and fundamental guarantees granted to the citizens for the exercise of public liberties; the obligations imposed by National Defense on the citizens personally or on their goods;

nationality, status and legal capacity of persons, matrimonial legal systems, inheritance, and gifts;

determination of crimes and misdemeanors as well as the corresponding penalties; criminal procedure; amnesty; the creation of new types of jurisdictions and the status of magistrates;

the basis, the rate, and the methods of collecting taxes of all types; the currency system.

Laws also determine the rules concerning:

The electoral system of parliamentary assemblies and of local assemblies;

the creation of categories of public corporate bodies;

the fundamental guarantees granted to civil and military state officials;

the nationalization of undertakings and the transfers of the ownership of undertakings from the public to the private sector.

Laws also determine the fundamental principles concerning:

the general organization of National Defense;

the free administration of local collectivities, their competences and their resources;

education;

the legal system of ownership, property rights, civil and commercial obligations;

labor law, trade-union law, and social security.

Finance laws determine the financial resources and obligations of the State according to the rules and subject to the restrictions stipulated by an organic law.

Program laws determine the objectives of the economic and social action of the state.

The provisions of this article may be made more specific and completed by an organic law.

*Article* 35. Parliament authorizes the declaration of war.

*Article* 36. A state of siege is decreed in the Council of Ministers.

Only Parliament may authorize an extension of the state of siege beyond twelve days.

*Article* 37. Matters other than those falling within the legislative field are of a regulatory nature.

Existing legislative texts concerning these matters may be modified by decrees issued after consultation with the Council of State. Such legislative texts passed after the coming into force of the present Constitution may be modified by decree only if the Constitutional Council has stated that they have a regulatory nature in application of the preceding paragraph.

*Article* 38. In order to carry out its program, the Government may ask of Parliament the authorization, valid for a specific period of time, to take, through ordinances, measures that are normally within the legislative field.

Ordinances are passed in the Council of Ministers after consultation with the Council of State. They come into force as soon as published but become void if the ratification bill is not submitted by the Government to Parliament before the date set by the enabling act.

At the end of the period mentioned in the first paragraph of this article, ordinances may be modified only by law with regard to those matters which are within the legislative field.

*Article* 39. The right to initiate legislation belongs to the Prime Minister and to members of Parliament.

Government bills are considered in the Council of Ministers after consultation with the Council of State and are tabled on the bureau of one of the two assemblies. Finance bills are tabled first in the National Assembly.

*Article* 40. Bills, resolutions, and amendments introduced by members of Parliament are not acceptable if their adoption would entail either a diminution of public financial resources or the creation or increase of a public expenditure.

*Article* 41. If it appears, during the legislative process, that a bill, resolution, or amendment is not within the field of law or is contrary to a delegation granted in virtue of Article 38, the Government may declare it to be unacceptable.

In case of disagreement between the Government and the Chairman of the Assembly concerned, the Constitutional Council, at the request of either, renders a decision within eight days.

*Article* 42. In the first assembly to which they are submitted, government bills are debated in the text introduced by the Government.

An assembly receiving a written document passed by the other assembly, considers the text as sent to it.

*Article* 43. At the request of either the government or the assembly concerned, government and private members' bills are sent for study to *ad hoc* committees, specifically set up for that purpose.

Government and private members' bills for which such a request has not been made are sent to one of the standing committees, the number of which is limited to six in each assembly.

*Article* 44. Members of Parliament and of the Government have the right of amendment.

After the debate is opened, the Government may veto the consideration of any amendment which has not previously been submitted to the committee.

If the Government so requests, the assembly concerned takes a single vote on all or part of the text under discussion, together with the amendments proposed or accepted by the Government.

*Article* 45. All government or private members' bills are examined successively by the two assemblies of Parliament with a view to passing an identical text.

When, following disagreement between the two assemblies, a government or private member's bill has not been passed after two readings by each assembly, or after a single reading by each of them if the Government has declared the matter urgent, the Prime Minister may call a meeting of a joint committee composed of an equal number of deputies and senators entrusted with proposing a text on the provisions still under discussion.

The text prepared by the joint committee may be submitted by the Government to the two assemblies for their approval. No amendment is in order, except with the Government's consent.

If the joint committee does not succeed in adopting a common text, or if this text is not passed in accordance with the conditions set in the preceding paragraph, the Government may after a further reading by the National Assembly and by the Senate, ask the National Assembly to cast the final decision. In that case, the National Assembly may consider either the text prepared by the joint committee, or the last text voted by the deputies, together, eventually, with one or several of the amendments passed by the Senate.

*Article* 46. The laws defined by the Constitution as organic laws are passed and modified according to the following procedure:

The government or private member's bill may come up for discussion and a vote in the assembly where it was first tabled only after fifteen days have lapsed following the tabling.

The procedure laid down in Article 45 is applicable. However, failing agreement between the two assemblies, the text may be passed by the National Assembly on a final reading only by an absolute majority of its members.

Organic laws concerning the Senate must be passed in identical terms by the two assemblies.

Organic laws may be promulgated only after the Constitutional Council has declared them to be in conformity with the Constitution.

*Article* 47. Parliament votes the government finance bills according to the provisions of an organic law.

Should the National Assembly fail to reach a decision on first reading within forty days after the tabling of a government bill, the Government refers it to the Senate, which must decide within fifteen days henceforth. The procedure described by Article 45 is followed.

Should Parliament fail to reach a decision within seventy days, the provisions of the bill may be enforced by ordinance.

Should the finance bill determining the revenues and expenditures for the fiscal year not be tabled in time for it to be promulgated before the beginning of that fiscal year, the Government urgently requests from Parliament the authorization to collect taxes and allocates by decree the funds required for the services previously approved by Parliament.

The time limits stipulated in this article are suspended when Parliament is not in session.

The Audit Court assists Parliament and the Government in supervising the execution of finance laws.

ORGANIC LAW NO. 59-2, JAN. 2, 1959

[*Article* 1. A legislative or a regulatory provision calling for new expenditures may not be passed or signed as long as such expenditures have not been stipulated, evaluated and authorized according to the procedure set by this ordinance.

*Article* 4. The authorization to levy taxes is valid for one year.

*Article* 11. In case of emergency, and provided that the Minister of Finance establishes that the financial balance fixed by the budget law is not affected, additional appropriations may be opened by decree taken in the Council of Ministers after consultation with the Council of State. Such appropriations must be ratified by Parliament in the following finance law.

In case of emergency and of imperious national interest, additional appropriations may be opened by decree in the Council of Ministers after consultation with the Council of State. A government finance bill calling for ratification of these appropriations is immediately tabled before Parliament or at the latest when the following parliamentary session opens.

*Article* 14. Transfers of appropriations may be made within given chapters of the finance law by orders from the Minister of Finance. Transfers of appropriations from one chapter to another may be made by decree provided the transfer be within the same title (*titre*) of a given ministry's budget and provided the transfer between chapters be not more than one-tenth of the original appropriation for the chapters concerned.

*Article* 31. The yearly budget bill is composed of two parts. The first is concerned with revenues, the second with expenditures. The second part is itself divided into two different sections. (1) the expenditures previously approved by Parliament; (2) new expenditures. The latter are divided into titles and ministries.

*Article* 33. The expenditures previously approved are the minimum expenditures that the Government considers necessary in order to carry on the public services approved by Parliament for the preceding year.

*Article* 34. The finance laws amending the budget are introduced in Parliament in the same way as the yearly budgets.

*Article* 37. The finance bills are prepared by the Minister of Finance under the Prime Minister's authority. They are approved in the Council of Ministers.

*Article* 38. The budget is tabled at the latest on the first Tuesday of October. It is immediately sent to a committee.

*Article* 40. Discussion of the second part of the budget may not start before an assembly as long as the first part has not been voted.

*Article* 41. Revenues are the object of a single vote as far as the general budget is concerned and of as many votes as there are appended budgets and special accounts categories.

The expenditures previously approved are the object of a single vote. New expenditures are voted per title and within each title, per ministry. Separate votes are taken for each appended budget and each category of special accounts in the same way as for the general budget.

*Article* 44. In application of Article 47 paragraph 4 of the Constitution, the Government has the use of the two following procedures:

1. Ten days at least before the end of the session, the Government may ask the National Assembly to vote separately on the whole of the first part (revenues) of the budget. This half bill is then sent to the Senate according to the urgency procedure.

2. If the above procedure has not been followed or has failed, the Government may, forty-eight hours before the end of the session, table before the National Assembly a special bill authorizing the government to continue levying existing taxes, until the budget be voted.

After having obtained this authorization the Government allocates funds by decree for the categories of expenditures known as expenditures previously approved.]

*Article* 48. Government bills and private member's bills accepted by the Government have priority on the assemblies' agenda. The Government determines in what order these bills are discussed.

One meeting a week is reserved, by priority, for questions from members of Parliament and for answers by the Government.

*Article* 49. After deliberation in the Council of Ministers, the Prime Minister stakes the Government's responsibility before the National Assembly on the Government's program or, eventually, on a declaration of general policy.

The National Assembly implicates the Government's responsibility by the vote of a motion of censure. Such a motion is acceptable only if signed by at least one-tenth of the members of the National Assembly. The vote may take place only forty-eight hours after the motion has been tabled. The votes supporting the motion of censure are the only ones to be tabulated. To be passed, a motion of censure requires a majority of the members of the Assembly. Should the motion of censure be defeated, its movers may not introduce another motion of censure during the same session, except in the case covered by the following paragraph.

After deliberation in the Council of Ministers, the Prime Minister may stake the Government's responsibility before the National Assembly on the passing of a written document. This document is then considered as passed, unless a motion of censure, tabled during the following twenty-four hours, is carried according to the provisions of the preceding paragraph.

The Prime Minister may request from the Senate approval of a declaration of general policy.

*Article* 50. When the National Assembly passes a motion of censure, or when it disapproves the Government's program or a Governmental declaration of general policy, the Prime Minister must tender the resignation of his Government to the President of the Republic.

*Article* 51. Eventually, the closure of ordinary or extraordinary sessions is postponed as of right in order to render possible the application of the provisions of Article 49.

ORGANIC LAW No. 58-1100, NOV. 17, 1958

[*Article* 6. Parliamentary committees of enquiry may not be created, or if they have been created, must cease their activities when a judicial action is opened regarding the facts subject to the investigation.

Parliamentary control committees are created to examine the management of public services and nationalized undertakings in order to report to the assembly concerned.

The members of control committees and of committees of enquiry are elected by a majority system.

Control committees and committees of enquiry may not last more than four months. They may be revived for the same purpose only twelve months after the end of the original committee's session.

Members of these committees are bound by the rule of secrecy. Only the assembly concerned may decide to publish part or whole of a committee's report.

*Article* 10. In peace time, parliamentarians may not be drafted in the armed forces, unless it be with their consent.]

## Chapter VI

*On treaties and international agreements*

*Article* 52. The President of the Republic negotiates and ratifies treaties.

He is kept informed of all negotiations leading to the conclusion of international agreements not subject to ratification.

*Article* 53. Peace treaties, commercial treaties, treaties or agreements relating to international organization, those that commit the finances of the State, those that modify provisions of a legislative nature, those relative to the status of persons, those that call for cession, exchange or addition of territory may be ratified or approved only by a law.

They take effect only after having been ratified or approved.

Cession, exchange, or addition of territory is not valid without the consent of the populations concerned.

*Article* 54. If the Constitutional Council, acting on a request made by the President of the Republic, by the Prime Minister, or by the Chairman of either assembly, declares that an international commitment contains a clause contrary to the Constitution, the authorization to ratify or approve this commitment may be given only after amendment of the Constitution.

*Article* 55. As soon as published, treaties or agreements duly ratified or approved have an authority superior to that of laws subject, for each agreement or treaty concerned, to being implemented by the other party.

## Chapter VII

*The Constitutional Council*

*Article* 56. The Constitutional Council consists of nine members, whose mandates last nine years and are not renewable. One-third of the membership of the Constitutional Council is renewed every three years. Three members are appointed by the President of the Republic, three by the Chairman of the National Assembly, three by the Chairman of the Senate.

In addition to those nine members, former Presidents of the Republic are ex-officio life members of the Constitutional Council.

The Chairman is appointed by the President of the Republic. He casts the deciding vote in case of a tie.

*Article* 57. The functions of members of the Constitutional Council are exclusive of ministerial and of parliamentary functions. Further restrictions are determined by an organic law.

ORGANIC LAW NO. 58-1067, NOV. 7, 1958

[*Article* 4. The functions of members of the Constitutional Council are exclusive of the functions of members of the Government, of Parliament, and of the Economic and Social Council.]

*Article* 58. The Constitutional Council ensures that the President of the Republic be regularly elected.

It investigates complaints and proclaims the results of the vote.

*Article* 59. In disputed cases, the Constitutional Council rules on the validity of the elections of deputies and senators.

*Article* 60. The Constitutional Council ensures that the referendum procedures be regularly conducted and proclaims their results.

*Article* 61. Organic laws, before their promulgation, and parliamentary standing orders, before their coming into force, must be submitted to the Constitutional Council, which rules on their constitutionality.

To the same end, laws may be, before their promulgation, submitted to the Constitutional Council either by the President of the Republic, by the Prime Minister or by the Chairman of one or the other assembly.

In the cases covered by the two preceding paragraphs, the Constitutional Council must render a decision within a month. However, at the Government's request, this period is reduced to eight days in case of urgency.

In these cases, moving the Constitutional Court suspends the time limit for promulgation.

*Article* 62. A provision declared unconstitutional may not be promulgated nor implemented.

The decisions of the Constitutional Council are not subject to any appeal. They are binding on the public authorities and on all administrative and judicial authorities.

*Article* 63. An organic law determines the rules of organization and administration of the Constitutional Council, the procedure to be followed before it, and in particular the time limits within which disputes may be submitted to it.

ORGANIC LAW NO. 58-1067, NOV. 7, 1958

[*Article* 14. The decisions and advice of the Constitutional Council are rendered by at least seven councilors, except in the case of *force majeure.*

*Article* 22. When the Constitutional Council declares that a law contains a provision contrary to the Constitution and that this provision is inseparable from the law as a whole, the latter may not be promulgated.

*Article* 23. When the Constitutional Council declares that a law contains a provision contrary to the Constitution without pronouncing this provision to be inseparable from the rest of the law, the President of the Republic may either send back the whole law to the assemblies or promulgate it with the exception of the unconstitutional provision.

*Article* 25. In the cases covered by Article 37 of the Constitution, the Constitutional Council renders its decisions within a month. This period is reduced to eight days if the Government has declared the matter to be urgent.

*Article* 31. When asked by the Government to determine whether the President of the Republic is incapacitated, the Council reaches its decision by an absolute majority of its members.

*Article* 33. A deputy's or a senator's election may be questioned by an appeal to the Constitutional Council within ten days following the proclamation of the election results. The appeal may be made by any registered elector.

*Article* 36. The Constitutional Council divides itself into three sections of three members chosen by lot from three groups of councilors: those appointed by the President of the Republic, those appointed by the Chairman of the Senate, and those appointed by the Chairman of the National Assembly. These three groups are represented equally on each section.

Each year, the Constitutional Council appoints ten vice-rapporteurs selected from the members of the Council of State and of the Audit Court.

*Article* 37. The Chairman of the Constitutional Council assigns each election case to a section and appoints a rapporteur who may be selected from the vice-rapporteurs.

*Articles* 38–42. The Constitutional Council may unseat members of Parliament irregularly elected and eventually may pronounce elected the candidate who had wrongly been declared to have been defeated.

*Article* 50. The Constitutional Council establishes whether irregularities have been committed in a referendum procedure and decides whether they are such as to cause the referendum to be declared void either partly or totally.

*Article* 52. When consulted by the President of the Republic in application of Article 16 of the Constitution, the Constitutional Council meets immediately.]

## Chapter VIII

### *On judicial authority*

*Article* 64. The President of the Republic is the guarantor of the independence of the judiciary.

He is assisted by the Superior Council of the Judiciary.

An organic law determines the status of magistrates.

Judges may not be removed from office.

Organic Law No. 58-1270, Dec. 22, 1958

[*Article* 3. The following magistrates are classified as *hors hierarchie* (above hierarchy): The Court of Cassation magistrates, the first presidents of the Appeal Courts, the state prosecutors (*procureurs généraux*) before the Courts of Appeal, the presidents of the Paris Appeal Court, the state attorneys general (*avocats généraux*) before the Paris Appeal Court, the president of the Seine Court, the state prosecutors, and the deputy state prosecutors (*procureurs de la République et procureurs adjoints*) before the Seine Court.

*Article* 4. Judges are irremovable. Consequently they may not be transferred nor promoted against their will.

*Article* 5. State prosecutors and state attorneys are under the authority of the Minister of Justice. However, during a trial they are free to express their opinions orally before the court.

*Article* 35. The promotion committee is composed of the first president of the Court of Cassation, the prosecutor general before the Court of Cassation, three members of the Court of Cassation, three magistrates, and the members of the administrative executive committee of the Ministry of Justice.

*Article* 37. The *hors hierarchie* judges are appointed by the President of the Republic in accordance with Article 65 of the Constitution.

*Article* 38. The *hors hierarchie* state prosecutors and attorneys are appointed by the President of the Republic in accordance with Ordinance No. 58–1136 of November 28, 1958.

*Article* 39. The rules concerning promotion do not apply to appointments to the *hors hierarchie* positions. However, no magistrate may be appointed to the Court of Cassation unless he has been either first president, prosecutor general, a president of the Seine Court, state prosecutor or deputy state prosecutor before the Seine Court, a president of an Appeal Court or state attorney general.

*Article* 42. The salaries of magistrates are determined by decree taken in the Council of Ministers.

*Article* 48. Disciplinary power is exercised by the Superior Council of the Judiciary as far as judges are concerned, and by the Minister of Justice as far as state attorneys and prosecutors are concerned.

*Article* 83. For a five-year period, at each competitive examination leading to the appointments of auditors of justice, 10 per cent of the positions are reserved to Algerian Moslems.]

*Article* 65. The Superior Council of the Judiciary is presided over by the President of the Republic. The Minister of Justice is ex-officio vice-chairman. He may deputize for the President of the Republic.

In addition the Superior Council includes nine members appointed by the President of the Republic in accordance with the conditions set by an organic law.

The Superior Council of the Judiciary proposes nominations

for the positions of judges on the Court of Cassation and of first presidents of the Appeal Courts. Regarding other judges, the Council gives its opinion on the nominations proposed by the Minister of Justice in accordance with the conditions set by an organic law. The Council is consulted on pardons under conditions determined by an organic law.

The Superior Council of the Judiciary renders decisions in its capacity as disciplinary council for judges. In such cases, it is presided over by the First President of the Court of Cassation.

ORGANIC LAW NO. 58-1271, DEC. 22, 1958

[*Article* 1. The Superior Council of the magistracy comprises nine members appointed by the President of the Republic, as follows:

Three members of the Court of Cassation including a state attorney general, and three judges. These six members are chosen from a list established by the bureau of the Court of Cassation. For each category of appointees, the list must include three times as many names as there are positions;

a State councilor chosen from a list of three names established by the general assembly of the council of State;

two competent personalities chosen outside the magistracy.

While serving on the Council no member may exercise a parliamentary mandate or exercise the profession of lawyer or attorney.

*Article* 2. Members of the Superior Council are appointed for four years.

*Article* 11. The quorum is six members including the chairman or the vice-chairman. Propositions and advice are passed by a majority vote.

*Article* 12. For appointments to the positions of judges on the Court of Cassation and to the positions of first presidents of Appeal Courts, the Superior Council submits nominations to the President of the Republic. Regarding the appointment of other judges, the Superior Council advises the President of the Republic on the nominations proposed by the Minister of Justice.

*Article* 13. When acting as disciplinary authority for judges, the Superior Council meets under the chairmanship of the first president of the Court of Cassation; the President of the Republic and the Minister of Justice do not have access to these meetings.

*Article* 66. No one may be arbitrarily detained. The judicial authority, guardian of individual liberty, ensures respect of this principle under the conditions stipulated by law.]

## Chapter IX

### *The High Court of Justice*

*Article* 67. A High Court of Justice is instituted.

It is composed of an equal number of deputies and senators elected by the National Assembly and by the Senate from their members following each general or partial election to these Assemblies. It elects its chairman from among its members.

An organic law determines the composition of the High Court, the rules concerning its working as well as the procedure to be followed when bringing a case before it.

### Organic Law No. 59-1, Jan. 2, 1959

[*Article* 1. The High Court of Justice is composed of twenty-four judges and twelve alternates.

*Article* 2. After each general election the National Assembly elects twelve judges and six alternates.

After each triennial election the Senate elects twelve judges and six alternates.

The ballot is secret. Election is by an absolute majority of the members comprising the assembly concerned.

*Article* 33. The High Court renders its decisions by an absolute majority. Voting is secret.

*Article* 34. If the accused is declared guilty, a vote is immediately taken concerning the penalty. If after two ballots no penalty has obtained a majority of the votes cast, the most severe sanction is eliminated and so on until a sanction is passed by a majority of the votes cast.

*Article* 35. High Court verdicts are not subject to appeals or cassation.]

*Article* 68. The President of the Republic is not responsible for acts performed in the exercise of his functions except in case of high treason. He may be impeached only by the two assemblies concurring in their votes. These votes must be by open ballot. An absolute majority of the members of the assembly concerned is required for passing the motion of impeachment.

The members of the government are responsible under criminal law for acts performed in the exercise of their functions provided such acts were qualified crimes or misdemeanors at the time they were committed. The procedure defined above is applicable to them, as well as to their accomplices, in case of a conspiracy against the security of the State. In the cases covered by this paragraph, the High Court is bound by the definition of crimes and misdemeanors, as well as by the determination of penalties as laid down in the criminal laws at the time the acts were committed.

## CHAPTER X

### *The Economic and Social Council*

*Article* 69. At the Government's request the Economic and Social Council gives its advice on the government bills, ordinances, and decrees, as well as on the private members' bills submitted to it.

A member of the Economic and Social Council may be appointed by this latter body to defend, before the parliamentary assemblies, the Council's opinions on the texts submitted to it by the Government or the Parliament.

*Article* 70. The Economic and Social Council may also be consulted by the Government on any problem of an economic or social nature concerning the Republic or the Community. Any plan, or any program-bill of an economic or social nature is submitted to it for advice.

*Article* 71. The composition of the Economic and Social Council and its rules of procedure are determined by an organic law.

### ORGANIC LAW 58-1360, DEC. 29, 1958

[*Article* 7. The Economic and Social Council includes:

a) forty-five members representing workers, employees, civil servants, technicians, engineers, and cadres;

b) forty-one members representing industrial, commercial, and artisanal undertakings, of whom six represent nationalized undertakings, nine represent commercial undertakings, ten represent artisans.

The representatives listed in (a) and (b), with the exception of those representing nationalized industries, are appointed by the more representative professional organizations concerned;

c) forty members appointed by the more representative agricultural organizations, including five for agricultural coöperatives;

d) fifteen personalities with economic, social, scientific, or cultural qualifications, five of whom representing the cultural domain;

e) fifteen members representing social activities such as housing, savings, public health, consumers coöperatives, construction coöperatives, and family associations, the latter having at least eight representatives;

f) seven members representing various activities, namely: two representatives of production coöperatives, one representative of tourism, two representatives of exports, two representatives of regional economic expansion;

g) two representatives of the more representative of middle-class organizations;

h) ten personalities qualified by their knowledge of overseas economic and social problems, or having an activity connected with the economic expansion of the franc zone.

These members are selected according to a procedure laid down by decree taken in the council of State.

*Article* 8. In addition, the Economic and Social Council includes: twenty representatives of economic and social activities in Algeria; ten representatives of economic and social activities in the overseas territories and the overseas *départements* (Martinique, Guadeloupe, Guyane, Réunion).

These members are selected according to a procedure laid down by decree taken in the council of State.

*Article* 9. The members of the Economic and Social Council are appointed for five years.

*Article* 15. The Economic and Social Council standing orders must be approved by decree.

*Article* 16. The Assembly of the Council meets every three months in ordinary sessions.

*Article* 17. Voting by proxy is not allowed.]

## Chapter XI

### *On territorial collectivities*

*Article* 72. The territorial collectivities of the Republic are the communes, the *départements* and the overseas territories. Any other territorial collectivity is created by law.

These collectivities administer themselves freely by means of elected councils and according to conditions determined by law.

In the *départements* and territories, the government delegate is entrusted with national interests, administrative supervision and observance of the laws.

*Article* 73. The legislative system and the administrative organization of the overseas *départements* may be subject to adaptations as required by specific conditions.

*Article* 74. The overseas territories of the Republic have a special organization, taking into account their own interests within the over-all interests of the Republic. This organization is defined and modified by law after consultation with the territorial assembly concerned.

*Article* 75. Citizens of the Republic who do not have common-law status, the only status covered by Article 34, preserve their personal status as long as they do not renounce it.

*Article* 76. The overseas territories may keep their status within the Republic.

If, by deliberation of their territorial assembly, the overseas territories express the will to do so, they become either overseas *départements* of the Republic or, singly or grouped, Member States of the Community.

## Chapter XII

### *On the Community*

*Article* 77. Within the Community instituted by the present Constitution, the States enjoy autonomy;

they administer themselves and manage their own affairs democratically and freely.

There is only one Community citizenship.

All citizens are equal before the law, whatever be their origin, their race, or their religion. They have the same duties.

*Article* 78. The Community's jurisdiction includes foreign policy, defense, currency, common economic and financial policy, as well as policy concerning strategic raw materials.

It also includes, unless specified by special agreement, control of justice, of higher education, of the general organization of external and common transports, and of telecommunications.

Special agreements may establish other common jurisdictions or regulate any transfer of jurisdiction from the Community to one of its members.

*Article* 79. Member states enjoy the benefit of the provisions of Article 77 as soon as they have exercised the choice envisaged in Article 76.

Until the entry into force of the measures necessary for the application of this chapter, the questions of common jurisdictions are settled by the Republic.

*Article* 80. The President of the Republic presides and represents the Community.

The Community's organs are an Executive Council, a Senate, and an Arbitration Court.

*Article* 81. The Member States of the Community take part in the election of the President in accordance with Article 6.

As President of the Community, the President of the Republic is represented in each State of the Community.

*Article* 82. The Executive Council of the Community is presided over by the President of the Community. It is composed of the Prime Minister of the Republic, of the heads of Government of each of the Member States of the Community, and of the ministers responsible for the Community's common affairs.

The Executive Council organizes the coöperation of the members of the Community at government and administrative levels.

The organization and the working of the Executive Council are determined by an organic law.

ORGANIC LAW NO. 58-1254, DEC. 19, 1958

[*Article* 1. The Executive Council of the Community has its seat in Paris. The President of the Community may decide to convene it in another city and in particular in the capital city of another State of the Community.

*Article* 2. The President of the Community presides over the Executive Council. He convenes it when the Senate of the Community meets in session and when political circumstances so require. The President establishes the agenda of the meetings of the Executive Council.

*Article* 3. The following are ex-officio members of the Executive Council: the Prime Minister of the French Republic, the heads of Governments of the other Member States of the Community and the ministers entrusted with common affairs by the President of the Community.

Members of the Executive Council sit personally. However they may exceptionally be replaced by a member of the Government to which they belong if the President of the Community gives his assent.

The President of the Community may ask ministers of the Member States of the Community to sit in the Executive Council when specific questions are debated.

*Article* 4. The Executive Council is the supreme organ of coöperation among Member States of the Community at the governmental and at the administrative level. The Executive Council may debate questions of Community general policy within the fields of jurisdiction covered by Article 78 of the Constitution.

The Council considers the expenses necessary for the creation and working of Community services and organs as well as the allocation among the Member States of the expenses and appropriations required for implementing common policies.

*Article* 5. The President of the Community sees to it that the Constitution, the organic laws of the Community, the Community agreements covered by Articles 78 and 87 of the Constitution, the decisions of the Community Arbitration Court, and the treaties and international agreements that bind the Community, be respected.

He formulates and serves notice of the measures necessary to the direction of common matters; he sees to it that they be implemented.

*Article* 6. The President of the Community may delegate part of his responsibilities to one or more members of the Executive Council. He may not however delegate the presidency of the Executive Council.

*Article* 7. The ministers in charge of Common Affairs and the ministers of the Member States concerned with the problems debated may meet before the Executive Council meetings to prepare its work.

*Article* 9. A secretary-general is appointed by the President of the Community in the Executive Council. He is present at Executive Council meetings; he keeps the minutes. He administers the Community bureaus and coördinates the work of the meetings covered by Article 7 above.

Community organs and services are created and organized by the President of the Community in the Executive Council. The staff is appointed by the President of the Community.

*Article* 10. The organs and services necessary to the Community's policy are placed under the President of the Community's high authority.]

*Article* 83. The Senate of the Community is composed of delegates selected by the Parliament of the Republic and by the legislative assemblies of the other members of the Community from among their own members. The number of delegates for each State is based on population and on the responsibilities assumed within the Community.

The Senate of the Community holds two sessions a year; they are opened and closed by the President of the Community and may not last more than one month each.

At the request of the President of the Community, the Senate of the Community considers common economic and financial policy before the laws on these matters come up for a vote in the Parliament of the Republic, and, eventually, in the legislative assemblies of the other members of the Community.

The Senate of the Community examines the acts and treaties

or the international agreements covered by Articles 35 and 53 if they commit the Community.

The Senate of the Community takes enforceable decisions in the fields for which it has received delegation of power from the legislative assemblies of the members of the Community. These decisions are promulgated in the same form as the laws enforceable on the territory of each of the states concerned.

An organic law determines the composition and the rules of procedure of the Senate of the Community.

ORGANIC LAW NO. 58-1255, DEC. 19, 1958

[*Article* 1. The Senate of the Community may not have more than three hundred members.

*Article* 3. The mandate of a Community Senator comes to an end at the same time as the mandate he holds in the assembly that appointed him. This mandate may not last more than five years. It is renewable.

*Article* 8. The Senate of the Community meets twice a year for regular sessions that may not last more than one month each.

*Article* 9. Extraordinary sessions may be called by the President of the Community. They may not last more than ten days each.

*Article* 14. The members of the Senate may question ministers entrusted with common affairs. Questions and answers are in written form.

*Article* 17. At the request of the President of the Community, the Senate of the Community considers proposed economic and financial policies of common interest.

*Article* 18. At the request of the President of the Community, the Senate of the Community studies the treaties and agreements covered by Article 53 of the Constitution, when they involve the Community.

*Article* 19. The Senate of the Community, called if need be in extraordinary session, is consulted by the President of the Republic on the authorization to declare war.

*Article* 20. The Senate of the Community takes executory decisions in the fields delegated to it by the legislative assemblies of the Member States.

*Article* 21. Organic laws concerning the Community are adapted, completed or revised according to the same procedure as that applicable to constitutional provisions.

*Article* 23. The Senate of the Community may initiate proposals for the harmonization of the laws of the Member States.]

*Article* 84. A Community Arbitration Court rules on litigations occurring between members of the Community.

Its composition and its competence are determined by an organic law.

ORGANIC LAW NO. 58-1256, DEC. 19, 1958

[*Article* 1. The competence of the Arbitration Court extends to legal disputes between members of the Community when these disputes bear on the interpretation or on the application of legal rules binding on the Member States of the Community.

*Article* 5. The President of the Community may seek the Court's advice on all questions of interpretation of Constitutional provisions concerning the Community, the organic laws concerning the Community, and the Community agreements.

*Article* 6. The Arbitration Court is composed of seven judges appointed for six years by the President of the Community.

*Article* 24. Court decisions are handed down by at least five judges. In the event of a tie, the chairman carries the vote.

*Article* 25. Court decisions are executory on the whole territory of the Community.]

ORGANIC LAW NO. 58-1257, DEC. 19, 1958

[*Article* 1. The Senate and the National Assembly select each one-half of the delegates of the Parliament of the Republic to the Senate of the Community.

*Article* 3. Algeria, the Sahara and the overseas departments must be fairly represented.]

*Article* 85. As an exception to the procedure prescribed by Article 89, the provisions of this chapter concerning the working of common institutions are revised by laws passed in identical terms by the Parliament of the Republic and by the Senate of the Community.

[The following paragraph was added to the Constitution in June, 1960.]

The provisions of this Chapter may also be revised by agreements concluded between all the States of the Community. The new provisions are brought into force according to the conditions prescribed by the constitution of each State.

*Article* 86. A change in the status of a Member State of the Community may be requested, either by the Republic, or by a resolution of the legislative assembly of the State concerned, confirmed by a local referendum, the organization and supervision of which are the responsibility of the institutions of the Community. The implementation of this change is determined by an agreement approved by the Parliament of the Republic and by the legislative assembly concerned.

Subject to the same conditions, a Member State of the Community may become independent. It then ceases to belong to the Community.

[The three following paragraphs were added to the Constitution in June, 1960.]

A Member State of the Community may also, by way of agreements, become independent without ceasing to belong to the Community.

An independent State, not member of the Community, may, by way of agreements, adhere to the Community without ceasing to be independent.

The position of these States within the Community is determined by the agreements concluded to that effect, in particular the agreements covered by the preceding paragraphs and eventually the agreements provided for by Article 85, paragraph 2.

*Article* 87. The specific agreements implementing this Chapter are approved by the Parliament of the Republic and by the legislative assembly concerned.

## Chapter XIII

### *On agreements of association*

*Article* 88. The Republic or the Community may conclude agreements with States wishing association in order to develop their civilizations.

## Chapter XIV

### *On Revision*

*Article* 89. The initiative for revising the Constitution belongs (a) to the President of the Republic acting on a proposal submitted to him by the Prime Minister, and (b) to members of Parliament.

The Government or private member's bill proposing a revision must be passed by the two assemblies in identical terms. The revision is final after it has been approved by a referendum.

However, a Government bill proposing revision is not submitted to a referendum when the President of the Republic decides to submit it to Parliament sitting in Congress; in that case, the revision bill is passed only if approved by a three-fifths majority of the votes cast. The bureau of the Congress is that of the National Assembly.

No revision process may be initiated or continued when the integrity of the territory is in danger.

The republican form of government is not subject to revision.

## Chapter XV

### *Transitional provisions*

*Article* 90. The ordinary parliamentary session is suspended. The mandate of the members of the National Assembly come to an end on the day the Assembly elected under the present Constitution convenes.

Until this meeting, the Government alone has the authority to convene Parliament.

The mandate of members of the Assembly of the French Union shall come to an end at the same time as the mandate of the members of the present National Assembly.

*Article* 91. The institutions of the Republic established by the present Constitution will be set up within four months of its promulgation.

This period is extended to six months as far as the institutions of the Community are concerned.

The powers of the President of the Republic now in office will come to an end when the results of the election prescribed in Articles 6 and 7 of the present Constitution are proclaimed.

The Member States of the Community will take part in this first election according to their status at the date of the promulgation of the Constitution.

The established authorities will continue to exercise their functions in these States according to the laws and regulations enforceable when the Constitution comes into force, until the establishment of the authorities provided for by their new systems of government.

Until finally constituted, the Senate is composed of the present members of the Council of the Republic. The organic laws that will settle the final constitution of the Senate must be passed before July 31, 1959.

Pending its establishment, the powers conferred on the Constitutional Council by Articles 58 and 59 of the Constitution are exercised by a committee composed of the vice-chairman of the Council of State, acting as chairman, the First President of the Court of Cassation, and the First President of the Audit Court.

The people of the Member States of the Community continue to be represented in Parliament until the coming into force of the measures necessary to the implementation of Chapter XII.

*Article* 92. Legislative measures necessary for the setting up of the institutions, and until they be set up, necessary to the functioning of the public authorities, will be taken in the Council of Ministers, after advice from the Council of State, in the form of ordinances having the force of law.

Subject to the same procedure and during the period set in the first paragraph of Article 91, the Government is authorized to determine, by ordinances having the force of law, the system of elections to the assemblies established by the Constitution.

During the same period and in the same conditions, the Government may also take all measures which it may deem necessary for the life of the nation, for the protection of the citizens and for the safeguarding of public liberties.

# Notes

*I*

## PAGES 1–11

[1] Raymond Cartier, editor of *Match*, a French version of *Life* magazine.

[2] Raymond Aron, *La Tragédie Algérienne* (Paris: 1957).

[3] See among others: P. H. Simon, *Contre la Torture* (Paris: 1957); J. J. Servan-Shreiber, *Lieutenant in Algeria* (New York: 1957); Roger Barberot, *Malaventure en Algérie* (Paris: 1957). For an analysis of the impact of such works on the settlers and the army see Edmond Michelet, *Contre la Guerre Civile* (Paris: 1957).

[4] Four politicians stand out: J. Soustelle (Gaullist), R. Duchet (Independent), G. Bidault (MRP) and A. Morice (Neo-Radical). Since the beginning of 1958 they had led an active campaign for the formation of a "government of public safety." They were among the leaders of the *Union pour le Salut et le Renouveau de l'Algérie Française* (USRAF) which played an important part in the events of May, 1958, in Algiers.

[5] The Algerian high command was not, at first, clearly committed to de Gaulle. According to the Brombergers, Massu was the only general in Algiers to be a convinced Gaullist before May 13. But if there were non-Gaullists, there were no anti-Gaullists to speak of. See S. and V. Bromberger, *Les 13 Complots du 13 Mai* (Paris: 1959). See also J. R. Tournoux, *Secrets d'État* (Paris: 1960).

[6] Lacoste's role is discussed in Alain de Sérigny, *La Révolution du 13 Mai* (Paris: 1958), pp. 20 ff. See Lacoste's comments in *Le Monde*, Aug. 22, 1958.

[7] The expression seems to have been coined by former Prime Minister E. Faure.

[8] See *Bulletin Intérieur du Parti S.F.I.O.* (July, 1958), p. 34.

[9] For the complete text of the letter see *Le Monde*, Sept. 16, 1958.

## 2

### Pages 14–25

[1] Albert Thibaudet, *La République des Professeurs* (Paris: 1927), p. 157.
[2] Emmanuel Berl, *La Politique et les Partis* (Paris: 1932), p. 206.
[3] André Siegfried, *Tableau des Partis en France* (Paris: 1930), p. 89.
[4] Walter Lippmann, *Public Opinion* (New York: 1922), Chapter 1.

## 3

### Pages 29–43

[1] According to party estimates. See Mario Einandi and others, *Communism in Western Europe* (New York: 1951), p. 72. For a discussion of the membership figures given by the party see below p. 40. Unless otherwise mentioned, the membership figures are those given by the Communist party.
[2] The CGT founded in the nineteenth century broke into the CGT (Socialist) and the CGTU (Communist) in 1920. The two organizations were reunified in 1936. In 1939 Communist leaders were expelled from the CGT because they refused to condemn the German-Russian aggression on Poland. They were reinstated in 1943. Socialists split from the Communist-dominated CGT in 1949 and formed the CGT-FO.
[3] The party has often found it difficult to meet such requirement. In 1950, M. Servin reporting before the Twelfth Congress stated that only 44 per cent of the federal secretaries and 37 per cent of the federal committees were workers. See P. Williams *Politics in Post-War France* (London: 1958), p. 53.
[4] The only addition to the central committee was that of Professor Joliot-Curie.
[5] M. Thorez had entered the secretariat in 1929 as one of the four secretaries.

[6] See *L'Humanité*, Dec. 10, 1958.

[7] See Alain Brayance, *Anatomie du Parti Communiste Français* (Paris: 1952), p. 209.

[8] The cards are renewed each year. Members are supposed to buy monthly stamps which affixed to the card show that the fees have been paid.

[9] See *Le Monde*, June 26, 1959.

[10] See *Les Cahiers du Communisme*, July, 1956, p. 208.

[11] See M. Thorez, *Une Politique Française* (speech before the 1945 congress) (Paris: 1945), p. 56. Quoted in M. Duverger, *Political Parties* (New York: 1955), p. 88.

[12] See *Le Monde*, June 26, 1959.

[13] See poll in Institut Français d'Opinion Publique, *Sondages*, No. 3 (1953). A summary of the poll findings is in P. Williams, *op. cit.*, p. 432.

[14] See chapter 2, p. 15.

## *4*

## PAGES 45–65

[1] See J. J. Chevallier and others, *Encyclopédie Politique de la France et du Monde* (Paris: n. d. [1947]), I, 94.

[2] See P. Louis, *Histoire du Socialisme en France de la Revolution à nos Jours* (Paris: 1925), pp. 289 ff.

[3] On the basis of the number of cards sold by party headquarters. Source: P. Rimbert, *Petite Histoire du Parti Socialiste Français 1905–1955* (unpublished manuscript).

[4] On the initiative of the Italian Socialist party, an international Socialist meeting had been held at Zimmerwald, Switzerland, in 1915. Neither the French nor the German Socialist parties had sent representatives. But a few French as well as German Socialists had gone to the meeting on their own initiative. The Zimmerwald conference had condemned the war and asked all Socialists to campaign for peace.

[5] Pivert founded the Parti Socialiste Ouvrier et Paysan which disappeared after the Second World War. It recruited mostly in the Paris area. Pivert was reinstated by the SFIO in 1946.

[6] At the time of liberation four Socialists were in de Gaulle's cabinet: A. Phillip, A. le Troquer, J. Monnet, and A. Tixier.

[7] The few advocates of a merger between the Socialists and Com-

munists were dropped from the Socialist executive committee in 1946.

[8] An attempt was made in 1947 to return partly to the group system by prescribing that the members of a section should also belong to a specialized professional group. This rule remained practically a dead letter.

[9] In 1957 the Socialist party claimed to have 60,000 municipal councilors most of whom can be assumed to be members of the party.

[10] See P. Rimbert "Sociologie du parti-socialiste," *La Revue Socialiste*, Feb.–March, 1952. The questionnaire had been sent to four hundred sections in 81 *départements*. Information was obtained for approximately 14,000 adherents.

# 5

## Pages 70–82

[1] Radical Socialist is a shortened version of "Radical Republican and Radical Socialist" party. Unless otherwise mentioned the term Radical is used with reference to that party.

[2] See C. Nicolet, *Le Radicalisme* (Paris: 1957), p. 20.

[3] *Ibid.*, p. 20.

[4] Secondary and University state education later became free of charge.

[5] For 1919 and 1924 the percentage of Radical votes cannot be determined exactly because of the number of coalition tickets. In 1924 the year most favorable to the Radicals, the *Cartel des Gauches* obtained 38 per cent of the votes and 46 per cent of the seats. About half of these seats went to Radicals. In 1936, the last election before the war, the Radicals obtained about 15 per cent of the votes.

[6] See *Le Monde*, May 6, 1955.

[7] In addition, a general councilor, a municipal councilor in the towns of more than 120,000 inhabitants, and a mayor in a city with more than 10,000 inhabitants are each considered as worth fifty members.

[8] See Alain (pseud. E. Chartier), *Le Citoyen contre les Pouvoirs* (Paris: 1926).

[9] See Alain (pseud. E. Chartier), *Eléments d'une Doctrine Radicale* (Paris: 1925), p. 280.

[10] See A. Siegfried, *Tableau des Partis en France* (Paris: 1930), p. 159.

# 6

## Pages 85–106

[1] The constitution was passed by a slight majority.

[2] This made Bernanos deplore that in the Christian-democratic compromise Christianity had to bear all the costs of the compromise.

[3] On the basis of the Ministry of the Interior Statistics which are far from accurate but less likely to be distorted than the statistics published by the various political parties. The classification of a large number of independent voters is difficult.

[4] According to figures given by party headquarters.

[5] If the MRP has no ministers in the government, the former ministers who sat at the previous national committee retain their seats.

[6] The total membership is usually approximately two hundred but attendance is often no more than half. In 1957 the committee met four times, in January, March, July, and November.

[7] If the MRP is not represented in the government, parliamentarians re-elect five former ministers.

[8] At the 1956 national congress, Vice-Secretary-General J. Fonteneau pointed out that in a number of federations CFTC had supported Socialist and Radical candidates. See *Le Monde*, May 12, 1956.

[9] Belgium, France, Germany, Holland, Italy, Luxembourg.

[10] The rule was accepted as a basis of discussion between the MRP and the *Rassemblement des Forces Démocratiques*, a Left-wing Christian-democratic fraction. Simmonet speaking for the MRP proposed that "be considered as workers: manual workers, workers on a monthly pay, technicians, civil servants and middle management." *Forces Nouvelles*, No. 277 (May, 1959), p. 3.

[11] See D. Pépy, "Note sur le Mouvement Républicain Populaire," *Partis Politiques et classes Sociales* (Paris: 1955), p. 213.

[12] According to figures given by the party secretariat.

[13] However, if one adds to the MRP's the votes polled by candidates running on Bidault's Christian-democratic's tickets the percentage is 11.6.

[14] In 1959 out of 53 MRP deputies, 18 came from the West; 11 from eastern *départements;* 7 from northern *départements;* 9 from scattered districts.

[15] The special religious status of Alsace-Lorraine, which is still under the concordate of 1802 while in the rest of France church and state

are separated, may also account for the lesser importance given by the eastern MRP electorate to confessional problems.

## 7

### Pages 111–116

[1] Pétain borrowed from the PSF the slogan "Travail, Famille, Patrie," meant to supersede "Liberté, Egalité, Fraternité."

[2] PRL, Independent Republicans, Independents' Democratic Union, Farmers Action, Democratic and Social Action, Independent Popular Republicans.

[3] Other Independents serving in the various cabinets between 1950 and 1952 included Pinay at the Ministry of Public Works; Jacquinot as minister for Veterans' Affairs, then as minister for the Overseas; Temple as minister for Veterans' Affairs; and Laniel and Duchet as Posts ministers. Antier of the Farmer's group was made Agriculture minister in 1951; Laurens succeeded him in 1952.

[4] The former RPF parliamentarians who had voted for Pinay, formed with the Independents a common parliamentary group, the *Groupe des Indépendents et Paysans d'Action Sociale.*

[5] For example in the Indre et Loire *département* in 1956.

[6] In 1956, for example, the congress heard reports from Peugeot, the car industrialist, and from H. Dubreuil, a theorist of coöperative syndicalism.

## 8

### Pages 123–137

[1] Vallon was a former Socialist, Capitant a member of the UDSR.

[2] A conservative newspaper, friendly to the RPF, estimated that close to one-third of the first 100,000 adherents were Socialists. *Le Pays,* April 18, 1947.

[3] *Combat,* Sept. 2, 1947.
[4] *Ibid.*
[5] In 1947 Soustelle was made secretary-general.
[6] Before November, 1959, the founders of the UNR, Soustelle included, were ex-officio members.
[7] Terrenoire, politically to the Center, was elected as caucus chairman in 1959 over Biaggi, an extreme nationalist. Terrenoire became minister of information in 1960.
[8] See *Le Monde,* May 19, 1959.
[9] See de Gaulle's criticisms of J. Monnet at a 1953 press conference, in *Le Monde,* Nov. 17, 1953.
[10] The working class is represented among UNR leaders by men like A. Jarrot, who have risen above their original social group, thanks to trade-union activities or by establishing small private businesses.

## *9*

### Pages 143–153

[1] Lecoeur later joined the SFIO.
[2] A majority of leaders and members of the *Jeune République* went to the new organization but the delegates at a national congress failed to muster the 75 per cent majority required by the JR's party rules to dissolve the organization.
[3] See *Combat,* July 7, 1945.
[4] Dorgère broke with Poujade in March, 1959. Dorgère approved de Gaulle's policies except on agriculture. Poujade was hostile on all counts.
[5] In 1958, Biaggi was elected as a UNR candidate. The *Parti Patriotique Révolutionnaire* was then dissolved by its founder. Biaggi left the UNR in 1959 and joined the Algerian group. Accused of plotting against the government, he spent some time in jail after the Algerian settlers' insurrection of January, 1960.
[6] Comte de Paris, *Esquisse d'une constitution monarchique et démocratique,* 1948.

# *10*

## Pages 157–166

[1] See C. Morazé, *Les Français et la République* (Paris: 1956), p. 40.
[2] After becoming a political party, the *Croix de Feu* lost much of their original antiparliamentarism.
[3] See *Le Monde*, Sept. 27, 1958.
[4] These and the following figures are based on estimates. For a discussion of union-membership figures see E. Dolleans and G. Dehove, *Histoire du Travail en France des Origines à nos Jours* (Paris: 1955), II, 234 ff. and J. Meynaud, *Les Groupes de Pression en France* (Paris: 1958), p. 71. In 1959 the official figure given by the CGT was 1,624,322 members. See *Le Monde*, June 20, 1959.
[5] See *Sondages*, No. 3 (1953) and revised figures in P. Williams, *Politics in Post-War France* (London: 1958), p. 452.
[6] See above, chapter 2, p. 15.

# *11*

## Pages 169–179

[1] The constitution of 1958 limits the term of office to seven years but allows reëlection which was forbidden in the draft of 1943. For a study of the Debré project of 1943 and more generally for the origins of the constitution of 1958 see N. Wahl, "Aux Origines de la Nouvelle Constitution," *Revue Française de Science Politique*, IX (March, 1959), 30–66.
[2] Before 1957, Socialists had individually proposed such reforms, among them L. Blum, J. Moch, and V. Auriol. But the party itself had done nothing to implement such proposals.
[3] See *Information Socialiste*, July, 1958, pp. 48 ff.
[4] The nominated members were: P. Reynaud, M. Blocq-Mascart, H.

Boukabeur, A. Bour, J. Chardonnet, R. Chazelle, R. Frey, M. Lauriol, A. Malterre, L. Noel, R. Pré, Van Graefschepe, M. Waline. The elected members included: *National Assembly:* four Independents, three Socialists, two MRP, one Radical, one dissident Radical, one RGR, one Social Republican, one former Poujadist, one RDA, and one PRA. *Senate:* three Independents, two Socialists, two Radicals, one MRP, one Social Republican, one PRA. The senators met in caucus to discuss the draft project. The National Assembly representatives seem not to have held similar meetings. See F. Goguel, "L'Elaboration des Institutions de la République dans la Constitution du 4 Octobre 1958," *Revue Française de Science Politique,* IX (March, 1959), 80.

[5] In this surprise move, de Gaulle must have been influenced not only by the debates in the Advisory Committee but also by two important decisions taken by overseas parliamentarians. First, on July 9, 1958, RDA and PRA parliamentarians sent a memorandum to the president of the council asking that the overseas territories be granted the right of self-determination and that such territories become autonomous states within a French-African federation. Second, on July 25–27, the PRA congress asked for the recognition of the overseas territories' right to independence and for the creation of a French-African confederation.

[6] The government had on this point asked the council to suggest ways of improving the constitutional text.

## 12

## Pages 183–206

[1] The deputies and senators who are also mayors, municipal or general councilors may appoint a substitute. Furthermore the municipal councils elect substitutes who replace, if need be, incapacitated members of the presidential college.

[2] See M. Duverger, *Droit Constitutionnel et Institutions Politiques* (Paris: 1959), pp. 518 ff. and G. Vedel in *Le Monde,* July 20, 1958.

[3] See Léon Blum, *La Réforme Gouvernementale* (Paris: 1930), p. 20.

[4] The terminology varies. In the Mollet government of 1950, Houphouët-Boigny was "minister delegate to the presidency of the council"; in the Debré government, Soustelle was made "minister delegate to the prime minister." In the lists of ministers published by the

government press services, Houphouët-Boigny was listed after all other ministers, while Soustelle was ranked second to Debré.

[5] *Le Monde*, Jan. 9, 1959.

# 13

## Pages 211–219

[1] The latter comprise: Comores, Somaliland, New Caledonia, Polynesia, Saint Pierre and Miquelon.

[2] The terms "executive-order's field" and "regulatory field" are used as synonyms for *domaine réglementaire*.

[3] As an exception to the rule, university professors, and priests and ministers in Alsace-Lorraine may cumulate a parliamentary mandate with their previous occupation. Unlike in the rest of France, in Alsace-Lorraine, church and state are not legally separated; priests and ministers are appointed and paid by the government.

[4] Ordinance No. 58-998, October 24, 1958.

[5] The cost of living was, at the time, only slightly lower in France than in the United States.

[6] The new terminology for "decree-law."

[7] To prevent such occurrences, the executive has to seek advice from the Council of State beforehand. However, the Council of State is not bound by its own advices. For an example of delegation-law see the law of February 4, 1960, giving to the government the right to legislate through ordinances for a year in order to "maintain order, safeguard the state and the constitution, pacify and administer Algeria."

# 14

## Pages 227–238

[1] *Forces Nouvelles*, Oct. 18, 1958.

[2] De Gaulle's government had been empowered by Article 92 of the constitution of 1958 to select an electoral system by decree. But the

electoral system could now be modified only by a law. The system could no longer be changed by the executive unless parliament were to delegate its electoral power to the cabinet.

[3] Peter Campbell, *French Electoral Systems and Elections 1789–1957* (London: 1958), p. 72.

[4] I defined Northern France as composed of the following *départements:* Nord, Pas de Calais, Somme, Seine-Inférieure, Oise, Aisne, Ardennes, Marne, Aube, Yonne, Meuse, Haute Marne, Côte d'Or, Moselle, Meurthe et Moselle, Vosges, Haute Saône, Bas-Rhin, Haut-Rhin, Territoire de Belfort, Doubs, Jura, Seine, Seine et Oise, Seine et Marne. The percentages are based on the population figures given in *Annuaire Statistique de la France, 1957* (Paris: 1958), p. 10.

[5] *Le Monde*, Oct. 18, 1958.

[6] From 1945 to 1956 the persons condemned for collaboration with the Germans during the occupation and the parliamentarians who had voted constitutional powers to Marshal Pétain in 1940 were also barred from election.

[7] The candidate elected in more than one district had to choose one. By-elections were held in the others.

[8] There is no evidence that multiple registration or registration of deceased persons leads to any significant distortion of electoral results but the fact that more names are on the rolls than there are people who could vote leads to an overestimation of abstentions. This should be kept in mind when electoral statistics are studied, especially for the elections of the immediate postwar period.

[9] The percentage of nonregistered eligible voters was at its lowest in November 1958 with 6.4 per cent; see *Le Monde*, Nov. 23, 1958. To obtain a higher degree of registration, the English system of canvassed registration would have to be used. The percentage of nonregistered eligible voters in Great Britain is estimated at 2 or 3 per cent. W. J. M. Mackenzie, *Free Elections* (London: 1958), p. 118.

[10] Parti Radical, Parti Communiste, Démocratie Chrétienne, MRP., Renouveau et Fidélité, Union des Forces Démocratiques, SFIO, Union pour la Nouvelle République, Centre de la Réforme Républicaine. Défense des Libertés (Poujade), Centre Républicain, Centre National des Indépendants.

[11] *Le Monde*, Nov. 20, 1958.

[12] The figures for this and the following examples are taken from *Le Monde*, Nov. 25 and Dec. 2, 1958.

[13] M. Duverger and others, *Les Elections du 2 Janvier 1956* (Paris: 1957), p. 119.

# 15

## Pages 249–276

[1] Under the Fourth Republic the membership was 627. Under the Third Republic membership varied from 526 in 1876 to 598 in 1936. It was at its highest in 1919 with 610.

[2] Among Socialists Lejeune is, with Lacoste, one of the staunchest defenders of French sovereignty in Algeria.

[3] If a deputy resigns or is expelled from his parliamentary group he ceases to be a member of the committee to which he had been assigned by his group.

[4] The minutes of committee debates are restricted to the deputies. The committee votes as well as a summary of the committee's work are published each week in the *Journal des Commissions*. Notwithstanding the secrecy of debates in the committees, well-informed newspapers such as *Le Monde* usually give informative and accurate descriptions of committee debates.

[5] In the parliamentary jargon, an isolated member is called "a savage."

[6] In the 1958 parliament the SFIO had 51 senators and 44 deputies.

[7] See *Journal Officiel. Débats Parlementaires, Assemblée Nationale*, p. 1421.

[8] *Ibid.*, p. 1343.

[9] However, ordinary as well as financial laws may be debated at both sessions.

[10] Or once if the bill has been declared "urgent" by the government.

[11] Unlike for ordinary laws, the National Assembly must then approve the budget by the special majority of its total membership, not solely of those voting.

[12] See M. Duverger, *Droit Constitutionnel et Institutions Politiques* (Paris: 1959), II, 622.

[13] See P. Williams, *Politics in Post-War France* (London: 1958), p. 266.

# *16*

## Pages 279–286

[1] In 1959, following the election of the first Senate, all senatorial districts were arranged in alphabetical order in either of three groups. The date at which each group of seats would face reëlection was determined by lot. Contrary to what might have been expected, the senators obliged to face reëlection only three years after being first elected, were generally pleased—the reason being that they would face again practically the same electorate. Their colleagues due for reëlection six or nine years later might be confronted with an entirely new electorate since municipal elections are scheduled for 1965.

[2] The 100,000 Frenchmen established in the United States are represented by two of thirty-four delegates.

[3] Eighty-five per cent of the senators in the last upper chamber of the Fourth Republic were elected to the new Senate.

# *17*

## Pages 291–299

[1] Except the powers held under Articles 11 and 12.

[2] However when the council decides on a president's incapacitation, the special majority of all the members of the council is required. See above p. 291.

[3] Ordinance No. 58-1271, December 22, 1958.

[4] Before 1946 the Court of Cassation had disciplinary authority over judges. Now the Court of Cassation judges have four out of ten seats; judges of lower orders of jurisdiction have another four seats.

[5] Ordinance No. 58-1270, December 22, 1958.

[6] There must be a total of eight magistrates, four of whom at least must be judges and include the first president of the Court of Cassation.

The representatives of the Justice ministry are the members of the administrative board of the Justice ministry.

[7] The members of the High Court may not vote on the impeachment.

[8] Ordinance No. 58-1360, December 29, 1958.

[9] Articles 6, 13, 23, 25, 27, 34, 47, 55, 57, 63, 64, 65, 67, 71, 82, 83, 84.

# 18

## Pages 302–314

[1] Ordinances: No. 58-1254, No. 58-1255, No. 58-1256, No. 58-1257, December 19, 1958.

[2] For a similar interpretation of Article 73, see M. Duverger, *Droit Constitutionnel et Institutions Politiques* (Paris: 1959), p. 700. But the parliament, the government, or the Constitutional Council could construe the article differently.

[3] Even to the point of granting full independence, as in the case of Mali and Madagascar.

[4] In order to emphasize the unity of foreign affairs, Africans were to be appointed to regular French diplomatic posts in Europe and Africa.

[5] The National Assembly elects 92, the Senate 93.

[6] The Assembly of the French Union was situated in the Versailles castle.

[7] As an exception, France alone financed the whole budget in 1959.

[8] See, among others, *Le Monde*, April 7, and Sept. 6, 1959.

[9] *Ibid.*, April 1, Sept. 4, Oct. 4, 1959.

# Selected Bibliography

## The End of the Fourth Republic

For studies on the Fourth Republic see Phillip Williams, *Politics in Post-War France* (2d ed.; London: Longmans, Green, 1958), the best scholarly study in English on French party politics and constitutional structures. See also: D. Thompson, *Democracy in France. The Third and Fourth Republics* (3d ed.; London: Oxford University Press, 1958); Maurice Duverger, *The French Political System* (Chicago: University of Chicago Press, 1958); André Siegfried, *De la IIIe à IVe République* (Paris: Grasset, 1956); A. Siegfried, *De la IVe à la Ve* (Paris: Grasset, 1958); F. Goguel, *France under the Fourth Republic* (Ithaca: Cornell University Press, 1952). Among the works written by newspapermen see in particular Hebert Lüthy, *France against Herself* (New York: Praeger, 1953); and David Schoenbrun, *As France Goes* (New York: Harper, 1957). Interesting but biased by Mendecian preferences are the works of Alexander Werth. See in particular Alexander Werth, *France 1940–1955* (London: R. Hall, 1956). Excellent is J. Fauvet, *La IVe République* (Paris: Fayard, 1959). An analysis of the effects of France's internal paralysis on her foreign policy is in E. S. Furniss, *France, Troubled Ally* (New York: Harper, 1960).

For specific criticisms of the government and of the party system see: Marcel Waline, *Les Partis contre la République* (Paris: Rousseau, 1948); René Massigli, *Sur Quelques Maladies de l'Etat* (Paris: Plon, 1958); Michel Debré, *Ces Princes qui nous Gouvernent* (Paris: Plon, 1957).

For an analysis of the army's reactions to the lack of political leadership see Jean Planchais, *Le Malaise de l'Armée* (Paris: Plon, 1958).

For a study of the Algerian question as well as for proposals for its solution, see among many others: R. Zenati, *Le Problème Algérien vu par un Indigène* (Paris: Comité de l'Afrique Française, 1938); and Jacques Soustelle, *Aimée et Souffrante Algérie* (Paris: Plon, 1957); both favorable to the integration of Algeria to France; R. Aron, *La Tragédie Algérienne* (Paris: Plon, 1957), suggesting the withdrawal of France from Algeria; and A. Fabre-Luce, *Demain en Algerie* (Paris: Plon,

1958), advocating a partition of the country. The best analysis of the sociological causes of the Moslem rebellion is in Germaine Tillon, *L'Algérie en 1957* (Paris: Editions de Minuit, 1957), translated as *Algeria the Realities* (New York: Knopf, 1958). For a history of the rebellion see Serge Bromberger, *Les Rebelles Algériens* (Paris: Plon, 1958); and M. K. Clark, *Algeria in Turmoil* (New York: F. A. Praeger, 1959).

The literature on the crisis of May 13 is already enormous, but only three of the persons who played a part of some importance in the events have published their memoirs. See Alain de Sérigny, *La Révolution du 13 Mai* (Paris: Plon, 1958); Raymond Dronne, *La Révolution d'Alger* (Paris: Ed. France-Empire, 1958); and Pascal Arrighi, *La Corse, Atout Décisif* (Paris: Plon, 1958). Among the better works of newspapermen see Jean Ferniot, *Les Ides de Mai* (Paris: Plon, 1958); D. Pado, *13 Mai* (Paris: Editions de Paris), 1958; J. R. Tournoux, *Carnets Secrets de la Politique* (Paris: Plon, 1958); and, best of all, S. and V. Bromberger, *Les 13 Complots du 13 Mai* (Paris: Fayard, 1959). For the role played by the Poujadists in Algiers see two articles in *Fraternité Française*, Oct. 25, 1958; Nov. 1, 1958. See also the statements made by two members of the Pflimlin cabinet, G. Mollet and J. Moch, before the national conference of the Socialist party of July, 1958, in *Bulletin Intérieur*, July, 1958. The important letter sent by G. Mollet to de Gaulle on May 25 was published in *Le Monde*, Sept. 16, 1958.

## Ideologies and Political Parties

For essays on French political attitudes and ideological conflicts see Albert Thibaudet, *La République des Professeurs* (Paris: Grasset, 1927); Robert de Jouvenel, *La République des Camarades* (Paris: Grasset, 1914); André Siegfried, *Tableau des Partis en France* (Paris: Grasset, 1930), translated as *France, a Study in Nationality* (New York: Yale University Press, 1930). See also Emmanuel Berl, *La Politique et les Partis* (Paris: Reider, 1932); Friedrich Sieburg, *Who are These French?* (New York: Macmillan, 1932); D. W. Brogan, *The French Nation, from Napoléon to Pétain* (London: Hamilton, 1952); and Charles Morazé, *Les Français et la République* (Paris: A. Colin, 1956). For specific analysis of Left and Right see the scholarly studies by René Rémond, *La Droite en France de 1815 à nos Jours* (Paris: Aubier, 1954); and R. Rémond "Droite et Gauche dans le Catholicisme Français," *Revue Française de Science Politique* (Sept.–Dec., 1958), VIII, 529–544, 803–820.

## The Communist Party

### *Communist sources*

Among the many Communist publications two stand out: the daily *L'Humanité*, and the monthly *Les Cahiers du Communisme*. The latter publish the proceedings of the party's congresses.

*France-Nouvelle* gives a popular version of Marxist and Communist thought. *La Pensée* and *La Nouvelle Critique* are intended for a more sophisticated public.

Among the writings of party leaders the most important are those of Maurice Thorez. See M. Thorez, *Fils du Peuple* (Paris: Editions Sociales, 1949); and M. Thorez, *Oeuvres*, 19 volumes (Paris: 1950–1959). See also J. Duclos, *Ecrits de la prison* (Paris: Editions Sociales, 1953); L. Casanova, *Le Parti Communiste, les Intellectuel et la Nation* (Paris: Editions Sociales, 1951); R. Garaudy, *Le Communisme et la Morale* (Paris: Edition Sociales, 1945); Pierre Hervé, *Individu et Marxisme* (Paris: Club-Maintenant, 1948); and L. Aragon, *L'Homme Communiste* (Paris: Gallimard, 1946).

Interesting are works of former Communists such as A. Marty, *L'Affaire Marty* (Paris: Deux Rives, 1955); A. Lecoeur, *L'Autocritique Attendue* (St. Cloud: Girault, 1955); P. Hervé, *Dieu et César sont-ils Communistes?* (Paris: Table Ronde, 1957); and P. Hervé, *La Révolution et les Fétiches* (Paris: Table Ronde, 1956).

### *Non-Communist sources*

For a general history of the French Communist party see G. Walters, *Histoire du Parti Communiste Français* (Paris: Somogy, 1948). For a historical study of French communism in the broader context of international communism see Franz Borkenau, *European Communism* (London: Faber and Faber, 1953). The best work on party organization is A. Brayance, *Anatomie du Parti Communiste Français* (Paris: Denoel, 1952). For a study of Communist tactics and policies during the Second World War see A. Rossi, *A Communist Party in Action* (New Haven: Yale University Press, 1949); A. Rossi, *La Guerre des Papillons, Quatre ans de Politique Communiste, 1940–44* (Paris: Plon, 1954); A. Rossi, *Les Communistes Français pendant le drôle de Guerre* (Paris: Plon, 1951).

For a psychological and sociological study of communism see Jules Monnerot, *Sociologie du Communisme* (Paris: Gallimard, 1949). See also Jean Lacroix "L'Homme Marxiste," *La Vie Intellectuelle*, Aug. and Sept., 1947.

For a general survey on the French Communist party see J. M. Domenach, "The French Communist Party" in Mario Einaudi, J. M. Domenach, and A. Garosci, *Communism in Western Europe* (Ithaca: Cornell University Press, 1951). For biographical data on party leaders see B. Lazic, *Les Partis Communistes d'Europe, 1919–1945* (Paris: Iles d'Or, 1957).

## SFIO

### Party publications

The best source of documentation on the SFIO is the *Bulletin Interieur du Parti Socialiste*, a party publication which gives the texts of the motions submitted before the congresses as well as a detailed analysis of the congress votes; the bulletin publishes the major decisions of the party's executive organs. The *Revue Socialiste*, the contributors to which belong mostly to the Left wing, is occasionally interesting. The party's newspaper *Le Populaire* and the monthly *Démocratie 60* may also be consulted.

### Writings by Socialists

See an anthology of Jaurès's writings in Louis Lévy, *Anthologie de Jean Jaurès* (Paris: Calman-Lévy, 1946). See L. Blum, *For All Mankind* (New York: Viking Press, 1946); L. Blum, *Oeuvres*, 2 volumes (Paris: A. Michel, 1954–1955); J. Moch, *Confrontations* (Paris: Gallimard, 1952); J. Moch, *La Folie des Hommes* (Paris: R. Laffont, 1954); M. E. Naegelen, *Grandeur et Solitude de la France* (Paris: Flammarion, 1956); A. Philip, *La Démocratie Industrielle* (Paris: Presses Universitaires, 1955); A. Philip, *Le Socialisme Trahi* (Paris: Plon, 1957); G. Mollet, *Bilan et Perspectives Socialistes* (Paris: Plon, 1958).

### Studies on the SFIO: Secondary sources

For a history of Socialist thinking see the works by Paul Louis, in particular his *Histoire du Socialisme en France* (Paris: Rivière, 1950); and the works by Maxime Leroy, in particular his *Histoire des idées sociales en France*, 3 volumes (Paris: Gallimard, 1946–1954). For short surveys see G. Bourgin and P. Rimbert, *Le Socialisme* (Paris: Presses Universitaires de France, 1955); and the May, 1956, issue of *Esprit*.

For more specific studies on the SFIO see A. Noland, *The Founding of the French Socialist Party* (Cambridge: Harvard University Press, 1956); J. T. Marcus, *French Socialism in the Crisis Year, 1933–1936* (London: Stevens and Sons, 1958). For a sociological analysis of party membership see P. Rimbert "Sociologie du Parti Socialiste" *La Revue Socialiste*, Feb. and March, 1952, and P. Rimbert "Le Parti Socialiste SFIO" in M. Duverger, ed., *Partis Politiques et Classes Sociales en France* (Paris: A. Colin, 1955). For studies of working class and trade-union attitudes toward the SFIO and socialism in general, see H. W. Ehrmann, *French Labor from Popular Front to Liberation* (New York: Oxford University Press, 1947); and V. Lorwin, *The French Labor Movements* (Cambridge: Harvard University Press, 1954).

## Radical Party

### *Party publications*

From the post-liberation period to 1958, the Radical party's official monthly *L'Information Socialiste* published a summary of congress proceedings, printed the most important speeches by party leaders and generally gave basic information on intraparty activities. The publication was discontinued in 1958. The party now publishes a small mimeographed monthly, the *Bulletin d'Information Radical Socialiste* and the review *Le Démocrate*. For a study of the Mendès-France Radical era consult the *Cahiers de la République*, a review edited by Mendès-France, and such Left-wing radical publications as *Le Jacobin* and *La Jeune Tribune*. See also the *Études sur la Doctrine du Parti*, a series of draft theses and questionaire prepared under Mendès-France's supervision and sent to party members in May, 1957.

### *Writings by Radicals*

E. Herriot, *Aux Sources de la Liberté* (Paris: NRF, 1939); E. Herriot, *In Those Days* (New York: Old and New World, 1952); Alain (pseud. for E. Chartier), *Eléments d'une Doctrine Radicale* (Paris: Gallimard, 1925); and Alain, *Le Citoyen contre les Pouvoirs* (Paris: Sagittaire, 1926). P. Mendès-France's major speeches and broadcasts are collected in P. Mendès-France, *Gouverner c'est choisir*, 3 volumes (Paris: Julliard, 1955–1958); and P. Mendès-France, *Dire la Verité* (Paris: Julliard, 1955); A. Bayet, *Le Radicalisme* (Paris: Valois, 1932); and A. Bayet, *Laicité XX^e^ Siécle* (Paris: Hachette, 1958).

### *Studies on the Radical party*

The section on radicalism in A. Siegfried, *Tableau des Partis en France* (Paris: Grasset, 1930), remains excellent. See also A. Charpentier, *Le Parti Radical et Radical Socialiste à travers ses congrès* (Paris: Giard et Briere, 1913); G. Maurice, *Le Parti Radical* (Paris: Rivière, 1929); Jamy-

Schmitt, *Les Grandes Thèses Radicales* (Paris: Portique, 1931); A. Milhaud, *Histoire du Radicalisme* (Paris: Caillard, 1951); C. Nicolet, *Le Radicalisme* (Paris: Presses Universitaires, 1957); A. Werth, *The Strange History of Pierre Mendès-France* (London: Barrie, 1958); J. A. Schlesinger "The French Radical Socialist Party and the Republican Front of 1956," *The Western Political Quarterly*, XI (March, 1958), 71–85; J. A. Laponce "Mendès-France and the Radical Party," *The Western Political Quarterly*, XI (June, 1958), 340–356. See also A. Gourdon "Le Parti Radical," in M. Duverger, ed., *Partis Politiques et Classes Sociales* (Paris: A. Colin, 1955) and L. Latty and J. M. Royer "Les Radicaux" in J. Fauvet and H. Mendras, eds., *Les Paysans et la Politique* (Paris: A. Colin, 1958).

## The MRP

### *Party publications*

The Christian-democratic newspaper *L'Aube* founded before the war by Francisque Gay and the review *Terre Humaine* founded after the war by Étienne Borne discontinued publication in the early 1950's. The MRP national headquarters now publish a small weekly *Forces Nouvelles* and a magazine *France Forum* intended for party members. The propaganda section of the national secretariat also puts out at more or less regular intervals a number of specialized publications geared to local leaders, such as *Pour l'Action des Elus Municipaux et Départementaux*, *Les Cahiers de Formation Politique*, and *Action Civique et Politique*. Summaries of the proceedings of national congresses and national committees are published in *Forces Nouvelles*, *Action Civique et Politique*, and occasionally in special booklets and pamphlets published by the party secretariat. The party's Left-wing opposition group publishes a monthly, *Rénovation Démocratique*, edited by P. Saint-Marc.

### *Writings by Christian Democrats*

See a selection of De Mun's speeches and writings in M. Sangnier, *Albert de Mun* (Paris: Presses Universitaires, 1957). See also M. Sangnier, *Discours 1891–1921*, 4 volumes (Paris: Bloud et Gay, 1910–1925); M. Sangnier, *Témoignages* (Paris: Bloud et Gay, 1950); F. Gay, *Les Démocrates Chrétiens à l'Epreuve du Pouvoir* (Paris: Bloud et Gay, 1951). Among the writings of postwar MRP leaders see E. Borne, *De Marc Sangnier à Marc Coquelin* (Toulouse: Privat, 1953); and P. Bacon, *Vers la Réforme de l'Entreprise Capitaliste* (Paris: S.E.R.P., 1948).

Among the many pamphlets published by the party's secretariat see in particular E. Borne, *Le MRP et les Courants Permanents de la Pensée*

*Française*, 1949. Docteur Anjoulat, *La Politique Coloniale*, 1945. E. Borne, *Le Sens de notre Engagement Politique, 1944–1954;* François de Menthon, *Notre Politique Economique*, 1946; R. Buron, *Le Libéralisme et l'Economie Moderne*, 1949; A. Colin, *Pour la République, pour la Famille, pour le Progrès, pour la Paix*, 1951; M. R. Simonnet, *La Voie du Progrès et du Mouvement*, 1955; A. Poher, *L'Europe nécéssaire à la Paix*, 1955; R. Lecourt, *La Crise de l'Etat*, 1955; P. H. Teitgen, *Pour Sauver l'Afrique Française*, 1956; R. Schuman, *La Politique Extérieure*, 1956; J. Fonteneau, *Pour un Mouvement Créateur*, 1956. See also the anonymous publications, *Le MRP, parti de la IVe République*, 1946 (?); *Jalons pour Rénover notre Agriculture*, 1945; *La Nationalisation*, 1945.

## *Studies on the MRP and on Christian democracy*

For the origins of Christian-democratic thought and parties in France see J. B. Duroselle, *Débuts du Catholicisme Social en France, 1822–1870* (Paris: Presses Universitaires, 1951); H. Rollet, *Action Sociale des Catholiques en France, 1871–1901* (Paris: Bovin & Co., 1948); J. Piou, *Le Ralliement, son Histoire* (Paris: Spes, 1928); E. Barbier, *Les Idées du Sillon* (Paris: Lethielloux, 1905); A. Dansette, *Destin du Catholicisme Français, 1926–1956* (Paris: Cerf, 1957); M. Vaussard, *Histoire de la Démocratie Chrétienne* (Paris: Seuil, 1956); R. H. de la Montagne, *Histoire de la Démocratie Chrétienne* (Paris: Arniot, 1948). For the creation and evolution of the MRP see J. M. Domenach, *Gilbert Dru, celui qui croyait au ciel* (Paris: E. L. F., 1947); M. Einaudi, and F. Goguel, *Christian Democracy in Italy and France* (Notre Dame: University of Notre Dame Press, 1952). See also A. J. Bouscaren, "The MRP in French Governments, 1948–1951," *Journal of Politics*, XIV (Feb., 1952), 104–131; J. T. Marcus, "Social Catholicism in Post War France," *South Atlantic Quarterly*, LVI (Summer, 1957), 299–313; S. H. Barnes, "The Politics of French Christian Labour," *Journal of Politics*, XXI (Feb., 1959), 105–122; D. Pépy, "Note sur le Mouvement Républicain Populaire," in M. Duverger ed., *Partis Politiques et Classes Sociales en France* (Paris: Colin, 1955); R. Plantade, "The MRP," in M. Duverger and H. Mendras eds., *Les Paysans et la Politique* (Paris: A. Colin, 1958). See also W. R. Yates, "Power, Principle and the Doctrine of the Mouvement Républicain Populaire," *American Political Science Review*, LII (June, 1958), 419–436.

## The Independents

### *Party publication*

The CNIP publishes the weekly *France-Indépendante* owned by the party's secretary-general, R. Duchet.

### *Writings by Independents*

See J. Rueff, *Discours aux Indépendants* (Paris: de Médicis, 1951); A. Pinay, "France's Political Problems," *International Affairs*, XXX (April, 1954), 149–155; R. Duchet, *Pour le Salut Public* (Paris: Plon, 1958). See also the works by P. Reynaud, in particular: *Jeunesse, Quelle France veux-tu?* (Paris: NRF, 1936); *Sauver le Pays et le Régime* (Paris: Imprimerie Nationale, 1939); *In the thick of the Fight, 1930–1945* (London: Cassell, 1955); *Unite or Perish, a dynamic program for a United Europe* (New York: Simon and Schuster, 1951).

### *Studies on the Independents*

A general study of French conservatism is in R. Rémond, *La Droite en France de 1815 à nos Jours* (Paris: Aubier, 1954). A sympathetic analysis of modern conservatism is given by P. Serant, *Où va la Droite?* (Paris: Plon, 1958). Descriptions of Independents in parliament is given by J. Isorni, *Le Silence est d'Or* (Paris: Flammarion, 1957).

## The UNR

### *Party publications*

The RPF used to publish *Le Rassemblement* and the *Courrier d'Information;* the Social Republicans published *Les Idées . . . , Les Faits,* and *La Nation Républicaine et Sociale.* Interesting also for the pre-1958 history of Gaullism is Debré's monthly magazine *Les Courriers de la Colère,* which, after de Gaulle's return to power, became *Les Courriers de la Nation.* Among the pamphlets put out by the RPF secretariat see *L'Association Capital-Travail,* 1952 (?); and *Devant la Politique Internationale,* 1952 (?).

The UNR publishes a monthly *Le Courrier de la Nouvelle République* which gives the secretariat's line and publishes brief summaries of the proceedings and decisions of the party's national organs. Slightly better coverage is given by the UNR's *Bulletin de Presse. L'Espoir des Jeunes* is intended for the party's younger members. J. Soustelle publishes

*Voici Pourquoi*, which voices the opinions of the more nationalistic wing among UNR leaders.

### *Writings by Gaullists*

Charles de Gaulle, *Le Fil de l'Epée* (Paris: 1932); *Vers l'Armée de Métier* (Paris: Berger-Leurault, 1934); *Discours de Guerre, 1940–42* (Fribourg: ed. M.U.R., 1944); *Discours aux Français* (Paris: Office Français d'Edition, 1945); and *War Memoirs*, 2 volumes (New York: Viking Press, 1956–1959). For the works of M. Debré and M. Blocq-Mascart on constitutional reform see below, p. 398. For the views of J. Soustelle on Algeria see his *Aimée et Souffrante Algérie* (Paris: Plon, 1956). For a general criticism of the Fourth Republic see the work of the first chairman of the Constitutional Council, L. Noël, *Notre Dernière Chance* (Paris: Geralde, 1956).

### *Studies on Gaullism*

For studies on the RPF see R. Barillon "Le Rassemblement du Peuple Français" in M. Duverger ed., *Partis Politiques et Classes Sociales en France* (Paris: A. Colin, 1955); M. Terrier, *Le RPF dans la tradition Politique Française* (Paris: Institut d'Études Politiques, 1952, thesis). A member of the RPF's Left wing analyzes the party's evolution in L. Vallon, *L'Histoire s'avance masquée* (Paris: Julliard, 1957). Studies of the RPF's failure are in R. G. Neumann "Formation and Transformation of Gaullism in France," *The Western Political Quarterly*, VI (June, 1953), 250–274; and R. Pierce "De Gaulle and the RPF. A post-mortem," *Journal of Politics*, XVI (Feb., 1954), 96–119. For studies on de Gaulle see F. Garas, *Charles de Gaulle seul contre les Pouvoirs* (Paris: Julliard, 1957). A. Fabre-Luce, *Gaulle-Deux* (Paris: Julliard, 1958); L. Hamon, *De Gaulle dans la République* (Paris: Plon, 1958); A. C. Robertson, *La Doctrine du Général de Gaulle* (Paris: Fayard, 1959); and H. Lüthy, "France in Person? General de Gaulle: His Memoirs and His Myth," *Encounter*, XL (May, 1957), 58–67.

## Minor Parties

### *Party publications*

Anarchists publish the newspaper *Le Libertaire;* Trotskyists control the weekly *La Vérité*. For an attempt at "national communism" see the monthly *La Nation Socialiste* before its editor, A. Lecoeur, joined the SFIO in 1958. Progressists publish the quarterly *Les Cahiers du*

*Progressisme*, and control the newspaper *Libération* and the monthly *Les Cahiers Internationaux.*

The publications by Left-wing "Labor" groups are numerous. See among others *La Tribune de Socialisme* published by the Autonomous Socialist party, *La Tribune du Peuple* published by the Union de la Gauche Socialiste. Necessary to the study of "laborism" are such weeklies as *L'Express, France-Observateur, Témoignage Chrétien,* and the monthlies *Esprit* and *Les Temps Modernes.*

The publications of splinter Center groups include the Right-wing Radical *La République,* and before the 1958 party split, the UDSR's *Combat Républicain.*

For splinter conservative groups see *Le Flambeau* published irregularly by the Réconciliation Française and *L'Unité Paysanne* published by Paul Antier.

For extreme Right-wing publications see Poujade's weekly *Fraternité Française;* Dorgère's *La Gazette Agricole;* the neofascist *Jeune Nation,* and the Pétainist *Rivarol.*

The Count of Paris publishes a monthly *Bulletin d'Information.* The monarchists in the *Action Française* tradition have two magazines *Aspects de la France* and *La Nation Française.*

### *Studies on splinter parties*

For Left-wing groups see E. D. Godfrey, Jr., *The Fate of the French Non-Communist Left* (New York: Doubleday Co., 1955); C. A. Micaud "The New Left in France," *World Politics,* X (July, 1958); R. Barrillon "Desseins et Destin de la Nouvelle Gauche," *Le Monde,* April 22, 1955.

For Right-wing groups see S. Hoffmann, *Le Mouvement Poujade* (Paris: A. Colin, 1956); R. Girardet "L'Héritage de l'Action Française," *Revue Française de Science Politique,* VII (Oct., 1957), 765–792; R. Barrillon "L'Extrème Droite en France," *Le Monde,* Feb. 14, 15, 16, 1958; S. M. Osgood "A Pretender's Concept of the French Monarchy," *Review of Politics,* XIX (Jan., 1957), 77–89.

## Pressure Groups

A general survey of French pressure groups and techniques is given by J. Meynaud, *Les Groupes de Pression en France* (Paris: A. Colin, 1958). For more specific studies see H. W. Ehrmann, *Organized Business in France* (Princeton: Princeton University Press, 1957); J. Fauvet and H. Mendras, *Les Paysans et la Politique* (Paris: A. Colin, 1958). A good case study of pressure politics is given by B. E. Brown "Alcohol and Politics in France," *American Political Science Review,* LI (Dec., 1957), 976–994. For an analysis of the military before the Second World War see R. Girardet, *La Societé Militaire dans la France Contemporaine* (Paris: Plon, 1953). For a brief analysis of political pressures and attitudes by veterans organizations see R. Rémond "Les Anciens Combattants et la Politique," *Revue Française de Science Politique,* V (May, 1955), 267–290. For studies on trade unions see R. Goetz-Girey, *La Pensée Syndicale Française. Militants et Théoriciens* (Paris: A. Colin, 1948); E. Dolléans and G. Dehove, *Histoire du Travail en France des Origines à nos Jours,* 2 volumes (Paris: Domat, 1953–1955); G. Lefranc, *Histoire du Travail et des Travailleurs* (Paris: Flammarion, 1957); Val R. Lorwin, *The French Labor Movement* (Cambridge: Harvard University Press, 1954); R. le Bourre, *Le Syndicalisme Français dans la Cinquième République* (Paris: Calman-Lévy, 1959). Studies of the structure of the Catholic church and of its political attitudes are made by V. L. Chaigneau, *L'Organisation de l'Eglise Catholique en France* (Paris: Spes, 1956); A. Dansette, *Destin du Catholicisme Français, 1926–1956* (Paris: Flammarion, 1957). For the minor religious groups see S. R. Schram, *Protestantism and Politics in France* (Alençon: Corbière et Jugain, 1954); and P. Aubery, *Milieux Juifs de la France Contemporaine* (Paris: Plon, 1957).

## The Drafting of the Constitution of 1958

### *Documents*

For the constitutional law of June 3, 1958, see *Journal Officiel, Lois et Decrets,* June 4, 1958. For the drafting of the constitution see *Avant Projet de la Constitution (soumis au Comité Constitutionnel le 29 Juillet 1958)* (Imprimerie du Journal Officiel, 1958); Comité Constitutionnel, *Avis du Comité Consultatif Constitutionnel* (Imprimerie du Journal Officiel, 1958); Secrétariat Général du Gouvernement, "Le Referendum des 26.27 et 28 Septembre 1958," *Notes et Etudes Documentaires,* No. 2504, 1959.

### *Secondary sources*

The best studies on the origins and drafting of the constitution are by N. Wahl in his "Aux Origines de la Nouvelle Constitution," *Revue Française de Science Politique,* IX (March, 1959), 30–66; and "The French Constitution of 1958: the Initial Draft and its Origins," *American Political Science Review,* LIII (June, 1959), 358–382. See also F. Goguel. "L'Elaboration des Institutions de la République dans la Constitution du 4 Octobre 1958," *Revue Française de Science Politique,* IX (March, 1959), 67–86; also two short studies published by members of the

Advisory Committee, A. Mignot, *La Nouvelle Constitution: Evolution ou Révolution* (Coulommiers: Brodard et Taupin, 1958); and P. Marcilhacy, "De l'Enfantement d'une Constitution," *Revue Politique des Idées et des Institutions*, XLVII (Sept., 1958), 421–425. For a study of the evolution of Debré's constitutional proposals see Jacquier-Bruère (pseud. for M. Debré and E. Monick), *Refaire La France: l'Effort d'une Génération* (Paris: Plon, 1945); M. Debré, *La Mort de l'Etat Republicain* (Paris: Gallimard, 1947); *La République et son pouvoir* (Paris: Nagel, 1950); *La République et ses Problèmes* (Paris: Nagel, 1953); *Ces Princes qui nous gouvernent* (Paris: Plon, 1957); *Refaire une Démocratie, un État, un Pouvoir* (Paris: Plon, 1958). See also an essay written shortly before the fall of the Fourth Republic by M. Blocq-Mascart, *La Prochaine République sera-t-elle Républicaine?* (Paris: Plon, 1958). See text of de Gaulle's Bayeux speech of June 1946 in *Revue Française de Science Politique*, IX (March, 1959), 188 ff.

## The Constitution of the Fifth Republic

### *Documents*

The text of the constitution and of the twenty-two organic laws of 1958 is in *Constitution. Ordonnances portant lois Organiques et Ordonnances relatives aux Pouvoirs Publics* (Paris: Imprimerie du Journal Officiel, No. 1119, 1959). For the parliamentary standing orders see *Règlement de l'Assemblée Nationale* (1st ed., Paris: Imprimerie de l'Assemblée Nationale, September, 1959); and *Règlement du Sénat* (1st ed., Paris: Imprimerie du Sénat, September, 1959). The Constitutional Council's decisions invalidating some of the articles of the draft parliamentary standing orders are in *Journal Officiel, Lois et Décrets*, July 3, 1959. For an English translation of the constitution with a brief commentary see P. Campbell and B. Chapman, *The Constitution of the Fifth Republic* (Oxford: Blackwell, 1958).

### *Secondary sources*

See M. Duverger, *Droit Constitutionnel et Institutions Politiques*, 2 volumes (Paris: Presses Universitaires, 1959); J. Chapsal, *La Constitution de 1958*, 2 volumes (Paris: Cours de l'Institut d'Études Politiques, 1959); M. Prélot, *Pour Comprendre la Nouvelle Constitution* (Paris: Centurion, 1958); J. Chatelain, *La Nouvelle Constitution et le Régime Politique de la France* (Paris: Berger-Levrault, 1959). See also an analysis of the constitution made on the basis of interviews with some legal advisors who helped Debré draft the constitution in "Commentaires sur la Constitution du 4 Octobre 1958," *Notes et Études Documentaires, serie française,* April 11, 1959. See also S. H. Hoffmann "The French Constitution of 1958. The Final Text and its Prospects," *The American Political Science Review,* LIII (June, 1959), 332–357. Still useful, although based on the experience of the Fourth Republic, are D. W. S. Lidderdale, *The Parliament of France* (New York: F. A. Praeger, 1953); P. Williams, *Politics in Post-war France* (2d ed., London: Longmans, Green, 1958); and E. Blamont, *Les Techniques Parlementaires* (Paris: Presses Universitaires, 1958).

## The Community

### *Documents*

The presidential decisions as well as other texts concerning the Community are published in *Le Journal Officiel de la Communauté* (Paris: Imprimerie du Journal Officiel). See in particular the constitutions of the member states in Nos. 5–15 (June, 1959).

### *Secondary sources*

The institutions of the Community are analyzed in the general works discussing the constitution of 1958. See also V. Silvera "Passé de l'Union Française et Avenir de la Communauté," *Revue Juridique et Politique de l'Union Française,* XII (Oct., 1958), 589–604, and the special issue of *Revue Française de Science Politique,* IX (Sept., 1959) on politics in French Black Africa. See also J. Ehrard, *Communauté ou Sécession?* (Paris: Calman-Lévy, 1959); and A. Blanchet, *L'Itinéraire des Partis Africains depuis Bamako* (Paris: Plon, 1958).

## Elections

### *Documents*

The laws and decrees governing elections have been compiled into a *Code Electoral* (Paris: Imprimerie du Journal Officiel). The election returns are published with about two years' delay by the Ministry of the Interior in their *Recueils et Monographies* series. The Ministry of the Interior also released election returns to the press following each election. Newspapers sometimes change the classifications suggested by the ministry, especially with regard to independent candidates. The most reliable classification is that of *Le Monde.* The statements of votes submitted before the credential committees of the National Assembly or the Constitutional Council may also be used.

## *Secondary sources*

The best historical survey of France's past electoral systems is P. Campbell, *French Electoral Systems and Elections 1789–1957* (London: Faber and Faber, 1958). For a discussion of the impact of electoral systems on party politics see M. Duverger and others, *L'Influence des Systèmes Electoraux sur la Vie Politique* (Paris: A. Colin, 1950); G. E. Lavau, *Partis Politiques et Réalités Sociales* (Paris: A. Colin, 1953). For studies of specific elections see among many others M. Duverger, F. Goguel, and J. Touchard, *Les Elections du 2 Janvier 1956* (Paris: A. Colin, 1957); H. G. Nicholas, P. M. Williams, S. Rose, and M. Thomas "The French Election of 1956," *Political Studies*, IV (1956), 139–175 and 250–282. The official regulations concerning electoral expenses are discussed in Mattei Dogan "Le Financement des Elections de Janvier 1956," *Revue Française de Science Politique*, VII (Jan., 1957), 88–98.

# Index

Accounting, 275–276
Accounting Court, 275
*Action Catholique.* See Catholic Action
*Action Démocratique et Sociale.* See Democratic and Social Action
*Action Française.* See French Action
*Action Paysanne.* See Farmers Action
*Action Républicaine et Sociale* (ARS). *See* Republican and Social Action
*Action Socialiste.* See Socialist Action
Advisory Constitutional Committee, 175, 176
African Democratic Rally (RDA) (Left of Center African party), 146, 149, 171, 379
African Rally party (PRA) (Left of Center African party), 379
Agrarian group, 23
Alain. *See* Chartier
Alduy, Paul, 128
Algeria: settlers and colons in, 2–4, 152, 157; and 13th of May, 3–5; and French public opinion, 4–5; and army in, 4–5, 157; and Communist party, 44; and SFIO, 68; and Radicals, 82; and MRP, 103; and Gaullists, 136; and Independents, 119
Algerian group in parliament, 149, 325
Alibert, Raphaël, 168
Allemane, Jean, 47
*Alliance Démocratique.* See Democratic Alliance
Anarchism and Anarchists, 15, 46, 141
Anticlericalism, 17–18, 21, 22, 24
Antier, Paul, 110, 111, 148, 376
Antiparliamentarism, 154, 175
Anxionnaz, Paul, 75
*Apparentements.* See Electoral system
Army: and 13th of May, 2, 4–6, 157; and Algeria, 4–5, 157; and politics, 157
*Arrêtés.* See Executive orders
Article 16. *See* President of the Republic
*Aspects de la France,* 140, 153, 154
*Association Catholique de la Jeunesse Française* (ACJF), 87
*Association des Parents d'Elèves des Ecoles Libres* (APEL), 159
Astier de la Vigerie, Emmanuel d', 143
*Aube, l',* 87
Audibert, 111
Audit Court. *See* Accounting Court
Auriol, Vincent, 11, 54, 191, 378
Autonomous Socialist party (PSA) (splinter Left-wing socialist party), 22, 144, 145, 180
Autonomous Syndicalist Federation (socialist trade union), 64
*Avenir, l',* 86

Babeuf, Gracchus, 45
Bacon, Paul, 87, 104
Bakounin, Michel, 141
Bamako congress, 171
*Banque Commerciale pour l'Europe du Nord,* 39
Barangé law, 117. *See also* school question
Barbé, 39

Bardoux, Jacques, 111, 168
Barrachin, Edmond, 245, 286
Barrès, Maurice, 109
Barthélémy, Joseph, 168, 169
Bastid, Paul, 169
Baumgartner, Wilfrid, 137
Bayeux speech. *See* De Gaulle
Baylet, Jean, 83, 235
Beaufort, Guy Grout de, 138
Belin, René, 51
Belleville, program of, 71. *See also* Radical party
Bendjelida, Ali, 149, 150
Berl, Emmanuel, 24
Bernanos, Georges, 375
Bevan, Aneurin, 259
Biaggi, Jean Baptiste, 129, 130, 152, 327
Bidault, Georges, 87, 88, 90, 91, 92, 96, 102, 103, 104, 255, 323, 371
Billères, René, 82
Billoux, François, 39
Bills. *See* Laws
Blanc, Louis, 46
Blanqui, Louis Auguste, 46, 47
Bloch-Lainé, François, 137
Blocq-Mascart, Maxime, 170, 378
Blum, Léon, 29, 49, 50, 52, 53, 64, 66, 68, 69, 73, 197, 378
Boivin-Champeaux J., 112
Bonaparte, descendants of, 186, 229
Bonapartism, 26–27
Bonnefous, Edouard, 146
Boukabeur, H., 379
Boulanger, Georges Ernest, 27, 157, 167, 185, 229
Boulloche, André, 309
Bour, A., 379
Bour, Louis, 87
Bourdan, R., 146
Bourdet, Claude, 144
Bouret, A., 90
Bourgès-Maunoury, Maurice, 114, 226, 323
Bouxom, Fernand, 87
Brayance, Alain, 40
Brazzaville speech. *See* De Gaulle
Brouillet, René, 138
Brousse, Paul, 47
Brutelle, Georges, 64
Budget. *See* Parliament; National Assembly; Senate
Buisson, Ferdinand, 71
Buonarroti, Filippo Michele, 45
Buron, Robert, 104, 309
Business. *See* Trade associations

Cabet, Etienne, 46
Cabinet, Council of. *See* Council of Ministers
Cabinet: of a minister, *see* Council of Ministers; President
Cachin, Marcel, 49
Cadillac Committee. *See* Radical party
*Cahiers du Progressisme,* 143
Caillaux, Joseph, 72
Canada, 269
Capitant, René, 123, 125, 127, 144, 146, 168, 169
Carré de Malberg, Raymond, 168
*Cartel des Gauches* (electoral alliance of Left-wing parties; Third Republic), 374
Casanova, Laurent, 39
Cassin, René, 173
Cassou, Jean, 144
Catholic Action, 94, 99
Catholic Church: and *Rerum Novarum,* 85; and Sillon, 86; and anticlericalism, 17–18, 71; and politics, 85–86, 107, 158–159; status in Alsace and Lorraine, 386
Caucus. *See* National Assembly
Cavaignac, Louis-Eugène, 157
Célor, 39
Central African Republic, 305, 314
Central Revolutionary Committee (nineteenth-century splinter socialist party), 47
*Centre National des Indépendants et Paysans* (CNIP). *See* Independent party
*Centre Républicain* (Neo-Radical group; Right of Center). *See* Republican Center
Chaban-Delmas, Jacques, 75, 129, 138, 251
Chalandon, Albin, 134, 137, 138
Chambrun, Gilbert de, 143
Champetier de Ribes, 87
Chappedelaine, L. de, 110
Chardonnet, J., 379
Chartier, Emile, 81
Chassin, Lionel Max, 152
Chatelet, Albert, 187
Chazelle, R., 379
Christian democracy, 18, 21, 23, 100–

103. *See also* Popular Republican Movement
Christian Democracy (Right of Center splinter group), 22–23, 91, 92
Churches: as pressure group, 158–159. *See also* Catholic Church
Churchill, Winston, 8
Civil rights, 289
Civil servants: in personal cabinets, 199; in Council of Ministers, 207
Claudius-Petit, Eugène, 146, 147
Clemenceau, Georges, 71
Clemenceau, Michel, 111, 112
Clostermann, Pierre, 128, 236
Colin, André, 87, 88, 90, 96, 97, 104, 286
Colons. *See* Algeria, settlers and colons in
Combes, Emile, 71
Cominform, 44
Comintern, 37
*Comité Consultatif Constitutionnel* (CCC). *See* Advisory Constitutional Committee
*Comité Révolutionnaire Central.* See Central Revolutionary Committee
*Commerçants, Artisans, Petits Industriels,* 38
Committees. *See* National Assembly; Senate
Commonwealth, comparison with, 302
Commune (1870), 30, 46
Communism, 15–16, 21, 22, 24. *See also* Communist party
Communist party (PCF): history of, 28–32; organization of, 32–39; and ancillary organizations, 38–39, 160; membership of, 29, 31, 40–44; leadership of, 34, 36, 39, 137, 372; purges, 29, 39, 144; electorate of, 29, 31, 40–44, 324; doctrine and program of, 15–16; 21, 22–23, 26, 43–44; caucus, 258; tactical changes of, 43–44; and the USSR, 44; seats in National Assembly, 325
Community: right of independence, 177, 308, 312, 314; Executive Council of, 193, 308–309; membership of, 303–305; the "new" Community, 303, 314–315; powers of, 305; President of, 306–308; organization of, 306–313; Senate of, 310; Arbitration Court of, 311; Budget of, 312; Secretariat of, 313; evolution of, 313–314; citizenship, 306; treaties of independence, 314–315; future of, 316
Comores, 184, 304
*Confédération Française des Travailleurs Chrétiens* (CFTC), 87, 99, 100, 160, 297
*Confédération Générale de l'Agriculture* (CGA), 161
*Confédération Générale des Cadres* (CGC), 160
*Confédération Générale du Commerce et de l'Industrie,* 38
*Confédération Générale du Travail* (CGT,) 30, 36, 38, 160, 297, 372
*Confédération Générale du Travail–Force Ouvrière* (CGT–FO), 64, 94, 142, 160, 297
Congo, 305, 314
*Conseil d'État.* See Council of State
*Conseil National de la Résistance* (CNR), 87, 169
*Conseil National du Patronat Français* (CNPF), 162, 239
Conservatism, 18–19, 21, 23, 24. *See also* Independents
Considérant, Victor, 46
Constitution of 1958: origins of, 167–171; drafting of, 171–181; revision of, 172, 201, 220, 301, 364; future of, 185; and Constitutional Council, 201; text of, 329–367. *See also* President; Parliament
Constitutional Committee: in 1946 constitution, 289, 293
Constitutional Council: article sixteen, 290; membership of, 191, 252–290; treaties, 216; and powers of, 219, 220; and parliament, 220, 274, 292; as electoral court, 231, 291; and incapacitated president, 291; and organic laws, 292, 299; quorum of, 293
Constitutionality, control of. *See* Laws
*Convention Républicaine.* See Republican Convention
Cornut-Gentille, Bernard, 138, 309
Corporatism, 15
Coste-Floret, Paul, 104
Cot, Pierre, 74, 84, 143
Coty, René, 111, 112, 113, 189, 190, 244
Council of Ministers: instability of,

Council of Ministers (*continued*) 7–8; differentiated from cabinet, 193; and president, 193; powers of, 195, 200–201; selection of, 197–198; types of ministers, 198–199; inner cabinet, 198; and parliament, 201, 202; personal cabinets of ministers, 199
Council of State, 178, 219, 269, 292, 295, 306, 380
Council of the Republic. *See* Senate Fourth Republic
Courcel, Geoffroy de, 138
*Courrier de la Nièvre*, 236
Court of Cassation, 295, 306, 383
Courts. *See* Judges
Couve de Murville, Maurice, 309
Croix de Feu. *See* Fiery Cross

Dahomey, 305, 314
Daladier, Edouard, 11, 38, 72, 73, 75, 82, 110, 111
David, Jean Paul, 145, 147
Déat, Marcel, 50, 167
Debré, Michel, 13, 75, 84, 128, 134, 168, 169, 173, 198, 199, 200, 205–206, 227, 244, 379
Decree Laws. *See* Ordinances
*Décrêts*. *See* Executive orders
Defferre, Gaston, 11, 64, 171, 286
de Gaulle, Charles. *See* Gaulle, Charles de
Delbecque, Léon, 9, 129, 130, 138
Demarquet, Jean, 151
Democratic Alliance (conservative party), 110
Democratic and Social Action (conservative group; Fourth Republic), 376
Democratic and Social Union of the Resistance (UDSR), 145, 146–147, 180
Democratic Center (Neo-Radical group in Senate), 325
Democratic Entente (Center Radical group), 158
Democratic Labor Union (UDT) (Left-wing Gaullist group), 144
Democratic Left (conservative group; Third Republic), 110
Democratic Renovation (Left-wing MRP group), 94, 100, 104
Democratic socialism. *See* Socialism
Democratic Socialist party (splinter Right of Center party), 147
*Démocratie Chretiènne*. *See* Christian Democracy
Denis, André, 90, 144
*Dépêche de Toulouse*, 235
Depreux, Edouard, 54, 145, 161, 180
Dia, Mamadou, 314
Dissolution, right of, 168, 202, 207
Dorgère, Henri, 148, 377
Doriot, Jacques, 167
Doumergue, Gaston, 27
Drop off agreements, 235, 237
Dru, Gilbert, 88
Dubreuil, Hyacinthe, 376
Duchet, Roger, 103, 112, 114, 115, 117, 120, 371, 376
Duclos, Jacques, 30, 39, 286
Dumas, J., 96
Duverger, Maurice, 184

*Echo d'Oran*, 149
Economic and Social Council, 162, 297–298
Economic Council: in 1946 constitution, 297, 298
Economic Liberalism. *See* Liberalism
*Editeurs Français Réunis*, 38
*Editions Sociales*, 38
Eisenhower, Dwight, 291
Elections: to the presidency, 168, 182–188; to the Senate, 211, 279, 280–281, 286; to the National Assembly, 229–244; in Algeria, 246–248; results of (1946–1958), 324
Electoral systems: *scrutin d'arrondissement*, 76, 222–223, 226, 243, 286; proportional representation, 183, 224, 243, 282; history of, 221–226; *apparentements*, 225; and districting, 228; proposed reforms of, 244–246; in Australia, 245; in Germany, 245; in Great Britain, 245; in Ireland, 245
Electorate: by socioeconomic groups, 328. *See also* Communist party, Socialist party
Ely, Paul, 309
*Ere Nouvelle*, 86
Erhard, Ludwig, 118
*Esprit*, 100, 140
*Eure-Eclair*, 236
European assemblies, 257, 260, 263

European Defense Community (EDC), 60, 69, 91, 102, 261
Europeanism, 20, 21, 23
Europeans in Algeria. *See* Algeria, settlers and colons in
Executive. *See* President; Prime Minister; Council of Ministers
Executive Orders, 168, 169, 173, 210, 215–220, 274, 292, 293
*Express, l'*, 239

Fabians, 86
Fajon, Etienne, 39
Farmers, as pressure group, 162, 207; as parliamentary group, 111, 325
Farmers Action (conservative party; Fourth Republic), 376
Farmers parties, 15, 111, 148, 376
Fascism, 15, 21
Fauchon, Maxime, 110
Faure, Edgar, 77, 82, 83, 145, 147, 150, 190, 226, 286, 323, 371
Faure, Maurice, 83
Faure, Paul, 49, 51, 147
*Fédération des Travailleurs Socialistes.* See Socialist Workers Federation
*Fédération Nationale des Syndicats d'Exploitants Agricoles* (FNSEA), 116, 161
*Fédération Républicaine.* See Republican Federation
Fiery Cross (veterans' Right-wing league; Third Republic), 159, 378
Flandin, Pierre Etienne, 110
Fonteneau, Jean, 375
Food and Agricultural Organization (FAO), 306
Fourcade, Jacques, 138
Fourier, Charles, 45
Fourth Republic: end of, 1–13; and party system, 6; paralysis of, 6–8, 317
Frachon, Benoit, 38, 39
*France-Indépendante,* 117
*France-Observateur,* 144
*Fraternité-Matin,* 239
Fraissinet, Jean, 115, 236
Frédéric-Dupont, Edouard, 110, 111
Freedom Republican party (conservative party; Fourth Republic), 112, 376
Freemasons, 159
French Action (Royalist extreme Right-wing party; Third Republic), 154, 167
French Fraternity Union. *See* Poujadist party
French National Front (extreme Right-wing group), 153
French Reconciliation (conservative group), 140, 147, 148
French Socialist party (splinter socialist party; nineteenth century), 47
French Social party (conservative party; Third Republic), 111
French Union and Fraternity (UFF). *See* Poujadist party
French Women's Union, 38
Frey, Roger, 138, 379
*Front National.* See National Front
*Front National des Combattants.* See National Front of Combatants
*Front National Français.* See French National Front
*Front Populaire.* See Popular Front

Gabon, 305, 314
Gaillard, Félix, 58, 77, 82, 83, 114, 226, 323
Gambetta, Léon, 71
*Gauche Démocratique.* See Democratic Left
*Gauche Révolutionnaire.* See Revolutionary Left
Gaudy, Georges, 154
Gaulle, Charles de: and 13th of May, 8–13, 27, 157; as a myth, 8, 27; and Communist, 8; and Pétain, 8; and economic and social policy, 8, 127, 136; 1958 government of, 12, 261; postwar government of, 73, 88; and foreign policy, 83, 135–136, 207; and Algeria, 103, 136, 207; and RPF, 114, 124–127; and UNR, 122, 130, 134, 204; and constitution of 1958, 122–123, 190, 207; and Left-wing Gaullists, 123, 129; Bayeux speech, 123; Strasbourg speech, 124; and Soustelle, 124, 205; and Fourth Republic, 127; and constitutional problems, 134–135, 171, 179; and European integration, 135; and former colonies, 135, 171; and 1946 constitution, 170; and drafting of the

Gaulle, Charles de (*continued*) 1958 constitution, 171, 173, 174; Brazzaville speech, 178
Gaullism and Gaullists, 26–27, 122–130; Left-wing, 123, 128. *See also* UNR; French People's Rally; de Gaulle; Gaullist Union
Gaullist Union, 75, 89, 123, 146
Gay, Francisque, 87, 88, 91, 104
Gazier, Albert, 64
Germany, comparison with, 266, 294
Gilibert, Jean, 88
Gingembre, Léon, 162
Giraudoux, Jean Pierre, 89
Giscard d'Estaing, Valérie, 120
Gouin, Félix, 52, 64
Government. *See* Council of Ministers; Prime Minister
Graefschepe, Van, 379
Great Britain, comparison with, 168, 210, 251, 269, 274, 289
Grenier, Fernand, 251
Guadeloupe, 303
Guesdes, Jules, 47, 48
Guillaumat, Pierre, 309
Guinée, 181
Guyane, 303

Hamon, Léo, 90, 144
Heinki, Bishop, 125
Herbaut, Pierre, 64
Herriot, Edouard, 49, 72, 73, 83, 149, 234
Hersant, Robert, 236
Hertzog, Maurice, 199
High Court of Justice, 291, 296
High Volta (*or* Upper Volta), 305, 314
Holy See, 85, 86
Houphouët-Boigny, Félix, 11, 13, 146, 173, 199, 313, 379
*Humanité, l'*, 36, 49

Ideologies: and parties, 15, 21–23; lesser important, 166
*Indépendants d' Action Populaire*. See Independents for Popular Action
*Indépendants d'Outre-Mer*. See Overseas Independents
*Indépendants et Paysans d'Action Sociale*. See Independents and Farmers for Social Action
Independent Democratic Union (conservative group; Fourth Republic), 376
Independent Popular Republicans. *See* Independent Republicans
Independent Republicans (conservative party; Third and Fourth republics), 110
Independent Socialists (nineteenth-century splinter socialist party), 47
Independents (CNIP): doctrine and program of, 21, 22, 23, 26, 118–120; history of, 109–115, 148; electorate of, 110, 111, 113, 114, 121, 324; organization of, 115–117; membership of, 116, 150; and Algeria, 119; and European integration, 120; leadership of, 120–121; and referendum of 1958, 179; and electoral system, 226; seats in National Assembly, 325
Independents and Farmers for Social Action (dissident Gaullists; Fourth Republic), 376
Independents for Popular Action (conservative party; Third Republic), 110
Inspectorate of Finance, 175
*Institut Français d'Opinion Publique*, poll by, 42, 66, 84, 106, 120, 138
*Intergroupes*, 163
International: first, 46, 142; second, 47; third, 49
International Communist party (PCI) (Trotskyists), 142
International Labour Organization (ILO), 306
Isorni, Jacques, 11, 120
Ivory Coast, 305, 314

Jacquinot, Louis, 13, 110, 198, 376
Janot, Raymond, 138, 173
Jarrot, André, 377
Jaurès, Jean, 28, 47, 48, 244
Jean Jaurès Club, 64
*Jeune Nation*. See Young Nation
*Jeune République*. See Young Republic
*Jeunesse Agricole Chrétienne* (JAC), 87, 94, 99
*Jeunesse Etudiante Catholique* (JEC), 94
*Jeunesse Ouvrière Chrétienne* (JOC), 87, 94, 99
Jews, 159

Joliot-Curie, Frédéric, 372
Judges, appointment of, 194, 294; promotion of, 295
Judicial Review. *See* Laws, control of constitutionality of
Juskiewenski, Georges, 128

Kayser, Jacques, 74
Keita, Modibo, 314
Kir, Félix, 111, 120

Labor splinter parties, 143–145
Lacordaire, Jean Baptiste Henri, 86
Lacoste, Robert, 4, 6, 64, 371, 382
Lafay, Bernard, 82, 140, 146, 147, 285
Lagaillarde, Pierre, 9, 150, 153
Lamennais, Hughes Félicité Robert de, 86
Laniel, Joseph, 110, 111, 112, 120, 323, 376
La Rocque, François de, 27, 110, 111, 148
Laurens, Camille, 111, 120, 148
Lauriol, Marc, 150, 379
Laws: promulgation of, 195; initiative of, 200, 210, 269; government bills, 201, 208, 269; drafting of, 208; organic laws, 220, 299; private members bills, 252, 256, 269, 270; finance bills, 269, 271–276; riders, 271; control of the constitutionality of, 172; program laws, 272, 298
Lay Primary School Teachers Union, 64
League of the Rights of Man, 159, 163
Lecoeur, Auguste, 39, 143, 377
Le Corre, Darius, 143
Lecourt, Robert, 87, 104, 198
Lefèvre, Dr. Bernard, 9, 152
Left and Right, notions of, 23–26; and constitutional reform, 168
Legendre, Jean, 164
Lejeune, Max, 64, 251, 382
Lenin, 28, 38, 142
Léotard, Pierre de, 148
Le Pen, Jean-Marie, 151
Leroux, Pierre, 45
Le Trocquer, André, 64, 373
L'Huillier, R., 87
Liberal splinter parties, 145–148
Liberals: political, 17, 21, 22, 24; economic, 17, 21, 22, 24, 114, 118
*Libération* (newspaper), 143
*Libertaire, le*, 141
*Ligue des Droits de l'Homme*. See League of the Rights of Man
Lipkowski, Jean de, 123, 128, 144
Lippmann, Walter, 25
Lisette, Gabriel, 177, 199
Lop, Ferdinand, 186
Lussy, Charles, 11
Lyautey, Louis Hubert G., 157

Madagascar, 305, 314, 315
Mali federation, 303, 314
Mallem, Ali, 129
Malraux, André, 124, 127, 137, 198
Malterre, A., 379
Mandel, Georges, 110
Marçais, Philippe, 150
Marie, André, 113, 323
Marin, Louis, 110, 111, 112
Marquet, Adrien, 50
Marrane, Georges, 187
Martel, Robert, 152
Martinet, Gilles, 144
Martinique, 303
Marty, André, 39
Marxism, 16, 30, 46, 47, 49, 142
Massis, Henri, 154
Massu, Jacques, 9, 371
Mauritania, 305, 314
Maurras, Charles, 154
Maurrassism, 15
May-13 Popular Movement (extreme Right-wing group), 152
May 13, Rebellion of, 1–13, 151
Mayer, Daniel, 52, 53, 54, 180
Mayer, René, 77, 323
Medecin, Jean, 111
Melun, Armand de, 86
Mendès-France, Pierre, 11, 54, 72, 73, 75, 76, 77, 81, 82, 83, 140, 145, 147, 150, 161, 180, 187, 197, 226, 234, 236, 257, 323
Menthon, François de, 11, 87, 169, 170
*Méridional, le*, 236
Michelet, Edmond, 137, 138, 309
Millerand, Alexandre, 47, 49, 167, 168, 236
Mitterrant, François, 11, 146, 147, 171, 228, 286
Moch, Jules, 10, 31, 64, 378
Moderates, 109–113. *See also* Independents

Mollet, Guy, 10, 11, 13, 53, 60, 64, 68, 69, 114, 173, 234, 260, 323, 379
Monarchism and Monarchists, 15, 21, 153–154
Monnet, Jean, 69, 373, 377
Montagne, Rémy, 236
Montalembert, Charles de, 86
Montesquieu, Charles de, 168, 288
Morazé, Charles, 157
Morice, André, 84, 103, 145, 147, 371
Moslems: discrimination against, 3; and 13th of May, 3–5; and elections, 248. *See also* Algerian group in parliament
Moulin, Jean, 73
*Mouvement de Libération du Peuple.* See People's Liberation Movement
*Mouvement Populaire du 13 Mai.* See May-13 Popular Movement
*Mouvement Républicain de Libération,* 88
*Mouvement Républicain Populaire* (MRP). See Popular Republican Movement
Movement for Agricultural and Social Union (Farmers party), 148
Mutter, André, 111
Multipartism, 140, 154, 211, 243

*Nation Française,* 153, 154
*Nation Socialiste, la* (dissident Communist group), 143
National Assembly: seating arrangement in, 25; geographical distribution of members (1958), 165; and president, 188, 189, 190, 195, 207, 269; vote of nonconfidence by, 202, 203, 266, 267; and prime minister, 202, 263; dissolution of, 208, 268; elections to, 211, 229–244; substitutes in, 229; members of, 249–250; caucuses, 203, 257–262; Algerians in, 250, 252; overseas representatives in, 250, 262; standing orders of, 250; organization of, 250–262; chairman of, 250–251, 293; chairmen's conference of, 251, 253, 266; questors of, 252; secretaries of, 252; bureau of, 252, 256, 257; committees of, 253–257, 263, 270; finance committee of, 253, 256; agenda of, 253, 257, 266; and pressure groups, 254; and European assemblies, 257, 263; and Community Senate, 257, 263; and High Court of Justice, 263; functions of, 263–275; question period in, 264–266; interpellations by, 266; and constitutional council, 266, 274; legislative procedure in, 268–272; debates in, 270–271
National Communism. *See* Titoism
National Front (electoral alliance of Right-wing parties; Third Republic), 111
National Front of Combatants (extreme Right-wing group), 152, 153
Nationalism, 19–20, 21, 23, 24, 114, 119
Naudet, Pierre, 128
Neo-liberals, and constitutional reform, 168
Neo-Socialist party (post-World-War I splinter socialist group led by Déat), 50
New Caledonia, 184, 304
New Left (Left-wing labor group; Fourth Republic), 144
Newspapers and elections, 235
Niger, 305, 314
Nocher, Jean, 146
Noël, Léon, 379
Nomination, politics of, 234
*Nouvelles Equipes Françaises,* 87
*Nouvelle Gauche.* See New Left

Oceania, 304
Ordinances, 219
*Ordre des Médecins,* 99
Ortiz, Joseph, 153
Overseas departements: representation in parliament, 249–250, 279; status of, 303–304
Overseas Independents (IOM) (Center group of African parliamentarians; Fourth Republic), 149
Overseas territories: representation in parliament, 249–250, 279; status of, 304
Ozanam, Antoine Frédéric, 86

Palewski, Gaston, 124
Pardon, 194, 295
Paris, Count of, 153, 186, 230
Parliament: members of, 202; overseas representatives in, 211; sessions of, 212; credentials, 213; and local politics, 213; and parliamentary profes-

sion, 213–214; immunities, 214, 253; committees of, 162; and executive, 200; extraordinary sessions of, 200, 207, 212; legislative field, 210, 215–220; and budget, 216; delegation of powers to the executive by, 219–220; declining powers of, 276. *See also* National Assembly; Senate
*Parti Communiste Français* (PCF). See Communist party
*Parti Communiste Internationaliste* (PCI). See International Communist party
*Parti Démocrate Populaire.* See Popular Democratic party
*Parti du Regroupement Africain.* See African Rally party
*Parti Ouvrier.* See Workers party
*Parti Patriotique Révolutionnaire.* See Revolutionary Patriotic party
*Parti Radical Socialiste.* See Radical party
*Parti Républicain de la Liberté* (PRL). See Freedom Republican party
*Parti Républicain et Social de la Réconciliation Française.* See French Reconciliation party
*Parti Républicain Radical.* See Radical Republican party
*Parti Républicain Radical et Radical Socialiste* (also referred to as *Parti Radical Socialiste* or *Parti Radical*). See Radical party
*Parti Socialiste Autonome* (PSA). See Autonomous Socialist party
*Parti Social Français* (PSF). See French Social party
*Parti Socialiste de France.* See Socialist Party of France
*Parti Socialiste Démocratique.* See Democratic Socialist party
*Parti Socialiste Unifié* (PSU). See Unified Socialist party
*Parti Socialiste Unitaire.* See Unitary Socialist party
*Paysans.* See Farmers
Pébellier, E., 110
People's Liberation Movement (MLP) (extreme Left-wing, Christian party), 144
Pépy, Daniel, 105
Pétain and Petainists, 154, 157, 168
*Petit Bleu des Côtes du Nord,* 236
*Petites et Moyennes Entreprises* (PME), 113, 162, 164
Petsche, Maurice, 110, 137
Peugeot, 376
Peyrolles, Germaine, 87
Pflimlin, Pierre, 2, 6, 9, 10, 11, 13, 91, 96, 103, 104, 157, 173, 323
Philip, André, 53, 373
Physicians. See *Ordre des Médecins*
Pierre, Abbé (pseudonym of Henri Grouès), 90
Pinay, Antoine, 13, 90, 113, 118, 119, 120, 121, 126, 137, 198, 227, 244, 309, 323, 376
Pineau, Christian, 11, 53, 64
Pivert, Marceau, 51, 373
Plantade, R., 87
Pléven, René, 137, 146, 147, 180, 189, 210, 236, 323
Poincaré, Raymond, 109
Poinso-Chapuis, Germaine, 87
Political parties: and ideologies, 2, 14–27; and electorates, 23, 166; and pressure groups, 67, 164; and Fourth Republic, 140, 317; representativeness of, 156; and constitution of 1958, 182, 211, 317. *See also* Multipartism; Socialist party
Polls, public opinion. See *Institut Français d'Opinion Publique*
Polynesia, 184
*Populaire, le,* 60, 63, 73
*Populaire-Dimanche, le,* 60, 63, 73
Popular Democratic party (PDP) (Right of Center Christian democratic party; Third Republic), 87
Popular Front (alliance of Left-wing parties; Third Republic), 29, 50–51
Popular Republican Movement (MRP): doctrine and program of, 21, 22–23, 26, 88, 93, 100–103; history of, 85–92; and de Gaulle, 88, 92; electorate of, 89, 90, 91, 106–107, 324; membership of, 89, 105–106; and church, 89, 99, 100–101, 107, 158; and school question, 90; and European integration, 91, 102; caucus of, 91, 103, 262; organization of, 93–99; and ancillary organizations, 99–100, 161; leadership of, 104–105, 137; and referendum of 1958, 179; preferred ministries in the cabinet,

Popular Republican Movement (*cont.*) 197; and electoral system, 226; seats in National Assembly, 325
Poujade, Pierre, 14, 84, 148, 162, 180, 377
Poujadist party (UFF), 14, 114, 137, 150–152, 161, 187, 213, 324, 325
*Pouvoir Réglementaire*. See Executive orders
Pré, R., 379
President of the Republic: elections of, 168, 182–188; and prime minister, 174, 179, 194, 200–201, 206; powers of, 188–195; and parliament, 188–190, 191; and article sixteen, 191–192, 290; and constitutional council, 191, 291, 293; impeachment of, 192; incapacitation of, 192, 291; as head of state, 193–194; and right of pardon, 194; and treaties, 194; and judiciary, 194; and decrees, 195; and power to validate, 195; and laws, 195, 269; and veto, 195, 205, 207, 211, 212; as president of the Community; *See also* Gaulle, Charles de, 306–309, 314
Pressure groups, 156–166, 297
Prime Minister: selection of, 188, 196–197; investiture of, 200–201; powers of, 196, 200; and ministers, 196–199; and parliament, 201–204; and Constitutional Council, 201, 293; list of prime ministers under the Fourth Republic, 323; and president, *see* President, and prime minister
Progressive Union (pro-Communist party), 143
Proportional Representation (PR). *See* Electoral systems
Protestants, 159
Proudhon, Pierre Joseph, 16, 46, 71

Queuille, Henri, 73, 82, 125, 278, 323

Racism, 3, 15, 21
Radical Party: doctrine and program of, 21–22, 23, 26, 71–72, 81–83; origin of name, 70; history of, 70–76; and school question, 71, 81–82; electorate of, 71, 72, 74, 75, 82, 84, 324; and church, 71, 80, 82; absence of discipline in, 72, 77, 83; and Mendès-France, 75–76; Cadillac committee, 79; membership of, 76, 83–84, 148; and parliamentary system, 76, 81; organization of, 76–80; and Algeria, 82; and European integration, 82; leadership of, 83, 137; splits from, 141, 147; and referendum of 1958, 180; preferred ministries in cabinet, 197; and electoral system, 226; caucus of, 258; seats in National Assembly, 325
Radical Republican party (nineteenth-century Left-wing party), 71
Radical Socialist party (nineteenth-century Left-wing party), 71
Radio and elections, 231
Rally of Democratic Forces (Christian Democratic group), 375
Rally of the French People (RPF) (Gaullist party): history of, 8, 79, 89, 112, 113, 114, 124–127, 146, 170, 225; membership of, 124, 376; electorate of, 126; leadership of, 126; program of, 126; splits in, 126; organisation of, 125–126
Rally of Republican Leftwingers (RGR) (Right of Center group), 145, 147, 179
Ramadier, Paul, 31, 53, 58, 64, 113, 197, 323
*Rassemblement Démocratique Africain* (RDA). See African Democratic Rally
*Rassemblement des Forces Démocratiques*. See Rally of Democratic Forces
*Rassemblement des Gauches Républicaines* (RGR). See Rally of Republican Leftwingers
*Rassemblement du Peuple Francais* (RPF). See Rally of the French People
*Réconciliation Française*. See French Reconciliation
Referendum: of 1958, 179, 180–181; in 1958 constitution, 188, 216
Renaudel, 50
Renouvier, Charles, 71
*Rénovation Démocratique*. See Democratic Renovation
*Républicains Sociaux* (RS). *See* Social Republicans
Republican and Resistance Union

(pro-Communist group; Fourth Republic), 143
Republican Center (Neo-Radicals), 22, 23, 140, 145, 147, 179
Republican Center for Rural and Social Action (farmers' group), 148
Republican Convention (Right-wing Gaullist group), 129
Republican Federation (conservative party; Third and Fourth republics), 110, 112
Republican Radicals. *See* Radical Republican party
Republican Unity (conservative parliamentary group; Fourth Republic), 111
Republicans and Social Action (ARS) (dissident Gaullists), 127
*Rerum Novarum*, 85
Resistance, parties during: Communists, 30, 44; SFIO, 52; MRP, 87; Independents, 110; Gaullists, 137; UDSR, 146; Radicals, 73
Réunion, 303
Revision process, 299–301
Revolutionary Left (post-World-War I Left-wing SFIO faction led by Pivert), 51
Revolutionary Patriotic party (extreme Rightist party), 152
Reynaud, Paul, 110, 111, 113, 119, 120, 175, 251, 378
Right. *See* Left
Rivarol, 140, 152
Rivet, Paul, 144
Rochet, Waldeck, 39
Roclore, Marcel, 111, 113
Rousseau, Jean Jacques, 288
Rueff, Jacques, 118

Sahara, 303
Saint Pierre et Miquelon, 184, 304
Saint Simon, Claude Henri, 45
Sakhiet, 5
Salan, Raoul, 9
Sangnier, Marc, 86, 88
Sarrault, Albert, 72
Saugé, G., 152
School question, 52, 71, 81–82, 90, 117, 125, 147, 148, 159
Schuman, Robert, 102, 104, 113, 162, 199, 323
Schumann, Maurice, 87, 88, 104
*Scrutin d'arrondissement.* See Electoral system
Secession, right of. *See* Community, right of independence
*Section Française de l'Internationale Ouvrière* (SFIO). *See* Socialist party
Sectionalism, 22, 42–43, 66, 84, 107, 121, 164, 375
Sedan, 46
Senate: before 1958, 199, 277–278; elections to, 211, 279, 280–281, 286; and budget, 274, 283; membership of, 279; organization of, 282–283; functions and powers of, 283; and High Court of Justice, 283; and Constitutional Council, 283; and Senate of the Community, 283; and European assemblies, 283; and legislative process, 283; chairman of, 283, 293; and National Assembly, 283–284; and government, 283, 284, 285; committees of, 285; question period in, 285; and Constitutional Council, 285
Senate of the Community. *See* Community, Senate of
Senegal, 305, 308, 314
Senghor, Léopold, 171, 175, 177, 314
Servin, Marcel, 39, 40, 372
Settlers, in Algeria. *See* Algeria, settlers and colons in
Sid Cara, Chérif, 9
Sidos, brothers (Jacques, François, Pierre, and Henri), 152
Siegfried, André, 24, 82
*Sillon* (Christian Democratic group; Third Republic), 86
Simmonet, Maurice, 87, 97, 104, 375
Simon, Jules, 71
Social Republicans (RS) (Gaullists; Fourth Republic), 127, 173, 179
Socialism: first use of word, 45; as a doctrine, 16, 21, 23, 24. *See also* Socialist party
Socialist Action (splinter socialist party; Fourth Republic), 144
Socialist Friends, 62
Socialist party (SFIO): and Algeria, 11, 53, 68; doctrine and program of, 22–23, 26, 47, 49, 50, 51, 66–69; history of, 28, 47–54; membership of, 48, 49, 64–66; electorate of, 48, 52,

Socialist party (*continued*)
53, 66, 324; splits in, 50–52, 61, 144, 261; and school question, 52; organization of, 54–63; and ancillary organizations, 63–64, 161; leadership of, 64, 137; and trade unions, 65; and European integration, 68–69; preferred ministries in cabinet, 197; caucus of, 259–260; and electoral system, 226; seats in the National Assembly, 325
Socialist Party of France (nineteenth-century splinter socialist party), 47
Socialist Party of France (post-World-War I splinter socialist group led by Renaudel), 50
Socialist Radicals. *See* Radical Party
Socialist Unity (splinter socialist party; Fourth Republic), 144
Socialist Workers Federation (nineteenth-century splinter socialist party), 47
Socialist Workers Party (nineteenth-century splinter socialist party), 47
*Sociétés de Pensée*, 140
Somaliland, French, 184, 304
Soustelle, Jacques, 9, 103, 124, 128, 129, 130, 132, 138, 146, 198, 227, 371, 377, 379
State of siege, 201, 217
Strasbourg speech. *See* Gaulle, Charles de
Strauss, Paul, 72
Superior Council of Frenchmen in foreign countries, 282
Superior Council of the Judiciary, 193, 294–296
Superior Council of National Defense, 193
Syndicalists, 142

Tahiti, 303
Tardieu, André, 168, 169
Targé, A., 71
Teitgen, Henri, 102, 104
Teitgen, Pierre Henri, 87, 89, 104, 169
Television and elections, 231
*Témoignage Chrétien*, 100, 141, 144
Temple, Emmanuel, 110, 376
*Temps Modernes, les*, 141
Terrenoire, Louis, 89, 129, 138, 377
Thibaudet, Albert, 14
Thomazo, Jean, 9, 130, 229
Thorez, Maurice, 29, 30, 37, 39, 40, 372
Tillon, Charles, 39
Titoism, 15, 21
Tixier, A., 373
Tocqueville, Alexis de, 19
Trade associations, 161, 297
Trade unions, 159–162, 297
Treaties, 194, 216
Triboulet, Raymond, 129, 138
*Tribune du Communisme* (Left-wing labor group), 145
*Tribune du Peuple*, 144
Trotskyism, 15
Tsiranana, Philibert, 177, 199

UNESCO, 306
Unified Socialist party (PSU) (Left-wing labor party), 145, 161
*Union Civique pour le Référendum* (Gaullist group; Fifth Republic), 129
*Union de Défense des Commerçants et Artisans* (UDCA) (Poujadist pressure group), 150, 161
*Union Démocratique du Travail* (UDT). *See* Democratic Labor Union
*Union Démocratique et Sociale de la Résistance* (UDSR). *See* Democratic and Social Union of the Resistance
*Union des Chrétiens Progressistes.* See Union of Progressive Christians
*Union des Femmes Françaises.* See French Women's Union
*Union des Forces Démocratiques* (UFD). See Union of Democratic Forces
*Union de la Gauche Socialiste* (UGS). *See* Union of the Socialist Left
*Union des Républicains et d'Action Sociale* (URAS). See Union of Republicans and of Social Action
*Union et Fraternité Française* (UFF). *See* Poujadist party
Union for French Revival (Right-wing Gaullists), 129
Union for the New Republic (UNR) (Gaullist party): doctrine and program of, 14, 21, 22–23, 26, 134–138; electorate of, 114, 129, 138–139, 325; and de Gaulle, 123, 130, 134, 204; history of, 122–130; organization of,

130–134; leadership of, 137–138; membership of, 138, 148, 150; splits in, 130; and European integration, 136; and overseas, 136; and Algeria, 136; future of, 139; caucus of, 262; seats in National Assembly, 325
*Union Gaulliste.* See Gaullist Union
*Union Nationale des Combattants,* 158
*Union Nationale des Etudiants de France,* 99
Union of Democratic Forces, 54, 140, 187
Union of Progressive Christians (pro-Communist group), 143
Union of Republicans and of Social Action (URAS) (Gaullists; Fourth Republic), 127
Union of the Republics of Central Africa, 314
Union of the Socialist Left (splinter labor party; Fourth and Fifth republics), 144, 145
*Union pour la Nouvelle République* (UNR). *See* Union for the New Republic
*Union pour le Renouveau Français.* See Union for French Revival
*Union pour le Salut et le Renouveau de l'Algérie Française* (USRAF), 371
*Union Progressiste.* See Progressive Union
*Union Républicaine et Résistante.* See Republican and Resistance Union
Unitary Socialist party (pro-Communist group), 143
*Unité de la République* (Algerian parliamentary group). *See* Algerian group
United States, comparisons with, 168, 210, 251, 256, 289, 290, 294
*Unité Républicaine.* See Republican Unity
Unité Socialiste. *See* Socialist Unity

Vaillant, Edouard, 47
Vallat, Xavier, 154
Vallon, Louis, 123, 376
Varende, Jean de la, 154
Vedel, Georges, 184
Verdier, Robert, 11, 52, 260
*Vérité, la,* 142
Vermeersch, Jeannette, 39
Veterans, 157
Vignau, Pierre, 150
Villiers, Georges, 162
Vinceguerra, René, 150
Viviani, René, 47

Waldeck-Rousseau, René, 47, 109
Waline, M., 379
Wallis and Futuna, 304
Walter, Michel, 110
War, in the constitution, 217
Weygand, Maxime, 157
Workers Party (nineteenth-century Marxist party led by Guesde), 47

Young Nation (extreme Rightist group), 152, 153
Young Republic (Left-wing Christian Democratic party), 86, 87, 88, 91, 141, 144, 377

Zay, Jean, 73
Zimmerwald conference, 373